Sir Robert Filmer (1
and the patriotic m

CW00822474

Manchester University Press

Politics, culture and society in early modern Britain

General editors

PROFESSOR ANN HUGHES
PROFESSOR ANTHONY MILTON
PROFESSOR PETER LAKE

This important series publishes monographs that take a fresh and challenging look at the interactions between politics, culture and society in Britain between 1500 and the mid-eighteenth century. It counteracts the fragmentation of current historiography through encouraging a variety of approaches which attempt to redefine the political, social and cultural worlds, and to explore their interconnection in a flexible and creative fashion. All the volumes in the series question and transcend traditional interdisciplinary boundaries, such as those between political history and literary studies, social history and divinity, urban history and anthropology. They thus contribute to a broader understanding of crucial developments in early modern Britain.

Already published in the series

Black Bartholomew's Day   DAVID J. APPLEBY

The 1630s   IAN ATHERTON AND JULIE SANDERS (*eds*)

Reading and politics in early modern England   GEOFF BAKER

Literature and politics in the English Reformation   TOM BETTERIDGE

'No historie so meete'   JAN BROADWAY

Republican learning   JUSTIN CHAMPION

This England: Essays on the English Nation and Commonwealth   PATRICK COLLINSON

Cromwell's major-generals   CHRISTOPHER DURSTON

The spoken word   ADAM FOX and DANIEL WOOLF (*eds*)

Reading Ireland   RAYMOND GILLESPIE

Londinopolis   PAUL GRIFFITHS and MARK JENNER (*eds*)

Brave community   JOHN GURNEY

'Black Tom': Sir Thomas Fairfax and the English Revolution   ANDREW HOPPER

The boxmaker's revenge   PETER LAKE

The politics of the public sphere in early modern England
PETER LAKE AND STEVEN PINCUS (*eds*)

Henry Neville and English republican culture   GABY MAHLBERG

Royalists and Royalism during the Interregnum   JASON McELLIGOTT AND DAVID L. SMITH (*eds*)

The social world of early modern Westminster   J. F. MERRITT

Laudian and Royalist polemic in Stuart England: ANTHONY MILTON

Courtship and constraint   DIANA O'HARA

The origins of the Scottish Reformation   ALEC RYRIE

Catholics and the 'Protestant nation'   ETHAN SHAGAN (*ed.*)

Communities in early modern England   ALEXANDRA SHEPARD
and PHILIP WITHINGTON (*eds*)

The later Stuart Church, 1600–1714   GRANT TAPSELL (*ed.*)

Civic portraiture and political culture in the English local community   ROBERT TITTLER

Aspects of English Protestantism, c. 1530–1700   NICHOLAS TYACKE

Charitable hatred   ALEXANDRA WALSHAM

Crowds and popular politics in early modern England   JOHN WALTER

Sir Robert Filmer (1588–1653) and the patriotic monarch

Patriarchalism in seventeenth-century political thought

CESARE CUTTICA

Manchester
University Press

Published by Manchester University Press
Altrincham Street, Manchester M1 7JA, UK
www.manchesteruniversitypress.co.uk

British Library Cataloguing-in-Publication Data is available

Library of Congress Cataloging-in-Publication Data is available

ISBN 978 0 7190 9918 2 *paperback*

First published by Manchester University Press in hardback 2012

This paperback edition first published 2015

Printed by Lightning Source

Contents

ACKNOWLEDGEMENTS—vii
ABBREVIATIONS AND CONVENTIONS—IX

Introduction   1

PART I

1 Filmer: his life and cultural interests   21
2 From Kent with anger. *Patriarcha* versus Thomas Scott's country
   patriotism   51
3 Filmer's patriarchalism versus Jesuit political ideas   91
4 Filmer's patriarchalism in context: 'popularity', King James VI and I,
   Parliament and monarchists   104
5 Writing in the early Caroline regime and the issue of *Patriarcha*'s
   non-publication   143
6 Filmer in the 1640s and 1650s: political troubles and intellectual
   activism   161

PART II

7 Publishing in the Exclusion Crisis (1679–81): *Patriarcha* between
   fatherhood and fatherland   187
8 *Much ado about nothing*? Edmund Bohun's rehabilitation of
   Patriarcha, the issue of allegiance and Adamite anti-republicanism   212
9 Patriarchalism versus patriotism in practice: *Patriarcha* from the Rye
   House Plot (1683) to the Glorious Revolution (1688–89)   231

Conclusion   246

Appendix 1: The treasury of the scholar: Filmer's library   251

SELECT BIBLIOGRAPHY—254
INDEX—275

Acknowledgements

During the completion of this book I benefited from the precious help of a number of people without whom this research would not have been accomplished. I am most indebted to my doctoral advisors Martin van Gelderen and Johann P. Sommerville. The former has been helpful, encouraging, and always enthusiastic about the project. Johann has provided me with great scholarly insight into the history of early modern European political thought. He has helped me to better understand a complicated century and its political discourses. In addition, his support during my stay at the University of Wisconsin and afterwards has been pivotal to the writing of this book. His comments and scholarship can only be described as exceptional. Moreover, I owe a great intellectual debt to Jonathan Scott, who gave me the opportunity to spend a very productive semester in a congenial environment at the University of Pittsburgh. Jonathan offered his invaluable knowledge and admirable patience. He read the entire manuscript and made essential comments, without which this book would be a much lesser achievement. Last but not least, I owe much to Peter Lake for having believed in this project since 'day one'. He too read my work several times and several times put me straight back on the right track.

A number of other scholars have been generous with their help, time, or material. Amongst them are Glenn Burgess, Dario Castiglione, David Cleggett, James (Jim) Collins, Richard Cust, Jacqueline Eales, Rachel Foxley, Marco Geuna, Janelle Greenberg, Mark Greengrass, Matthew Growhoski, Knud Haakonssen, Rob Iliffe, Robert Kingdon, Gaby Mahlberg, Emilio Mazza, Jason McElligott, Anthony Milton, Eleonora Montuschi, Linda Levy Peck, Maria Luisa Pesante, Sue Petrie, Arfon Rees, Giuseppe Ricuperati, Julia Rudolph, Mark Somos, Naomi Tadmor, Ann Thomson, Edward (Ted) Vallance, Richard Whatmore, and Blair Worden. I am also grateful to my first mentors, Gianni Francioni and the late Fiorella De Michelis, who fuelled my early interest in the history of ideas and have been constant guides for all these years. The 'Politics, Culture and Society in Early Modern Britain' series editors at MUP and the anonymous referees helped me to correct mistakes and reorganise the material here presented.

My PhD thesis – from which this book partly originates – would not have been written without the financial support of the European University Institute (Florence). I am also grateful to a number of institutions and research boards whose financial help made this project possible. I would like to thank, above all, the University of Pavia, the Luigi Einaudi Foundation (Turin), the University of Wisconsin, and the Scaliger Institute (Leiden). Last but not least, a Marie Curie Intra-European Fellowship enabled me to complete this project at the Sussex Centre for Intellectual History at the University of Sussex. Here I found a warm and stimulating environment, and two excellent tutors in Knud Haakonssen and Richard Whatmore.

At different stages Ken Goodwin, Kris Grint, Kerry Mason, Tom Roper, Amy Smith, and Janet Summerton provided me with editorial help. A big thank you goes to my family, to whom the name Filmer probably represents my long absences from Piedmont. Friends have been generous with their encouragement, humour, and intellectual stimuli. A special mention goes to Adrian, Amy, Ben, Charlie, Chris, Clair, David, Florence, Gerben, Ian, Jake, John, Lucy, Massimo, Matthew, Miriam, Nick, Rico, Romy, Ruth, Sam, Seonad, Stefaan, and Tatiana. A particular thank you to Mark, who has accommodated an unseen and discreet lodger, Filmer, for many years. Last but not least, my deep gratitude towards Karin whose *company* has kept me sane.

Brighton, October 2011

List of abbreviations and conventions

SELECTED WORKS BY FILMER (POLITICAL)

AN   *The Anarchy of a Limited or Mixed Monarchy*, in J. P. Sommerville (ed.), *Robert Filmer. Patriarcha and Other Political Writings* (Cambridge, 1991), pp. 131–71.

DO   *Directions for Obedience to Governours in Dangerous and Doubtfull Times*, in Sommerville (ed.), *Patriarcha*, pp. 281–6.

FH   *The Free-holders Grand Inquest Touching Our Sovereraigne Lord the king and His Parliament*, in Sommerville (ed.), *Patriarcha*, pp. 69–130.

OA   *Observations Upon Aristotles Politiques Touching Forms of Government*, in Sommerville (ed.), *Patriarcha*, pp. 235–81.

OG   *Observations Concerning The Originall of Goverment, Upon Mr Hobs* Leviathan, *Mr Milton against* Salmasius, *H. Grotius* De Jure Belli, in Sommerville (ed.), *Patriarcha*, pp. 184–234.

PT   *Patriarcha or The Naturall Power of Kinges Defended against the Unnatural Liberty of the People*, in Sommerville (ed.), *Patriarcha*, pp. 1–68.

SELECTED WORKS BY FILMER (OTHERS)

AD   *An Advertisement to the Jurymen of England, Touching Witches. Together with A Difference between An English and Hebrew Witch* (edition printed from the original manuscript by *The Rota*, at the University of Exeter, 1975).

BHG *Of the Blasphemie against the Holy-Ghost* (London, 1647).

QQ   *Quaestio Quodlibetica or A Discourse, Whether it may bee Lawfull to take Use For Money* (London, printed for Humphrey Moseley, 1653).

VW   'In Praise of the Vertuous Wife', in M. Ezell, *The Patriarch's Wife. Literary Evidence and the History of the Family* (Chapel Hill and London, 1987), Appendix I, pp. 169–90.

OTHER ABBREVIATIONS

BDO   Bodleian Library, Oxford
BL   British Library, London
CCL   Canterbury Cathedral Library
DNB   *Dictionary of National Biography*
EEBO Early English Books Online
EHR   *English Historical Review*
HJ   *Historical Journal*
HPT   *History of Political Thought*

List of abbreviations and conventions

JBS   *Journal of British Studies*
KAO   Kent Archive Office, Maidstone
ODNB *Oxford Dictionary of National Biography* (new edition online)
OED   *Oxford English Dictionary*
PP 1610 E. Read Foster (ed.), *Proceedings in Parliament 1610* (New Haven and London, 2 vols., 1966), vols i and ii
PP 1628 R. C. Johnson et al. (eds), *Proceedings in Parliament 1628* (New Haven and London, 6 vols., 1977–83), vols ii, iii, vi (Appendixes and Indexes)
PRO   Public Record Office, London

PLACES OF PUBLICATION

The place of all publications is London unless otherwise stated.

DATES

All dates are given with the year beginning on 1 January.

TITLES

Titles of primary sources are given in short when they are too long and when this does not compromise their general meaning. Titles of secondary sources have been capitalised. The name of authors of primary sources is given in full, whilst only the initials and the surname are provided in the case of secondary literature.

TRANSLATIONS AND SPELLING

Translations of non-English sources that have no English edition are the author's own. The notes direct the reader to the original text.

MANUSCRIPTS

Recto and verso of manuscript pages are indicated both by 'r'–'v' and by 'a'–'b'.

Everything has been said before. But since nobody listens we have to keep going back and begin again. (André Gide, *Le traité du Narcisse*, 1891)

Introduction

This book explores the patriarchalist theories of Sir Robert Filmer (1588–1653) in relation to early modern English and European political cultures. The nine chapters – divided into two parts and chronologically structured – focus on Filmer's life and intellectual activity; on his main political treatise, *Patriarcha*; on the context in which it was produced and on its reception since the seventeenth century; on the theoretical importance of the two doctrines of 'patriarchalism' and 'patriotism'; on the intellectual role as well as ideological place of Filmer's major political ideas throughout the Stuart dynasty. They address central questions regarding *Patriarcha* (and Filmer's oeuvre) that have been hitherto ignored or, at best, left unanswered. More broadly, by studying the language of the Filmerian treatise, this book rethinks some crucial issues in the reading of seventeenth-century English history. Likewise, it also invites new reflections on the theory of patriarchalism in European political thinking.

Making use of unexplored primary material and adopting an innovative contextual approach to *Patriarcha*, this book provides a response to the following points: who was the 'real biographical' Filmer? What do we know about the much commented upon *Patriarcha*, namely about the document itself? When was it conceived and in connection with what milieu of publications? Did it respond to a particular target and, if so, what were the offending texts or political languages in question? What factors drove Sir Robert to compose his writing? Moreover, to what extent were Filmer's doctrines compatible with those of his contemporaries? Did Filmer shape his principles in conjunction with the discourses of other authors? What is the political and argumentative value of patriarchalism? Why did *Patriarcha* find a vast audience in the 1680s in England? Lastly, what aspects of Filmer's theory contribute to explain some of the most politically and culturally relevant dynamics concerning the seventeenth century?

Generally identified in the scholarly mainstream as the *villain* of early modern political thinking, Filmer has been depicted as a narrow-minded representative of a patriarchal society; as a conventional absolutist; or, simply, as the target of John Locke (1632–1704) and the republicans Algernon Sidney (1623–83) and James Tyrrell (1642–1718). In contrast to these approaches, this study focuses on the political and religious contexts where Filmer wrote and on the intellectual debates in which he was involved during his lifetime. Specific attention is paid to *Patriarcha* (written in the late 1620s but not published until 1680) with the aim of unveiling the theoretical cornerstones of the language of patriarchalism, its goals and political message(s). Filmer's ideas are thus examined both in conjunction with the Caroline regime (1625–49) – with its cultural standards and ideological trends – and as a response to European debates centred on questions of liberty and sovereignty. In particular, the book connects Filmer's patriarchalist theories to the debates on the Oath of Allegiance (1606); to the controversies engendered by the Jesuit theory of the active role of the Pope in the temporal sphere; to the emergence of a strong patriotic discourse of parliamentary power in the 1620s in England; to claims of popular participation in government and the right to resist tyrannical or heretical princes in European disputes; to the Exclusion Crisis period (1679–81) when they enjoyed a revival. Thematically rich and multivalent in scope, Filmer's oeuvre is thus presented as the articulation of a European mind at work to clarify the same topics which had engaged Jean Bodin and the French *politiques*, King James VI and I, Thomas Hobbes, and Jesuit thinkers like Cardinal Robert Bellarmine and Francisco Suarez, John Locke and Jacques-Bénigne Bossuet.

By no means a hagiographic portrayal of Filmer nor an unhistorically sympathetic account of his ideas, the following pages show how his works – caught in the heat of debates – sometimes presented contradictory statements and discrepancies between their content and what was going on in the arena of political affairs. Indeed, our aim is to restore Filmer's thought and *Patriarcha* to precisely those debates and their time.

Any analysis of Filmer's work should start with the study of an important doctrine in the history of Western political thought: patriarchalism. This is a term used in different ways and fields. It is traditionally employed in the theological sphere where references are made to biblical patriarchs. In this context the word 'patriarch' as attached to biblical personages comes from the Septuagint version, where it is adopted in a broad sense, including religious and civic officials like in Chronicles. In a more restricted sense it is applied to the antediluvian fathers of the human race, and more particularly to the three great progenitors of Israel: Abraham, Isaac, and Jacob. In the New Testament the term is also extended to the sons of Jacob and to King David. As far as social theory is concerned, 'patriarchalist' normally indicates a pre-modern societal organisation at the centre of which stood the absolute authority of the male landowner over a large familial unit. In economic parlance 'patriarchalism' describes a specific structure of production and distribution of goods and labour characterising the household as an entity. Political theorists generally associate it with a form of oppressive, archaic, and anti-modern power (patriarchy) whereby the father of the household had absolute dominion over the members of his family. This kind of personal and personalised authority has generally been considered antithetical to a liberal, conventional, and artificial conception of politics. Furthermore, feminist scholars depict patriarchalism as the quintessence of women's subjugation to men and their consequent oppression under a rigorous system made of duties and no rights, obedience and no liberties.

As for the history of political thought, patriarchalist theory maintained the supremacy of monarchs since they held the same authority as Adam, to whom God had assigned absolute power over all creatures. From the progenitor of mankind, power had passed to kings through the ancient patriarchs. On the whole, patriarchalism had a significant impact on the organisation of politics, society, and family in early modern Europe for it claimed that order and submission to higher authorities ought to be preserved in all human institutions. It thus followed that kings in the political realm, fathers in the family, and masters in the household wielded the same authority over their subjects, wives, children, and servants. Equally, the theoretical implications of these ideas profoundly influenced many traditions of political thought in Europe. In seventeenth-century England it was Filmer who became known as the representative of the patriarchalist theory since he had insisted on the superior role of Adam as first king on earth. In consequence, *Patriarcha* came to be seen as the ideological bedrock of patriarchalism.

PATRIARCHALISM IN THE THEATRE OF IDEAS: HISTORIOGRAPHICAL LIMITS AND A NEW APPROACH

The most extensive and pervasive use of the family in political thought was made by patriarchalists. The analogy between the familial and the political spheres served to justify the divine right theory of kings. According to several historians, this doctrine 'fitted well with the prescriptions of the writers of household manuals'.[1] Patriarchalism, Gordon Schochet maintained, was the political language adopted by Plato, Aristotle, Bodin, and Hooker to identify and define 'the organizational precursor of the political order'.[2] More specifically, Schochet argued that in seventeenth-century England the idea that the household represented the source of governmental authority became 'the basis of an absolutist theory of political obligation'.[3] However, even though 'the familial symbol had played a significant role in political thinking' throughout the early modern era, for Schochet there was no developed patriarchalist doctrine that could be employed in political debates.[4] Patriarchalism thrived until it had the 'ability to "fit into" a culture and to incorporate and rely upon the principles that [were] widely accepted or taken for granted' within that culture. Defeated by the Lockean paradigm, patriarchalism became 'outmoded, irrelevant, and therefore unacceptable'.[5] Its demise was due to 'the collapse of two attitudes':

'the appeal to origins to discover the nature of political authority' and the juxta-position of political and familial societies.[6]

This approach presents two main problems. Firstly, Schochet assumed that patriarchalism exclusively referred to the origins of authority. It followed that it had to do with the normative phase of the development of political govern-ment. Moreover, by focusing univocally on its historical and anthropological connotations, Schochet failed to see patriarchalism in relation to cultural meanings, metaphorical references, gendered paradigms permeating the broader intellectual context of early modern England and Europe.[7] He ignored that treatises like *Patriarcha* participated in the multiple process of image-construction that the Stuart monarchy set up through cultural, aesthetic, moral mediums to convey various politico-ideological messages. Secondly, Schochet neglected patriarchalism's role as a political language employed both to depict a distinct sketch of monarchy and to counterattack rival political paradigms. Patriarchalism entailed a stringent configuration of power that promoted a specific form of absolutism. It also provided a thorough model for the method of government and set forth a fully-fledged account of sovereignty. In other words, patriarchalism was more than the codification of archaic beliefs failing to succeed in the theatre of ideas when confronted by the typhoon of modern philosophy, empirical science, and social change.

Equally problematic is Glenn Burgess' view of patriarchalism as 'an impor-tant sub-language closely attached to order theory'.[8] Following William H. Greenleaf's interpretation,[9] Burgess associated patriarchalist discourse with the notion that society had to be preserved by means of a hierarchical struc-ture, for which the theologically laden theory of patriarchalism represented the strongest justification. As he put it, the 'sub-languages' of 'order theory, patriarchalism, millenarianism ... possessed an uncontested capacity to make statements of *moral* duty', which 'in *political* matters was vague and unspe-cific'.[10] For Burgess patriarchalism functioned in a prescriptive mode. It was employed either to enforce subjects' obedience or to emphasise the unselfish role of the king to promote the common good.[11] That subjects had 'to love kings as one loved one's father' did not imply any 'particular political or ideological points' other than the mere imposition of instructions with which society could be aptly controlled.[12]

Despite their acumen, these interpretations did not see that patriarchalism articulated a specific vision of politics through rational arguments, historical research,[13] analogical reasoning. Filmer did not transpose social prejudices into his political theories. His work cannot be schematically reduced to the antithesis of '[i]ndividualism, political conventionalism, and rational justifica-tion'. Nor can it be branded as the systematisation of a 'more communitarian view, naturalism, and the use of genetic-historical arguments'.[14] To think so obscures the fact that Filmer adopted a conservative vocabulary with a radical meaning.[15] In substance, 'anthropological' and 'ideological' readings of patriarchalism need to be replaced with interpretations that highlight its *political* dimension. And it is from this angle that the following pages consider this intellectual category.

Thus, it is argued that political patriarchalism was not simply a strong reaction to the idea that a voluntary contract formed civil society. Nor was it merely a fierce rejection of the concept that human consent was the wellspring of government. This was the theoretical performance that patriarchalist theorists played when it came to analysing the origins of political society.[16] Yet there was another stage on which authors like Filmer knew it was fundamental to act. This regarded governance (the method of governing a polity), and entailed a different representation of power. Nor can patriarchalism as a forceful theory of absolute and arbitrary government be identified *tout court* with the theory of the divine right of kings.[17] In this respect, whilst the latter doctrine claimed that kings had been entrusted with power either directly by God or indirectly through the irrevocable mediation of the people, the patriarchalist Filmer rejected all forms of popular participation in politics and made Adam the exclusive founder of political authority. Besides, divine right theory applied to republics too, in that it concerned government per se, which made it all the more incongruous with the Filmerian viewpoint.

Through his free will, the patriarchal sovereign regulated political interaction with no consideration for assemblies and fundamental laws. The arbitrary power of Adam represented the guiding model of political organisation. The Adamite paradigm fused absolute and arbitrary power. Moreover, if royalist thinkers like John Hayward, Adam Blackwood, and John Barclay[18] admitted that men had originally been free and had, therefore, set up different kinds of government, Filmer denied that a state of nature had ever existed. Likewise, he rejected Hobbes' claims that in the beginning people had been free of government and that, as such, polities stemmed from a contract. Whilst these royalists saw the king as the embodiment of the persona of the *respublica*, Filmer dismissed the fictional element of this argument, opting, instead, for a configuration of sovereignty where king and State coincided thanks to the Adamite argument and its fatherly metaphors. For Filmer the sovereign was not a fictional character on the political stage. He was the real (genetic) source of the body politic. The sovereign *was* the body politic. In contrast to the Hobbesian model,[19] the Filmerian ruler did not act in the name of the State because he *was* the State.

Contrary to received scholarly views, contractualists were not the sole target of patriarchalists. A major part of their criticism in early seventeenth-century England discredited claims that Parliament was the true representative of the people. This conflict centred on the identity of the nation.[20] Its key element was the identification of the head of the nation either with Parliament as the cornerstone of liberties or, instead, with the absolute monarch as *pater patriae*.[21] This last image is here taken as the theoretical fabric of what we call *political patriarchalism*.[22]

THE CONDESCENSION OF POSTERITY: FILMERIAN HISTORIOGRAPHY[23]

As for the main scholarly interpretations of Filmer's political theory to date, the older view – with few notable exceptions[24] – portrayed it as obsolete and superseded already in the sixteenth and seventeenth centuries. Based on a Lockean-conditioned and supposedly modern standpoint, a largely liberal and Whiggish (but also Marxist) approach failed to place Filmer's ideas in context.[25] As a result, it gave a caricatured picture of *Patriarcha* as a relic of the past that received surprisingly close scrutiny from intellectual heavyweights such as Locke,[26] Sidney,[27] and Tyrrell.[28] Following a tradition which had in Jean Barbeyrac and Jean-Jacques Rousseau two influential precursors,[29] the historiographical mainstream denied Filmer the status of independent thinker within the history of English political thought and considered him as an 'inconspicuous' figure.[30] Reputed as an unoriginal theorist to whom only the devastating criticism of Locke and Sidney lent any significance, Filmer and his works were thus studied exclusively in connection with the astringent remarks made by Whigs and republicans against them.

A small number of new historiographical readings of Filmer's thought came into the debate by promoting a novel critique of his patriarchalism. Ironically, the first scholar to do so was Peter Laslett, the modern editor of Locke's *Two Treatises* and of Filmer's political works (1949), with a brief but remarkable study of Sir Robert's Kentish intellectual milieu (1948–49).[31] For Laslett, Filmer set up a code of 'conscious and unconscious prejudice' typical of his county environment.[32] Sir Robert's 'brash naivety and his obviously amateur outlook' made him an 'extremely rare phenomenon' whose name by 1750 'had already become a rather dreary appendage to the name of John Locke'.[33] *Patriarcha* was the quintessential expression of a patriarchal society, that is, of what with a much celebrated phrase Laslett named 'the world we have lost'.[34] Subsequently, Gordon Schochet (1975)[35] and James Daly (1979)[36] studied – in somewhat mutually exclusive ways – patriarchalism as the ideological cornerstone of Filmer's work.[37] Schochet argued that almost all seventeenth-century thinkers subscribed to the idea that fathers and masters had dominion over their families. Hence he concluded that the positions of Filmer and Locke were 'not vastly different'.[38] By contrast, Daly stressed the originality of Filmer's principles and their distance from seventeenth-century English royalism.[39] His political ideas were too controversial and, therefore, were followed up only by a 'minority of authors' supporting the Stuart monarchy.[40] Daly coined the term 'Filmerism' to define his 'splendid isolation' from the arguments of other monarchist writers.

Despite their important contributions, Laslett and Schochet looked at patriarchalism through the interpretative category of 'the unity of meaning'. Conditioned by a sort of 'syndrome of the social historian',[41] they clung to a concept of social causation (patriarchy) as the quintessential explanation for intellectual discourse (Filmer's ideas).[42] In brief, their approach recalls what Gareth Stedman Jones has named 'the determinist fix'.[43] This fixity of meaning applied to Filmer's patriarchalism also had the effect of obscuring the context in which *Patriarcha* was composed.[44] As for Daly, his insightful research painted Filmer as a fundamentally English character on a stage which, instead, was more open to continental ideas. Furthermore, reflecting on the role of Filmer's political opinions in the debates of post-Restoration England, Daly examined them as though there had been no monarchist thinkers in England before the 1640s and very few before the 1680s.[45] In summary, by opposing tradition versus originality as templates for their readings of Filmer's doctrines, these perspectives epitomised the most distinct and influential interpretations in Filmerian scholarship.

This was so until Johann P. Sommerville's new edition of Filmer's political works appeared in 1991.[46] Sommerville deftly criticised those who read Sir Robert's writings only in relation to Locke, and paid much needed attention to the connections between English monarchists and their continental counterparts.[47] Underscoring *Patriarcha*'s importance in early modern political thought, Sommerville conceded that 'much of what Filmer had to say against contractualist theories of government remains compelling'.[48] Therefore, 'if we want to understand Filmer it makes little sense to approach him through Locke ... or through the debates on the Exclusion Crisis. ... Rather, we must read him in the context of his own time'.[49] And yet, Sommerville dismissed the date of composition of *Patriarcha* as 'of relatively minor historical interest, since the political doctrines expressed in it were mostly unoriginal'.[50] This – it will be shown throughout – is not true. Lastly, Sommerville's anti-revisionist work on absolutism (1986 and 1999)[51] as well as Burgess' book on absolute monarchy and the Stuart constitution (1996)[52] recognised the value of Filmer's analysis of power and acknowledged his forceful criticism of popular government and resistance.

What follows is thus an attempt to develop these fruitful perspectives in unexplored directions and, at the same time, reject some of their assumptions.[53] In so doing, we should be enabled to approach *Patriarcha* and patriarchalism from a different and innovative angle.

CONTENTS

Being mainly about the ideological origins, political contexts, arguments and effects of *Patriarcha* (and its wide implications for the political thought and culture of the period), the structure of this book tries to reflect that as directly as possible. This is why it presents a formal break between Part I dealing with issues down to the 1650s and Part II addressing the 1670s and 1680s.

Chapter 1 provides a new biographical account of Filmer and a complete picture of his native Kent's intellectual and political environment. It foregrounds the traces he left both as a thinker engaged in a specific social milieu and as a late humanist whose writings articulated questions amply debated in the republic of letters. New light is cast on the personal relations and cultural scene that animated his life and context up to the 1640s. In addition, unprecedented attention is given to Filmer's non-political tracts on usury, the household and witchcraft. As a result, the orthodoxies of the historiographical mainstream whereby he was a backwoodsman or, at best, an uninteresting erudite whose ideas had no relevance in the pantheon of seventeenth-century culture will be once and for all put to rest.

If Kent provided the terrain on which Filmer moved both as a wealthy gentleman and as a prolific thinker, this county also constituted an important springboard for Filmer's patriarchalist reaction to the so-called (parliamentary and county) 'patriots'. These represented the first target he chose in *Patriarcha*. The other attack was reserved for some Jesuit theorists whose works Filmer saw as spreading lethal principles on the nature of monarchical power. The next two chapters deal with patriots and Jesuits in their respective contexts and, in so doing, they explain the arguments Sir Robert deployed in *Patriarcha* and the languages in which they were couched.

Relying upon an extensive range of historical texts and archival material, chapter 2 elucidates two important conflicting paradigms of political thought elaborated in the disputes of the late Jacobean (1603–25) and early Caroline eras. The first paradigm is here identified as 'patriotism', the second one as 'patriarchalism'. Based on very different notions of liberty and sovereignty, these paradigms – it is argued – entailed distinctly opposing models of political power and civic life in the body politic. In the last three decades seventeenth-century English patriotism[54] and patriarchalism[55] have been studied separately, but they have not been considered as part of the same ideological battle. The political doctrines the 'patriots' articulated to criticise the Stuart monarchy have never been seen as the emerging rebellious force against which the political discourse of patriarchalism was deployed. Most importantly, this conflict provides the background against which to elucidate the goals and targets of *Patriarcha*. This chapter shows that the treatise intended to provide an answer to the 'image crisis'[56] affecting the Crown at the time of the Forced Loan (1626–27) and the Petition of Right (1628), and that it derived from Filmer's alarm at the popularity that quasi-republican[57] and godly patriotic ideas obtained in the 1620s. These were set forth by the likes of his cousin, the interesting but little-studied figure of local MP and radical thinker Thomas Scott of Canterbury (1566–1635).[58] In his extraordinary political and religious diary (c. 1614–35) and in *A Discourse of Polletique and Civell Honor* (c. 1619), Scott attacked the supporters of the monarch and opposed kingly supreme prerogative. By contrast, Filmer centred his patriotism on the fatherly power of the ruler considered as *pater patriae*.[59] In so doing, he both rejected the discourses of those defending – in Parliament and on paper – the publicly active 'honest patriot' and freeborn Protestant freeholder, and targeted the theories of papal temporal power advanced by Bellarmine and Suarez. In this respect, chapter 3 unravels Filmer's principles as part of a wider European framework of political theories.[60] This had to do with monarchist (both Catholic and Protestant) rejections of the Jesuit tenet of papal deposing power and opposition to their justification of tyrannicide. In writing *Patriarcha* Filmer did not miss the chance to have his say in this important debate.

By means of a comparative approach, chapter 4 then sheds light on *Patriarcha*'s place within the Jacobean and early Caroline monarchist canon. The treatise is analysed in conjunction with the reinforcement of kingship pursued in the late 1620s in England. A major section of the chapter focuses on the pungent rhetoric of King James VI and I's (1566–1625) monarchist tracts and his Parliament-speeches devoted to dismantling the ideological apparatus of 'popularity'. James' opinions are compared with Filmer's. This comparison highlights their differences rather than simply assessing their similarities. By concentrating on the rhetoric MPs and pamphleteers employed to depict events in the country, to conceive ideal constitutional arrangements and to counterattack any attempts to enlarge the royal prerogative, this chapter also opens up new ground for a much needed discussion of patriarchalism and its role in early seventeenth-century political parlance. En route to mapping out the intellectual territory in which Filmer's concept of kingship developed, light is cast on the English theorists who claimed the supreme power of the fatherly ruler by resorting to the metaphor of the *pater patriae*.[61] Finally, Filmer's political use of fatherhood (and masculinity) is studied together with the process of image-construction which the Stuart monarchy undertook in the 1620s and 1630s through the paintings of Anthony van Dyck.

Chapter 5 follows and expands this line of enquiry by focusing on the reign of Charles I (1600–1649), especially from the start of the so-called 'Personal Rule' (1629). It thus considers the King's policies, both at home and abroad; financial strategies; ideal of command; cultural taste. In particular, it examines their repercussions for thinkers who, like Filmer, were at work to carve out a successful image of the ruler and a forceful narrative of sovereignty. In addition, the chapter endeavours to establish how *Patriarcha* took part in the ideological enterprise of fortification of monarchical authority involving different types of cultural codification: political, pictorial, theological, literary. This approach involves references to models of royalty other than Charles': Prince Henry (1594–1612) and Gustavus Adolphus of Sweden (1594–1632) feature as leading figures on a stage where the key issues were the defence of Protestantism as well as the promotion of English identity. In this context attention is then paid to Charles' refusal to give permission to publish *Patriarcha* (1632). New questions are here raised: how compatible was *Patriarcha* with the Caroline narrative of kingship (e.g. with the writings of Roger Maynwaring and Robert Sibthorpe)? What significance did Filmer's theories have for Charles' own vision of power? As Laslett's ground-breaking research (1960)[62] changed our perspective on Locke's *Two Treatises*, so the fact that Filmer tried to publish his famous work in the early 1630s prompts a significantly different reading of it both as a political text and as an ideological manifesto. This portion of the book also illustrates the importance of patriotism for many monarchists and assesses the developments and (significant) changes the term 'patriot' underwent through the sixteenth and seventeenth centuries.

Resuming the account of Sir Robert's life and his public engagements detailed in chapter 1, chapter 6 concentrates on the period of the Civil War and the troubles he experienced then; on his close friendship with Peter Heylyn; on his little-known but insightful theological views; finally, on his prolific phase of intense political writing that occurred between 1648 and 1652, when he combined what we might term 'high theory' with a more immediately polemical involvement with the issues and arguments of the day. The status of these later works as in effect applications of some of the doctrines laid out in *Patriarcha* to recent events and debates will thus be rendered apparent.

With Part I the process of excavation of the origins of *Patriarcha* in early seventeenth-century Kent is concluded, whilst, at the same time, a lively, polarised and sophisticated intellectual milieu in the heart of the English shires, which contradicts Alan Everitt's perspective on the county as the paradigm for his localist account of the interests and instincts of the local gentry, is evoked.

Following the work of Jonathan Scott, Mark Knights and others, Part II begins by clarifying the continuities in political theory as much as in political practice that accompanied the composition and the publication of *Patriarcha* in the 1620s and 1680s, respectively.[63] Coupled with this general historical narrative, chapter 7 complements previous ones in that it discusses patriarchalism as an alternative model to republican, parliamentarian and Whig claims to patriotic values. It also pays new attention to why Locke felt compelled to try to overthrow Filmer's theories. Against the grain of mainstream scholarship, the chapter details how widely employed Filmer's political patriarchalism was in late seventeenth-century England, and why this was the case. In particular, it is here shown that both in the 1620s (and frequently until the 1640s) and then in the 1680s, namely at times of crisis for the monarchy, monarchist theorists resorted to patriarchalist concepts in order to depict the king as *pater patriae* and advance a new configuration of governance. In practice, it is here demonstrated that Filmerian doctrines formed a theoretical asset for the political edifice erected by important figures such as Sir Roger L'Estrange (1616–1704).

One of the main characters in this panorama is the absolutist Edmund Bohun (1645–99) with his steadfast defence of Filmer and edition of *Patriarcha* (1685). To Bohun's Filmerian works is dedicated chapter 8 where they are placed in conjunction with the polemics engendered by the political problematic of exclusion and the assault on *Patriarcha* carried out by Sidney, Tyrrell, Neville and others. Bohun's texts – which remain off the historiographical radar – are dissected as a direct product of that genus of patriarchalism that re-appropriated patriotic discourse to promote the cause of absolute monarchy. And this whole process mirrored the increasing resonance of Filmer's name.

In chapter 9 a number of references to important post-Restoration propagandists will be made, whilst a variety of sources – from treatises to pamphlets, petitions, sermons and periodical papers – will also be examined. These have to do with the aftermath of the Popish Plot (1678) and, especially, of the Rye House Plot (1683) when the rhetoric of 'patriots' and 'parricide' was *again* amply deployed on the ideological battlefield of pre-Williamite England where rival interpretations of the nation's political ethos and religious texture strongly collided with one another. Such a picture of the 1680s serves to further confirm the relevance of Filmerian language in society at large and the appeal of his arguments in theoretical disputes at that time. It also depicts the intellectual scenario leading to the Glorious Revolution (1688–89) when concepts, meanings and implications carved out in *Patriarcha* became once more the object of bitter controversy and vehement polemics as much as of full endorsement and appreciation.

Although *Patriarcha* is central to its general narrative,[64] this book hopes to make an important contribution to the study of the political thought and culture of the entire seventeenth century. In fact, the paradigms of patriarchalism and patriotism work as lenses that bring into focus a series of decisive facets of early modern political theory and practice. Lastly, before concluding this introduction, a few considerations on the methodological angle taken here seem to be in order.

METHODOLOGICAL REMARKS

This book does not adhere to revisionist interpretations according to which pre-Civil War England was immune to ideological conflict.[65] Its approach differs from that of historians[66] who see the beginning of the Caroline reign as a phase with no political tension, no discrepancies at theoretical level and no competing political groups.[67] By contrast, it argues that English political theorists did not all speak 'the same language' and that early seventeenth-century debates were informed by a vibrant plurality of dissonant discourses of liberty and sovereignty. In this sense, *Patriarcha* was the outcome of a phase characterised by a 'formidable insurgent temper' which 'was taking possession of the English people ... to fever height'.[68]

What follows mostly relies on Quentin Skinner's theory of 'contextualism',[69] whereby it is necessary to look at texts as the articulation of stances in a dialogue in which a great role is played both by the exchange of ideas and by the constant invention of arguments and counter-arguments in controversies. Endorsing this view enables us to ask which works and which theorists monarchist texts responded to and why specific languages were chosen to defend absolute monarchy. Skinner aims at grasping political concepts by concentrating on the multifarious ways in which language(s) and paradigms functioned. Moreover, he stresses the importance of exploring the meaning(s) of texts in conjunction with their specific linguistic context and the debates in which their authors were involved. In line with this perspective, the present study considers Filmer's doctrine as one of a host of theoretical strategies adopted to rethink the notion of kingship. Thus, *Patriarcha* is seen not as an unalterable and timeless discursive performance expounding uniform cultural patterns or social typologies. Rather, it is considered as a character acting on a stage of ongoing exchanges of texts and opinions. Hence our chief goal is – paraphrasing Skinner's words – to try and *see things Filmer's way*.[70] For this reason the book focuses, first of all, on the thinkers Filmer attacked as much as on his (rhetorical) configuration of absolute power. Secondly, it explores his historical setting. Thirdly, it analyses how he took part in debates occurring both in his own time and afterwards through other people's readings of his works. This way of proceeding should lead us to assess what he *was doing*.[71]

The study of Filmer's context is, therefore, interwoven with the textual analysis of his treatises. The close attention paid to his sources and political languages serves as a platform for a larger historical investigation of the disputes and questions in the foreground in his time. In the words of Dominick LaCapra, this corresponds 'to formulate as a problem what is so often taken, deceptively, as a solution: the relationship between texts and their various pertinent contexts'.[72]

Perhaps *unfaithfully* to the Skinnerian method, the author attempts to overcome one of its limits: its focus on mainstream thinkers.[73] That here presented is a plea for the study not only of the 'winners' (the Grotiuses and the Lockes) but also of the 'losers' in the arena of political thinking. In this respect, the book is about a significant group of 'losers' and their ideas: monarchist theorists.[74] As a result, it raises essential questions on the nature of theoretical absolutism in early modern Europe.[75] This means to take into account the opinions of those who supported the supreme authority of the monarch; the indivisibility and inalienability of his power; the idea that he was accountable only to God for his decisions and actions and not to his subjects; the notion that the latter had, instead, to obey him unconditionally; the principle that the authority to make laws pertained exclusively to the ruler.[76]

By no means a fully comprehensive intellectual biography of Filmer, let alone an exhaustive presentation of his entire political production – a task which would require, at least, twice the space here provided – this study nonetheless equips the reader with a long-overdue account of the most important and interesting biographical and intellectual aspects of a thinker who has been unjustly associated with oppressive political dogmas or, at best, derided as an appendix to the history of political thought. In fact, despite having been and still being referred to by theorists, polemicists, pamphleteers and modern scholars alike since the days of Locke's virulent tirade against his ideas, Filmer and *Patriarcha* have still not completely made it onto the stage of academic scholarship and its readership. This book attempts to provide precisely such an intellectual springboard.

NOTES

1 S. D. Amussen, *An Ordered Society. Gender and Class in Early Modern England* (Oxford, 1988), p. 55.

2 G. Schochet, *Patriarchalism in Political Thought. The Authoritarian Family and Political Speculation and Attitudes Especially in Seventeenth-Century England* (Oxford, 1975), p. 268.

3 *Ibid.*, p. 268.

4 *Ibid.*, p. 56.

5 *Ibid.*, p. 57.

6 *Ibid.*, p. 274.

7 This is an aspect more recently taken into consideration by Gaby Mahlberg: 'the concern with patriarchalism provides a continuity in the political debates [of the seventeenth century] that has often been overlooked in a historiography focusing on ever smaller periods of time' (G. Mahlberg, 'Republicanism as Anti-patriarchalism in Henry Neville's *The Isle of Pines* (1668)', in J. Morrow and J. Scott (eds), *Liberty, Authority, Formality. Political Ideas and Culture, 1600–1900. Essays in Honour of Colin Davis* (Exeter, 2008), pp. 131–52, p. 143).

8   G. Burgess, *The Politics of the Ancient Constitution. An Introduction to English Political Thought, 1603–1642* (University Park (Pennsylvania), 1992), p. 134.

9   See W. H. Greenleaf, *Order, Empiricism and Politics* (1964), *passim*.

10 Burgess, *The Politics of the Ancient Constitution*, p. 134.

11 *Ibid.*, pp. 134 ff.

12 *Ibid.*, p. 138.

13 Greenleaf argued that Filmer's historical arguments were endowed with irrefutable 'cogency' (W. H. Greenleaf, 'Filmer's Patriarchal History', *HJ*, 9 (1966), pp. 157–71, pp. 157–8).

14 Schochet, *Patriarchalism in Political Thought*, p. 276.

15 On the methodological propriety to apply 'radicalism' and/or 'radical' to pre-1820 contexts see G. Burgess and M. Festenstein (eds), *English Radicalism, 1550–1850* (Cambridge, 2007), esp. G. Burgess, 'Introduction', pp. 1–16. See also chapter 2 below.

16 Filmer explained that 'at the creation one man alone was made' (*OA*, p. 252). For this reason, all ideas of a 'contract of people' was 'imaginary', that is, 'a fancy not improbable only, but impossible, except a multitude of men at first had sprung out and were engendered of the earth' (*ibid.*, p. 253).

17 The theory of divine right primarily revolved around 'the duty of obedience' and 'much less frequently' around 'the specific nature of royal authority' (G. Burgess, *British Political Thought, 1500–1600. The Politics of the Post-Reformation* (Basingstoke, 2009), p. 149).

18 On this see chapter 2 below. It has to be noted that Filmer probably meant John Barclay's father, William (author of the anti-Bellarmine *De Potestate Papae*), but confused the two.

19 Q. Skinner, *Visions of Politics. Volume II. Renaissance Virtues* (Cambridge, 2002), p. 403.

20 Derek Hirst spoke of the 'growing sense of English identity' in the first decades of the century (D. Hirst, *England in Conflict 1603–1660. Kingdom, Community, Commonwealth* (1999), p. 29). However, he played down the place national political issues had in the mind of local freeholders before the 1630s, with the exception of highly divided counties like Norfolk and Kent (D. Hirst, *The Representative of the People? Voters and Voting in England under the Early Stuarts* (Cambridge, 1975), pp. 140ff.).

21 Hirst, *The Representative of the People?*, pp. 192–3.

22 The patriarchalist theories here analysed are also distinguished from the doctrines normally classified as 'paternalism'. According to Nicola Matteucci, paternalism represented 'an authoritarian and, at the same time, benevolent type of politics, a sort of charitable activity pursued from above and set out to help the people with purely administrative methods' (N. Matteucci, 'Paternalismo', in N. Bobbio, N. Matteucci, and G. Pasquino (eds), *Dizionario di Politica* (Turin, 1983), pp. 804–5). By the same token, those theorists who assumed the family to be the original community from which the State derived are not considered as political patriarchalists.

23 For a detailed account of Filmerian historiography see C. Cuttica, 'Sir Robert Filmer (1588–1653) and the Condescension of Posterity: Historiographical Interpretations', *Intellectual History Review*, 21 (2011), pp. 195–208.

24 J. N. Figgis, *The Divine Right of Kings* (Cambridge, 2nd edn, 1914), pp. 148–52, 155–6, 252, 254–5. See also J. W. Allen, 'Sir Robert Filmer', in F. J. C. Hearnshaw (ed.), *The Social and Political Ideas of Some English Thinkers of the Augustan Age A.D. 1650–1750. A Series*

of *Lectures Delivered at King's College, University of London During the Session 1927–1928* (1928), pp. 27–46, p. 27). For an unusual eulogy of Filmer by none other than T. S. Eliot see D. Bradshaw, 'Lonely Royalists: T. S. Eliot and Sir Robert Filmer', *The Review of English Studies*, 46 (1995), pp. 375–9, p. 376.

25 For instances of this die-hard scholarly tendency see G. P. Gooch, *Political Thought in England. From Bacon to Halifax* (1915), pp. 160–1; H. Laski, *Political Thought in England from Locke to Bentham* (1920), pp. 9, 15–16, 38–9; G. H. Sabine, *A History of Political Theory* (1937), pp. 512–14, 524; P. Zagorin, *A History of Political Thought in the English Revolution* (1954), pp. 28, 200–1; J. Plamenatz, *Man and Society. A Critical Examination of Some Important Social and Political Theories from Machiavelli to Marx* (2 vols, 1963), vol. 1, pp. 173, 182, 186–7; J. Dunn, *The Political Thought of John Locke. An Historical Account of the Argument of the Two Treatises of Government* (Cambridge, 1969), pp. 58–9; D. Wootton, *Divine Right and Democracy* (1986), p. 31.

26 See John Locke, *Two Treatises of Government*, a critical edition with an introduction and apparatus criticus by P. Laslett (Cambridge, 1960), e.g. bk i, 'The Preface', pp. 155–6; bk i, ch. i, § 1, p. 159 and *passim*.

27 See Algernon Sidney, *Discourses Concerning Government*, ed. T. G. West (Indianapolis, 1990), e.g. bk i, ch. i, p. 7 and *passim*.

28 See James Tyrrell, *Patriarcha non Monarcha. The Patriarch Unmonarch'd* (1681), *passim*.

29 See Jean Barbeyrac, 'Notes', in Samuel Pufendorf, *Of the Law of Nature and Nations* (8 bks, 1729), bk vi, ch. ii, § x, p. 606; Jean-Jacques Rousseau, 'Discours sur l'Économie Politique', in *Jean-Jacques Rousseau. Oeuvres Completes* (Paris, 1964), vol. iii, pp. 239–78, p. 244; Jean-Jacques Rousseau, 'Du Contract Social ou Essai sur la Forme de la République', in *Oeuvres Completes*, vol. iii, pp. 279–470, pp. 298, 354; Jean-Jacques Rousseau, 'Discours sur l'Origine et les Fondements de l'Inégalité parmi les Hommes', in *Oeuvres Completes*, vol. iii, pp. 109–223, pp. 182, 182, n. 1. For a more positive opinion of Filmer's doctrines see Gottfried Wilhelm Leibniz, 'Meditation on the Common Concept of Justice', in *Leibniz. Political Writings*, ed. and trans. P. Riley (Cambridge, 2nd edn, 1988), pp. 45–64, pp. 60–2.

30 J. G. A. Pocock, *The Machiavellian Moment. Florentine Political Thought and the Atlantic Republican Tradition* (Princeton, 1975), p. 376.

31 See P. Laslett, 'Sir Robert Filmer: The Man versus the Whig Myth', *William and Mary Quarterly*, 5 (1948), pp. 523–46; P. Laslett, 'The Gentry of Kent in 1640', *Cambridge Historical Journal*, 9 (1948), pp. 148–64; P. Laslett, 'Introduction', in *Patriarcha and Other Political Works*, ed. P. Laslett (Oxford, 1949), pp. 1–43.

32 Laslett, 'Introduction', p. 37.

33 *Ibid.*, p. 41.

34 P. Laslett, *The World We Have Lost* (1965).

35 See G. Schochet, 'Patriarchalism, Politics and Mass Attitudes in Stuart England', *HJ*, 12 (1969), pp. 413–41; G. Schochet, 'The Family and the Origins of the State in Locke's Political Philosophy', in J. W. Yolton (ed.), *John Locke. Problems and Perspectives* (Cambridge, 1969), pp. 81–98; Schochet, *Patriarchalism in Political Thought*; G. Schochet, 'Patriarchalism, Naturalism and the Rise of the "Conventional State"', in F. Fagiani and G. Valera (eds), *Categorie del Reale e Storiografia* (Milan, 1986), pp. 111–27.

36 See J. Daly, *Sir Robert Filmer and English Political Thought* (Toronto, 1979).

37 Whilst Schochet distinguished between 'anthropological', 'moral', and 'ideological' patriarchalism (Schochet, *Patriarchalism in Political Thought*, pp. 10–16), Daly referred to the 'anthropological', 'analogical', and 'legal' types (Daly, *Sir Robert Filmer*, pp. 151–2).

38 Schochet, 'The Family and the Origins of the State', p. 91. For a similar but more original perspective on Filmer (as both 'a traditionalist and an innovator') see A. C. Houston, *Algernon Sidney and the Republican Heritage in England and America* (Princeton, 1991), pp. 94–8.

39 Daly, *Sir Robert Filmer*, pp. 152–3.

40 *Ibid.*, pp. 124–5.

41 G. Eley, 'Is All the World a Text? From Social History to the History of Society Two Decades Later', in G. M. Spiegel (ed.), *Practicing History. New Directions in Historical Writing after the Linguistic Turn* (New York and London, 2005), pp. 35–61, p. 50.

42 This stance is most evident in e.g. Laslett, 'The Man', pp. 544, 545 (although Laslett eventually acknowledged the necessity to bypass a reading of Filmer 'as a socially determined spokesman of a threatened dominant group', especially for matters such as witchcraft: see *ibid.*, p. 546).

43 See G. Stedman Jones, 'The Determinist Fix: Some Obstacles to the Further Development of the Linguistic Approach to History in the 1990s', in Spiegel (ed.), *Practicing History*, pp. 62–75.

44 For a thorough interpretation placing *Patriarcha* 'in the context of the debate over the *Petition of Right*' see L. Levy Peck, 'Kingship, Counsel and Law in Early Stuart Britain', in J. G. A. Pocock, G. Schochet, and L. Schwoerer (eds), *The Varieties of British Political Thought, 1500–1800* (Cambridge, 1993), pp. 80–115, pp. 106–9.

45 See Daly, *Sir Robert Filmer*, pp. 124–50.

46 *Robert Filmer. Patriarcha and Other Political Writings*, ed. J. P. Sommerville (Cambridge, 1991).

47 J. P. Sommerville, 'Introduction', in Sommerville (ed.), *Patriarcha*, pp. vii–xxxvii. This was so especially with regard to Hadrian Saravia's (alleged) influence on Filmer and their similar vision of monarchy (J. P. Sommerville, 'Richard Hooker, Hadrian Saravia and the Divine Right of Kings', *HPT*, 4 (1983), pp. 229–45, pp. 244–5).

48 Sommerville, 'Introduction', p. xxiv.

49 *Ibid.*, p. xv.

50 J. P. Sommerville, 'Absolutism and Royalism', in J. H. Burns and M. Goldie (eds), *The Cambridge History of Political Thought 1450–1700* (Cambridge, 1991), pp. 347–73, p. 358.

51 J. P. Sommerville, *Royalists and Patriots. Politics and Ideology in England 1603–1640* (London and New York, 2nd edn rev., 1999).

52 G. Burgess, *Absolute Monarchy and the Stuart Constitution* (New Haven and London, 1996).

53 A more recent interpretation of Filmer's political writings has insisted on their dependence on Lutheran theology, its political *Weltanschauung*, and the English Erastian tradition of Tyndale and Cranmer (L. Ward, *The Politics of Liberty in England and Revolutionary America* (Cambridge, 2004), pp. 28–31). Despite his stimulating views, Ward problematically juxtaposes patriarchalism and theory of the divine right of kings; fails to provide sufficient evidence to maintain Luther's influence on Filmer; and overplays

the role of God in Sir Robert's work to the detriment of the sovereign's supreme and absolute power in the body politic (on Ward's reading see also chapter 2 below).

54 See T. Cogswell, 'The People's Love: The Duke of Buckingham and Popularity', in T. Cogswell, R. Cust and P. Lake (eds), *Politics, Religion and Popularity in Early Stuart Britain. Essays in Honour of Conrad Russell* (Cambridge, 2002), pp. 211–34; R. Cust, 'Politics and the Electorate in the 1620s', in R. Cust and A. Hughes (eds), *Conflict in Early Stuart England. Studies in Religion and Politics 1603–1642* (London and New York, 1989), pp. 134–67; R. Cust, 'Charles I and Popularity', in Cogswell, Cust and Lake (eds), *Politics, Religion and Popularity*, pp. 235–58; R. Cust, '"Patriots" and "Popular" Spirits: Narratives of Conflict in Early Stuart Politics', in N. Tyacke (ed.), *The English Revolution c.1590–1720. Politics, Religion and Communities* (Manchester, 2007), pp. 43–61; Sommerville, *Royalists and Patriots, passim*.

55 See Schochet, *Patriarchalism in Political Thought, passim*; Daly, *Sir Robert Filmer, passim*.

56 See K. Sharpe, *Remapping Early Modern England. The Culture of Seventeenth-Century Politics* (Cambridge, 2000), *passim*.

57 See P. Collinson, *De Republica Anglorum or History with the Politics Put Back* (Cambridge, 1990), esp. pp. 22 ff.

58 This Thomas Scott is not the well-known pamphleteer and author of *Vox Populi* (1619–20).

59 John Neville Figgis is the only scholar to have underlined the importance of the idea of the king as *pater patriae* in Filmer's work (Figgis, *The Divine Right of Kings*, pp. 150–1).

60 For criticism of scholarly approaches that maintain the 'distinctiveness' of English political reflection see J. P. Sommerville, 'English and European Political Ideas in the Early Seventeenth Century: Revisionism and the Case of Absolutism', *JBS*, 35 (1996), pp. 168–94, e.g. pp. 169, 190. For a more *European* approach to English political thinking see also J. H. M. Salmon, *The French Religious Wars in English Political Thought* (Oxford, 1959); Pocock, *The Machiavellian Moment*; J. Scott, *Algernon Sidney and the English Republic 1623–1677* (Cambridge, 1988); R. Tuck, *Philosophy and Government, 1572–1651* (Cambridge, 1993); Q. Skinner, *Reason and Rhetoric in the Philosophy of Hobbes* (Cambridge, 1996).

61 Despite its importance in the early modern period, this moment of monarchical representation is nowadays historiographically underestimated (R. Bast, *Honor Your Fathers. Catechisms and the Emergence of a Patriarchal Ideology in Germany 1400–1600* (Leiden, New York and Köln, 1997), p. 147, n. 5).

62 See Laslett, 'Introduction'.

63 John Pocock pointed out that '[w]hat Filmer "was doing" ... when he wrote *Patriarcha*' differs 'significantly from what his publishers were doing in 1679', so that 'the meanings he had intended to convey at the later date were not necessarily those read into his text half a century later'. This serves to differentiate 'between the intention of writing and the intention of publishing' (J. G. A. Pocock, 'Quentin Skinner: The History of Politics and the Politics of History', *Common Knowledge*, 10 (2004), pp. 532–50, p. 535).

64 Sir Robert's other writings are, nonetheless, analysed throughout so as to show both continuity of motifs and changes in his intellectual oeuvre.

65 On the debated revisionism in the (broadly defined) field of early modern British history see G. Burgess, 'On Revisionism: An Analysis of Early Stuart Historiography in the 1970s and 1980s', *HJ*, 33 (1990), pp. 609–27. See also the special issues dedicated to

'Revisionism Revised: Two Perspectives on Early Stuart Parliamentary History' in *Past & Present*, 92 (1981), pp. 55–124 and to 'Revisionisms' in *JBS*, 35 (1996), pp. 135–256. An important contribution is also R. Cust and A. Hughes, 'Introduction: After Revisionism', in Cust and Hughes (eds), *Conflict in Early Stuart England*, pp. 1–46.

66 See e.g. C. Russell (ed.), *The Origins of the English Civil War* (1973); J. S. Morrill, *The Revolt of the Provinces. Conservatives and Radicals in the English Civil War, 1630–1650* (1976); K. Sharpe (ed.), *Faction and Parliament. Essays on Early Stuart History* (Oxford and New York, 1978); M. Kishlansky, *Parliamentary Selection. Social and Political Choice in Early Modern England* (Cambridge, 1986); C. Russell, *Unrevolutionary England, 1603–1642* (London and Ronceverte, 1990); Burgess, *The Politics of the Ancient Constitution*; K. Sharpe, *The Personal Rule of Charles I* (New Haven and London, 1992); Burgess, *Absolute Monarchy*; M. Kishlansky, *A Monarchy Transformed. Britain 1603–1714* (1996).

67 A clear explanation of why the revisionist approach to seventeenth-century political thought is unconvincing can be found in Sommerville, 'English and European Political Ideas', *passim*.

68 P. Zagorin, *The Court and the Country. The Beginning of the English Revolution* (1969), p. 106.

69 On Skinner's methodology see Q. Skinner, *Visions of Politics. Volume I. Regarding Method* (Cambridge, 2002). See also J. Tully (ed.), *Meaning and Context. Quentin Skinner and His Critics* (Cambridge, 1988), esp. pp. 29–132.

70 See Skinner, *Visions of Politics. Volume I. Regarding Method*, e.g. pp. vii, 3, 6, 47.

71 *Ibid.*, pp. 82–3.

72 D. LaCapra, *Rethinking Intellectual History. Texts, Contexts, Language* (Ithaca, 1983), p. 16.

73 See S. Stuurman, 'The Canon of the History of Political Thought: Its Critique and a Proposed Alternative', *History and Theory*, 39 (2000), pp. 147–66, pp. 150–1, n. 6.

74 Whereas scholars have traditionally pointed out that 'loyalists' were those whose allegiance was to the office and authority of the monarch, whilst 'royalists' corresponded to those whose obedience was directed to the person of the king, for Jason McElligott and David L. Smith the two terms can be used interchangeably because they were employed as synonyms in the seventeenth century (J. McElligott and D. L. Smith, 'Introduction: Rethinking Royalists and Royalism', in J. McElligott and D. L. Smith (eds), *Royalists and Royalism during the English Civil Wars* (Cambridge, 2007), pp. 1–15, pp. 13–14).

75 For a recent contribution to these themes see C. Cuttica and G. Burgess (eds), *Monarchism and Absolutism in Early Modern Europe* (2012), esp. 'Introduction', pp. 1–17.

76 Sommerville, *Royalists and Patriots*, p. 228.

Part I

Chapter 1

Filmer: his life and cultural interests

Apart from Peter Laslett, no scholar has taken any significant heed of the background in which Filmer grew up, nor of what this environment was *really* like. Sir Robert has simply been pinned down either as a traditionalist representative of a backward patriarchal society unworthy of exploration[1] or as 'a byword for obscurity'.[2] For this reason, he has never received any attention as a seventeenth-century controversialist writing about widely debated philosophical topics and important social issues. In fact, his analysis of usury, housewifery and witchcraft has gone almost entirely unnoticed or deemed negligible.[3] As a result, scholars have failed to understand Filmer as an innovative and original thinker whose intellectual horizons were wide and whose central concerns were of immediate interest and engagement. By contrast, the following pages unravel the complexity of political, religious and cultural factors that shaped Filmer's vibrant intellectual life.[4] It is thus hoped that this chapter will correct all reading of his work as the emblem of intellectual narrow-mindedness and archaic thinking.

FILMER IN KENT:[5] FAMILY, LIFE AND EDUCATION

Since the fourteenth century the Filmers had been one of the most influential Kentish families. Sir Robert's father was Sir Edward Filmer, Prothonotary (i.e. the principal clerk) of the Court of Common Pleas during the reign of Elizabeth I. In 1564 Sir Robert's grandfather had enhanced the standing of the family amongst the members of the local community by marrying the daughter of Sir Robert Chester, Gentleman Usher to King Henry VIII. Yet the founder of the family fortune was Sir Edward.[6]

Sir Edward – who had married Elizabeth Argall, sister of Sir John Argall from whom he had bought the Manor House of East Sutton – played an important role in the public and administrative life of the county.[7] In 1593 Edward was nominated Justice of the Peace at Maidstone where, as his notebook shows, he fulfilled his duties with great zeal.[8] At the Kent Quarter Sessions he contributed to draw up petitions and orders directed to the High Constables. Together with Thomas Argall, one of his numerous brothers-in-law, Edward was involved in the Levy of Arms called by Sir William Twysden in 1595. Active on many fronts, he was finally appointed High Sheriff of Kent and was knighted. Edward was a devout man[9] and owned properties all over Kent as well as a house in Knightrider Street, London. He died in 1629 leaving a very detailed will in which he promised his son Henry £40, provided the latter commenced his 'M. A. in University of Cambridge'.[10] On 10 February 1632 a letter patent of King Charles I authorised Sir Robert to enter into inheritance after his father's death.[11]

Sir Edward Filmer contributed to a fertile exchange of historical manuscripts within the county. Together with Sir Roger Twysden and the renowned Anglo-Saxon scholar William Somner, Sir Robert's father was one of the main antiquaries in Kent. Thus, Filmer probably owned many of Lambarde's works, including the famous *Pereambulation of Kent* (1570); Richard Lynche's account of Noah's travelling after the Flood (1601); writings like Anthony Murray's *A Briefe Chronicle of the Success of Times, from the Creation of the World to this instant* (1611) that told events from the Creation up to the seventeenth century and that Sir Robert very likely consulted when writing *Patriarcha*.[12] Another well-known work was the *Genethliacon* of William Slatyer, a clergyman who probably knew Filmer since in 1625 he had been appointed rector of the church of Ottenden, near East Sutton. A few Kentish landowners were also on good terms with Sir Robert Cotton, 'the father figure of early Stuart historiography',[13] whose *A Short View of King Henry the Third his Reigne* (1614) Filmer owned in manuscript.[14] As Appendix 1 shows,[15] books constituted an essential part of the Filmers' life and interests: their collection was rich in a variety of topics (ethics, politics, philosophy, theology, gardening, architecture) and served Sir Robert to engage in political debates and helped him create his commonplace lists.[16]

Robert Filmer was born in 1588[17] at East Sutton, near Maidstone. He was the eldest of eighteen children. He spent his childhood at the family household and attended the local school at Sutton Valence. In 1604 at Easter he matriculated at Trinity College, Cambridge, where he never graduated. The following year, on 24 January, he was admitted to Lincoln's Inn. Eight years later Filmer enrolled as a member of the Bar despite the fact that he probably never worked as a lawyer.[18] In this respect, his formative years were not dissimilar from those of many young members of the gentry who attended the Inns of Court because of their prestige.

Sir Robert met Anne Heton (d. 1671), elder daughter and heiress of Martin Heton, the powerful Bishop of Ely during James I's reign. They married in August 1618 'at St. Leonard, in precinct of St. Martin-le-Grand. 8 Aug. 1618. D. [Dean and Chapter of Westminster]'.[19] They lived at Sir Robert's house in London, in the Porter's Lodge at Westminster Abbey, until the death of Sir Robert's father. Sir Robert was knighted by James I at Newmarket on 24 January 1619.[20] The following year Sir Robert and Anne had their first son, Edward, who was baptised – as well as one of his brothers (1622) and one of his sisters (1624) – at St Margaret's, Westminster.[21]

Looking at the family album, we find that amongst his brothers one was a courtier (Edward, 1589/90–1648); one a merchant active in the City (Reginald, 1596–1638); one an influential member of the Virginia Company (Henry, 1607–91). However, only the former deserves a historical mention. An undergraduate at Trinity College, Cambridge, like Sir Robert, in 1618 Edward entered Gray's Inn and eleven years later became Esquire of the King's Body. He always held important roles at court and was a good friend of Ben Jonson and of the poet and dramatist Thomas Randolph. Edward was also a successful lawyer with a strong passion for music. In 1629 he published in English some *airs de cour* amongst which was a collection of works of Pierre Guedron and Antoine Boesset with lute accompaniments by Gabriel Bataille. To Edward's work Ben Jonson prefixed and dedicated the poem *What Charming Pearls Are These*.[22] The same poem had been added to *French Court-Aires, with their Ditties Englished* written and translated by Edward himself the year before.[23] Although only Edward was a professional musician, the Filmers patronised and associated with musicians and – being *à la mode* – possessed many English, French, Italian, Dutch part books.[24] Less driven by melody but worth being remembered because of a curious anecdote, was Sir Robert's son Samuel (c. 1624–70), who on 29 May 1646 played cricket at Coxheath near Maidstone in what is thought to be the first recorded cricket match.[25]

Besides being a wealthy landowner, Filmer was a refined and meticulous scholar.[26] From an early age he applied his philological acumen to make commentaries in Latin and Greek on works such as Plato's *De Legibus* and Aristotle's *De Categorys*.[27] These exercises served Sir Robert to accumulate material he would then use in his political works. Of the latter the first he composed was indeed *Patriarcha*, a version of which was ready for publication in 1632. As we will see in the next chapters, the treatise was refused the licence to be published and did not come out until 1680.[28] In any case, the mid 1630s saw Filmer write his first philosophical work.

QUAESTIO QUODLIBETICA: THE UTILITY OF USURY AGAINST TRADITIONALISTS AND AN OUTLOOK ON GOVERNANCE

Dedicated to the important issue of usury,[29] *Quaestio Quodlibetica or A Discourse, Whether it may bee Lawfull to take Use For Money*[30] was published in 1653,[31] even though in the 'Preface to the Reader' (9 October 1652) Sir Roger Twysden clarified that it had actually been written 'almost thirty yeares since'.[32]

Having undertaken a historical survey of the ways in which different authors had addressed this matter, Twysden declared that his knowledge was insufficient to carry this discussion any further. By citing sources as diverse as several Popes, Emperors and Councils of the Church, authorities such as St Augustine, Aquinas, Cardinal Cajetan, Calvin, and by separating prescriptions to the clergy from prescriptions to laymen, Twysden argued that no definite answer to the question of the legitimacy of usury could be advanced. Hence he thought it necessary to present to the public 'this peece ... written ... by a very Learned Gentleman'. '[F]earing the thing it self might receive injury by ill transcribers', Twysden had 'adventured the putting it to the press, not knowing how the Auctor may interpret this my bold attempt in doing it without his command'. The 'Reader therefore cannot expect it should come out so perfect as it might have done, had it past his [Filmer's] last eye'. In fact, Twysden continued, 'the gravel stone and some infirmity' had made 'the Writer unable to give' readers and 'the world further satisfaction'.[33]

The issue of whether it was legitimate to take money at interest on loans certainly troubled several of Filmer's wealthy neighbours and probably some of his relatives too. Amongst these were the Argalls and the Scotts, who were involved in the development of Virginia and needed money to pursue both their financial and colonial projects. *Quaestio*'s main target was Roger Fenton's *A Treatise of Usurie* (1611).[34] Sir Robert compared his thesis with Fenton's and dismantled (not without irony) the theoretical apparatus of his adversary.[35] He confronted head-on Fenton's idea that usury was a morally evil, economically ruinous and legally dubious practice.[36] By contrast, Filmer claimed that not only was usury in line with divine prescriptions, but that it promoted the public good. In this respect, *Quaestio* provides important insights into the Filmerian view of the relations between ruler and subjects. Sir Robert argued that, due to his superiority, the monarch never acted against the financial interest of his subjects. The latter could thus safely practise activities such as commerce, money-lending, agriculture.[37] In turn, the sovereign did not have to fear his subjects as they were individuals (*singuli*) and, accordingly, were not an autonomous community (*universi*) since this would place them above the king.[38] In other words, with his absolute authority the ruler guaranteed that the members of his polity pursued 'lawfull things' that 'have no need of a permission'.[39]

For Filmer usury was a matter as '*indifferent* (as *eating*)'.[40] Indeed, he thought it 'unlikely that the State should tolerate such a Bank [of usury] if all *Vsury* were of it self unlawfull, and also so pernicious to the Commonwealth by the oppression of it as Dr. *Fenton* pretends'.[41] Being 'the meanes of plenty in a kingdome',[42] usury was not only not 'hurtful to a state' but stimulated general growth. Even Fenton 'cannot shew how any particular person is oppressed by *Vsury*', so that 'he flies for Sanctuary to the Common-wealth, to hide himself in the croud, whilest he must confess he cannot tell who is oppressed, but yet the Commonwealth or some body in it (God knowes who) is oppressed'.[43] Fenton's and George Downam's[44] 'pretences of the oppression of the Common-wealth by taking *Vsury* of the Rich' stemmed from what Filmer caustically described as 'a mere *Sanctuary of ignorance*, a fiction which can never be proved, since it is practised in the Richest Common-wealths'.[45] Moreover, the 'Civill Law' allowed usury. And the same applied to commerce, which had to be freed from moral constraints and stifling statutory regulations.[46]

Filmer accused '*Canonists* and *School-men*' of being 'the first broachers of these descriptions of *Vsury*' condemning 'all *Contracts* of gain for the use of money'. However, this 'popish question'[47] was 'now' being 'pressed upon us by some few Modern Divines'.[48] Both 'the Papists'[49] and 'the Ministers of the Gospell' made of usury 'one of the Crying sins', even though it was 'never ... named for a sin in the whole New Testament'.[50] Docrinally as well as morally, usury was not 'unnatural, ungodly, or uncharitable' since the Bible did not proscribe it. Politically, 'unless the lawes of the Land do prohibit or moderate it, as a point of state or policy', usury was legitimate too.[51]

On financial grounds, Filmer maintained that Fenton was wrong in assuming that usury 'makes *things dearer & enhaunces* the prices *of the Mercat*'. The increase of prices was not caused by usury, but rather 'either by the scarcity of the things themselves, or by the plenty of mony'. In contrast to Fenton, Sir Robert argued that 'merchants and others (who by *Usury* are enabled to trade) do export such things as are cheaper and plentifuller here than in other Countries, that so they may gain *there*'.[52] Equally, they 'bring back such things as are dearest and of most necessity at home', making another profit. Borrowing and lending were free activities pertaining to private agents on the market. They could be conditioned neither by external regulators nor by biblical precepts.[53] To follow Mosaic laws to the detriment of 'the rules and principles of naturall reason' was a pure absurdity.[54] Praising the 'artificial' nature of 'increase or gain',[55] Filmer held that '[n]either God nor Nature' had established a fixed value for land, commodities or money. There was 'no Text' which could 'prove an Acre must be sold at such a price, or a commodity at such a rate' since 'the worth of things in proportion one to another is a *humane arbitrary custom*, grounded upon the several necessities or particular opinions of each particular Nation'.[56] Thus, people had the freedom to sell and buy as they wanted 'since mony hath a gainfull use in it self'.[57] Human affairs like usury ought to be regulated by '*right reason or common justice*'.[58]

Despite acknowledging that 'men who are fit for Callings' and 'live idlely on Usury' did 'sinne', Filmer thought they did so 'no otherwise than those that let their lands'. Not satisfied, he added that 'they may and ought to serve God and their Country in some Calling, if they do not, it is no fault of *Usury*, but an abuse of it'.[59] In line with this argument, he indicated that it was wrong to 'fear that *Usury* will bring idleness in the world, for if all men be idle there can be no *Usury*'.[60] That many '*Usurers*' were 'Covetous' did not depend on usury.[61] As he rejected idleness because it yielded no progress to society, so Filmer fully endorsed the practice of usury since it brought riches to people and their country.[62]

That Filmer supported the lawfulness of usury should not surprise if we consider that around 1630 in a royal grant he was named as one of the two creditors (the other was Sir Edward Duke, c. 1604–71, a Suffolk MP who sat in the Commons in 1640) of Edmund Randolph. The latter had 'died outlawed', so that Duke and Filmer were to receive 'the benefit which accrued to the King by the said outlawry, for the payment of Randolph's debts to them, or his debts for which they were sureties'.[63]

THE 1630S: FILMER AMONGST THE KENTISH LITERATI

The 1630s were mainly a period of public commitment for Sir Robert. He participated in the administrative life of the county and carried out his duties as an officer of the county militia. He divided his time between the affairs related to the household and from about 1635 the magistrates' bench in Maidstone. Here he most likely exchanged opinions and shared ideas with his colleagues and men of letters, Sir Edward Dering,[64] Sir John Marsham,[65] Sir Thomas Culpeper (1578–1662)[66] and Sir Roger Twysden (1597–1672).[67]

The latter – county politician[68] and antiquarian[69] – was a good friend and neighbour[70] for whom Filmer stood bail to free him from jail where Twysden had ended up because of his involvement in presenting to Parliament the Petition in favour of the King at the Maidstone Assizes in April 1642. In his journal, Twysden reported that he had found 'my very noble friends, my uncle, Francis Finch, Sr Robert Filmor, ready to joyn, each in a bond of 5,000, and myself of 10,000, I did, in ye end, submit unto it, though tyed not to make a steppe into Kent'.[71]

Another man of letters on familiar terms with the Filmers was the cavalier poet Richard Lovelace (1618–58), who dedicated a poem to Sir Robert's niece Elizabeth, commending her youth and beauty.[72] Mainly known for his *To Altea, From Prison* (1649),[73] Lovelace maintained strong royalist convictions throughout his life. In 1640 he took part in two expeditions to Scotland as an officer under the Earl of Northumberland. Afterwards, he retired to Kent where he became Justice of the Peace. As a royalist partisan, he courageously led the county's protest against impositions levied by Parliament. His vehemence caught the attention of Edward Dering, who then bestowed Lovelace the leadership of the turbulent group of Kentish protesters that presented their remonstrance to the Commons. Amongst them the staunch loyalist Edward

(1619/20–69), Filmer's eldest son, played a crucial role and was very likely forced to go abroad precisely because of his royalism.[74] Edward – a Gentleman of the Privy Council to both Charles I and Charles II who was knighted on 15 February 1642 – joined the King's headquarters and, subsequently, followed the royal family to France. A Francophile close to Queen Henrietta Maria, Edward also travelled to Portugal in the mid 1630s and to France in 1640.[75] However, he returned to England at his father's death in order to prove his will. He died unmarried in Paris on 12 August 1669. After his death, one of his friends, G. Frere, dedicated a few lines to him in a letter in which it was said that Edward 'took his flight thither from France, and out of respect to that place died in the religion of the country – a Roman Catholic'.[76]

In April 1642 these angry and frustrated royalists invaded Maidstone Court House, tearing up the latest counter-petition drawn up by the parliamentarian Thomas Blount.[77] In his *Journal* Twysden reported that, at the Kentish Assize summoned in July 1642, he had found 'certain young gentlemen, Sir John Mayney, Sir John Tufton, Sir Edward Filmer, Mr. Wm. Clark… with a petition' (*The Humble Petition of the Gentlemen and Commoners of Kent*. Presented to His Majesty, 1st August 1642) in which they demanded the restoration of Hull and the Navy to the King, the 'laying aside' of the militia and, moreover, the convocation of Parliament in an 'indifferent place'. In fact, it was Lovelace that 'tore in pieces a disloyal petition in the presence of its makers shortly before he delivered the Kentish Petition to the House of Commons'.[78] As a result, he was jailed for seven weeks and had to pay a heavy fine for his release, whilst the others were sent away as misled young men.

Whilst Filmer and Lovelace might have met and shared political ideas through the former's son, Sir Robert sat on the magistrates' bench in Maidstone with the Egyptologist and chronologer Sir John Marsham (1602–85). Widely travelled and member of the circle patronised by Sir Thomas Edmondes, ambassador extraordinary at the court of Louis XIII,[79] Marsham was a staunch royalist who joined the King at Oxford. After the surrender of Charles' supporters, he retired to private studies in Kent where he owned a very well-furnished library, of which many of his literary acquaintances could make use.

These glimpses of Filmer's cultivated connections portray a richer picture of his life than that given in the scholarship. And this is further confirmed by the fact that such an array of contacts extended to the world of the arts. The Filmers had under their patronage the portrait-painter Cornelius Johnson (born in London around 1594 of Dutch parents), who during the 1620s and 1630s had become 'the fashionable depicter of the court nobility and gentry in England'.[80] Since he resided near Canterbury, Johnson – who painted a portrait of Sir Robert (c. 1623)[81] – had many clients amongst the Kentish gentry and at some stage became a protégé of the Filmers and the Sandys.

In this context Sir Edwin Sandys[82] was the patron of Richard Hooker; Robert Fludd the Rosicrucian was an active scientist associated with several Kentish gentlemen; Sir Cheyney Culpeper of Leeds Castle and Hollingbourne was one of Samuel Hartlib's friends and correspondents. Moreover, amongst Kentish patrons who most actively promoted erudite contacts and provided intellectual and financial resources was Sir Peter Manwood (1571–1625). Together with his father Roger, Sir Peter protected the historian Richard Knolles during his stay in Kent, fostered his literary skills and encouraged him to compose his famous *Generall Historie of the Turkes* (1603). In Kent Knolles also translated Camden's *Britannia* and completed the translation of Bodin's *République* (1606).

In this environment, the library of Sir Edward Dering (1598–1644) – prominent Kentish politician,[83] renowned bibliophile and patron – constituted a valuable fount of material for thinkers at work in disparate fields of learning.[84] The Derings' family estates were concentrated around the village of Pluckley and their seat was Surrenden-Dering in the same village where Sir Edward set up his library. The Filmers' household was thus half-way between Dering's Pluckley and Twysden's East Peckham.[85] Most importantly, Dering knew Filmer personally because of their involvement in the county's public affairs. In a letter written in 1638 to his brother-in-law, the (fickle) royalist Earl of Thanet, Dering mentioned Filmer: 'it is necessary for ye country that I remayne heere, where (since your Lord is now a Sussex man) there is from east to west for 20 mile in length between Sir John Honywood and Sir Robert Filmer, but one Justice of the peace'.[86]

Dering was a well-read scholar who often travelled in Europe and maintained contacts with such figures as Ben Jonson, Cotton, Selden.[87] The outcome of his activity as a book-collector was the creation of the Surrenden Library, which contained over two thousand titles covering many subjects from religion to the theatre.[88] In a list of books and manuscripts formerly at Surrenden, including material which used to be in Twysden's library, can be found treatises of many European thinkers amongst which are Filmer's *Necessity of the Absolute Power of all Kings* (1648) and *Monarchy, The Anarchy of a Limited or Mixed Monarchy* (with Autograph and Manuscript Notes by Twysden).[89]

Friendship and admiration for Filmer's writings, however, were not confined to Kent.

FILMER IN CAMBRIDGE AND LONDON: HIGHBROW CONTACTS AND POLITICS

Outside his county, Filmer's early intellectual contacts included one of 'the most picturesque and pathetic figures of his generation':[90] the blind man of letters and erudite dramatist Ambrose Fisher (d. 1617).[91] Fisher's works were released posthumously: *Pathomachia or loves loadstone* was published anonymously in

London in 1630 with the slightly different title of *Pathomachia: or, The Battell of Affections. Shadowed by a faigned siedge of the citie Pathopolis.*[92]

Fisher was chiefly known as the author of *A Defence of the Liturgie of the Church of England* (1630), which – according to the author of the preface 'Iohn Grant' – was dedicated 'To his Much Honoured Friend Sir *Robert Filmer*, Knight'. Addressing Filmer, Grant interestingly stated that '[i]t was *your care* that preserved this *treatise*; and it will bee *your honour* that you have preserved it'.[93] As Grant clarified, '[f]rom you I had it in *writing*; to you I returne it *printed*'.[94] Grant went on to laud 'this *Monument* of his [Fisher's] *Learning*, and *Love* to *his* and *our* Dear Mother, (the English Church)'.[95] He thought that *A Defence* had been 'unrewarded' till then and that it was now important to publish it. Fisher's work was 'a *th[o]rough defence*' of the Church against the 'opposers' of '*Our Common Prayer Booke*'[96] and those who '*despised Rits of Our Church*'.[97]

A Defence was conceived as a dialogue that both presented 'the Laconicall brevitie' and 'the Socraticall disputing, on *Irenaeus* part', and showed 'the Ramisticall *Dichotomies*, on the part of *Novatus*'. In the frontispiece of Book 1 Novatus was branded a 'curious Corrector, of things indifferent' whilst Ireneus was defined as a 'peaceable Conformer to the state of the present Church'.[98] This set the tone of the argument and confirmed that the dispute centred on Anglican reactions to the mounting tide of non-conformism. In fact, it was mainly thanks to Filmer's effort to preserve the manuscript that *A Defence* could now guide people on doctrinal and ecclesiastical matters. In this respect, the work casts some light on Filmer's religious sympathies. Whilst surviving sources show Sir Robert as reluctant to express his theological positions, Fisher's dedication provides good evidence that Filmer was highly esteemed amongst Anglican divines and, most of all, in tune with the doctrines of the Church.

Grant explained that Fisher and Filmer had met at Trinity College Cambridge where '(as your selfe [Filmer] remembers) we were *coequalls* in time, and *companions* in *studies*'.[99] This sodality of learning continued and bore important fruits: *A Defence* 'was conceived in the *braine* and *brest* of this *learned Authour* in your [Filmer's] Uncle *Argall's* house at *Colchester*',[100] where poets such as John King, Henry King, Izaac Walton, George Sandys, John Donne and Ben Jonson were all habitués.[101]

Another literary friendship Filmer might have cultivated whilst away from Kent was with George Herbert (1593–1633), to whom in a manuscript note he referred as 'the divine Poet and my intimate friend Mr. Geo. Herba[e]rt'.[102] Since the latter's patron Philip Herbert, Fourth Earl of Pembroke, was High Steward of Westminster (1628–49/50), it is likely that Filmer had met the poet amongst the literati and scholars who lived or spent time near his house there. In his *Lives* John Aubrey claimed that Filmer was also on close terms with William Camden, which can be explained in light of the latter's being master at Westminster School. Camden had revealed to Sir Robert how King James had prevented him from making public his account of the Bothwell scandal involving the King's mother, Mary Queen of Scots. In Aubrey's account, 'Mr Camden told Sir Robert Filmore that he was not suffered to print many things in his *Elizabetha*, which he sent over to his acquaintance and correspondent Thuanus, who printed it all faithfully in his *Annals* without altering a word'.[103]

Together with pursuing intellectually stimulating contacts, Filmer continued to reflect on various cultural issues. One such little-known but highly significant effort saw the light of day in the mid 1640s.

AN UNEXPECTED EULOGY: FILMER, THE *VERTUOUS WIFE*[104] AND THE 'NOT VERY PATRIARCHAL PATRIARCH'

In Praise of the Vertuous Wife[105] is, firstly, a practical and moral eulogy of women's general characteristics and, above all, an illustration of their role as wives.[106] Secondly, it is a polemical dialogue based on an exchange of objections formulated by a hypothetical misogynist pamphleteer and the consequent attempts to answer them. Lastly, it expounds Filmer's views on the argument as a result of a thorough examination of his own propositions.

Filmer began his treatise arguing that historically women had often proved their abilities by giving birth; by suffering the consequences of their difficult condition as widows; by experiencing martyrdom. Placing 'courage' at the centre of his account, he explained that 'Huswifrie', '*Labour*' and '*temperance*' were 'meanes to attaine' this virtue.[107] Subsequently, he criticised traditional images of Eve as the evil creature who had corrupted Adam and ruled out the idea that 'the pain and difficulty of childbirth in the human female' were evidence of God's justice for Eve's sin. He then reminded the reader that Eve 'was created in *Paradise*, lastly out of man['s] *Ribb* not out of the earth' and also that 'the incarnation and resurrection of Christ were first revealed to women'. This meant that these 'priviledges had not beene granted if weomen could not be vertuous'.[108] Most importantly, against those who accused them to '*have beene most wicked*', Filmer forthrightly argued that '[i]f some weomen have beene worst, then some weomen have beene better then men'.[109] Hence he did not hesitate to affirm that men should 'emulate even the courage of women'.[110] By revisiting the interpretation of the creation of Eve and her subsequent role in sinning against God,[111] Filmer challenged the traditional view whereby women's inferiority stemmed from the account of the Fall and questioned the old typology of Eve as the symbol of irredeemable depravity intrinsic to her gender.[112]

These considerations served Sir Robert to introduce his novel perspective on the role of women in the household. Far from the hypocrisy of household manuals that, despite advocating the necessity to respect women in public, de facto considered the social station of the husband and his reputation as the only important aspects of marriage,[113] Filmer called attention to the damaging effect of instilling fear in the wife to the detriment of 'love of vertue' and 'the family'.[114] Consequently, he attacked those 'wicked men' who 'kill the spirit of the wife wth bitter lookes, wordes, deedes'[115] and, as he vividly put it, 'make her of a rib to become an excrement'.[116]

It was precisely against patriarchal positions of this kind that Filmer depicted the figure of the virtuous woman. Her principal traits were courage and strength. These made her 'not ... afraid of any terror' and gave her 'true vertue'.[117] In tune with this, Filmer maintained that she expressed her wisdom not just in practices that gave pleasure such as 'Musique' and the *'curious Artes'*, but also in important fields like 'Huswifrie' and in disciplines such as *'Phisicke and Chirurgery'*.[118] In order to improve their social conditions women needed to be enabled to pursue activities which fostered their skills. As a form of apprenticeship, it was important that 'they be broken of the(ir) will when they are younge'; 'they be kept in service farre from home'; 'they be not marri(ed) untill they be skillful in huswifrie'.[119] They also had to act with 'moderation' in order to marry husbands who were neither *'Spendthrifts* nor medlers wthin doores'; they ought not to have *'concurrent mothers* or any other to command'; they had to be strong so as to organise their household effectively and increase its incomes. In contrast, a *'foolish woman* [who] *wth her owne handes destroieth her house'* was likened to people who 'pull downe their owne houses, in time of fire or when the enemie approacheth'.[120]

Most importantly, through this image of the virtuous wife, Filmer shaped some of his political views on the role of Parliament. In particular, he emphasised the necessity that those who were in a position of responsibility always fulfil their duties even under the harshest circumstances. To leave the household or abandon the kingdom (and, consequently, the sovereign) in case of danger or conflict represented the most despicable decision that a housewife, or an assembly, could take.[121] Good housewifery and good governance symbolised the safeguard of the household and the State, respectively. Moreover, as a virtuous woman *'shal build her house* ... First by saveinge. Secondly by encreasinge. Thirdly by absolute raisinge of a mans estate',[122] so counsellors should act according to the same criteria in order to make their kingdom (and king) prosper. The woman who was incapable of governing her household with competence and authority was a *'Contintious wife'*. A 'contintious wife' caused damages similar to 'a *continual droppinge* wch eateth through the hardest stone, and being let in rotteth the strongest houses'.[123] By the same token, such a situation occurred when a weakened king was confronted with an increasingly hostile Parliament. Indeed, whilst *'the foolish sonne is a heavynesse to the father,* much more a *contintious wife'*: as a subject towards the ruler, so 'the sonne is not *equal* to his father' and as such 'he may be *restrained, disinherited, dismissed'*; yet 'all theise [measures] fail in a wife', just as they did in relation

31

to Parliament.[124] The reference to the mid 1640s political scenario could not be lost. Thus, the wife represented the English Parliament: 'he [the king] may trust her [Parliament] for speech or silence if he tell her no *secrets* wch either go beyond her understanding as matter of state, or may drive her into suspition, greife, anger: or wherein she can give neither counsail nor helpe'.[125]

By and large, the marital relationship should be founded not on financial, familial or political interests, but on the profound compatibility of the spouses' personalities and on '*vertue*'.[126] For Filmer, mutual independence and love were the core of their union. He valued both men and women as individuals. Respect and self-confidence were defining elements of their bond. Likewise, a full understanding of their environment helped husband and wife to judge each other and take decisions in the household. In this regard, Filmer subscribed to Plato's philosophical model whereby moral and political virtues in the community were always intertwined with the capacity of each individual to govern themselves. He articulated a form of Platonic paradigm according to which a rational *régime des désirs* constituted the foundations that made possible the good organisation of ethical and political life in society.[127]

Equally, Filmer underlined the fundamental role (both practical and moral) the wife held in preserving the unity of the household. The '*vertuous wife*' saved her husband from sexual lust ('whoredome'); from irrational behaviour ('drunkinesse' and '*anger*'); from passions like '*Jealousie*'.[128] Coupled with this, women and men had to be productive through work. Filmer rejected '*carelessnesse*' and deplored the lack of '*earilynesse*', '*vehemency*', '*continuance*' and '*method*' on the part of the wife with regard to the management of the household. He considered '[h]elpe' and '*allacritye*' key traits of her personality without which she showed neither wisdom nor intelligence. He despised gentlemen and ladies 'who live by their lands in sloth, not in publique labour of profitable huswifry'.[129] Extolling zeal in work-activities (like he had done in *Quaestio*), Filmer also offered some practical advice with the aim of improving the quality of the couple's well-being.[130] A good lifestyle enhanced not simply physical health but also spiritual strength since this 'sharpneth the wit', 'lengtheneth the memory' and 'cheereth the hart'.[131] The opposite was true of '*disuse of labour*' that 'enfeeble their bodies and disable their mindes'.[132]

In Praise of the Virtuous Wife shaped a model of the woman as an independent '*housekeeper* that is no gadder abroade, but a traveller for lawfull businesse wth unsuspected company'.[133] It also described her as active for her country by means of commercial activities – '[s]he must seeke out such thinges as are profitable for her country'.[134] Most importantly, it acknowledged that

> there is no vertue in men so differen(t) wch weomen may not hope in some sort to attaine, for e[ven] sayling and warre and goverment of kingdomes have been often times well handled by weomen, *Queene Dido* may be example for all, or rather Q *Elizabeth* in whose tim(e) theis things flourisht.[135]

Placing merit centre stage, Filmer made clear that 'if any woman excell in *Chirurgery, Phisick, government* of a commonwealth she shall be no more bound to the *wheele* then a prince is to ye *Plough'*.[36] Far from patriarchal views defended by many of his contemporaries, he gave an innovative and enlightening account of womanhood and rejected the principle that conventions or customs were the cornerstone of judgement.

The virtuous wife deserved to be praised both by her children, whom she treated 'wthout partiality', and by her spouse. Her '*Constancie*', 'wisedome', '*Arte*' ought to be 'honor[ed]'.[37] Likewise, her '*Justic(e,) Clemencie, Liberalitye*' should be recognised, so that her children would regard her with respect after the death of the father.[38] The widow had the right to 'enjoy a convenient and honorable portion' of her husband's properties and she had to be respected in her decisions even 'though she marrye againe'. Consequently, her offspring should not 'grudge ... at that wch she enioyes'. Most significantly, '[i]f she be accused in the gates of *Judgement*, either// for *witchcraft* or *whoredome*, or be molested in suites of lawe', they had the duty to 'defend her by declaring her former innocencye'.[39] In recognising that women were too often identified with crimes like witchcraft and prostitution, Filmer closed *In Praise of the Vertuous Wife* with a defence of their virtues, skills and superiority over men in many fields. Above all, he urged husbands to respect their wives as equal, loyal and loved companions.

Unusual for the views expressed in it, *In Praise of the Vertuous Wife* was no isolated attempt on Filmer's part to investigate fields of knowledge other than politics. One of these domains – conspicuously absent from the historiographical radar – is witchcraft. In 1652 he wrote one of his most interesting but least-studied works: *An Advertisement to the Jurymen of England, Touching Witches,*[40] which the bookseller to three Stuart monarchs, Richard Royston, published on 28 March 1653. This was to be Sir Robert's last intellectual effort.

'A SUCCESSFUL SPELL': FILMER AND WITCH-HUNT

It was after having witnessed a trial against a group of women accused of witchcraft, which took place at the Maidstone Assizes on 30 July 1652, that Filmer began writing *An Advertisement.*[41] The outcome of the Maidstone trial was that, whilst some of those accused were imprisoned and others put in the stocks, six of them were sentenced to be hanged. The latter were judged guilty of having lethally bewitched adults and children, horses and livestock. They were also held responsible for having destroyed chattels and property by means of enchantments and evil spells.

It was precisely this customary tale that Filmer – having revisited his previous views[42] – came to abhor. Together with the conditions in which trials were generally carried out, it was the treatment of the accused – often poor, old women, uneducated and excluded within their communities – that appalled Filmer the most. Hence he saw it necessary to distinguish between biblical witches, to whom judges still referred so as to found their accusations, and those who were prosecuted in seventeenth-century England for what was regarded as the same crime. This enabled him to expose the absurd ways in which judges dealt with proofs, witnesses and circumstances.[143]

Interest in witchcraft ran in Sir Robert's family: a distant relative of his through his grandmother was Reginald Scott (d. 1599), author of the famous *The Discoverie of Witchcraft* (1584).[144] As his ancestor had proclaimed that to believe in the existence of witches and in their power was 'a probable matter to children, fooles, melancholike persons and *papists'*,[145] so Filmer considered 'those of the reformed churches, as well as these of the roman' equally propagators of the conviction that witchcraft existed and that its pursuers should be punished.[146] Sir Robert was also writing in the wake of the 1604 repeal of the Statute of 1563, which had established the death penalty for crimes of witchcraft.[147] Hence he carried out his discourse along two lines. On one level, he denounced the archaic procedures of which the legal system made use when treating this matter and highlighted their lethal consequences on the social order. On another level, he fused the former type of argument with a more direct doctrinal examination and with a philosophically thorough textual critique of his adversaries' positions on witchcraft.

First of all, *An Advertisement* shed light on the lack of a precise definition in the Statute of 1604 of 'what a conjuror, a witch, an enchanter, a charmer and sorcerer is'.[148] This had engendered disorder from a legal perspective as well as raising problems of a moral nature. Therefore, Filmer called the attention of judges, lawyers and legislators to the unfair treatment reserved for those accused of witchcraft. Manifesting his strong scepticism towards practices like the swimming test, whose origins he traced in Germany,[149] Filmer also aimed at preventing hysteric behaviours and irrational beliefs from replacing the law. Against prejudice and superstition, he insisted on the necessity to embrace scientific innovations and accept historical change. As he put it, 'ignorance in the times of darkness ... and credulity in these days of light' had hindered a necessary transformation in the ways with which witchcraft was dealt.[150] Traditional approaches to nature needed to be replaced with the new spirit of empirical investigation: 'for there be daily many things found out and daily more may be, which our forefathers never knew to be possible in nature', but with which it was now imperative to reckon.[151] This method, Filmer argued, would enlighten 'such as have not deliberately thought upon the great difficulty in discovering, what, or who a witch is'.[152] Those sitting on the magistrates' bench in Maidstone were certainly amongst the audience addressed. However, they were not the only ones Filmer had in mind.

The latter comprised the Puritan William Perkins (1558–1602),[153] author of *A Discourse of the Damned Art of Witchcraft* (published posthumously in 1608),[154] and the Jesuit Martin Del Rio (1551–1608), who wrote *Disquisitionum Magicarum Libri Sex* (published at Louvain in 1599).[155] Perkins' demonology was deeply influenced by his Calvinist theology, at the heart of which was the tenet of the covenant between man and God. He stressed the importance of divine election whereby some men had been endowed by the Almighty with His light, and insisted on inscrutable godly grace and predestination. In stipulating their covenant, the elected and God acted as equal: despite His omnipotence, Perkins argued, God had conceded a large degree of autonomy to covenanting men. In stark contrast to Perkins, Filmer stated that '*Covenants* and *Contracts* ... are grounded only upon the laws of *Nature* and *Nations*'.[156]

Filmer attacked the Calvinist by resorting to paradoxes and irony: if 'the witch doth not work the wonder but the devil only' (as maintained in *A Discourse of the Damned Art of Witchcraft*), it followed 'that the devil is the worker of the wonder and the witch is but the counsellor, persuader or commander of it, and only accessory before the fact and the devil only principal'.[157] Hence it was difficult to explain 'how' the witch 'can be "duly and lawfully convicted and attainted" according as our statute requires, unless the devil who is the principal be first convicted, or at least outlawed, which cannot be because the devil can never be lawfully summoned according to the rules of our Common Law'.[158] By emphasising the absurdity of Perkins' propositions, Filmer also cast doubt on the adequacy of the common law to confront and resolve problems stemming from the complexity of public life.

He subtly criticised both 'the public faith of the present age' and the literati for failing to provide a clear explanation for the alleged existence of witches. Accordingly, he ridiculed Perkins' conviction that in order to know a witch, one had to resort directly to Satan. Filmer remarked that this consideration was totally absurd 'except [where] the devil be bound over to give in evidence against the witch'.[159] This conspicuously unfounded assumption 'discredits all' of Perkins' 'Proofs'. Equally, the evidence provided by 'K. James [VI and I], who as I remember hath but 3. arguments for the discovery of a witch', had to be dismissed.[160] The King's idea that 'disability in a witch to shed tears' represented unmistakable evidence of her guilt was no less erroneous. However, James' views (advanced in 'his book of daemonologie [composed] in his youth'[161]) had a great influence not only on popular opinions, but also on thinkers like Perkins and Del Rio whose theories – Sir Robert showed – were replete with inconsistencies.

Perkins saw witchcraft as a 'craft' to accomplish miracles thanks to the Devil's help. Similarly, Del Rio underlined that the contractual 'league' between Satan and witches had the power to generate wonders which overcame common human knowledge. In substance, Perkins had not only failed to conform to Scripture but he had also ignored the rules of logic: as Filmer ironically observed, 'if every man that hath invocated the devil or desired his help must have formerly made a league with him, then the whole nations are' full of 'witches, which I think none will say'.[162] By resting his argument on an 'intimation only' taken from the Psalms rather than from empirical facts, Perkins had also contradicted another Puritan '*Rabby*', Henry Ainsworth (1569–1622).[163] Whilst Perkins thought that the stipulation of the contract determined the characteristics of the deal between the witch and the Devil, Ainsworth had argued that sorcerers held their own right in the contract. In this respect, Del Rio's opinions proved to be no less unreasonable: despite having 'no confidence in this text of Mr Perkins, for he doth not cite it to prove a contract', the Jesuit thinker 'hath also one text of his own to that purpose': this was 'Isaiah 28.15. where it is said, "we have made a covenant with death, and with hell we are at an agreement"'. The outcome was the same since Del Rio's argument

> proves nothing at all, ... for it is not possible to make a covenant with death, which in it self is nothing but a mere not being; and whereas it is called an agreement with hell, it may be translated, as well, if not better in this place an agreement with the grave.[164]

As a result, Filmer asserted that 'neither Mr Perkins nor the Jesuit'[165] could 'prove this contract between the witch and the devil'. In fact, both of them said 'very little ... of this great point, but pass it over perfunctorily'. Things, however, did not improve if one considered King James' *Daemonologie* of 1597. In fact, Filmer did 'not find that he doth meddle with it at all, but takes it for granted that if there be witches, there must needs be a covenant, and so leaves it without further proof'.[166] In this caustic *reductio ad absurdum* of his targets' theory, Filmer astutely argued that in 'the agreement between the witch, and the devil' the likes of Perkins 'call a covenant' a situation in which 'neither of the parties' was 'any way bound to perform their part, and the devil without doubt notwithstanding all his craft hath far the worst part of the bargain'.[167] Nor was Del Rio's argument much better set out. In fact, despite conceding that the Devil was always free to break the agreement, *Investigations into Magic* still implied the freedom of 'the witch to frustrate the devil's contract'.[168]

Filmer's unbroken stream of criticism was then addressed to both Perkins' idea that 'witches renounce God and baptism' and Del Rio's opinion that it 'is common to all contracts with the devil, that first they must deny the faith and Christianism and obedience to God', and second 'reject the patronage of the Virgin Mary and revile her'.[169] By embracing this last view, it followed that 'none can be witches but ... Roman Catholics'.[170] Thus, Filmer showed the foolish conclusion of the Jesuit's thesis by rhetorically asking: if Del Rio is right, 'who else can renounce the patronage of the Virgin Mary? And what shall be said then of all those idolatrous nations of Lapland, Finland and of diverse parts of Africa, and many other heathen nations which our travellers report to be full of witches?'[171]

Filmer then pointed out the absurdity of condemning a witch merely by claiming that she was in contact with Satan. After all, if Perkins was correct in maintaining that 'witch-craft' was the 'working of wonders', 'it must be understood that the art must be the witches' art and not the devil's, otherwise it is no witchcraft, but devils-craft'.[172] Yet since the Puritan writer had declared that 'it is a rare art for a witch by her art to be able to do nothing her self', how could it be legitimate to condemn her, who could only 'command another to practise the art'?[173] Such an argument served Filmer to further unveil Perkins' contradictory approach to witchcraft. On the one hand, the latter claimed that Satan's main goal was 'to obtain thereby the soul and body of the witch' so as to persuade a human being to stipulate a pact. On the other hand though, Perkins argued that '"the Precepts of witchcraft are not delivered indifferently to every man, but to his own subjects, the wicked; and not to them all, but to special and tried ones"'.[174]

From this Filmer concluded that the logic of the covenant was at odds with the logic of God. Perkins himself admitted that it was thanks to divine grace that one could be freed from the influence of Satan, so that contracts proved to be of no use. In addition, Filmer pointedly unfolded the difficulty of combining the impenetrable arbitrariness of divine grace with human free will to justify the contractual agreement. This fictitious arrangement yielded confusion in the mind; deprived people of their cognitive faculties; obfuscated their memory; weakened their soul; intoxicated them to the extent that they fell prey to hallucinations and delusions. Those who stipulated a covenant ceased to be themselves, so that they confessed to the most implausible stories.[175] As the belief in the power of magic drifted people away from God,[176] so in the body politic – Filmer reminded his readers throughout his political writings – contractualist tenets diverted subjects' allegiance from the superior care of the fatherly sovereign.

An Advertisement received attention soon after its publication: the well-known diarist Thomas Burton referred to the 1652 'judicial tragedy at Maidstone' as the event that called forth '"An Advertisement to the Jurymen of England, touching Witches", by Sir Robert Filmer, whose *Patriarcha* has been long exploded, but who in this pamphlet, as well as in a later one on *Usury*, has anticipated the good sense and just reasoning of our times'.[177] Burton's extolling words were not wide of the mark and confirmed Filmer's contemporaries' recognition of his talent. Not as quick and/or willing was the historiographical mainstream.

Expression of an intellectual activity whose spectrum of interests went beyond the realm of political ideas for which he is known, *An Advertisement* – exactly like *Quaestio* and *In Praise of the Vertuous Wife* – offers novel insights into an important but almost totally neglected part of Filmer's work. These three writings explored the implications of order, authority and harmony in the public arenas of the market and the courtroom, and in the private space of the household. They ridiculed die-hard prejudices; dismantled rooted social attitudes; questioned traditional methods of enquiry into natural phenomena. Moreover, they investigated the nature of power in conjunction with the cohesion of the community (as in the case of usury and witchcraft) and the image of the self (as for the organisation of the household). Money, love and witches represented three theoretically fertile 'normative analogues'[178] with which Filmer enquired into relevant political, social and cultural dynamics affecting the body politic and its structure. Thanks to his argumentative lucidity, moral understanding and powerful scepticism, he advanced knowledge to eradicate unsubstantiated claims against usury; condemned brutal and misogynistic treatments of women; ridiculed fatuous credulity in the supernatural, dismissing the pretences of witch-mongering charlatans.

An Advertisement was Filmer's last work before his death around 23 May 1653. He was buried a week later in the church at East Sutton. His will shows the extent of his connections across Kent as well as the size of his properties, which included land not only near East Sutton but also in Boughton and Boxley, manors in Bartley in Lamborhirst and Berst in Ottinden. As for his possessions, Sir Robert announced that he would leave to his son Sir Edward 'all my money, books, and other Goods not formerly disposed of'.[179] He then bequeathed his wife Anne gold and jewels together with his house at Westminster and his manor at Witchling and other land in the Romney Marsh. To his daughter Anne, he guaranteed 2500 pounds for her marriage and wedding dowry.

Given his sedulously anti-republican stances, it is rather ironic that on 13 January 1653 'Oliver Lord Protector of the Commonwealth of England and Scotland ... lawfully authorised the last will of testament of Sir Robert Filmer'.[180] A more significant moment of posthumous recognition came in 1674 when his second son, also named Robert (1622–75), was nominated baronet 'in consideration for his father's sufferings for the Crown'.[181]

As we will see in chapter 6, Filmer's practical sufferings occurred during the Civil War. Problems of a more theoretical nature, instead, date back to the late 1620s/early 1630s when Sir Robert completed the highly controversial *Patriarcha or The Naturall Power of Kinges Defended against the Unnatural Liberty of the People*. And controversy was part and parcel of the milieu in which this work was first thought and written. In particular, the 1620s witnessed a decisive process of ideological radicalisation mirrored in the opposition between the narratives of 'patriots' and 'popularity'. Whilst the former emphasised the role of the 'good commmonwealthmen' in contrast to corrupted courtiers and treacherous papists, the latter virulently criticised all forms of popular participation in politics. It was, indeed, 'over a period stretching from at least the 1580s to the 1640s' that 'these two narratives played an important role in structuring political attitudes and responses'.[182] The peaceful literary world of cordial exchanges, rich libraries and vibrant scholarly collaboration delineated in this chapter, and in which Filmer was an active participant, was not immune to this type of contrast.[183] In fact, *Patriarcha* turned out to be the strongest absolutist response to the patriots' defence of 'the common people'.[184]

Interestingly, since the patriot paradigm found a particularly fertile ground in Kent our discourse comes full circle: one of its most strenuous representatives was not only a Kentish man but also one of Filmer's cousins: Thomas Scott of Canterbury.

NOTES

1 See my introduction. For a brief sketch of Filmer's life see also Sommerville, 'Introduction', pp. vii-xxxvii.

2 Laslett, 'Introduction', p. 1.

3 The only exception is a study dedicated to Filmer's conception of marital life: M. Ezell, *The Patriarch's Wife. Literary Evidence and the History of the Family* (Chapel Hill and London, 1987).

4 It has to be noted that archival material on Filmer, his life and public activity is scarce, which has made it all the more difficult to track down his conduct in relation to why, for example, he did not serve as an MP; his activity on the magistrates' bench in Kent; where he paid ship money; how he responded to the Protestation; whether he took the Negative Oath or the Engagement. In fact, the Filmer MSS at the KAO are not complete as many of them were lost in 1945 (I am grateful to Mr David Cleggett for help on this matter). As for the KAO material, since it is sometimes made up of unnumbered loose sheets, it has not always been possible to separate them for purposes of citation.

5 On Kent see e.g. M. Zell (ed.), *Early Modern Kent, 1540–1640* (Woodbridge, 2000).

6 B. J. Filmer, *Filmer Family Notes. Part One* (1984), p. 43.

7 See KAO, U120/C1–3 (File B, 13 documents) and KAO, U120/C6, A5.

8 See KAO, U120/O9, 'Notebook kept by Sir Edward Filmer as a Justice of the Peace' (dated 1609–25).

9 See KAO, U120/F21.

10 See KAO, T200/10 (Edward's will) and KAO, T200/12 (Dame Elizabeth's will).

11 See KAO, U120/T1/36/2.

12 The same can be said of Henry Lythe's *The Light of Britanyne. A Recorde of the honourable Originall & Antiquitie of Britaine* (1588) and John Taylor's *A Memorial of All the English Monarchs ...* (1622) (Greenleaf, 'Filmer's Patriarchal History', p. 165).

13 P. Clark, *English Provincial Society from the Reformation to the Revolution. Religion, Politics and Society in Kent 1500–1640* (Hassocks (Sussex), 1977), p. 219.

14 See D. A. H. Cleggett, *The Filmer and Wilson Families*, Leeds Castle Foundation (Maidstone, 2003), ch. 4, which refers to an eighteenth-century inventory drawn up at East Sutton.

15 A quick glance at Sir Robert's library catalogue suffices to dispense with the assumption that he was a backward gentleman with narrow cultural views.

16 See A. Grafton and A. Blair (eds), *The Transmission of Culture in Early Modern Europe* (Philadelphia, 1990).

17 1588 is accepted as the year of his birth (although there is no sure evidence proving this).

18 Laslett, 'Introduction', pp. 1–2.

19 J. Foster (ed.), *London Marriage Licences, 1521–1889* (1887), p. 484. Laslett wrote that the marriage took place in 1610, but that a marriage settlement to be found in the East Sutton Papers was agreed in 1618. This, Laslett continued, was due to the fact that Filmer and 'his young wife did not live together until after 1618: this sometimes occurred when a child heiress was married to a grown man' (Laslett, 'The Man', p. 526). However, Laslett was wrong and must have misread '1618' as '1610'. I thank Johann Sommerville for his help on this issue. St Leonard, Foster Lane was a Church of England church in the city of London that served as a parish church for those who lived on St Martin's Le Grand. It was destroyed in the Great Fire in 1666 and never rebuilt.

20 Around this time, Filmer wrote *In praematuram Mortem disperati Juninis G. W. Funebris Elogia*, an epitaph dedicated to G. Wyatt, a son of George Wyatt, influential member of the Virginia Company and related to the Filmers through the Scotts. This G. Wyatt had fallen ill with a fever and had died at the age of seventeen. The reasons why Sir Robert wrote this piece are unclear (BL, Additional MS 62135, fos 68–9).

21 Of the Westminster parishes, St Margaret's was the most conservative and most attached to ceremony; it kept church music and was lavishly decorated (J. F. Merritt, *The Social World of Early Modern Westminster. Abbey, Court and Community, 1525–1640* (Manchester, 2005), pp. 322, 325–7). Interestingly, in 1622 the minister appointed there was the absolutist Isaac Bargrave under whose ministry more strikingly anti-Catholic positions were taken (*ibid.*, p. 340).

22 B. J. Filmer, *Filmer Family Notes. Part Three* (1992), p. 26.

23 See Ben Jonson, 'To My Worthy Friend, Master Edward Filmer', in *Ben Jonson, The Complete Poems*, ed. G. Parfitt (1996, repr.), Miscellaneous Poems, xx, p. 270.

24 These presented a variety of dance music, villanelles, sonnets, madrigals, songs, dialogues and other vocal pieces (R. Ford, 'The Filmer Manuscripts: A Handlist', Notes, *The Quarterly Journal of the Music Library Association*, 34 (1978), pp. 814–25).

25 See R. M. Filmer, *Deep-Rooted in Kent. An Account of the Filmer Family* (1977).

26 For instance, he punctiliously singled out a mistake in Denis Lambin's Latin translation of a passage taken from a French edition of Aristotle's *Politics* published in Paris in 1619 (see BL, Harley MS 6867, fos 251a–2a, signed R. F. at fo. 252a). Here Filmer also referred to Casaubon's work on Aristotle (*ibid.*, fo. 251a). In *Patriarcha* he remarked that 'not only our English translator of Aristotle's Politics is, in this place, misled by following Lambin Aristotles Politiques, p. 179, but even the learned Monsieur Duval in his analytical Synopsis bears them company' (*PT*, p. 13).

27 See the book-list in G. Schochet, 'Sir Robert Filmer: Some New Bibliographical Discoveries', *The Library: The Transactions of the Bibliographical Society*, 5th series, 26 (1971), pp. 135–60, p. 151, where these commentaries are defined as 'possibly' part of 'a school exercise-book'. There survives a manuscript with extracts on these texts and other commentaries in Latin and Greek, which might have been Filmer's (see BDO, uncatalogued and part of the late Peter Laslett's library papers, item f on the list

titled 'Manuscripts from East Sutton Park', 88 fos, quarto; for details of this series of manuscripts see Appendix 1).

28 As will be further specified in chapter 2, I assume that the 1632 manuscript is textually the same as the version that we now have or, at least, that if there were any differences, they would not change the content of the book.

29 On usury in the early modern period see e.g. C. H. George, 'English Calvinist Opinion on Usury, 1600–1640', *Journal of the History of Ideas*, 18 (1957), pp. 455–74; R. Ashton, 'Usury and High Finance in the Age of Shakespeare and Jonson', *University of Nottingham Renaissance and Modern Studies*, 4 (1960), pp. 14–43; B. Nelson, *The Idea of Usury. From Tribal Brotherhood to Universal Otherhood* (Chicago, 2nd edn enl., 1969); J. O. Appleby, *Economic Thought and Ideology in Seventeenth-Century England* (Princeton, 1980); M. MacDonald, 'An Early Seventeenth-Century Defence of Usury', *Historical Research*, 60 (1987), pp. 353–60; N. Jones, *God and the Moneylenders. Usury and Law in Early Modern England* (Oxford, 1989); E. Kerridge, *Usury, Interest, and the Reformation* (Aldershot, 2002).

30 The Latin *quodlibet* means 'what you please'. In common usage it referred to a subtle or debatable point. The expression *quaestio quodlibetica* held a technical meaning in the medieval university system. During the academic year in Advent and Lent, specific topics would be singled out for discussion and special disputations open to a wide array of people would take place. These focused on 'any topic whatever (*de quodlibet*) and could be initiated by any member of the audience (*a quolibet*)' (A. Kenny and J. Pinborg, 'Medieval Philosophical Literature', in N. Kretzmann, A. Kenny, and J. Pinborg (eds), *The Cambridge History of Later Medieval Philosophy from the Rediscovery of Aristotle to the Disintegration of Scholasticism, 1100–1600* (Cambridge and New York, 1982), pp. 11–42, p. 22). Such disputations were characterised by intense 'question-answer' exchanges. Given their format and argumentative structure, it is likely that Filmer chose this title to suit his treatment of a publicly important argument where the author's pungency could be fully deployed.

31 On the difficulty in establishing when *Quaestio* was composed see J. P. Sommerville, 'Sir Robert Filmer, Usury and the Ideology of Order', in D. Carey (ed.), *Money and the Enlightenment* (Oxford, 2007), pp. 1–37 (I am grateful to Johann Sommerville for letting me read a copy of his paper ahead of publication). Sommerville argues that, since Filmer referred to the statute of 1624 that fixed usury at 8%, 'the book is clearly later than that' (*ibid.*, p. 6). Sommerville bases his attribution of *Quaestio* to a date later than the mid 1620s mainly on the fact that Filmer quoted from Lancelot Andrewes' *De Usuris*, which was published only in 1629, and referred to Salmasius' *De Usuris Liber*, which was published in 1638. According to Sommerville, this proves that 'Filmer cannot have completed the preface to the *Quaestio* before 1638' (*ibid.*, p. 7). Yet this does not exclude that Filmer conceived the main part of his text between the mid 1620s and early 1630s and that he added the preface where he mentioned Salmasius after 1638 (though it is certain that Salmasius wrote his work shortly before its publication date of 1638; on this see C. Salmasius, *De Usuris Liber, Claudio Salmasio auctore*, Lugd. Batavor. (Leiden), Ex Officina Elseviriorum, 1638. The preface is addressed to Ioh. Cloppenburgius, at Brill, 13 January, 1638 (sig. *4a–*5°)). It is also possible that Filmer knew Andrewes' writings before their publication and that he had read them in manuscript, whilst Salmasius' positions on usury might have been well known before their publication. Considering how often Filmer quoted from and referred to works of other authors engaged in the same intellectual fields as his, it is odd that he did not mention John Blaxton's important *The English Usurer; or Usury Condemned* published in 1634. Thereby, it seems plausible

to infer that at least by this date Sir Robert had completed his work. Finally, it is worth pointing out that, since Filmer stated to have singled out Roger Fenton's treatise 'because it is the latest' and considering that this work came out in 1611, it is reasonable to assign to Filmer's treatise an early date rather than a late one when Fenton's writing was not 'the latest' any more (*QQ*, 'Preface', sig. A5a). The same applies to the reference Filmer made to George Downam as 'now Bishop of London-derry' in consideration of the fact that the latter had been appointed to that position in 1616.

32 *Ibid.*, sig. A2r. Filmer placed his discussion of usury in relation to both English – 'Bishop Babington, *Mr.* Perkins, *Dr.* Willet, *Dr.* Mayer, *Mr.* Brinsley' – and continental authors – 'Calvin, Martyr, Bucer, Bullinger, Danaeus, Hemingius, Zanchius, Vrsinus, Bucanus, Junius, Polanus, Molineus, Scultetus, Alstedius, Amesius, Grotius, Salmasius' (*ibid.*, A4a).

33 Roger Twysden, 'To the Reader', in *QQ*, A14.

34 Fenton (1565–1616) was a Church of England clergyman and author, preacher and scholar (see *ODNB*, 'Fenton, Roger').

35 Filmer accused Fenton of having borrowed his arguments 'from *Dr. Downam*', who in turn had taken his 'from *Melancthon* and *Chemnitius*, and these two fetch it from *Canonists, Casuists*, and *School-men*' (*QQ*, pp. 17–18).

36 See e.g. *ibid.*, pp. 142–3.

37 *Ibid.*, pp. 133–5.

38 M. L. Pesante, 'L'Usura degli Inglesi: Lessico del Peccato e Lessico della Corruzione Politica alla Fine del Seicento', in G. Boschiero and B. Molina (eds), *Politiche del Credito. Investimento Consumo Solidarietà*, Atti del Congresso Internazionale Cassa di Risparmio di Asti (Asti (Italy), 20–22 March, 2004), pp. 113–38.

39 *QQ*, pp. 63–4.

40 *Ibid.*, p. 116.

41 *Ibid.*, p. 14.

42 *Ibid.*, p. 45.

43 *Ibid.*, p. 43 (misnumbered as p. 42 in the Thomason Tracts, BL 1312).

44 Downam (also spelt Downham, d. 1634) had written *The Christians Sanctuarie* (1604).

45 *QQ*, p. 56. See also *ibid.*, p. 137.

46 *Ibid.*, pp. 113–14.

47 *Ibid.*, 'Preface', sig. A4b–5a.

48 *Ibid.*, pp. 16–17.

49 *Ibid.*, p. 92.

50 *Ibid.*, 'Preface', sig. A8b–9a.

51 *Ibid.*, 'Preface', sig. B5.

52 *Ibid.*, p. 44.

53 *Ibid.*, pp. 46, 53.

54 *Ibid.*, p. 55. See also *ibid.*, p. 85. As he put it, 'there is no faith but it is mingled with some doubting'. Indeed, 'if a man be perswaded of any thing by the light of *Reason*, or by *Sense*, he is justly said to beleeve it' (*ibid.*, pp. 117–18; see also *ibid.*, pp. 120, 121–2).

55 *Ibid.*, pp. 127, 122.

56 *Ibid.*, pp. 131–2.

57 *Ibid.*, p. 135.

58 *Ibid.*, p. 136.

59 *Ibid.*, p. 146.

60 *Ibid.*, p. 147.

61 *Ibid.*, p. 149.

62 *Ibid.*, pp. 182–3.

63 *Calendar of State Papers Domestic, Series of the Reign of: Charles I 1629–31*, ed. J. Bruce (1860), vol. 178, undated 1630, pp. 423–30, p. 423.

64 Please see page 28 (this chapter).

65 Please see page 27 (this chapter).

66 The Cavalier Sir Thomas Culpeper was the author of *Tract Against the High Rate of Usurie* (1621), where he claimed that, both on commercial and moral grounds, it was necessary to decrease the legal interest rate from 10% to 6% (*DNB*, 'Culpeper, Thomas').

67 See Laslett, 'The Man', p. 533.

68 Roger Twysden of Roydon Hall, East Peckham (Kent), had been knighted in 1620 and by 1636 had become Justice of the Peace in Kent. He was a widely learned man with a strong interest in legal, constitutional and ecclesiastical history. He numbered Sir Simonds D'Ewes, John Selden, Sir Henry Spelman and Sir William Dugdale amongst his friends. Twysden collaborated with many other scholars on different subjects and wrote extensively (see *DNB*, 'Twysden, Sir Roger'). On Twysden see S. Petrie, 'Sir Roger Twysden 1597–1672: A Re-appraisal of His Life and Writings', PhD Thesis, University of Kent, 2006.

69 Twysden found in Paolo Sarpi's works a model of knowledge and a platform for doctrinal reconciliation in Europe. Twysden was familiar with the *Historia del Concilio Tridentino* and the *Trattato dell'Interdetto*, just as with the works of Marc'Antonio De Dominis and Fulgenzio Micanzio (J. L. Lievsay, *Venetian Phoenix. Paolo Sarpi and Some of His English Friends (1606–1700)* (Lawrence, Manhattan and Wichita (Kansas), 1973), p. 88). In fact, he exchanged letters with Micanzio as well as with others of Sarpi's friends and pupils. Twysden's reputation as a historian earned him the praise of Manasseh Ben Israel, the mastermind of the re-settlement of the Jews in England (*ibid.*, p. 92).

70 On 16 December 1638 Twysden wrote to Sir Robert 'excusing his searching a substitute horse, and ruler, and giving reasons' (KAO, U120, C6, A4); whilst on 20 December 1642, it was Sir Robert that wrote to 'my Honord friend Sir Roger Twisden K. and Baronet at his house in Red Cross Streete' referring to 'these times ... of troubles', during which he had been fined 'of some mony', and expressing his distress at the fact that the parliamentarians were 'searching him money for Yalding Bridge' (*ibid.*, A6).

71 'The Journal of Sir Roger Twysden. From the Roydon Hall MSS', *Archaeologia Cantiana* (vols 1–4 1858–61), vol. 2, pp. 175–220, p. 180. Twysden's account is confirmed by the official report in 'House of Commons Journal Volume 2: 09 April 1642', in *Journal of the House of Commons 1640–1643* (1802), vol. 2, pp. 518–21, p. 520.

72 Laslett, 'The Man', p. 528.

73 C. H. Wilkinson (ed.), *The Poems of Richard Lovelace* (Oxford, 1930), p. xxii.

74 P. Lindsay, *For King or Parliament* (1949), pp. 186–7.

75 See *Historical Manuscripts Commission*, Third Report, Appendix, 'The Manuscripts of Sir Edmund Filmer, Bart., at East Sutton Park, Co. Kent' (1872), p. 246.

76 Cited in Filmer, *Filmer Family Notes, Part One*, p. 100.

77 'The Journal of Sir Roger Twysden', vol. 2, p. 186.

78 *The Poems of Richard Lovelace*, p. xxiv.

79 See *DNB*, 'Marsham, Sir John'.

80 J. T. Cliffe, *The World of the Country House in Seventeenth-Century England* (New Haven and London, 1999), p. 40. Later variants of his name include 'Jansen' and 'Janssens'.

81 For reproductions of it see the cover of this book and both *ODNB*, 'Filmer, Sir Robert' and Ezell, *The Patriarch's Wife*.

82 Together with one of Filmer's sons and with George Herbert, Sandys was amongst the most influential members of the Virginia Company (see N. Malcolm, 'Hobbes, Sandys, and the Virginia Company', *HJ*, 24 (1981), pp. 297–321).

83 On the stormy phase of Dering's political career in the 1640s a direct testimony is 'The Journal of Sir Roger Twysden', esp. vol. 1, pp. 184–214. See also *ODND*, 'Dering, Sir Edward'.

84 On Dering see N. H. Krivatsy and L. Yeandle, 'Sir Edward Dering', in R. J. Fehrenbach and E. S. Leedham-Green (eds), *Private Libraries in Renaissance England. A Collection and Catalogue of Tudor and Early Stuart Book-Lists* (Binghamton (New York), 1992), vol. 1, pp. 137–63.

85 Dering dedicated his energies to antiquarian studies and to scholarly interests that enabled him to 'spend the tyme in reading, walking, or somewhat else that will beguile it' with people like Twysden ('On the Surrenden Charters', *Archaeologia Cantiana*, vol. 1 (1858), pp. 50–65, p. 62).

86 BL, Stowe MS 743, fos 132–3, *Letter to the right honourable my ever honest Lord the Earl of Thanet, Surrenden-Dering 7 March 1638* (included in the volume of manuscripts titled *Dering Correspondence*, vol. 1570–1640, Jas I-Geo II).

87 M. Butler, *Theatre and Crisis 1632–1642* (Cambridge, 1984), pp. 128–9.

88 'On the Surrenden Charters', pp. 50–1.

89 See *A Sale Catalogue of the Collections of Sir Edward Dering, 1st Bart., and his son, and Sir Roger Twysden ...* (1858). I am grateful to Sue Petrie for letting me consult this list.

90 Laslett, 'The Man', p. 527.

91 There are no sources on his life: neither the *DNB* nor the *ODNB* provides an entry for Fisher.

92 See *Pathomachia or loves loadstone* (BL, Harley MS 6869, item 1). Although the work had been traditionally ascribed to Fisher, Gordon Schochet has attributed it to Filmer (Schochet, 'New Bibliographical Discoveries', p. 147, n. 1). In EEBO *Pathomachia* is attributed to Henry More (1614–87).

93 Ambrose Fisher, *A Defence of the Liturgie of the Church of England ...* (1630), 1a.

94 *Ibid.*, 1a.

95 *Ibid.*, 1a–b.

96 *Ibid.*, 1b.

97 *Ibid.*, 2b.

98 *Ibid.*, 1b–2a.

99 *Ibid.*, 2a.

100 *Ibid.*, 1b.

101 Laslett, 'The Man', p. 527.

102 BDO, Tanner MS 233, fo. 147a. However, no evidence of their friendship survives from Herbert's hand.

103 O. Lawson Dick (ed.), *Aubrey's Brief Lives* (1960), p. 51.

104 On this image see D. J. Latt, 'Praising Virtuous Ladies: The Literary Image and Historical Reality of Women in Seventeenth-Century England', in M. Springer (ed.), *What Manner of Woman. Essays on English and American Life and Literature* (Oxford, 1977), pp. 39–64.

105 This was an essay on 'Proverbs', 12.4, 'A virtuous woman is the Crowne of her husband ...'. The version of *In Praise of the Vertuous Wife* used here can be found in Ezell, *The Patriarch's Wife*, Appendix I, pp. 169–90 (the following symbols have been inserted in the passages extracted from Filmer's text: () = editor's addition; < > = author's deletion; // = end of manuscript page; [ ] = my addition. One manuscript copy can be found at the Cambridge University Library, Trinity, Add. MS a/406 ('Manuscript on Woman') and another at the BDO (uncatalogued and part of the late Peter Laslett's library papers, item g, 17 fos, quarto). According to Ezell, 'its abrupt ending and the blank sheet at the end of the volume suggest that although the argument set out in the opening of the piece is complete, the copy itself lacks some part of its conclusion' (Ezell, *The Patriarch's Wife*, p. 130). In a previous manuscript titled *Touching marriage and adultery* Filmer had dealt with biblical directives on marriage, especially Hebrew, so as to confirm the sanctity of the marital institution (see N. Tadmor, 'Women and Wives: The Language of Marriage in Early Modern English Biblical Translations', *History Workshop Journal*, 62 (2006), pp. 1–27, pp. 1–2). In this piece, which for Schochet was 'perhaps ... a lay sermon' (Schochet, 'New Bibliographical Discoveries', p. 147), Filmer spoke of the 'great benefits of conjugal society' and 'mutual consent'. He referred to 'parental power' rather than to 'paternal power'. Despite holding adultery a punishable offence, Filmer also acknowledged the status of unmarried women unrestrained by any marital contracts and that of concubines too (*Touching marriage and adultery*, BL, Harley MS 6866, fos 514r–22r). Ezell, instead, suggested that this tract was a survey on the practice of polygamy in the Old Testament and the debate about it that followed (Ezell, *The Patriarch's Wife*, pp. 130–1). It focused on texts such as 'Genesis', 'Exodus', 'Numbers', 'Deuteronomy' and on biblical characters like Sarah, Hagar, Moab, Rachel, Salomon, David and Abraham.

106 On gender in seventeenth-century England see e.g. L. Stone, *The Family, Sex and Marriage in England 1500–1800* (1977); L. Bernikow, *The World Split Open. Women Poets 1552–1950* (1979); P. Malekin, *Liberty and Love. English Literature and Society 1640–1688* (1981); A. Fraser, *The Weaker Vessel. Woman's Lot in Seventeenth-Century England* (1984); S. D. Amussen, 'Gender, Family and the Social Order, 1560–1725', in A. Fletcher and J. Stevenson (eds), *Order and Disorder in Early Modern England* (Cambridge, 2nd edn, 1987), pp. 196–217; Ezell, *The Patriarch's Wife*; A. Fletcher, *Gender, Sex and Subordina-*

tion in England 1500–1800 (New Haven and London, 1995); M. R. Sommerville, *Sex and Subjection. Attitudes to Women in Early-Modern Society* (1995); S. W. Hull, *Women According to Men. The World of Tudor–Stuart Women* (1996); P. Springborg, 'Mary Astell and John Locke', in S. N. Zwicker (ed.), *The Cambridge Companion to English Literature 1650–1740* (Cambridge, 1998), pp. 276–306; A. Shepard, *Meanings of Manhood in Early Modern England* (Oxford, 2003).

107 *VW*, pp. 172–3.

108 *Ibid.*, pp. 170–1.

109 *Ibid.*, p. 171.

110 *Ibid.*, p. 172.

111 Despite departing from traditional teachings whereby Eve's subordinate status was justified since she had been created 'after', 'for' and 'from' Adam (*ibid.*, p. 170), Filmer (still) admonished to 'let none therefore wth Adam lay the blame upon her, but rather blame him that should have beene the wiser of the two' (*ibid.*, p. 175). As Margaret Sommerville observed, '[e]ven when sinning – the only thing she was remembered for – Eve had less impact than Adam', who was considered the sole culprit for the sin (Sommerville, *Sex and Subjection*, p. 22).

112 For a similarly positive view of Eve see e.g. I. G., *An Apology for Womankind* (1605). For the opposite opinion see e.g. John Wing, *The Crown Conjugal or, The Spouse Royal …* (1620).

113 An exception to this trend can be found in Daniel Tuvil, *Asylym Veneris or a Sanctuary for Ladies* (1616).

114 *VW*, p. 182.

115 *Ibid.*, p. 171.

116 *Ibid.*, pp. 182–3. Like Filmer, the post-Restoration Tory and proto-feminist champion Mary Astell (1666–1731) argued that underlying husbands' treatment of wives stood the conviction that those 'who make the Idols, are the greater Deities'. For husbands 'set' wives 'up', it was in the former's 'power to reduce' the latter to their 'first obscurity, or to somewhat worse, to Contempt' (Mary Astell, *Some Reflections upon Marriage …* (1700), p. 24). For a modern edition of Astell's work see P. Springborg (ed.), *Mary Astell. Political Writings* (Cambridge, 1996), pp. 1–80.

117 *VW*, pp. 169–70.

118 *Ibid.*, p. 176.

119 *Ibid.*, p. 176.

120 *Ibid.*, p. 176.

121 Parliamentary theorists often resorted to the image of houses burning down as a metaphor to decry the incapacity of monarchs to face up to emergencies (J. Daly, 'John Bramhall and the Theoretical Problems of Royalist Moderation', *JBS*, 11 (1971), pp. 26–44, p. 33). Consequently, Filmer's passage could well be an answer to this argument.

122 *VW*, p. 176.

123 *Ibid.*, p. 177.

124 *Ibid.*, p. 177.

125 *Ibid.*, pp. 180–1.

126 *Ibid.*, p. 180. For Filmer the 'first' to be 'condemned' were those 'that will not marry where *vertue* is separated from *wealth*'.

127 See *ibid.*, p. 178. On the concept of '*régime des désirs*' see M. Foucault, *L'Usage des Plaisirs* (Paris, 1984).

128 VW, pp. 180, 182.

129 *Ibid.*, p. 186.

130 *Ibid.*, p. 183.

131 *Ibid.*, pp. 183–4.

132 *Ibid.*, p. 186.

133 *Ibid.*, p. 182.

134 *Ibid.*, pp. 182–3.

135 *Ibid.*, p. 183.

136 *Ibid.*, pp. 186–7.

137 *Ibid.*, pp. 177–8. See also *ibid.*, p. 182.

138 *Ibid.*, p. 189.

139 *Ibid.*, p. 189.

140 The original manuscript is BL, X.519 25563. There is also a copy in the Thomason Collection (E. 690 (6), Wing F 909). Here the page numbers refer to the edition printed from the original manuscript by *The Rota*, at the University of Exeter 1975. Although it was published anonymously, *An Advertisement* was attributed to Filmer in the anonymous preface of his *The Power of Kings* (1680).

141 Whilst for Laslett it was the emotional impact of the Maidstone trial that prompted Filmer to compose *An Advertisement* (Laslett, 'The Man', p. 543, n. 59), Ian Bostridge identified doctrinal convictions as the main reason that led Sir Robert to write this work (I. Bostridge, *Witchcraft and its Transformations c. 1650–c. 1750* (Oxford, 1997), p. 19; for an account of Filmer's positions vis à vis witchcraft see *ibid.*, pp. 13–21). I think that the 1652 trial provided Filmer with the stage on which to expound ideas he had elaborated and matured over a longer period of time.

142 On Filmer's early belief in the existence and right punishment of witches see *Theologie: or Diuinity* (BDO, uncatalogued and part of the late Peter Laslett's library papers, item c, esp. fos 5–6), where 'witchcrafte' was associated with 'ydolatrie' and 'changing of religion' (all had to do with 'false feare'), and where it was defined as 'an arte', based on 'Faith in a covenant … made with Sathan' (*ibid.*, fo. 5). Filmer distinguished between 'theoreticall' and 'Practicall' witchcraft: the former had to do with knowledge and was either 'ymediatlie' or 'by means', which in turn was either 'pollitique (as diuinge lotts)' or 'Supernaturall (as raising the dead)'. Practical witchcraft, instead, attempted 'things aboue nature, in healing, or huntinge' (see *ibid.*, fo. 6 where he also spoke of dreams). As for the legal aspect, Filmer declared that 'Witches are to be condemned either by their owne witnesse, voluntary, or extorted by the rack: or by the witnesse of others'. Death was thus due onto them 'for theire league' with Satan (*ibid.*, fo. 6). For brief mentions of *Theologie: or Diuinity* see Schochet, 'New Bibliographical Discoveries', p. 151 and Bostridge, *Witchcraft and its Transformations*, pp. 14, n.31, 18.

143 On witchcraft in England and its social, juridical and epistemological features see e.g. H. R. Trevor Roper, *The European Witch-Craze of the 16th and 17th Centuries* (Harmondsworth, 1969); K. Thomas, *Religion and the Decline of Magic* (New York, 1971); S. Anglo (ed.), *The Damned Art. Essays in the Literature of Witchcraft* (1977); D. Underdown, 'The Taming of the Scold: The Enforcement of Patriarchal Authority in Early Modern England', in A. Fletcher and J. Stevenson (eds), *Order and Disorder in Early Modern England* (Cambridge, 2nd edn, 1987), pp. 116–36; L. Roper, *Oedipus and the Devil. Witchcraft, Sexuality and Religion in Early Modern Europe* (London and New York, 1994); J. Sharpe, 'Women, Witchcraft and the Legal Process', in J. Kermode and G. Walker (eds), *Women, Crime and the Courts in Early Modern England* (1994), pp. 106–24; J. Sharpe, *Instruments of Darkness. Witchcraft in England 1550–1750* (1996); Bostridge, *Witchcraft and its Transformations*; G. Geis and I. Bunn, *A Trial of Witches. A Seventeenth-Century Witchcraft Prosecution* (London and New York, 1997); S. Clark, *Thinking with Demons: The Idea of Witchcraft in Early Modern Europe* (Oxford, 1997, repr. 2005).

144 Scott deftly targeted Jean Bodin's *De la Démonomanie des Sorciers* (1580); totally denied the existence of witches in contemporary England; argued that those executed for witchcraft were innocent; objected to the traditional opinion that there was a biblical sanction for executing witches; and reduced witchcraft to an impossible crime since words had no effect on reality (see *ODNB*, 'Scott, Reginald' and Laslett, 'The Gentry of Kent', p. 158, n. 30).

145 Cited in S. Anglo, 'Reginald Scot's *Discoverie of Witchcraft*: Scepticism and Sadduceeism', in Anglo (ed.), *The Damned Art*, pp. 106–39, p. 110 (italics added). Reginald Scott, Thomas Ady (author of *A Candle in the Dark* published in 1655) and Filmer were the three main sceptics in the early modern English debate on witchcraft (S. Clark, 'King James's *Daemonologie*: Witchcraft and Kingship', in Anglo (ed.), *The Damned Art*, pp. 156–81, p. 173). Keith Thomas suggested that amongst English thinkers who saw the belief in the existence of witches as a continental habit were 'Reginald Scot, Samuel Harsnet, Sir Robert Filmer, Thomas Ady, John Wagstaffe, John Webster, Francis Hutchinson' (Thomas, *Religion and the Decline of Magic*, p. 570).

146 *AD*, p. 3.

147 See Geis and Bunn, *A Trial of Witches, passim*.

148 *AD*, p. 2.

149 *Ibid.*, p. 11.

150 *Ibid.*, pp. A2a–b. Departing from his previous views, Filmer questioned the legitimacy of employing torture as a means to obtain information in the course of judicial proceedings against alleged witches (*ibid.*, p. 12).

151 *Ibid.*, p. 8. Here he attacked faith in miracles and belief in the supernatural as completely antithetical to the enquiries of 'philosophers' concerning 'the power of nature'. Seeing 'things done the like whereof they had never seen nor heard of', credulous people would 'believe them to be miracles'. Accordingly, they would consider those who talked without opening their mouth but only using their belly as possessed by a 'Familiar Spirit' instead of realising that they exploited a particular physical skill (*ibid.*, p. 19).

152 *Ibid.*, p. A2.

153 On Perkins see e.g. D. K. McKim, *Ramism in William Perkins's Theology* (New York, 1987). Perkins was a widely read author whose doctrine of the absolute predestination (prior to the Fall) represented the chief position on divine grace amongst English Calvinists.

154 See William Perkins, *A Discourse of the Damned Art of Witchcraft, so farre forth as it is revealed in the scriptures and manifest by true experience* (1608). It was printed several times afterwards.

155 This work became one of the most read texts of demonology right up to the 1650s. Del Rio's approach to witchcraft was strongly influenced by the thought that magic was a phenomenon which needed to be solved by the Church as the only repository of 'Truth'. Del Rio associated witchcraft with transgression of the Church's teachings and with separation from God (Martin Del Rio, *Investigations into Magic*, ed. and trans. P. G. Maxwell-Stuart (Manchester and New York, 2000), esp. 'Introduction', pp. 1–23, p. 23).

156 *QQ*, p. 55. Filmer's view of magic also differed from Hobbes' in that they disagreed with regard to the role of witchcraft in the State (see Thomas Hobbes, *Leviathan*, ed. C. B. Macpherson (Harmondsworth, 1968), esp. Part 1, ch. 2, p. 92; Part 4, chs 44–5, *passim*; for similarities between the two thinkers see *ibid.*, Part 3, ch. 37, pp. 474–5).

157 *AD*, p. 7.

158 *Ibid.*, pp. 7–8.

159 *Ibid.*, p. A3.

160 *Ibid.*, p. A4.

161 *Ibid.*, p. A4.

162 *Ibid.*, p. 17.

163 *Ibid.*, p. 4. In calling Perkins a '*Rabby*' Filmer was suggesting that the Puritan thinker belonged to the philosemitic group of scholars who sustained the necessity for all Christians to abide by both the moral law *and* the judicial law (criminal law). They argued that the Mosaic law ought to be largely revived, whilst others claimed that only those aspects of it that were also deducible from the Ten Commandments (i.e. those which coincided with the moral law) were still valid.

164 *Ibid.*, p. 5.

165 For Filmer, Del Rio agreed with '*Bellarmine*' (*ibid.*, p. 20).

166 *Ibid.*, pp. 5–6.

167 *Ibid.*, p. 5.

168 *Ibid.*, pp. 5–6.

169 *Ibid.*, p. 6.

170 *Ibid.*, p. 6.

171 *Ibid.*, p. 6.

172 *Ibid.*, pp. 6–7.

173 *Ibid.*, p. 7.

174 *Ibid.*, p. 8.

175 *Ibid.*, p. 13.

176 *Ibid.*, pp. 22, 16.

177 'The Diary of Thomas Burton 5 December 1656', in *Diary of Thomas Burton esq., July 1653–April 1657* (1828), vol. 1, pp. 20–37, p. 26.

178 This notion is employed in Sharpe, *Remapping*, esp. pp. 38–123.

179 KAO, U120, T200/14.

180 Cust, '"Patriots" and "Popular" Spirits'.

181 Cited in Laslett, 'Introduction', p. 9.

182 Cust, '"Patriots" and "Popular" Spirits', p. 58.

183 See J. Eales, 'The Rise of Ideological Politics in Kent, 1558–1640', in Zell (ed.), *Early Modern Kent*, pp. 279–313.

184 Hirst, *The Representative of the People?*, e.g. pp. 12, 139. Hirst defined *Patriarcha* as 'the most extreme English statement of what may be called absolutism' (Hirst, *England in Conflict*, p. 125). These common people can be identified with small property householders who stood below the gentry. In general, in the late 1620s there was a convergence of interests between commoners and members of the gentry on the issue of the extension of the franchise (*ibid.*, esp. pp. 75–89 with regard to voting as 'the birthright of the subjects of England'). See also D. Underdown, *A Freeborn People. Politics and the Nation in Seventeenth-Century England* (Oxford, 1996), pp. 53–4; R. Cust and P. Lake, 'Sir Richard Grosvenor and the Rhetoric of Magistrates', *Bulletin of the Institute of Historical Research*, 54 (1981), pp. 40–53.

Chapter 2

———◆———

From Kent with anger: *Patriarcha* versus Thomas Scott's country patriotism[1]

In concluding the previous chapter, we briefly referred to the kind of political tensions that informed early seventeenth-century England. To unravel this last scenario we do not need to look further than Canterbury and Maidstone.[2] Thus, the leading characters of this chapter are the two Kentish cousins Thomas Scott of Canterbury and Robert Filmer. The interesting but little-studied Scott belonged to the 'patriots', the group of thinkers and countrymen who in the 1620s claimed to be the true defenders of the nation and its subjects' liberties. Although they did not constitute a coherent party, Filmer took their stance as a serious threat to the unity of monarchy. Accordingly, in *Patriarcha* he rejected their opinions; criticised ideas of popular government; developed a different version of patriotism grounded on the fatherly power of the sovereign.

The first part of the chapter traces the origins and developments of the language of patriotism and underscores its importance in early modern England. Scott is then singled out as one of its representative mouthpieces. Both in his rich diary (c. 1614–35) and in *A Discourse of Polletique and Civell Honor* (c. 1619) he set forth a rhetorically radical stream of vitriolic political and religious observations. In line with the patriot narrative, his discourse centred on the essential role of Parliament as England's constitutional representative. Subsequently, *Patriarcha* is analysed not simply as one of many tracts produced in the Caroline absolutist milieu,[3] but more specifically as a text whose prime goal was to protect the nation against both internal and external threats. A stringent examination of its content will unearth the reasons behind the outspoken patriarchalist message it delivered.

Even though both cousins were more extreme than most of their fellow countrymen (patriot critics of the government and of the Laudian establishment, and monarchist theorists),[4] the study of Scott and Filmer provides useful insights into the political and ideological conflicts of the first two Stuart reigns.

'LANGUAGE MATTERS': SCOTT AND FILMER IN THEIR POLITICAL CONTEXT

In *Volpone* (1607) Ben Jonson referred to 'such as were knowne *Patriots*' and clarified that they were '[s]ound louers of their country'.[5] In the parliament of 1610 the ardent government-critic Sir Henry Neville 'ranged himself with those Patriots that were accounted of a contrary faction to the Courtiers'.[6] The following year, in *A Dictionarie of the French and English Tongues*, Randle Cotgrave defined 'Patriote' as '*A patriote, ones countrey-man*' whilst calling 'Royaliste' somebody 'Taking the Kings part, siding with the King'.[7] In November 1621, having in mind his friend Sir Dudley Carleton, ambassador to the United Provinces, Sir John Ogle spoke of 'many good patriots on both sydes that bear up agaynst the Pope and Spaniard'.[8] Three years later, one political commentator interestingly claimed that England was divided into two categories of partisans: 'regians and Republicans'. The former maintained that the king's 'absolute will' was the sole authority and 'the principall rule of all proceedings & obedience in the Commonwealth', whilst the latter held that 'the peoples good is the chiefe of all civill proceedings, and the rule of all such proceedings to be only the lawe of the land'.[9]

Few years went by, the incumbent ruler changed but the rhetoric persisted. In the course of 1627 the well-known Parliament historian Thomas May published his widely read translation of Lucan's *Pharsalia* in which different volumes were dedicated to important personages. Amongst these was the Third Earl of Pembroke[10] whom May extolled by maintaining that he was not only '[f]ree from ambition, free from faction' but, above all, '[a]n honest Lord, a noble Patriot' like the republican heroes Cato and Brutus.[11] The same fate befell the Earl of Devonshire, who accomplished a solid reputation as a 'patriot peer'.[12]

Writing in 1628 on the strict censorship 'in presse, or pulpit', John Russell addressed the issue of tyranny. Taking as models Demosthenes, Cicero and Solon, in the tellingly titled *The Spy Discovering the Danger of Arminian Heresie and Spanish Trecherie*, Russell defined himself as one of the 'true Patriots' seeking 'publique preservation'.[13] His aim was to avoid the internal discord that had destroyed '[t]he Graecian Monarchy' and Roman 'greatnes'.[14] Referring to the 'Catilines' in ancient Rome, Russell identified their modern counterparts in those who supported 'Spanish designes'. These were corrupted statesmen who were plunging England into ruin. Russell thought the commonwealth was perishing under George Villiers, Duke of Buckingham, and his group of courtly acolytes whose principal end was to enthrone the Duke with Spanish help.[15]

In the same crucial year, another commonwealth man, the religious controversialist Alexander Leighton, sent copies of his *Sions Plea* from the Netherlands to every English MP, emphatically calling for full support of the common cause. Coupled with a staunch anti-Catholicism, the abolition of episcopacy and the promotion of Protestant doctrines across Europe, the cause pursued by Leighton entailed the preservation of the country against those who discredited Parliament and its important role. Thus, he invited MPs to embrace the model of the *vita activa* as the most pertinent to their task. They had to fight for the common good and refuse to privilege private interests. Insisting on the instructive example of classical history, Leighton stressed that '[w]ee [true Englishmen] neede not tell you of the Roman Patriots, or the Athenian Kings; who were willinge to dye [so] that the glorie of their nation might live'.[16]

Reporting on the parliamentary elections of 1628, the Venetian ambassador Alvise Contarini tellingly remarked that '[a]ll the counties have uniformly rejected candidates who had even a shadow of dependence upon the Court, electing members who refused the late subsidies, who are now everywhere called good patriots'.[17] Most importantly, the murder of Buckingham (1628) left the English political and ideological landscape increasingly divided.[18] In anti-Stuart circles Buckingham became the byword for foreign effeminacy and moral degeneration. Instead, his murderer John Felton was held as the true patriot who had exercised Parliament's will and fulfilled God's design for the sake of the English nation.[19] As an anonymous poet put it, Felton had 'wonne / The prize of Patriots to a British sonne'.[20]

The advent of the Personal Rule did not alter this wave of patriotism. In *Truth's Triumph* (1629) Henry Burton spoke of the 'kinde usage of the natives and patriots of the country'.[21] In 1630 Richard Brathwaite, the renowned author of one of the most widely read conduct books, *The English Gentleman*, associated the 'honest patriot' with the republican orators of ancient Greece and Rome.[22] He underpinned their role as one of opposition to the greatest enemies of State and underlined their activism for the liberty of the citizens since they placed 'the safetie and peace' of the 'countrey' before private gain.[23] These few examples prove that, if the *Oxford English Dictionary* is mistaken in stating that '"Patriot", for "good patriot", is *rare* before 1680', it is nonetheless true that the term was 'applied to one who supported the rights of the country against the King and court'.[24]

Besides the realm of literary and philosophical debates, many MPs in the 1620s proclaimed themselves 'patriots'. As we will see in chapter 4, they staunchly defended the nation against the tyrannical policies of the Crown. They promoted the Protestant Cause both at home and abroad; claimed the fundamental role of a freely-elected parliamentary assembly; stressed their (republican) abhorrence of corruption; rejected the absolute prerogative of the king. They were strongly attached to the England of freeborn individuals and overtly hostile to foreign powers and customs (mainly Spanish). Modelled on Cicero's ideal of the virtuous citizen actively engaged in the life of the *respublica*, the patriot narrative fostered the service in Parliament of good Englishmen. This entailed firm opposition to the satisfaction of private interests; to vicious courtiers; to tyranny. The patriot's essential goal was the safeguard of the commonweal.[25]

The patriotic discourse had strong rhetorical appeal, especially at a time when the Stuart government implemented unpopular policies like the Forced Loan (1626–27) and manifested sympathy for Catholicism. In contrast to Elizabeth's skilful elaboration of the royal image, both James I and his son Charles I failed to provide their subjects with a popular and successful account of monarchy and its values.[26] Because of its divisive religious policy (Arminianism), controversial political strategy at home (taxation, billeting of troops, imprisonment without cause shown) and disastrous diplomatic campaigns abroad (the Spanish Match, the Palatinate), the Crown was alienating consensus upon which it had previously been able to rely.[27] The decisive outcome of this situation was that the Stuart regime was losing support even amongst those members of the local communities who had always been faithful royalists.[28] In this context Elizabeth's reign and her victorious foreign policy became a byword for what England – as 'true Englishmen' claimed – ought to be and was no longer. Mutual trust between the Queen and her subjects had fostered successful external expansion as well as internal peace. Instead, Charles' political conduct was viewed – in many contexts, at least – as badly damaging to the English nation.[29] Therefore, he had to confront (on an unprecedented scale) the emergence of 'the threat from popularity'. In fact, the widespread idea that a popular conspiracy was imminent affected Charles I's 'personal and ideological formation'.[30] This attitude he undoubtedly inherited from his father.

In 1616 James I had delivered a speech in which he had identified the most dangerous opponents of monarchy with those who could not 'be content with the present forme of Gouernement, but must haue a kind of libertie in the people, and must be gracious Lords, and Redeemers of their libertie'. These 'in euery cause that concernes Prerogatiue, giue a snatch against a Monarchie, through *their Puritanicall itching after Popularitie*'.[31] According to James, such a challenge to royal sovereignty was the first disastrous step towards the establishment of democracy. In line with the King's fears and scathing opinion of popularity, during the same period in Kent some manuscript collections containing 'Curious Citations' taken from Plato, Guicciardini, Tacitus, Fuller,[32] Virgill, Livy, Cicero and Dallington warned against the dangers and 'Levity of the Common People'.[33] In a similar vein, on 28 April 1622 Walter Curll, Dean of Lichfield Cathedral (Staffordshire), preached a sermon at Whitehall in which he warned that peace and order were under fire from both internal and external fomenters of sedition. As he put it,

> desire of change and alteration, it is the mother, and mover, and marker of much
> sedition; and they that are troubled with this itch of Innovation, they cannot but

be rubbing upon Majestie it selfe, and could be content to turne Monarchy into Anarchy, or into any thing, so they might be doing. And some turbulent Tribunes there are in every State, who out of their glorious, vaineglorious humur of *popularity* would be counted Angels, though it bee but for stirring and troubling of the waters.[34]

At this point, the fracture between those who considered Parliament as the bastion of English liberties in opposition to the supreme prerogative of kings and those who saw the unlimited defence of the sovereign as a priority widened considerably. These conflicting political views of liberty and sovereignty mirror the works of Scott and Filmer. In fact, their writings revolved to a great extent around highly debated questions connected to the 1628 electoral campaign to Parliament. Scott's actions and words epitomised the increasing discontent of many MPs, whilst *Patriarcha* was a vigorous attempt to regain to the monarchical cause those who had become dissatisfied with Charles I's policies.[35] In other words, Scott's sedulously developed criticism of the government and the Laudian establishment and Filmer's forceful patriarchalist theory serve as lenses to bring into focus a pivotal series of larger issues concerning English politics and political thought in the pre-Civil War era. As this chapter will illustrate, their ideas of what the nation was and what it ought to stand for moulded two mutually exclusive models of England.[36]

Thus, the Kentish literati Scott and Filmer took the disputes on monarchical power and the role of Parliament very seriously. Both cousins were shocked by what they saw and heard, read and confronted in their locality and at national level too.[37] Hence they refuted the dangerous 'heresies' of their adversaries. The patriotic and Puritan explosions of one prompted the other to fire back using the fatherly cannon of patriarchalism.[38] The comfortable social world of the Kent gentry provided the arena for a spirited battle. As David Underdown observed, Filmer 'was related to Scott by marriage, had certainly met him, and ... he must have heard enough from Scott and from others like him to cause him to fear that the very foundations of his world were threatened'.[39] Liberty and sovereignty became central objects of public discourse as much as of theoretical dispute. Indeed, they touched family ties and often undid them.

THOMAS SCOTT: ENGLISH PATRIOTISM AND 'REPUBLICAN' DEFENCE OF LIBERTY[40]

Thomas Scott, Esquire of Egerton was born in Kent around 1566. He attended Canterbury Grammar School and then proceeded to university (probably at Cambridge) where he never took a degree. Thomas was the son of Charles Scott, Esquire and Justice of the Peace, who had married Jane, daughter of Sir Thomas Wyatt, the leader of the 1554 rebellion against Queen Mary. Thomas Scott was also the grandson of Sir Reginald Scott (Scot) of Scots' Hall near Ashford. Filmer was a second cousin – great-grandson to this Reginald Scott through his mother.[41] Thomas Scott was a Parliament man. He had been Sheriff of Kent (1601) and was elected as one of the two MPs for Canterbury in 1624 and again in 1628 (he had also stood in 1625 and 1626 but had been defeated). By 1612 he had moved to Canterbury, which became the main stage of his public activity as a polemicist. It was in the same year on 14 July that he sent a letter titled *To My Brother Knatchbull* where he referred to 'my cosen, and your Brother Robert Filmer [who] hath this day related unto me, that I am left to be put unto you ...'.[42] Even though fragmentary, this passage denotes that the two cousins were in contact and certainly aware of one another.

Most importantly, Scott kept a diary that he wrote in different phases of his life. The first part dates from 1613–14 whilst the second refers to the late 1620s and presents a continuous sequence of events until the end of the decade. Lastly, there exist a few fragments concerning the early 1630s until just before his death in 1635. The diary is not only a very valuable historical source on early seventeenth-century England, but is also an interesting account of the political and religious situation in Kent and London as it was seen by an active urban polemicist.[43] In particular, the diary shows the extent to which 'popular' voices – that is, outside the elite circles of politics and, instead, rooted in the localities[44] – were attaining visibility in the country. It casts light on the increasing presence of those Filmer branded as the 'common people everywhere',[45] who supported limited monarchy and extended participation in politics. According to Peter Clark, Scott's diary is 'a collage of correspondence, excursive religious and genealogical memoranda, political comment, and personal jottings – all within the rough framework of a journal'.[46] Its narrative form elucidates the interplay of political ideas, doctrinal tenets and ideological sentiments that were to become the key factor 'in the growth of urban opposition to the Crown from the late 1620s'.[47] The diary was thus the repository of the products of Scott's mind. It centred on his staunch commitment to godly religion, but it also worked as a vehicle through which he defined his political agenda and established his ideological identity.

This explains why Scott constantly referred to the connections his family could boast with other important Kentish dynasties such as the Wyatts, the Finches, the Palmers. These genealogical interests were not only the studious fruits of an erudite mind but they held a crucial political meaning. In particular, Scott thought that being a member of one of the most ancient families in Kent gave him the right to have a say in the county community.[48] These genealogical surveys proved that his family derived from the Scots north of the Border. As such he claimed that his countrymen had courageously resisted the Romans and, subsequently, the Norman Yoke. By focusing on genealogy, Scott also recalled the doctrinal lineage that connected him to the marked anti-Catholicism of many Elizabethan Protestants. Similarly, when addressing historical matters or referring to biblical accounts, he targeted fundamental political questions. In contrast to monarchical theorists like Filmer[49] and Peter Heylyn,[50] who argued that the Norman Conquest had completely altered the juridical and political organisation of Saxon England, Scott – in line with the approach taken in François Hotman's *Francogallia* (1573) – played down the impact of the Conquest on the legal and political structure of the reign. In so doing, he rejected all arguments defending royal impositions and justified the claims of Parliament.

Accordingly, Scott emphasised his kinship with the Wyatts with the aim of comparing his Puritan[51] hostility to the Spanish Match in the 1620s, whereby Prince Charles had to marry the Spanish Infanta, with that of his ancestor Sir Thomas Wyatt, who seventy years earlier had led the rebellion against Mary's proposed marriage to Philip of Spain.[52] Scott's investigation of the past in search of meaning to clarify events in his own time also elucidates his identification with a cause whose goal was fierce opposition to the Duke of Buckingham.

Combining the pursuit of the godly[53] cause with 'civic radicalism',[54] Scott attacked Catholicism as the deepest root of 'all our [English] diseases'.[55] If this sentiment was shared by many, Scott went farther than most by suggesting that the most effective remedy to put an end to popish threats on England's religious and political life was to promote the active participation of freeholders in the election process.[56] By exercising their rights, they could ensure that 'men of redoubted courage and grounded in the love of god and their countrye' – men like Sir Edwin Sandys (a vehement critic of the 'tyrannical government' of James I)[57] and Edward Scott – became MPs for their counties.[58] Imbued with these opinions and in reaction to the 1614 local electoral success of the anti-Puritan faction,[59] Scott himself made his debut on the Canterbury political scene. His support of John Finch, 'the notorious Speaker of the Commons',[60] was to bring him into civic office as a common councillor (1618). Yet both Finch and Scott were deprived of their positions because of their Puritanism.[61] Amidst growing tension in the county, Scott based his political activity mainly on the strenuous defence of his civic community against oligarchic impingement and external interference of 'any Forrenner, Non freehoulder, or Non-Resiants'.[62]

Never short of polemical verve, around 1619 Scott composed *A Discourse of Polletique and Civell Honor*,[63] addressing it to Thomas Howard, Earl of Arundel. The treatise criticised James I's policy on knighthood and proposed a humanist ideal of nobility. Scott lambasted James' decision to knight more than two thousand people and create two hundred baronets[64] (several of whom were unsuitable to receive this distinction) in a desperate attempt to save his increasingly shaky authority. Scott centred his criticism on the bribe-soaked mechanisms of distribution of honours in society. He vented his anger on social climbers by remarking that at court '[a]n upstart, a stalking puppitt, is more esteemed and countenanced then hee that is honorably descended, and not degenerated'.[65] The assigning of honours had become so patently common as to discourage knights from embracing courage and fortitude.[66] Deploying his mordant rhetoric Scott spoke of the 'plague of sellinge and prostituting of honour' and pointed out that the lavish distribution of knighthoods had engendered a situation in which 'Learning, Wisedome, Justice, Pietie' were 'very idle and unprofitable quallities'.[67] Adhering to Montaigne's opinion that 'The way to disanull honor is to make a largesse of it', Scott compared the current trend with that in which a fool of a king put on a 'triple Crowne, and [assumed the] title of *Rex regum*, [wearing] gay clothing, and boordes end'.[68]

To consolidate his views on honour and virtue Scott couched his discourse in the language of Cicero and Seneca. He referred to the 'Roman State, and [to] all other flourishing Commonwealths, which ... were carefull of this rule of well ruling' according to which authority pertained to those who were morally and intellectually able to govern and not to 'Rustiques' or 'Mechaniques' who were merely involved in their private activities.[69] Following the traditional humanist account of nobility,[70] Scott argued that honour 'is the proper reward of virtue' and

> none can meritt honor but the honorable, and none but such as are capable of it, though Princes can do what they will, yet they may doe noe otherwise then is fitt and seemely, and therefore not make them honorable for whome Honor is not fitt and seemely: and if they doe otherwise, they doe wronge to themselves, to honor, and the honorable.[71]

The abuse of privileges like the knighthood deprived men of their duty to seek after 'true Religion, vertue, learning, and good deeds'. They promoted, instead, vice, corruption and idleness. Scott defined this practice of granting undeserved honours as '[a]n Evill, a visible and sensible evill, and an Error, the error of Rulers, an unseemely evill, a noysome evill, an Intolerable evill', which 'disquiets the lande'.[72] Therefore, 'it must be remeadied, or we shall bee ruinated'. In fact, Scott fervently added, '[a]llreadie it disquiets us, it will not bee longe before it will be our distruction'.[73] Whilst nobility was transmitted from fathers to their eldest son, Scott argued that knighthood 'of whatsoever order, in England is temporarie, and dies w[i]th him that first receaved it'.[74] Despite covering his contentions with a veil of respect towards authority, these passages suggest that Scott considered the sovereign responsible for the vicissitudes of the nation.[75]

A Discourse also addressed the question of the inheritance of reigns. Scott declared that, although difficult to prove, kings had to present evidence of their kinship with ancestors whose roles and origins were indisputable.[76] He pointed out that there were cases where nobility by birth could not be applied to the choice of kings. Instead, he continued, 'virtue' and 'abilitie' had to replace nobility by birth so as to avert 'great inconvenience and mischeife' in political matters.[77] For this reason, 'honor and magistratie, are for the honorable and worthie', being these things 'peculier', whereas 'other good things are common to all'.[78] In order to have a commonwealth where excellent men governed, it was necessary to promote education and 'endeavours to make good'.[79] This would encourage love of the *res publica*. Likewise, Scott stressed that nobility did not simply derive from inheritance, but it implied skills enabling a poor and obscure man 'to stand before kings'.[80] Remarking that in England 'men are soe much respected for theire birth and other greatnesse' and not for their wisdom,[81] Scott's critique was directed at the Stuart regime. His forthright defence of honour as the outcome of virtue and merit carried strands of republican values. It recalled the tradition of civic humanism focused on people's active role within the body politic. Public duty and courage were not exclusively modelled on the achievements of the godly, but they also entailed political connotations based on the classical tradition and the stoic philosophy of life.[82] Above all, they were important for the life of both local community and commonwealth.[83]

Relying on Melanchthon, Scott emphasised the importance of 'worthinesse' as the only criterion suitable to gauge governors' eligibility.[84] Through Melanchthon he also strengthened his idea that the primary duty of the citizen was the defence of the commonwealth. Very likely from Lutheran political discourse Scott then elicited the concept that inferior magistrates had to protect their fatherland and that, animated by a strong civic sentiment, they had to mobilise citizens to safeguard the *patria*.[85] In fact, in 1538 Melanchthon had underlined that 'the love of fatherland was inscribed into the hearts of men by God'.[86] These opinions sharply contrasted with Filmer's view of fatherly power. For Scott it was impossible to maintain a clear thread of hereditary authority throughout history, whereas Filmer's political discourse was founded on the intelligibility of the transmission of power from God to Adam and from the first man to patriarchs and, consequently, to kings. In this respect, Scott's dismissal of hereditary lineage and primogeniture dealt a blow to the Filmerian configuration of sovereignty because it eroded the line of patriarchalist continuity that – as will be shown below – Filmer reinforced in order to guarantee stability in the nation.

Although *A Discourse* does not predominantly focus on political doctrines, it presents some of Scott's most interesting and confrontational ideas on government. He asserted that the rule of 'right ruling, ought still to rule Rulers',[87] dismissing the opinions of those theorists for whom only God could force kings to do so. He also attacked the absolutist idea that the sovereign was immune not only to criticism but also to all forms of legal control. Scott maintained that 'the rule of choosing Rulers was made' for man and by man 'it ought to be observed'.[88] He emphasised the separation between God's absolute authority and man's limited power. By arguing that 'men should choose theire

Rulers' by 'the rule of lawe', he also pleaded the cause of a constitutional government.[89] In expressing these thoughts Scott no doubt had in mind the conduct of the first Stuart towards Parliament and his appropriation of more and more legislative powers.

After *A Discourse*, there followed a time of intense political and religious activity during which Scott tried to set up a Puritan lectureship in the parish of St Alphege (Canterbury) where he became a close friend of Herbert Palmer, a Puritan preacher who was also the first to hold the lectureship there. Furthermore, given what he considered the gloomy state of public affairs, in 1624 Scott consented to stand as MP for Canterbury. It was in this context that his electoral campaign revolved around growing fear of Catholic plotting and the so-called 'civic radicalism' whose exponents claimed the necessity to embrace the Protestant Cause both at home and abroad.[90]

The final years of the Jacobean reign saw Scott fiercely opposed to what he deemed Catholic attempts to seize an important portion of public life in the country. He regarded the Spaniards as fomenters at work to sustain 'the incroaching ambition of Popes' that had 'of very late dayes' tried to interfere in 'Kent, for example, and Canterburie' with 'temporall power'.[91] In his deeply militant approach to events in his county as well as in the country at large, Scott pointed to the menace that 'now the Spaniards, or [the] French Arminian faction' aided by 'Buckinghams Arminian Ministers' bore for 'the nation of England'. Such a threat was for him 'as dangerous' as that brought by the Danes whose actions had made 'English men ... even poorer and bare'.[92]

In 1625 Scott was persuaded to stand again as a candidate for the parliamentary election. Despite obtaining a number of votes equivalent to one third of the total electorate formed of freemen, he lost the contest.[93] Most revealingly, his followers were not only Puritan radicals or tradesmen holding godly views, but they also included moderates. Scott fought to restore effective parliamentary action aimed at protecting the liberties of the free members of the commonalty. Above all, he advocated a general parliamentary reform.[94] In 1626 he drew a proposal in which he questioned the legal structure of the Commons: he criticised the absurd situation in which the benches were filled with burgesses who did not reside in their constituencies. His goal was, therefore, to make parliamentary assemblies more regular so as to guarantee continuity between one session and another, and limit the power of the monarch.[95]

It was in January 1626 that, amongst disputes over the nature of government and the role of kings towards people and Parliament, Scott sent a letter to Sir Dudley Digges in which he declared that the latter 'shall never be able to proove that his cosen Scott [himself] and those worthies and true Patriotts that joyned wth him in the Election of Syr Ed. Sandys did either unworthily, or unadvizedly, or otherwise, then yf it were to doe agayne *Rebus sic stantibus*'.[96] Similarly, two months later Scott referred to 'the Offence of Godly and just (men and) Judges ([and] the) Patriots throughout England, and Parliament Judges' whose primary task 'consisteth, not only in not wronging or invading the Liberties of any other person ... but also in Defending and Maintaining those Lawfull Liberties', as 'with God (nature, reason, and lawe)' they had been 'ordained to Protect the People from iniuries'.[97] At this historical juncture, Scott was well aware of the importance of gaining a reputation as an 'honest patriot' to succeed in the electoral campaign in Kent.[98] Therefore, he carved out an image of himself as a defender of parliamentary and Protestant England both in his political activity and on paper.

In tune with the principles expressed in *A Discourse*, a few years later in the midst of the heated controversies of the late 1620s concerning the Petition of Right (1628) and the growing anxiety at what was perceived as absolutist ruling on the part of Charles I, Scott pointed out that '[k]ings may and do err, and in such cases it is the subjects' duty not to do against right ... and the people's safety' by blindly obeying the ruler.[99] Having underlined the fallibility of governors, he outspokenly declared that '[h]e is the best subject that will rather displease his prince than not discharge his duty to his prince, and to his God also, the Church and commonwealth'.[100] In practice, Scott asserted – more radically than most – the right of the subject to disobey rulers that acted against the common good. In tone and content his discourse was reminiscent of that articulated by the seventeenth-century German monarchomachs Johannes Althusius, Reinhard König and Christian Liebenthal to fight tyrannical ruling in the imperial territories.[101] Like these authors', Scott's concept of disobedience was intertwined with the idea of a community of citizens-patriots engaged in protecting their fatherland. Holding the protection of 'the ancient and undoubted birthright and inheritance of the Subjects of England' as the most important task of governors, he justified disobedience to tyrannical princes who, following the evil example of Caesar, oppressed the *leges patriae*.[102]

As for England, Scott deemed Buckingham the main culprit for the miserable condition that free Englishmen had to endure. In his view, the Duke wanted 'to do us [Parliament men] a mischief' by recruiting 'Irish popish soldiers ... together with the rutters[103] [reiters, that is German horsemen the favourite wanted to bring to England[104]], popish and Arminian and Maynwarian faction, and the rogues whereof this city [Canterbury] and the country is full'.[105] For Scott, Buckingham aimed to 'help set up popery and the excise and, as some of them do already give out, cut the Puritans' throats'.[106] Espousing anti-popish and anti-absolutist stances Scott tellingly grouped 'Irish ... the Germans, Papists, Arminians, Maynwarians, and other Dukists' as members of the same unpatriotic group.[107]

Thus, Scott shaped his role within the public arena of the 1620s both as a victim of the oppressive Stuart regime and as a fierce patriot. Likewise, his authorial identity fused the role of prophet and that of citizen. By drawing on the rhetoric of freeborn Englishmen and their attachment to liberty, he questioned Stuart rule. He employed biblical passages and historical examples to remark that children were better governors than an old and foolish king.[108] He eloquently referred to Israel with its king who oppressed 'the Commonwealth; poyson[ed] the Church; with Idolatrie, heresie Schisme, and atheisme'. This was a king who did 'break the fundamentall Lawes of libertie, free elections, and free Parliaments; onely to please their minion, or his mistress; or for his owne covetous, ambitious and tyrannous ends'.[109] As his allusive language shows, for Scott the situation that had afflicted Israel presented striking similarities to the England of the 1620s. And he argued that kings like these 'doth iniurie the State, and Kingdome, for whose goods and advice Kings are ordained'.[110]

In contrast to tyrannical sovereigns, Scott emphasised how honest, grave and morally integral were those elected to Parliament as 'guides and lights of the Cittie'.[111] He called them 'discreet and able men' who were 'sincere, and voide of any factious humor'.[112] In depicting the role of these 'public mindes',[113] he carved out a new picture of the ideal citizen based on the image of 'a knowne and renowned Protestant Patriot ... and faithfull Counsellor of State'[114] whose principal task was to protect the 'fundamentall libertie'.[115] Without their political activism, Scott thought that the body politic could not survive: '[f]or so it is with infected States, as it is with sick men; yf theire accustomed ill diet, and other disorders, hurt them, healed they cannot be, untill they leave these evill usages, and choose to themselues which is more for theire recoverie and preservation'.[116]

Scott strongly countered the absolute prerogative of kings. He maintained that mere obedience to the will of the sovereign denied 'lawe, right and libertye'.[117] Like Cicero, he deplored the concept of kingly *summum ius*: he defined it as *summa iniuria* because it meant that 'there is noo ... limitation or quallification' to sovereign power.[118] By the same token, he insisted upon the deleterious effects caused by 'the absolute obedience, due to the meere will, voice or words, of him who Comaunnds'. Therefore, 'from him' who 'is above all lawes' cannot derive anything but an 'Unjust, Unnatural, and Empious' form of government.[119] Scott also contended that, 'yf the Commonwealth be well ordered, the wealth of the Commons is conserved and increased; [whilst] on the other hand, yf the government be corrupt the people perish'.[120] For Scott the England of Charles I was succumbing exactly to this kind of tragic scenario.

These passages reveal that Scott's views were the blending of a localist, religious and legal-constitutional perception of tyranny prior to 1640. Yet his ideas and rhetoric often took him further than the majority of his contemporary political pamphleteers. As such Scott explicitly reminded his fellow countrymen that '[y]f wee desire to know how to SECURE and how to

INCREASE the prosperitie and glorie of Great Brittaine, there needs no more then this, let us thoughly reforme our church and common wealth, changing our evill ordinances and usages for such as right'.[121] He unhesitatingly declared that England was beset by a 'Babylonian Monarch', who curbed liberties, created disorder and caused disharmony in the nation. Given this increasingly difficult situation, and feeling that all the values he was fighting for were under siege, Scott thought it was fundamental to be 'readie ... to defend the truth of God (of religion, of lawe; of right, of libertie ... for the Parliament)'.[122] Thus, he urged Englishmen

> to remember ..., to maintayne your Antient Liberties; not suffering any ... to set themselves up above you and therein to imitate your own noble predecessors, who, (even in the dayes of greatest blindnesse) did divers times couragiously oppose themselves ... to the incroaching Prince.[123]

At the heart of this political vocabulary stood the defence of the birthrights of 'freeborn Englishmen'.[124] Scott advocated the role of the ancient law as the most grounded constitutional guarantee of the rights of subjects. His discourse embodied a mixture of immediate parliamentary anxiety towards what Scott viewed as Buckingham's treacherous manoeuvring to set Arminianism in England and Puritan dislike for the unruly 'rogues' threatening the godly settlement in society. Scott's self-proclaimed Puritanism certainly influenced his political ideas of liberty and sovereignty and shaped his civic radicalism. It helped him, first, to formulate and, subsequently, to consolidate his political principles. Yet this was not the only theoretical source of which Scott made use to pursue his goals. As shown above, he employed history and genealogy as useful argumentative tools to spell out his political and religious opinions. By interpreting historical events from an anti-absolutist perspective, he justified the claims of Parliament. At the same time, he forged an image of England's national identity at odds with the Stuart narrative of the nation's past. Above all, Scott brought to light a fundamental question on people's right to punish the monarch who did not condemn to death his tyrannical chief minister. Thus, Parliament and subordinate magistrates had 'to doe Justice' because they were 'noe lesse gods ordinance then the Sovraigne Magistrate'.[125]

He also attacked 'Earthly Jesuites, and other Papists, the Arminians' conspiring against England.[126] In fact, it was to respond to a sermon preached by the absolutist Isaac Bargrave (1627)[127] that Scott markedly rejected ideas of passive obedience and asserted subjects' right to disobey.[128] Soon afterwards, he radicalised these views: 'we will turne this State upside downe in time' and 'remove this contagion out of this kingdome as soone as possibly wee can', for this was 'harmefull to the wealth of the Commons; and consequently of the king and his whole kingdome'.[129] Whilst he was sceptical about kings' honesty to admit or 'confesse that they erred through too much hast, and passion',[130] in 1628 Scott was trenchant about the duty of the good Puritan:

[i]t is true that the puritan's conscience consists [in some cases] in disobedience; they dare not but disobaye Pharaon or Herod yf they command to massacre the infants; their conscience bindes them to disobaye Nebuchadnezzar yf hee commaund them to worshipp his goulden image; their Geneva puritan Bible saith that the three puritans despised the King's Commaundment and that the twoe midwives theire disobedience was lawfull. Naye (their puritan meaning is) it was their duety. Their Conscience in this matter consisted in Disobedience; and in generall all Juditious puritans houlde that it is against conscience to yeald obedience to Tyrannicall and lawlesse commaunds as of duety.[31]

Explicit and direct, Scott's delineation of a Puritan code of conduct had political implications that could only worry people like his cousin Filmer. In fact, Scott's overt justification of disobedience relied on a well-established tradition of political thought recalling the works of George Buchanan, Théodore de Bèze, François Hotman, Philippe du Plessis-Mornay. In addition to the idea of absolute obedience to God and the belief in the integrity of individual conscience, Scott founded his argument on the constitutional principle of the popular origins of the body politic and of kingly power. He referred to the biblical episode of Saul and the Amalekites to show how Puritans ought to act under a tyrant. He declared that, in opposing and killing Agag, Samuel had intervened not as prophet (as monarchist thinkers held) but as an inferior 'publique Magistrate' delegated to depose the evil ruler and save the reign.[32] In sanctioning disobedience to tyrannical governors, Scott argued that good Puritans had the responsibility to oppose all malignant persecutors and deprive them of their authority.[33] People had not simply the right, but they also had the duty to oppose the oppressor of their liberties. Those subjects who did not free their country from the plight of the monstrous tyrant ruined 'the people and the wealthe and strength of the Kingdome'.[34] As he had pointed out in 1626 at the time of the impeachment proceedings against the Duke of Buckingham for high treason, which had prompted Charles to dissolve Parliament in June of that year,[35] history provided many examples of such evil actions on the part of monarchs:[36] 'Lodovic Sforce' was a tyrant against whom it had been the duty of the citizen to resist so as not to be branded a 'traytor'.[37] Hence Scott maintained that

when by these kinde of men and the like, Republiques are governed, Justice and truth ... and the common good are held but for shadowes. Gold and glorie is that these men hunt after. They knowne, or acknoledge, at the least, no other happinesse, in earth or heaven, then have clothes, abundance of riches, high place, domination, and dayly riot, and earthly and sensuall delights. As for their owne true libertie, and safetie, and of their posterity and Countrie, they have no care or feeling of them.[38]

Together with assigning a fundamental role to the third estate, Scott listed the dangers that every monarchical government entailed. He expressed his abhorrence of kings who were free from the control of laws and unbridled by constitutional checks. Most importantly, he forthrightly poured his scorn on 'the Monarchicall forme of Government' itself, for it was 'the most apt to degenerate into a Tyrannie and lawless soveraigntie' and as such the most likely to cause 'oppression and detriment of the Commons' and the 'common good'.[39]

Helped by the relative privacy of the medium with which he conveyed his thoughts,[40] Scott's vocabulary was more extreme than the majority of his contemporaries'.[41] His radicalism was not simply the outlet of an angry and impulsive hothead. Rather, it developed in relation to the changing political landscape of the 1620s.[42] Despite being silent in Parliament, both his private and his public writings account for the important intellectual and ideological development of an opposition to the Stuart regime. In contrast to the monarchist idea that the prime fount of allegiance within the realm was the king, Scott emphasised the protection of the body politic as the primary duty of the citizen-patriot. He rejected the concept that obedience to the monarch recalled submission to the father and identified the duty of the active citizen to defend the *respublica* as the highest political goal. In this sense, Scott can be viewed as an 'earlier radical Puritan antecedent of [Algernon] Sidney's Calvinist republicanism ... indirectly responsible for the creation of *Discourses*', which were written in Scott's spirit against Filmer's un-Christian, devilishly and heretical political arguments.[43]

By and large, what had started as forcible libelling of Buckingham progressively turned into a head-on attack on the person responsible for the general crisis in which the country was now enmeshed. Only one name stuck out and this was 'Charles'. Unsurprisingly, ideas like those held by Scott left one member of his family particularly concerned. Even though evidence that the two Kentish men directly addressed and responded to each other is lacking, we can assuredly maintain that it was precisely the type of opinions conveyed by Scott's vitriolic rhetoric that prompted Filmer's reaction.[44] In consequence, Sir Robert adopted a political language that enabled him to dismantle the patriotic discourse and shape a powerful model of kingship. It is now time to consider how he did so and unveil his opposite views of liberty and sovereignty.

AT THE HEART OF *PATRIARCHA*: ORIGINS, GOALS, TARGETS

In February 1632 – a week after Charles I had officially proclaimed his intention to prevent writers from addressing matters of state since they led to 'scandall of gouvernment and disadvantage of our service'[45] – Georg Rudolph Weckherlin, the government press licenser from 1627 to 1638, brought to the King two manuscripts seeking licence for publication. One of them was a version of Filmer's *Patriarcha*.[46] In Weckherlin's own words,

> Sir Robert Filmer brought me a *Discourse* to bee licensed for printing, written of Government and in praise of Royaltie and the supreme authority thereof. I most humbly crave your Majesties wise Censure, whether such a subject at this time is fitter to bee made publick or kept in Non licet.[147]

Charles attributed great importance to what his subjects read. Therefore, Weckherlin regularly gave him a brief summary of the contents of the works ready for publication. The Stuart had explicitly warned that 'nothing ... should bee printed without the view ... and approbation of my servaunt Weckherlin'.[148] Interestingly, in the case of Filmer's treatise the licenser did not express his opinion, but asked Charles for advice on whether it was sensible to send the book out for publication at that time. In the end, *Patriarcha* was not licensed and it had to wait fifty years before finding its way into print.[149] What constellation of reasons prompted the King to deny permission to send *Patriarcha* out in the public arena?[150] An initial answer might come from the analysis of Filmer's text.

As its subtitle enunciates, the principal goal of *Patriarcha* was to assert 'The *Naturall* Power of Kinges Defended against the Unnatural Liberty of the People'.[151] By employing 'Theological, Rational, Historical, Legall' arguments, Filmer aimed at defending the superiority of monarchical authority. In stark contrast to the likes of Thomas Scott and to a host of natural rights theorists, he began by stating that men were born dependent on those who had begotten them.[152] The 'tenet' that mankind was 'naturally endowed and born with freedom from all subjection, and at liberty to choose what form of government it please ... according to the discretion of the multitude' was 'first hatched in the schools [of the Jesuits] and hath been fostered by all succeeding papists for good divinity'.[153] Yet Filmer was quick to add that also the

> divines ... of the reformed churches have entertained it, and *the common people every-where* tenderly embrace it as being most plausible to flesh and blood, for that it prodigally distributes a portion of liberty to the meanest of the multitude as if the height of human felicity were only to be found in it – never remembering that the desire of liberty was the cause of the fall of Adam.[154]

Filmer opened up his argument by firing a few rhetorical bullets at his adversaries, making sure that none of them went amiss. Not only did he criticise Catholic (popish) theorists and Protestant thinkers in one shot, but – most importantly – he subtly targeted 'the common people'.[155] These were urbanised parliamentary countrymen like Scott who, on Filmer's account, represented a very dangerous category of subjects. He pointed out that, as a consequence of their immoderate love of liberty, they irresponsibly conceded political space to the rabble.[156]

In choosing these targets Filmer articulated his discourse on two different levels. On the one hand, he engaged in a well-established theoretical dispute on the origins of government and the natural role of men in assigning power to governors. On the other hand, he addressed his pungent critique to a 'vulgar opinion [that] hath of late obtained great reputation' and of which '[i]t is hard to say whether it be more dangerous in divinity or dangerous in policy'.[57] Thus, in the first case Filmer attacked those who spread the 'pestilent' theory of 'the supposed natural equality and freedom of mankind'.[58] Amongst these were 'both Jesuits and some over zealous favourers of the Geneva discipline'.[59] He singled out Parsons, Buchanan, Bellarmine and Calvin as supporters of the right of the people to depose and punish their rulers in case the latter flouted the law.[160] As he was to vividly explain in *The Anarchy of a Limited or Mixed Monarchy* (1648), this brigade supporting the 'new doctrine of the limitation and mixture of monarchy' had 'crucified' kings 'between two thieves, the pope and the people'.[161]

In the second case, Filmer knew very well that he did not need to look for sophisticated treatises to discover how widespread 'the whole fabric of this vast engine of popular sedition' had become.[162] It was, in fact, sufficient to pay attention to one particular opinion (a 'faith') many people held in his county and into which 'many an ignorant subject hath been fooled'.[163] This was the belief according to which 'a man may become a martyr for his country by being a traitor to his prince'.[164] Accordingly, Puritan and quasi-republican stalwarts considered the people above the king (just as papists argued that the Pope was superior to secular monarchs), so that the former could judge the latter and re-appropriate the power they claimed to have conceded to the sovereign. Filmer believed that this seditious opinion had become so popular that 'many out of an imaginary fear pretend the power of the people to be necessary for the repressing of the insolencies of tyrants, herein they propound a remedy far worse than the disease'.[165] Stressing that 'the disease' was not 'so frequent as they would have us think', he fiercely challenged these factious spirits (the likes of Scott) on their ground by admonishing to 'be judged by the history of our own nation'.[166] Most importantly, he explained that 'the new coined distinction of subjects into *royalists* and *patriots* is most unnatural, since the relation between king and people is so great that their well-being is reciprocal'.[167] This passage unveils a fundamental argument of *Patriarcha* that has been overlooked in the historiography. It casts light on one of the main reasons why Filmer put forth his patriarchalist philosophy at the end of the 1620s.

This is to say that Sir Robert had fully understood the strength of (the discourse of) the self-proclaimed English patriots in that they claimed to protect the country from the tyranny of monarchical government. He saw the patriotic rhetoric gain increasing weight in a country where the separation between monarchy and a significant portion of the people was spiralling. Filmer accused the patriots – whom he misleadingly took as a homogenous group – of proposing an alternative political allegiance and of undermining the unifying role of the monarchy. They depicted the interest of the country as incompatible with the monarch's and argued that only Parliament protected patriotic freeholders. To counterattack this proposition Filmer suggested that the two parts could only live in perfect harmony under an absolute monarchy and not in the chaotic polity advocated by the patriots. Dismissing the role of Parliament as the main defender of the English people, he declared that 'the rights or liberties of this or any other nation ... are derived ... from the grace and bounty of princes'.[168] And the latter's 'desire and hope' were indeed 'that the people of England may and do enjoy as ample privileges as any nation under heaven'.[169]

From these initial few steps into Filmer's thought, we can infer that his idea of the nation greatly differed from Scott's. On Sir Robert's account, only the supreme king represented the whole of the nation as he subsumed it under his care. Those who, like his cousin,[170] impudently identified the nation with the people inevitably excluded a part or more parts of it. Since the supporters of the natural liberty of men were ambiguous on the meaning of 'people', Filmer concluded that they did not intend to comprehend all.[171] Instead, the absolute monarch made everyone equal because he was the only superior in the body politic.[172] For this reason, the nation was and ought to be powerless to control and judge the decisions of the sovereign. In line with this opinion, Filmer uncompromisingly argued that '[t]he causes and ends of the greatest politic actions and motions of state dazzle the eyes and exceed the capacities of all men, save only those that are hourly versed in managing public affairs'.[173] Politics was not for all. It was a complex domain that required specific competence.

In sharp contrast to this view, Scott had strenuously asserted that 'good patriots' had to defend the liberties of the nation because 'if free parliaments be gone, all is lost; and free parliaments cannot long continue if the freedom and right of elections be violently and deceitfully taken from us'.[174] For him free elections represented 'the liberty, honour, and happiness of England if duly observed; and the only way to prevent slavery and ruin'.[175] Likewise, Scott had also said that politics had to be in the hands of 'religious, grave, learned, wise, and honest men (true to the realme) free from all dependence on those that have other than public and English ends'.[176]

To reject these ideas of active citizenship, Filmer adopted a form of encompassing naturalism. He dismissed the political languages of virtue; of rights; of nation, history and law for they presupposed a dangerous amount of activism on the part of the subject. Yet the absence of virtue from the arguments set out in *Patriarcha* did not extend to the ruler, who embodied the utmost expression of virtue. At the centre of Filmer's political account was an alternative form of activism to that professed by humanists of Aristotelian legacy. Transferred to politics, the activism of the father in the household became the political activism of the sovereign in the body politic. The latter was the only and ultimate repository of sovereignty.

In accordance with his theory of fatherly authority, Filmer conceived sovereignty as the power to give laws in an unbounded manner: 'in a monarchy the king must be of necessity above the laws. There can be no sovereign majesty in him that is under them. That which giveth the very being to a king is the power to give laws; without this power he is but an equivocal king'.[77] Sovereignty consisted of one, absolute, arbitrary, unique, indivisible power. It could be compared to a beam of light descending from the sky. Sovereignty was the force to act and modify things. It was strong power in action.[78] Filmer adopted a powerful image to underpin the backbone of sovereignty: '[t]he people cannot assemble themselves, but the king, by his writs, calls them to what place he pleases, and then again scatters them with his breath at an instant, without any cause showed them than his will'.[79]

For Filmer the notion of sovereignty was intertwined with the principle of efficiency. A monarchical sovereignty best guaranteed peace and stability. The monarch was above all, so that he could act in a rapid and competent way. He was always present within the legislative and administrative life of the realm.[80] He could delegate his judicial power but he remained the last and supreme ruler when it came to taking decisions. He alone held the authority to judge in the highest causes and last appeals. There was no limit to his power and no constraints could hinder him. In order to be sovereign the prince had to be *legibus solutus*.

Filmer also associated sovereignty with the concept of interest. He stated that the king ought to contribute to the wealth of his realm so as to preserve unity within it. Indeed, '[i]t is the multitude of people and the abundance of their riches which are the only strength and glory of every prince'. The profit of the subjects was interwoven with the prince's:

> [t]he bodies of his subjects do him service in war, and their goods supply his public wants. Therefore, if not out of affection to his people, yet out of natural love to himself, every tyrant desires to preserve the lives and protect the goods of his subjects, which cannot be done but by justice, and if it be not done, the prince's loss is the greatest.[81]

On their part, subjects must 'allow' their king 'royal maintenance by providing revenues for the Crown, since it is both for the honour, profit and safety of the people to have their king glorious, powerful and abounding in riches'.[82]

Being guided by the 'natural law of a father', a patriarchalist monarchy was the best form of government to guarantee people's prosperity and preserve the wealth of the kingdom. That even a tyrant would look after the properties of his subjects better than a democratic regime was easy to grasp. As Filmer remarked, 'in a popular state every man knows that the public good doth not depend wholly on his care, but the commonwealth may be well enough governed by others though he tend only his private benefit. He never takes the public to be his own business'.[183] The same careless attitude towards the public good manifested by those who lived in a democracy was mirrored in the magistrates of popular states. These, 'being for the most part annual, do always lay down before they understand it, so a prince though of a duller understanding, by use and experience must needs excel them'.[184] It followed that only absolute monarchies ensured continuity to the political process.

Above all, for Filmer monarchical sovereignty was the encompassing force that not only created laws but also shaped the structure of the body politic (its *ethos*). In this sense, the Adamite model neutralised the consequences of a political scenario comparable to the chaos of Babel. Whilst patriarchalism advocated order in the body politic and guaranteed unity of sovereignty in the person of the *lex loquens* ruler, country patriotism led to a polity where the (linguistic) confusion of Babel had been restored. For this reason, Filmer underlined that 'the safety of' the ruler's 'kingdom be his chief law ... and that the public is to be preferred before the private'.[185] This helped to maintain an equal 'balance' between 'the particular profit' and 'the counterpoise of the public, according to the infinite variety of times, places, persons'.[186]

Nothing was worse for Filmer than the tyranny of the multitude. As he put it, 'there is no tyrant so barbarously wicked' to act with the same degree of oppression as the headless populace. In fact, 'his own reason and sense will tell him that though he be a god, yet he must die like a man'.[187] Whilst tyrants such as 'Tiberius, Caligula and Nero' always suffered from 'panic fears' because of their evil actions towards specific individuals, the tyranny of the multitude was worse in that it prevented people from knowing 'who hurt' them, 'or who to complain of, or to whom to address' themselves 'for reparation'. In popular assemblies, men always behaved towards their fellow citizens with more 'malice and cruelty'.[188]

By contrast, the absolute monarch promoted efficiency in the State and provided subjects with (fatherly) security. After all, as historical examples had proved many times, 'the last refuge in perils of states is to fly to regal authority'.[189] Being above all laws and endowed with their prerogative, kings protected those who were under them and defended people's liberties.[190] Instead, Parliament was a fragile political body entirely dependent on the 'good will' of MPs whose actions were conditioned by their fear of losing consent at each election. Thus, Filmer thought it inevitable that those who sat in Parliament were only interested in maintaining their position without any consideration for the future benefit of the nation, whereas the patriarchalist prince guaranteed certainty of power and safeguarded the commonweal against lawless anarchy. As he emphasised anew, even usurpers and tyrants were 'bound to preserve the lands, goods, liberties and lives of all their subjects, not by any municipal law of the land, but by the natural law of a father'.[191]

These considerations unfold Filmer's vision of sovereignty and politics as dimensions that coincided. Politics had an all-embracing function and was never absent. The moment in which man was born represented the moment in which politics had originated. In this sense, Sir Robert conceived politics as strictly intertwined with generation. As such men's original freedom was a mere impossibility. Filmer was interested in the first generative moment in which political government had been created. He focused on the *punctuality* and immediacy of the decision-making act. He did not believe in the immemorial aspects of law and customs as his adversaries did. He stressed the origins of government so as to cast light on the generation of those laws and customs. In *Patriarcha* temporality was the touchstone that determined the existence and the role of the law. In other terms, Filmer established the tempo of the law-making process. He insisted on the *instantaneousness* that the creative moment held in the legislative sphere.[192]

Sovereignty conveyed the eminence of power. As seen above, Sir Robert thought it was vital to achieve efficiency and continuity in the State. Hence he sought to establish the unequivocal source of power from which authority and laws had their clear origin. This certainty was a fundamental asset in government. Whilst democracy lacked such soundness because laws were always the result of chaotic and unstable popular decisions, monarchy found the strongest guarantee in the absolute sovereign. The latter symbolised certainty in governance and visibility of power, whereas the common law engendered uncertainty and failed to ensure efficiency in the legislative process. Moreover, since the law was at times too rigid in its application and incapable of covering the multiple aspects of life in the polity, the king could bypass those fundamental rules that he judged to be infringing the pursuit of the common good. This idea is connected to the principle of the '*excessum iuris communis propter bonum commune*' which, developed in the sixteenth century, was interpreted as the theoretical cornerstone of the paradigm of reason of State. Amongst those who supported it was Scipione Ammirato, author of *Discorsi su C. Tacito* (1594). Ammirato's work was a detailed critical comment on Botero's *Della Ragion di Stato* (1589) and an attempt to clarify the ambiguous statements of the latter. Thus, for Ammirato *Politica* dealt with the ordinary course of life in the body politic whilst reason of State addressed extraordinary situations. Despite insisting on honesty and religion as indispensable limits which reason of State could not overcome, Ammirato opened the way for more radical authors like Gabriel Naudé to focus on the problem of derogation of the law (*deroga*). Ammirato realised that positive legislation was insufficient to cover all aspects of life in the State and, therefore, needed to be ignored in order to pursue the general interest. It was exactly this principle that Filmer employed in *Patriarcha*. Yet Sir Robert radicalised it and personalised it by placing the power of derogation exclusively in the hands of the sovereign. His formulation was on the same line of thought that Ammirato had developed thirty years earlier by ruling out the authority of lawyers in favour of politicians' (*politici*) with regard to derogation. Filmer's defence of the *legibus solutus* model of kingship against the attacks of natural rights theorists was thus part of this long-term battle developed in sixteenth-century Italy.[193]

Moreover, whereas contractualists referred to a pre-political state of humankind and depicted man as 'naked' and 'pure', equal to all and deprived of social identity, patriarchalism did not conceive man as an essentially isolated individual, but rather as 'subject' (endowed with a specific role) of a natural relationship of which the family represented the core. Adam's family was also a commonwealth. There was no distinction between his absolute paternal authority and his unrestricted political power. The Adamite account of the origins of humankind explained how political society had formed and evolved after the Flood throughout the centuries.

Accordingly, Filmer delineated his concept of sovereign power by contesting Aristotle's idea of the family and the State as separate spheres. Like John Buckeridge and Hadrian Saravia before him, Filmer thought the only difference between œconomical and political power was one of size.[194] Indeed, he asserted that 'Aristotle gives the lie to Plato and those that say that political and economical societies are all one, and do not differ *specie* [in species], but only *multitudine et paucitate* [in greatness and smallness of number]'.[195] Sir Robert never argued that monarchs were the biological fathers of their subjects since, through generations, human beings had divided into numerous and different entities. And 'yet, ... they all either are, or are to be reputed, as the next heirs of those progenitors who were at first the natural parents of the whole people, and in their right succeed to the exercise of supreme jurisdiction'.[196] Fatherhood and politics were, therefore, part and parcel of the same process.

The foregoing analysis enables us to confidently maintain that *Patriarcha* presented two theoretical cornerstones. First, Filmer employed the patriarchalist discourse with its focus on the story of the Creation and the derivation of kingly authority from God through Adam. This explained the origins of power and provided an indisputable justification for all the supreme fathers to come. Through the biblical account of 'Genesis' Filmer demonstrated that obedience was naturally embedded in humankind and that subjection to absolute power stemmed from the paternal authority of Adam. Moreover, he established that fatherhood guaranteed continuity to the body politic through the hereditary mechanism. The patriarchalist model provided the foundations on which sovereignty grounded its existence and legitimacy. In brief, this part of *Patriarcha* elucidated the normative moment. Most importantly for Filmer, to govern was related not only to the two notions of 'principality and power' ('αρχυ')[197] but also to that of 'beginning' ('*principium*'). Hence 'prince' and 'principality' embodied the idea of the beginning of government. As creation had 'made man prince of his posterity',[198] so the lawmaker – and not the law – was the *'primum mobile'* of the political universe. The *'culmen* or *apex potestatis'* resided in the monarch.[199]

The second keynote of the Filmerian discourse regarded how the State should be efficiently and righteously governed: it had to do with governance. This other cardinal moment mirrored the new course that had begun at the time of Nimrod's unjust appropriation of power.[200] Filmer made of Nimrod – who had increased his power by invading neighbouring countries 'against right' and by depriving other legitimate heads of families of their authority – 'the author and first founder of monarchy'.[201] Hence Filmer concentrated on the identity of the sovereign as the chief actor on the political stage. He saw the role of the ruler in conjunction with the ability to wield power.

To summarise, the power of the father represented the foundation of politics, whilst the position of the king in government symbolised stability and unity in the polity. Therefore, the authority of a father was limited to his household whilst the might of a king resided in the legislative power. In consequence, the latter was above fathers: his was 'the transcendent fatherly power of the supreme prince'.[202] As Filmer was to specify in the 1640s, 'the fifthe commandement' entailed 'Privat' and 'Publique' 'duties': of the former type were those pertaining to the 'duty of the wife, of Parents and Children, or Serv(ants) and Masters', whilst the public sphere regarded 'the office of a Kinge'.[203] Therefore, in case of a crime committed by a wife, Filmer distinguished between the position of the husband and that of the magistrate.[204] Likewise, he established that 'the power of the father over his child gives place and is subordinate to the power of the magistrate'.[205]

In Sir Robert's world, politics had priority over all other dimensions of life. Its pertaining to the public sphere rendered it substantially more important than any private domain: '[i]f we compare the natural duties of a father with those of a king, we find them to be all one, without any difference at all but only in the latitude or extent of them'. The analogy continued: '[a]s the father over one family, so the king, as father over many families, extends his care to preserve, feed, clothe, instruct and defend the whole commonwealth'. In terms of rhetorical appeal, this message could not but be persuasive. Equally convincing was Filmer when, against those who rejected the absolute power of the king because of its alleged oppression, he rebutted that

> [h]is wars, his peace, his courts of justice and all his acts of sovereignty tend only to preserve and distribute to every subordinate and inferior father, and to their children, their rights and privileges, so that all the duties of a king are summoned up in an universal fatherly care of his people.[206]

By defining the role of the father, Filmer retraced the original moment of the foundation of political dominion. But, above all, the image of fatherly care he employed served him to persuasively depict the patriotic king. As he put it, 'many a child, by succeeding a king, hath the right of a father over many a grey-headed multitude, and hath the title of *pater patriae*'.[207] At this point, Filmer had completed in the most stringent way the indissoluble link between Adamite fatherhood, household, patriarchy and kingly care for the polity and its subjects.

Patriarcha then explained that the arbitrary power of Adam represented the guiding model of all political communities. This is an important thesis because it highlights that Filmer did not support inequality in society. Rather, he considered the sovereign as the only non-equal in the State.[208] Such a perspective resembled the Platonic idea of organic unity from which the sole unequal member outside the pattern of general equality in the *polis* was the absolute fatherly sovereign. This conception of the body politic greatly differed from the Aristotelian model. In the Stuart period, as Vaughan Hart observed, Platonic harmony 'shifted from emphasising the monarch's duty to the body politic to underlining his virtues as an absolute ruler':[209] Filmer was at the centre of this transition. As such, he clarified that '[i]t skills not which way kings come by their power, whether by election, donation, succession or by any other means', which comprised force and usurpation. Since the origins were indisputably Adamite, what *really* mattered was 'the manner of the government by supreme power that makes them properly kings'.[210]

That, after having analysed the different forms of government, Sir Robert should pick absolute monarchy as the best political settlement is no more than standard logic. What is original political thinking is that for him this was so because here the will of the sovereign not only gave being to the law, but coincided with the law. Absolute monarchies were superior because in them the king was *'lex loquens* – a speaking law'.[211] As he commented in *The Free-Holders Grand Inquest* (1648): '[a] king with a negative voice only is but like a syllogism of pure negative propositions, which can conclude nothing'. In fact, 'it must be an affirmative voice that makes both a king and a law, and without it there can be no imaginable government'.[212] It followed that the law compelled, prohibited and punished. The model of kingship he proposed was, in fact, founded on the idea of 'the charismatic leader who speaks the law'.[213] This meant that it was always imperative to have for every law 'some present known person in being, whose will it must be to make it a law for the present'. The same could not be said of assemblies and parliaments where confusion and endless disputes reigned. Thus, against the faceless dimension of the law typical of republican polities, Filmer was to stress (1652) the importance of knowing 'the commander or willer of it'. In so doing, he relied on none other than Hobbes whose *Leviathan* had so clearly stated that '[n]othing is law where the legislator cannot be known'. It had to be manifest that it stemmed 'from the will of the sovereign'. A 'declaration' was not sufficient: 'the author and the authority' of the law needed to be known too.[214] This concept came straight from *Patriarcha*, where Filmer had insisted that the legislator was not only sovereign but also one and *alone*.[215]

Accordingly, Filmer distinguished between '*directive*' and '*coactive*' power to prove that, as even medieval Catholic schoolmen had argued, 'kings are not bound by the positive laws of any nation'. Whilst the former represented only the power of 'advice and direction which the king's council gives the king' (and as such this was not 'a law to the king'), the latter was 'the compulsory power of laws' that 'properly makes laws to be laws' (and as such it implied punishment and obedience).[216] Since the monarch was 'the sole immediate author, corrector and moderator' not only of statutes but also of common laws,[217] Filmer concluded that

> [t]he greatest liberty in the world (if it be duly considered) is for people to live under a monarch. It is the Magna Carta of this kingdom. All other shows or pretexts of liberty are but several degrees of slavery, and a liberty only to destroy liberty.[218]

Defining his opponents' theories of liberty as merely illusory, Sir Robert explained that popular governments were always embroiled in turbulent sedition 'because the nature of all people is to desire liberty without restraint, which cannot be but where the wicked bear rule'.[219] To show (once more) that monarchy was superior, safer and more stable than democracy, Filmer also resorted to a powerful analysis of Roman history. He compared the political situation at the time of the tribunes of the multitude with the phase of the dominion of the emperors. From this he inferred that endemic bloodshed and scarce 'durability', disorder and limited extension[220] characterised the very being of democracy. In order to make it shine in all its monstrosity, he subjected the idea of 'popularity' to a corrosive bath of historical scrutiny.[221] The history of Rome served Filmer as a rhetorically persuasive device to counterattack his adversaries and dismiss their arguments as lacking credibility. This is to say that he identified the England of his time with ancient Rome so as to alert readers that their nation was on the verge of falling prey to the folly of seditious popular fomenters. Hence he fervently depicted 'the imperfections of popular government'. He observed that, although '[m]any have exercised their wits in paralleling the inconveniences of regal and popular government', through 'experience' rather than by means of 'speculations philosophical', it could not 'be denied but that this one mischief of sedition, which necessarily waits upon all popularity, weighs down all the inconveniences that can be found in monarchy, though they were never so many'.[222] Likewise, he emphatically reminded the reader that in democratic Rome '[m]any citizens under their grave gowns came armed unto the public meetings, as if they went to war'. Prey to 'contrary factions' that 'fell to blows, sometimes with stones and sometimes swords', Rome had witnessed a staggering series of crimes and violence. In Filmer's vivid prose, '[t]he blood hath been sucked up in the market-place with sponges: the river Tiber hath been filled with the dead bodies of citizens, and the common privies stuffed full with them'.[223] No doubt, for him this chilling picture of Roman life should have sent a cold sweat down the spine of his countrymen.

To think that a multitude was naturally free and able to gather together in order to choose its government was for Filmer absurd. It would be necessary to have the universal consent of all the people of the world in one instant. Instead, he argued that a commonweal stemmed from a hereditary process through primogeniture or, in certain cases, from the deliberative act of one man (even a usurper). But it was never the outcome of a compact stipulated by the populace. Otherwise, anyone could set up as many new polities as there were families on earth. This would lead to a state of anarchy and irrational private dominion.[224]

Finally, Filmer rejected the idea of an intermediate body placed between sovereign and subjects because this would inevitably hinder the supreme authority of the former. Such a power was not only supreme and arbitrary; prime and pristine; original and indivisible; inviolable and absolute. It was also one. 'For the having of this [sovereignty] alone, and nothing but this, makes a king to be a king', whilst to 'once admit the people to be his companions' was for the monarch tantamount to ceasing to be a king, so that 'the state becomes a democracy'. This arrangement would make him into 'a titular and no real king, that hath not the sovereignty to himself'.[225] There was no sharing element in sovereignty. No institutional body could govern in conjunction with kingly power. The ruler had to be alone. As Filmer stated in *The Anarchy*, referring to the term 'μόνος, *solus*, one alone', '[t]he monarch must not only have the supreme power unlimited, but he must have it alone – without any companions'.[226]

These passages encapsulate *Patriarcha*'s essential message: both the solitude of the monarch and the solitude of power were indispensable and irrevocable conditions for the working of all good politics.

To end this chapter by referring to the element of 'solitude' might be appropriate in light of the positions of Scott and Filmer in the ideological spectrum of the early seventeenth century. This is to say that, whilst both Scott's opinions and Filmer's doctrines reflected (in some respects, at least) the mood of many people in the country, this chapter hopes to have shown that the former's rejection of Stuart policies and the Filmerian defence of patriarchalist rulership were unusually radical.[227]

If my analysis of Scott agrees with Richard Cust's,[228] it goes further in exploring how Filmer's cousin was not simply a Puritan zealot pursuing the godly cause, but, above all, a patriotic countryman that created the ideological platform which two decades later contributed to bring down the monarchical regime.[229] Thus, the conflicts of the Civil War had certainly something to do with the 'most unnatural' mid–late 1620s 'new coined distinction of subjects into royalists and patriots'.[230] Filmer proved to be well alerted to the perils arising from attempts such as Scott's to mould an alternative identity for the English nation at the centre of which stood out the freeborn Protestant freeholder and 'honest patriot'. Indeed, it was for this reason that he resorted to patriarchalism: a theory that depicted the sovereign as the father of the realm whose patriotic care for the nation was greater than the patriots'.[231]

However, the latter's political vocabulary was not the only one *Patriarcha* sought to dismantle. The next chapter shows how Filmer identified Jesuit thinkers like Cardinal Robert Bellarmine (1542–1621) and Francisco Suarez (1548–1617) with the promoters of a deleterious form of external political allegiance. This did not centre on the secular national monarch, but on the external authority of the Bishop of Rome, whom Jesuit theorists considered superior and authorised to depose kings.[232] Once again, a major part of the controversies in which Filmer engaged concerned political betrayal and patriotism.

NOTES

1 This chapter partly draws on C. Cuttica, 'Kentish Cousins at Odds: Filmer's *Patriarcha* and Thomas Scott's Defence of Freeborn Englishmen', *HPT*, 28 (2007), pp. 599–616.

2 My general argument departs from Alan Everitt's interpretation whereby the early seventeenth-century Kentish gentry was politically moderate, ideologically neutral, largely dominated by family ties and inherently conditioned by a deeply localist view of both society and intellectual activity. According to Everitt, Kentish gentlemen were often unaware of the problems, issues and principles that informed the political nation at large (see A. Everitt, *The Community of Kent and the Great Rebellion 1640–60* (Leicester, 1966), e.g. pp. 45–55, 56–83, 116–24, 207, 220). For Everitt, *Patriarcha* was entirely a product of Sir Robert's Kentish environment (*ibid.*, p. 49).

3 See Laslett, 'Introduction'; Schochet, *Patriarchalism in Political Thought*.

4 Departing from Richard Cust's picture of Scott as an instance of a 'substantial body' of country opposition to court policies (see below), Conrad Russell considered Scott most untypical (Russell, *Unrevolutionary England*, p. xxviii).

5 Ben Jonson, *Ben: Ionson his Volpone, or, the Foxe* (1607), Act iv, Scene i, 'Politiqve. Peregrine'.

6 *Reports and Calendars issued by the Royal Commission on Historical Manuscripts, Buccleuch* (1899), i, p. 102.

7 Randle Cotgrave, *A Dictionarie of the French and English Tongues* (1611). Interestingly, Cotgrave gave of 'Patriot' the more monarchist definition of '*A father, or protector of the countrey, or Commonwealth*'.

8 Cited in P. Lake, 'Constitutional Consensus and Puritan Opposition in the 1620s: Thomas Scott and the Spanish Match', *HJ*, 25 (1982), pp. 805–25, p. 813, n. 39.

9 Cited in Sommerville, *Royalists and Patriots*, p. 249.

10 After the Duke of Buckingham's murder (1628), Pembroke – a long-term opponent of the Duke – became the most likely 'candidate for leadership of a patriot coalition' whose goal was the pursuit of the Protestant Cause (R. Cust, 'Was There an Alternative to the Personal Rule? Charles I, the Privy Council and the Parliament of 1629', *History*, 90 (2005), pp. 330–52, p. 337).

11 Thomas May, *M. A. Lucan, Pharsalia: or the civill warres of Rome, between Pompey the Great, and Iulius Caesar: then bookes*, trans. (1627), A2–4.

12 Cited in R. Cust, 'The "Public Man" in Late Tudor and Early Stuart England', in S. Pincus and P. Lake (eds), *The Politics of the Public Sphere in Early Modern England* (Manchester, 2007), pp. 116–43, p. 129. I would like to thank Richard Cust for letting me consult this piece ahead of publication.

13 John Russell, *The Spy Discovering the Danger of Arminian Heresie and Spanish Trecherie* (Strasbourg [i.e. Amsterdam], 1628), A1–2.

14 *Ibid.*, C2.

15 *Ibid.*, E4–F1.

16 Alexander Leighton, *An Appeal to the Parliament; or Sions Plea against the Prelacie ...* (Amsterdam?, 1628), esp. 'Epistle to the ... Parliament'. See also M. Peltonen, *Classical Humanism and Republicanism in English Political Thought, 1570–1640* (Cambridge, 1995), p. 274.

17 *Letter from Alvise Contarini ... to the Doge and Senate in Venice, on March 15*, in R. Brown (ed.), *Calendar of State Papers and Manuscripts relating to English Affairs, existing in the archives and collections of Venice, and in other libraries of Northern Italy* (1864), vol. xxi, 1628–29, pp. 21–2, p. 21.

18 A. Bellany, '"The Brightnes of the Noble Leiutenants Action": An Intellectual Ponders Buckingham's Assassination', *EHR*, 118 (2003), pp. 1242–63.

19 *Ibid.*, p. 1251.

20 Cited in T. Cogswell, *The Blessed Revolution. English Politics and the Coming of War, 1621–1624* (Cambridge, 1989), p. 84.

21 Henry Burton, *Truth's Triumph* (1629), p. 285.

22 Cust, 'The "Public Man"', p. 123.

23 Richard Brathwaite, *The English Gentleman Containing Sundry Excellent Rules or Exquisite Observations ...* (1630), p. 145.

24 *OED*, 'patriot, n. and adj.'.

25 Cust, '"Patriots" and "Popular" Spirits', pp. 51–2.

26 I. Roy, 'Royalist Reputations: The Cavalier Ideal and the Reality', in McElligott and Smith (eds), *Royalists and Royalism*, pp. 89–111, p. 92.

27 P. Clark, 'Thomas Scott, and the Growth of Urban Opposition to the Early Stuart Regime', *HJ*, 21 (1978), pp. 1–26, p. 20.

28 This issue was to become central in the Civil War (Hirst, *England in Conflict*, pp. 205–6, 233 and *passim*).

29 See Sharpe, *Remapping, passim*.

30 Cust, 'Charles I and Popularity', p. 236.

31 King James VI and I, *A Speach in the Starre-Chamber, the XX. Of June Anno 1616*, in J. P. Sommerville (ed.), *King James VI and I. Political Writings* (Cambridge, 1994), pp. 204–28, p. 222 (italics added).

32 To signify the persistent importance of the rhetoric of patriotism and its conflict with monarchism we find that in 1657 one of Thomas Fuller's works was published with the suggestive title of *The Soveraigns Prerogative and the Subject's priviledge, discussed betwixt courtiers and patriots in Parliament ...* (1657). Incidentally, the same work had been published three years earlier with the title of *Ephemeris Parlamentaria ...* (1654). In his edition of documents from the parliamentary session of 1628–29, Fuller (1593–1667) distinguished between two rival parties: 'the upholders of the Royal Prerogative & the Asserters of the Subjects Liberties' (*ibid.*, 'Preface').

33 KAO, U269/F35, Coll. 16 'Curious Citations' (Hand of Sir Richard Weston c. 1625?). The opinion that the common people were dangerous and their intervention in politics calamitous was widespread throughout the 1640s too (C. Hill, 'The Many-Headed Monster in Late Tudor and Early Stuart Political Thinking', in C. H. Carter (ed.), *From the Renaissance to the Counter-Reformation* (1966), pp. 296–324, pp. 307–11). On 22 November 1641, addressing the Speaker of the House of Commons, Sir Edward Dering clarified that, 'I neither looke for cure of our complaints from the Common people, nor doe desire to be cured by them' (Edward Dering, *A Collection of Speeches Made by Sir Edward Dering Knight and Baronet, in matter of Religion ...* (1642), Section xv, p. 70).

34 Walter Curll, *A Sermon preached at White-Hall on the 28. of April in 1622* (1622), pp. 21–3 (italics added).

35 Despite erroneously maintaining that Filmer wrote *Patriarcha* at the end of the 1630s, Peter Clark correctly pointed out that Sir Robert wanted to avoid that the increasing disaffection of his fellow county gentlemen towards the Crown culminated in an unbridgeable separation between country and court (Clark, *Kent 1500–1640*, p. 219).

36 Scott and Filmer were in various respects more extreme than the majority of their counterparts, especially when it came to dividing the political and religious spectrum of their time and interpreting it. However, they were also representative of a mental trend widely diffused in the early modern period: 'a predisposition to see things in terms of binary opposition' (S. Clark, 'Inversion, Misrule and the Meaning of Witchcraft', *Past & Present*, 87 (1980), pp. 98–127, p. 105).

37 Hirst, *England in Conflict*, p. 125.

38 On Scott and Filmer in this milieu see Eales, 'The Rise of Ideological Politics in Kent', pp. 280–1, 312–13.

39 Underdown, *A Freeborn People*, p. 44.

40 This part is largely based on archival research pursued at the KAO, CCL, BDO and BL. The manuscripts referred to in the text are listed as KAO U951/Z/9, U951/Z/10, U951/Z16, U951/Z17 (Knatchbull Papers); CCL, MS Urry 66 ('Thomas Scott's Papers on the Elections to the Parliament of 1626', fos 1a–141a); BDO, Ballard MS 61; BL, Harley MS 7018, Add. MS 62135, n. 31. The majority of the material consists of Scott's diary and of a series of mostly unfoliated papers in Scott's own hand. Some portions of the diary are in secretarial hand whilst others are reproduced in *PP 1628*, pp. 126–37, 218–43 (where there are passages in both manuscript and printed form I refer to the latter). Amongst the miscellaneous Scott manuscripts two are in BDO, Rawlinson MS A 346,

fos 224a–34b, 285a–97b. These are transcribed and published in *Dorothea Scott, otherwise Gotherson and Hogben, of Egerton House, Kent, 1611–1680*, A New and Enlarged Edition by G. D. Scull (Oxford, 1883).

41 In fact, one of Reginald Scott's daughters, Mary, was the wife of Richard Argall. Amongst their children was Elizabeth, who had married Sir Edward Filmer. Elizabeth and Sir Edward were Sir Robert's parents (*ODNB*, 'Argall, Thomas').

42 *Letter to My Brother Knatchbull*, in BDO, Ballard MS 61, fos 79–80.

43 Clark, 'Thomas Scott', p. 2. Clark's study is pivotal to understanding Scott's religious background and the electoral situation in Kent in the 1610s and 1620s. Clark, however, did not analyse Scott's political ideas, especially his critical views of the monarchy. For another interpretation of Scott's ideas see C. Cuttica, 'Thomas Scott of Canterbury (1566–1635): Patriot, Civic Radical, Puritan', *History of European Ideas*, 34 (2008), pp. 475–89, where parts of this section on Scott appear.

44 They were often deprecatingly referred to as the most riotous, unstable and disorderly of the populace.

45 In the words of Douglas Bradburn, 'there is one group entirely absent from [Lee] Ward's [*The Politics of Liberty*]': the 'common people'. Thus, 'we get no sense of the truth or lack of truth of Filmer's assertion. Who are these "common people everywhere?" What role did they have in turning these high ideas into decisive action?' (D. Bradburn, 'The Origin of a Species: The Making of Whig Political Thought', *Book Review*, H-Atlantic@h-net.msu.edu (May 2005; accessed December 2009), p. 6). This and chapter 4 attempt to answer precisely these important questions.

46 Clark, 'Thomas Scott', p. 2.

47 *Ibid.*, p. 26.

48 *Ibid.*, p. 7.

49 See e.g. *PT*, pp. 33–4, 48, 53–4, 66; *FH*, pp. 76–7, 80–1, 96.

50 See Peter Heylyn, *The Stumbling-Block of Disobedience* (1658), *passim*.

51 Like the labels 'Arminian' and 'papist', 'Puritan' is a problematic word and needs to be used with caution. This is so because of its derogatory connotations in that it was originally (1564) applied to nonconformist clergy within the Elizabethan Church as 'a term of abuse' and as such it was often vociferously disavowed by the latter (J. Coffey and P. C. H. Lim, 'Introduction', in J. Coffey and P. C. H. Lim (eds), *The Cambridge Companion to Puritanism* (Cambridge, 2008), pp. 1–15, p. 1). As Nicholas Tyacke clarified, 'until the 1620s Puritan, as a technical term, was usually employed to describe those members of the English Church who wanted further Protestant reforms in liturgy and organization'. Afterwards, 'Puritanism' came to commonly include Calvinists (N. Tyacke, *Anti-Calvinists. The Rise of English Arminianism c.1590–1640* (Oxford, 1987), pp. 7–8, 8, n. 21, where Tyacke referred to 'Puritan' as 'an abusive epithet' to denote all aspects of 'Protestant religiosity' and remained unconvinced by interpretations that acknowledged the presence of radical Puritans in the phase preceding the Arminian rise in England). See also N. Tyacke, 'Puritanism, Arminianism and Counter-Revolution', in Russell (ed.), *The Origins of the English Civil War*, pp. 119–43.

52 See M. R. Thorp, 'Religion and the Wyatt Rebellion of 1554', *Church History*, 47 (1978), pp. 363–80.

53 To clarify, I use 'Puritan' and 'godly' interchangeably to define Scott's religious, political and, broadly speaking, ideological identity in the sense of 'a distinctive and particularly

intense variety of early modern Reformed Protestantism which originated within the unique context of the Church of England but spilled beyond it' (Coffey and Lim, 'Introduction', pp. 1–2). This form of Protestantism entailed Luther's principles of *sola fide, sola gratia, sola scriptura*; focus on 'personal salvation'; uncompromising anti-Catholic feelings and a complete rejection of its 'penitential system' as well as sacramental theology; identification of the Papacy with the anti-Christ; insistence on the Word as the sole pivot of faith; importance of preaching and reading the Bible; the Calvinist theory of absolute predestination; a constant tension with the establishment of the Reformed Church of England aimed at changing what was perceived as renmants of popery; piety, fasting, spiritual meditation often conveyed through the medium of the diary; sabbatarianism and family devotional exercises (*ibid.*, pp. 2–4). Most importantly, Puritanism was characterised, especially from the late sixteenth century, by a sense of identity that was both imposed upon people like Scott by their adversaries and the result of self-styled godliness (*ibid.*, p. 3). Their intense evangelical tendencies and zealous life distinguished Puritans from conformist Calvinists and turned them into militant Protestants. These traits encapsulate Thomas Scott's *radical* stances. In one word, he was no *moderate* Puritan (see Cuttica, 'Thomas Scott of Canterbury', esp. p. 489).

54 Scholars like Conal Condren and Jonathan Clark (exponents of a *'linguistic'* or 'nominalist' approach), and to a lesser degree Colin Davis (employer of a *'functional'* approach), warn against applying 'radical' and 'radicalism' to historical contexts – such as the early modern period – where these categories had not yet been coined (Burgess, 'Introduction', in Burgess and Festenstein (eds), *English Radicalism*, pp. 7–8). However, Davis' idea of 'the radical moments of actions devoid of a programmatic radicalism, that is the development of radically pragmatic responses under the sheer pressure of events and circumstances' aptly describes the situation in which Scott thought and acted. His radical views did not present the level of systematisation one might expect from a fully fledged radical agenda. But they certainly conveyed anger for, dissatisfaction with and disapproval of Stuart policies, ideas of kingly absolute prerogative and Church organisation in the 1620s. Thus, Davis' model of radicalism can include Scott as one of its most interesting and fiercest (even if little public) representatives. For Davis' position see J. C. Davis, 'Afterword: Reassessing Radicalism in a Traditional Society: Two Questions', in Burgess and Festenstein (eds), *English Radicalism*, pp. 338–72, p. 367. See also C. Condren, 'Afterword: Radicalism Revisited', in Burgess and Festenstein (eds), *English Radicalism*, pp. 311–37.

55 KAO U951/Z16.

56 Hirst, *The Representative of the People?*, pp. 29–43 and *passim*.

57 Hirst, *England in Conflict*, p. 96.

58 KAO U951/Z16. See also Cust, 'The "Public Man"', p. 131.

59 This occurred in the context of the newly summoned parliament (April 1614) when rivalry between the Puritan faction at court and the conservative group formed of the 'old-style' grandees faithful to the Church centred on the issue of recusancy (Clark, 'Thomas Scott', p. 10).

60 Everitt, *The Community of Kent*, p. 63.

61 Clark, 'Thomas Scott', p. 10. On the use of 'Puritanism' and 'Antipuritanism' see the 'sceptical' approach of P. Collinson, 'Antipuritanism', in Coffey and Lim (eds), *The Cambridge Companion to Puritanism*, pp. 19–33, where we are (again) reminded that 'Puritan' was only one of several pejorative nicknames applied to 'the hotter sort of

Protestants' (*ibid.*, p. 20) and that the two isms 'belong together' (*ibid.*, p. 24). For a complete account of 'Puritanism' as a legitimate scholarly term see P. Lake, 'The Historiography of Puritanism', in Coffey and Lim (eds), *The Cambridge Companion to Puritanism*, pp. 346–71. Lake speaks of 'Puritanism as a movement and a sensibility' (*ibid.*, p. 346). Most importantly, he defends the use of 'Puritanism (both name and thing, movement and polemically inflected construct, ascribed and internalised identity)' and underlines 'the continuing salience, the analytic relevance and bite, of the notion of Puritanism' (*ibid.*, p. 364). Indeed, my account of Scott's thoughts and actions confirms the validity of Lake's perspective.

62 CCL, MS Urry 66, fo. 2a.

63 See Thomas Scott, 'A Discourse of Polletique and Civell Honor', in *Dorothea Scott*, pp. 145–98. The treatise was originally in seven chapters but only three have been preserved. Whilst G. D. Scull maintained that it 'was no doubt written early in the reign of Charles I' (*Dorothea Scott*, p. 129, n. a), Clark argued that 'internal evidence and its dedication to the Earl of Arundel as a commissioner for the Earl Marshal's office' suggest that Scott composed this work around 1619 (Clark, 'Thomas Scott', p. 11, n. 36). In the dedication Arundel was called 'one of the Lords Commissioners for the Earle Marshallshipp of England' (Scott, 'Discourse', p. 149). Given that between 1604 and 1622 the 'Marshallshipp' was in commission and that Arundel did not become Earl Marshal until 1622, it seems more likely that Scott wrote his work in the late 1610s.

64 His cousin Filmer was amongst those knighted by James.

65 Scott, 'Discourse', p. 156.

66 *Ibid.*, p. 156.

67 *Ibid.*, p. 156.

68 *Ibid.*, p. 156.

69 *Ibid.*, p. 186.

70 Peltonen, *Classical Humanism*, p. 161. Markku Peltonen saw Scott's vision of politics as being 'close to the idea of an aristocracy' (*ibid.*, p. 173).

71 Scott, 'Discourse', p. 157.

72 *Ibid.*, p. 158.

73 *Ibid.*, pp. 158–9.

74 *Ibid.*, p. 160.

75 *Ibid.*, pp. 158–9.

76 *Ibid.*, p. 193.

77 *Ibid.*, p. 193.

78 *Ibid.*, p. 187.

79 *Ibid.*, p. 193.

80 *Ibid.*, p. 194.

81 *Ibid.*, p. 194.

82 These principles emerge not only throughout *A Discourse* but also in other parts of his writings (see e.g. CCL, MS Urry 66, fo. 91a; KAO, U951/Z16).

83 Peltonen, *Classical Humanism*, p. 161.

84 Scott, 'Discourse', p. 194.

85 See R. von Friedeburg, 'Civic Humanism and Republican Citizenship in Early Modern Germany', in M. van Gelderen and Q. Skinner (eds), *Republicanism. A Shared European Heritage* (Cambridge, 2 vols, 2002), vol. 1, pp. 127–45.

86 R. von Friedeburg, 'The Making of Patriots: Love of Fatherland and Negotiating Monarchy in Seventeenth-Century Germany', *The Journal of Modern History*, 77 (2005), pp. 881–916, p. 895.

87 Scott, 'Discourse', p. 195.

88 *Ibid.*, p. 196.

89 *Ibid.*, p. 197.

90 Clark, 'Thomas Scott', pp. 5, 12–13.

91 CCL, MS Urry 66, fo. 122b.

92 KAO, U951/Z17, fos 6a–b. See also *ibid.*, fos 9a, 11a, 14a. Scott remarked on the threat posed by Arminians well before MPs such as Francis Rous (in the Commons on 26 January 1629) accused people like Montague of stirring up an 'organized movement to subvert the established church' and set Arminianism in England (*ODNB*, 'Montague, Richard'). On Arminianism as 'the least misleading' of the 'various terms' employed to describe religious change in the early seventeenth century see Tyacke, *Anti-Calvinists*, p. 245. See also *ibid.*, pp. 245–7 for a succinct summary of the differences between Arminians and Calvinists.

93 Clark, 'Thomas Scott', p. 14.

94 CCL, MS Urry 66, fos 31b–2a.

95 *Ibid.*, fos 81b–2a. In this regard, Scott's stances belie Conrad Russell's claim that before the early 1640s there had been no voices asking for parliamentary reform on the basis of issues of principle and creed (Russell, *Unrevolutionary England*, pp. 27–9).

96 'An after thought or Postscript. Letter from Thomas Scott to Dudley Digges', in *Dorothea Scott*, pp. 142–3, p. 143.

97 CCL, MS Urry 66, *Thomas Scott Papers on the Elections to the Parliament of 1626*, fos 1a–141a, fo. 123a.

98 According to Derek Hirst, '[a] local politician increasingly had to keep his distance from the attractions of the court lest his local standing should suffer amongst his neighbours' (D. Hirst, 'Court, Country, and Politics before 1629', in K. Sharpe (ed.), *Faction and Parliament. Essays on Early Stuart History* (Oxford, 1978), pp. 105–37, p. 136).

99 'Letters and Miscellaneous Documents', in *PP 1628*, vi, p. 220.

100 *Ibid.*, p. 224.

101 See von Friedeburg, 'Civic Humanism and Republican Citizenship', pp. 130, 145.

102 CCL, MS Urry 66, fo. 96b.

103 See E. Weekley, 'The Etymology of "Roister"', *The Modern Language Review*, 7 (1912), pp. 518–19.

104 Charles had tried to raise cavalry in Germany claiming to employ it in France (Hirst, *England in Conflict*, p. 125). It is significant that the second manifesto of the Parisian *Seize* sent in 1587 to the other cities of the Catholic League singled out Henry III's intention to bring German *reitres* into the country as the definite sign of his evil and

dangerous designs to protect the heretics to the detriment of true religion and national integrity (F. J. Baumgartner, *Radical Reactionaries: The Political Thought of the French Catholic League* (Geneva, 1975), pp. 74–5). The analogy of discourses and polemical arguments between late sixteenth-century France and the 1620s in England is striking (even though in the latter case the heretical faction was identified with papist and Arminian unpatriotic elements).

105 *PP 1628*, vi, p. 220.

106 *Ibid.*, p. 220.

107 *Ibid.*, p. 232. Papism (or *papalism*) refers to a political doctrine that advocates papal supremacy, whilst 'popery' is a derogatory term applied to the doctrines, ceremonies and practices of the Roman Catholic Church at whose head is the Pope (often defined as the anti-Christ).

108 CCL, MS Urry 66, fo. 138a.

109 *Ibid.*, fo. 139b.

110 *Ibid.*, fos 139b–40a.

111 *Ibid.*, fo. 31b.

112 *Ibid.*, fo. 32a.

113 *Ibid.*, fo. 32b.

114 *Ibid.*, fo. 2b. The 'origins' and 'image' of the 'public man' can be found 'in the blending of zealous Calvinism and classical republicanism' (Cust, 'The "Public Man"', p. 126).

115 CCL, MS Urry 66, fo. 74a.

116 *Ibid.*, fo. 83a.

117 KAO, U951/Z10, Knatchbull MSS, A1.

118 *Ibid.*, A1.

119 *Ibid.*, A2.

120 CCL, MS Urry 66, fos 83b–4a.

121 *Ibid.*, fo. 88b.

122 *Ibid.*, fo. 122a.

123 *Ibid.*, fo. 122b.

124 On this concept see chapter 4. See also Underdown, *A Freeborn People*, p. 24; Hirst, *England in Conflict*, p. 91.

125 KAO, U951/Z10.

126 *Ibid.*, U951/Z17, fos 374a, 376a.

127 On Bargrave see chapter 5.

128 Scott had previously defined his position on the civic duty to oppose tyrants as 'Puritan' (KAO, U951/Z17, fos 130a ff.). According to Cust, this unusual step 'suggests the extent to which Scott viewed the broader political perspective in terms of division and polarization' already in the final phases of James I's reign (R. Cust, *The Forced Loan and English Politics 1626–1628* (Oxford, 1987), p. 177).

129 CCL, MS Urry 66, fo. 129b.

130 *Ibid.*, fos 138b–9a.

131 KAO, U951/Z10, A 7–8.

132 *Ibid.*, A8. Almost certainly with a tinge of identification, Scott spoke of Samuel as he who 'even to his sovereign' had said '"Thou has done foolishly"' (*PP 1628*, vi, p. 224).

133 KAO, U951/Z10, fos 4b ff.

134 *Ibid.*, A12.

135 It was in consequence of his mismanagement of the (failed) Cadiz expedition and also of his lavish policy of royal patronage that the Commons had tried to impeach Buckingham. The charges presented to the Lords on 8 May 1626 accused the Duke 'of holding too many offices; of delivering English ships into French hands for use against the Huguenots; of selling honours and offices; of procuring titles for his kindred; and, finally, of poisoning James I' (*ODNB*, 'Villiers, George').

136 Instead of deserting the royal favourite, in June 1626 Charles provided him with the prestigious office of the chancellorship of Cambridge University. In substance, the King held the Commons's attack upon Villiers as a strategic move to target him personally as much as monarchical rule generally. For this reason, Charles prevented the charges from being brought before the Lords and proceeded, instead, to dissolve Parliament.

137 CCL, MS Urry 66, fo. 104a. Scott spoke of those who did nothing to deprive the ruler of his tyrannical power as 'traytors' affected by 'many prettie pretences ... colourable enough, being dyed deepe in hypocrisie, policie and Courtcraft' (*ibid.*, fo. 105b). The reference to Sforce was a Machiavellian motif in that the Florentine had praised as a republican hero the fifteenth-century ringleader of a plot organised against the Milanese tyrant (see Niccolò Machiavelli, *History of Florence* ..., ed. F. Gilbert (New York, 1960), bk viii, ch. 4).

138 CCL, MS Urry 66, fos 81b–2a.

139 *Ibid.*, fos 124b–5a.

140 On censorship at the time of the Spanish Match and the extent to which criticism of the King slipped out see Cogswell, *The Blessed Revolution*, pp. 6–50.

141 This is certainly the case when his opinions are compared with those of vociferous MPs like Edward Alford (on Alford see R. Zaller, 'Edward Alford and the Making of Country Radicalism', *JBS*, 22 (1982), pp. 59–79). On 3 June 1626 one MP named Moore referred hypothetically to tyrants, immediately prompting Sir John Eliot to call for more caution against transforming freedom of speech into licence to criticise the sovereign (J. N. Ball, 'Sir John Eliot and Parliament, 1624–1629', in Sharpe (ed.), *Faction and Parliament*, pp. 173–207, p. 205, n. 75).

142 Scott's positions can be explained with the notion of 'situational disposition'. This interpretative model entails that radicals were 'the holders of certain ideas' that 'under pressure of certain events' took them 'in directions we may label radical' (G. Burgess, 'A Matter of Context: "Radicalism" and the English Revolution', in M. Caricchio and G. Tarantino (eds), *Cromohs Virtual Seminars. Recent Historiographical Trends of the British Studies (17th–18th Centuries)*, 2006–7, pp. 1–4, www.cromohs.unifi.it/seminari/burgess_radicalism.html; accessed 1 December 2009).

143 M. P. Winship, 'Algernon Sidney's Calvinist Republicanism', *JBS*, 49 (2010), pp. 753–73, pp. 770–1.

144 Burgess argued that the Levellers 'are, in a sense, the nightmare that Filmer envisaged in *Patriarcha*' (Burgess, 'A Matter of Context', pp. 1–4). Actually, Filmer was losing his sleep much earlier than the 1640s when he identified the ghosts of his 'nightmare' with patriots such as his cousin.

145 BL, Trumbull MS, Misc. Corr., xix, fo. 16.

146 As for the debate on the date of composition of *Patriarcha* see Schochet, 'New Bibliographical Discoveries'; J. M. Wallace, 'The Date of Sir Robert's Patriarcha', *HJ*, 23 (1980), pp. 155–65; J. Daly, 'Some Problems in the Authorship of Sir Robert Filmer's Works', *EHR*, 98 (1983), pp. 737–62; R. Tuck, 'A New Date for Filmer's Patriarcha', *HJ*, 29 (1986), pp. 183–6. There are two (partly) different original manuscripts of *Patriarcha*: the Cambridge manuscript and the Chicago manuscript. Laslett drew upon the former whilst Sommerville's edition is based on both manuscripts. I adhere to Richard Tuck's hypothesis that the greater part of the work was written in the late 1620s (Tuck, 'A New Date', pp. 183–6). In line with Tuck's dating of the Chicago and the Cambridge manuscripts, Sommerville concluded that '[p]erhaps the first two chapters of *Patriarcha* were composed in the 1620s and the third chapter about 1630' (Sommerville, 'Introduction', p. xxxiv; Sommerville did not focus on the 1632 attempted publication since it was only whilst proofs of his edition of Filmer's works were being prepared that he was drawn to this important document amongst the Trumbull Papers (*ibid.*, p. viii)). Whilst Laslett claimed that the Cambridge manuscript was composed between 1635 and 1642 since it made no references to books later than Selden's *Mare Clausum* (1635), Tuck pointed out that the Chicago manuscript omits Filmer's critique of Grotius' *De Iure Belli ac Pacis* and of *Mare Clausum* (Tuck, 'A New Date', pp. 183–4). The Chicago manuscript also leaves out a section on Selden's *Titles of Honour*, which however appears both in the Cambridge manuscript and in the 1685 edition by Edmund Bohun (see chapter 8 below). The passages referred to in Filmer's work 'are to be found not in the first edition of the work (1614) but in the greatly enlarged second edition (1631) in which Selden incorporated a famous essay on the history of parliament' (*ibid.*, p. 184). For Tuck, the fact that only two texts quoted in the Chicago manuscript were published after 1631 is 'compatible with a date for *Patriarcha* of before 1631'. Filmer quoted Raleigh's *Prerogative of Parliaments* (1628) and referred to the Petition of Right (1628), proving that the Chicago manuscript was ready for circulation 'in late 1628 or early 1629' (*ibid.*, p. 184). Tuck thought it plausible to maintain that *Patriarcha* in the form in which it is preserved in the Chicago manuscript, which is probably not the first draft, was composed between 1628 and 1631. After 1631 Filmer both incorporated new parts into the pre-existing account of Parliament (Chicago manuscript and 1685 Bohun edition) and modified his manuscript to deal with Selden's and Grotius' works. The result was a new manuscript which corresponds to the Cambridge version, which is still datable before 1642. Most importantly, Tuck and, partly, Sommerville agreed that the very first draft of *Patriarcha* might 'belong to the period between 1606 and 1614 when James I was in conflict with his Catholic opponents over the Oath of Allegiance' (*ibid.*, p. 185). To sustain this hypothesis is the evidence that the first section of the *Patriarcha*-Chicago manuscript does not refer to any work later than Raleigh's *History* (1614). Accordingly, Tuck argued that the original draft of *Patriarcha* was a contribution to the debate on the Oath of Allegiance.

147 'Reasons for refusing a licence to Sir Robert Filmer's Patriarcha of G. R. Weckherlin', London, 8 February 1632, BL, Additional MS 72439, fo. 8. See also A. B. Thompson, 'Licensing the Press: The Career of G. R. Weckherlin during the Personal Rule of Charles I', *HJ*, 41 (1998), pp. 653–78, p. 654, where Weckherlin's document is referred

to as BL, Trumbull MS, Misc. Corr., xlii, fo. 35.

148 Cited in Thompson, 'Licensing the Press', p. 654.

149 The other work was a rather hazardous comparison between Henry IV of France and the King of Sweden, Gustavus Adolphus, which Weckherlin deemed damaging to Charles' image. Unsurprisingly, the latter agreed with his licenser (see *ibid.*, pp. 668–9). From 1632 corantos reporting on Gustavus' German victories were banned (Hirst, *England in Conflict*, p. 146).

150 This issue will be more specifically addressed in chapter 5 below.

151 *PT*, p. 2.

152 *Ibid.*, p. 2.

153 *Ibid.*, p. 2.

154 *Ibid.*, p. 2 (italics added).

155 Interestingly, this Filmerian conviction that the common people were a serious threat to the monarchy became a leitmotif both in texts like *Eikon Basilike* (1648) and, above all, during the Restoration era. In his inaugural speech in the parliament of 1661 Edward Hyde, Earl of Clarendon, described the events of the preceding years as the rotten fruits of the actions of 'reformers' from 'all ages, sexes and degrees, all professions and trades'. These seditious elements had led to 'the confounding [of] the Commons of England, which is a noble representative, with *the common people* of England [which] was the first ingredient into that accursed dose, which intoxicated the brains of men with that imagination of a commonwealth' (cited in N. Tyacke, 'Introduction', in *The English Revolution c.1590–1720*, pp. 1–26, p. 20; italics added).

156 *PT*, p. 2.

157 *Ibid.*, p. 3.

158 *Ibid.*, p. 3.

159 *Ibid.*, p. 3.

160 Filmer also rebutted the opinions of monarchist authors such as Sir John Hayward, Adam Blackwood, John Barclay ('and some others') who, despite having 'learnedly confuted' the 'erroneous principle[s]' of Buchanan and Parsons, subscribed to the theory of 'the natural liberty and equality of mankind' (*ibid.*, p. 3).

161 *AN*, 'The Preface', p. 132. Filmer clarified that 'what principles the papists make use of for the power of the pope above kings, the very same (by blotting out the word pope, and putting in the word people), the plebists take up to use against their sovereigns' (*ibid.*, p. 132).

162 *PT*, p. 3.

163 *Ibid.*, p. 5.

164 *Ibid.*, p. 5. Filmer repeated this idea years later when he maintained that people 'flatter[ed]' themselves thinking 'that by resisting our superiors we may do our country laudable service without disturbance of the commonwealth' (*OG*, p. 220).

165 *PT*, p. 33.

166 *Ibid.*, p. 33.

167 *Ibid.*, p. 5 (italics added).

168 *Ibid.*, p. 4.

169 *Ibid.*, p. 4.

170 Once again, I think it important to repeat that Filmer never mentioned Scott. And yet the genus of opinions he opposed mirrored those expounded by his cousin and reported in the first section of this chapter.

171 *Ibid.*, p. 20.

172 See below in this chapter.

173 *PT*, p. 4.

174 Scott, 'Journal', in *PP 1628*, vi, p. 127.

175 *Ibid.*, pp. 127–8.

176 *Ibid.*, p. 127.

177 *PT*, p. 44.

178 Daly described Filmer's idea of sovereignty as 'an undiluted singleness of will' (Daly, *Sir Robert Filmer*, p. 13).

179 *PT*, p. 55.

180 According to Michael Zuckert, Filmer's absolutist doctrine has to be associated with the Reformed vision of God. Zuckert argued that 'in the background of Filmer's royalism' was the 'surpassingly sovereign God' shaped by 'the Reformation dispensation'. As Calvin's God was 'active and assertive' for he did not leave 'the world to run on its own', so Filmer's monarch was omnipresent in the body politic as he actively and constantly intervened to govern. Both the Protestant God and Filmer's ruler were no 'watchmaker[s]' (M. P. Zuckert, *Natural Rights and the New Republicanism* (Princeton, 1994), p. 48).

181 *PT*, p. 31. This could be read as an indirect admonishment to Charles I for his policies of heavy taxation at the end of the 1620s.

182 *Ibid.*, p. 37.

183 *Ibid.*, p. 31. In 1624 Edmund Bolton had declared that 'no Prince is so bad as not to make monarckie seeme the best forme of government' (Edmund Bolton, *Nero Caesar, or Monarchie Depraved* (1624), A3b): indeed, even Nero did more in favour of the public benefit than those who had attempted to dethrone him (*ibid.*, p. 69).

184 *PT*, p. 31.

185 *Ibid.*, p. 35.

186 *Ibid.*, p. 35.

187 *Ibid.*, p. 31. This sharp remark – which is an allusion to 'Psalms', 82.7 and which James I had quoted in Parliament in March 1610 – might also have been a reminder to Charles I of his tasks and role.

188 *Ibid.*, p. 31.

189 *Ibid.*, p. 26.

190 Evidently, these liberties were not derived from a natural right belonging to the people or to each individual in the polity. But they were the product of monarchical fatherly care for the subject.

191 *Ibid.*, p. 42.

192 This unveils the clarity, transparency and Cartesian simplicity of Filmer's discourse. His way of reasoning and expressing ideas denoted a nearly mathematical style. His prose was precise and it articulated a theoretical system recalling the new scientific mindset (on this last point see Daly, *Sir Robert Filmer*, pp. 155–6).

193 According to Rodolfo De Mattei, seventeenth-century natural law theorists and contractualists were the heirs of those who, in the previous century, had erected ethical barriers to the development of the derogation of power and the intertwined paradigm of (amoral) reason of State (R. De Mattei, *Il Problema della 'Ragion di Stato' nell'Età della Controriforma* (Milan and Naples, 1979), p. 108).

194 *PT*, pp. 15, 19.

195 *Ibid.*, p. 17.

196 *Ibid.*, p. 10.

197 Power is where one can act on something or somebody. It means to have the *puissance* (the potential) to act if one wants to; to have the force for doing so.

198 *Ibid.*, p. 6.

199 *AN*, pp. 137, 136.

200 See below.

201 *PT*, p. 8.

202 *OG*, p. 228.

203 *VW*, p. 169.

204 *Ibid.*, p. 174; see also *PT*, p. 18.

205 *PT*, p. 12.

206 *Ibid.*, p. 12.

207 *Ibid.*, p. 10. On this crucial argument of *Patriarcha* see chapter 4 below.

208 See e.g. *FH*, p. 99. See also J. Waldron, *God, Locke, and Equality. Christian Foundations in Locke's Political Thought* (Cambridge, 2002).

209 V. Hart, *Art and Magic in the Court of the Stuarts* (1994), p. 189.

210 *PT*, p. 44.

211 *Ibid.*, p. 40.

212 *FH*, p. 117.

213 Clark, *Thinking with Demons*, p. 623.

214 *OA*, pp. 279–80. In an assembly those who held the legislative power were in charge only 'in *possibility*' and 'not in *act*' since this corresponded to the moment of their casting their vote (*ibid.*, p. 280).

215 See *ibid.*, pp. 280–1 and *PT*, p. 32.

216 *PT*, p. 40.

217 *Ibid.*, p. 52.

218 *Ibid.*, p. 4.

219 *Ibid.*, p. 28.

220 He stated that 'no democracy can extend further than to one city' (*ibid.*, p. 25).

221 *Ibid.*, p. 26.

222 *Ibid.*, p. 29.

223 *Ibid.*, p. 28. See also *ibid.*, p. 27.

224 *Ibid.*, p. 20.

225 *Ibid.*, p. 32.

226 *AN*, p. 137.

227 However, Michael P. Winship has recently shown that, by the late 1620s, 'legal/ constitutional' views like those held by 'radical Puritans' such as William Bradshaw (1571–1618) in the 1580s and (implicitly) Thomas Scott a few decades later had become common amongst 'moderate Protestants'. These saw all too clearly what was going on in England: 'a constitutionally deluded monarch, divine right bishops and popish doctrinal rot' (M. P. Winship, 'Freeborn (Puritan) Englishmen and Slavish Subjection: Popish Tyranny and Puritan Constitutionalism, c. 1570–1606', *EHR*, 124 (2009), pp. 1050–74, pp. 1073–4).

228 See Cust, *The Forced Loan*; Cust, 'The "Public Man"'.

229 Thomas Cogswell identified the origins of the Civil War in what he called 'a domestic crisis of considerable proportions, one which casts a new light on events later in the decade and century' (Cogswell, *The Blessed Revolution*, p. 51). In this respect, Thomas Alured's *Letter sent to the Marquis of Buckingham touching the Spanish Match* (1621), the pamphlet *Tom Tell-Troath* (see chapter 4) and Thomas Scott of Canterbury's hostile comments on Queen Mary and Philip II's marriage proved that the Wyatt Rebellion had been provoked precisely by the type of tensions that ripened in the early 1620s (Cogswell, *The Blessed Revolution*, p. 50).

230 *PT*, p. 5. Although this consideration does not imply that there was a 'high road to Civil War', it is nonetheless distant from accepting Geoffrey Elton's conclusions on the lack of ideological conflict in the first decades of the seventeenth century in England (see G. R. Elton, 'A High Road to Civil War?', in Carter (ed.), *From the Renaissance to the Counter-Reformation*, pp. 325–47, esp. pp. 328–9).

231 On the 'dichotomy between republicanism and absolutism' as conflicting accounts of patriotism see M. Viroli, *For Love of Country. An Essay on Patriotism and Nationalism* (Oxford, 1995), esp. pp. 44–5 and von Friedeburg, 'The Making of Patriots', esp. pp. 915–16.

232 In 1570 Pope Pius V's bull had excommunicated Queen Elizabeth Tudor. Fifteen years later, Pope Sixtus V had intervened in French affairs by excommunicating the Protestant heir Henry of Navarre. In brief, the Pope had become 'a kind of super-king with straightforward secular authority over other monarchs, or at least Christian monarchs' (J. P. Sommerville, 'An Emergent Britain? Literature and National Identity in Early Stuart England', in D. Loewenstein and J. Mueller (eds), *The Cambridge History of Early Modern English Literature* (Cambridge, 2003), pp. 459–86, p. 473). In his mocking political satire *A Game at Chess* (1624), Thomas Middleton remarked that the Jesuits aimed at imposing a kind of 'universal monarchy' and that their theories divested people of any form of political allegiance to national states (Sommerville, 'An Emergent Britain', p. 469).

Chapter 3

Filmer's patriarchalism versus
Jesuit political ideas

Inflaming political literature in early seventeenth-century England, the doctrine of the Pope's (indirect) temporal power[1] had its major and most systematic exponent in Robert Bellarmine.[2] His ideas were hugely popular amongst Catholic theorists such as Jacob Gretser at Ingolstadt; Martin Becanus at Mainz; Francisco Suarez, Pedro de Ribadeneyra, Gabriel Vasquez in Spain; Emmanuel de Sâ in Portugal; Jean Guigard in France; the Gunpowder plotter Father Henry Garnet in England.[3] Contributing to such a popularity was also the fact that Bellarmine's political opinions came under heavy fire across Europe.[4] On English soil one of the most vehement reactions to them was set forth by King James VI and I.[5]

Branding the Jesuits a bunch of wicked 'preachers', in 1598 James (then still in Scotland) announced that in both England and France they had 'busied themselues most to stir vp rebellion vnder cloake of religion'.[6] He added that their theories promoted external intrusion into kingdoms, which led 'to expell and put out their rigtheous King'.[7] A few years later, at the time of the virulent polemics on the Oath of Allegiance (1606), James reminded 'what a Panegyricke Oration was made by the *Pope*, in praise and approbation of the Frier [Jacques Clément] and his fact, that murthered king *Henry* the third of *France*'. In 'that Oration', Sixtus Quintus had announced '*That a trew Frier hath killed a counterfeit Frier*'. Indeed, James sarcastically observed, 'besides that vehement Oration and congratulation for that fact, how neere it scaped, that the said Frier was not canonized for that glorious act, is better knowen to *Bellarmine* and his followers, then to vs here'.[8]

James' harsh views were not at all exceptional. Nor were they simply conditioned by the Gunpowder Plot of 1605. In fact, his opinions matched those of many who accused the Jesuits of having influenced the fanatical Catholics Jacques Clément (the murderer of Henry III, 1589) and François Ravaillac (the murderer of King Henry IV, 1610). Their doctrines came to represent the justification of parricide with which the killing of kings was associated.[9] It did not help that their coreligionist Juan de Mariana (1536–1624) admitted that a private subject could kill a tyrant for the safeguard of the nation. Since it was impossible for the community to assemble so as to proceed to dethrone the tyrannical prince, Mariana argued that it was legitimate for everyone to take up arms against he who oppressed the subjects and, above all, trod over the values of the *sacra patria*.[10]

It was precisely to contrast these ideas that monarchists targeted Jesuit theorists as unpatriotic fanatics justifying the most horrible and abominable of crimes. This was the parricide of the nation's most venerable father: the king.

THE 'HEAVYWEIGHTS' OF JESUIT THINKING: BELLARMINE AND SUAREZ[11]

As for the deposing power Jesuit theorists assigned to the Pontiff vis à vis the temporal authority of monarchs, Bellarmine was adamant that it was no 'probable' tenet but a 'certain' doctrine. Those who denied it were heretical propagators of falsities.[12] In one of his most political works, *De Laicis* (conceived as a section of *De Controversiis* of 1585), the Cardinal had concentrated on civil government, its origins and governance. He trenchantly separated the authority of the Pope – which derived immediately from God – from that of temporal rulers – which, instead, stemmed from God only through the consent of the people. One of Bellarmine's argumentative pillars was the notion that God had entrusted power to no one in particular, so that kings claiming to have supreme authority over the people erred or acted in bad faith. As he put it, 'Divine law gives ... power to the collected body' and 'in the absence of positive law, there is no good reason why, in a multitude of equals, one rather than another should dominate'.[13] Confirming this truth, the law of nature prescribed that 'this power is delegated by the multitude to one or several'.[14] Bellarmine explicitly said that not only 'political power resides in the people',[15] but that

> it depends on the consent of the people to decide whether kings, or consuls, or other magistrates are to be established in authority over them; and, if there be legitimate cause, the people can change a kingdom into an aristocracy, or an aristocracy into a democracy, and vice versa, as we read was done in Rome.[16]

Bellarmine pointed out that 'even if at the beginning those who founded kingdoms were usurpers for the most part, yet, by the passing of time, either they or their successors became lawful rulers of those kingdoms, since the people gradually gave their consent'.[17] Accordingly, he argued that 'it is absolutely necessary that the nation, if it is to be ruled rightly, must be ruled by laws, not merely by the will of the ruler'.[18] In stark contrast to monarchist theorists, the Cardinal also stated that whilst the multitude 'consider the law carefully', 'the ruler is only one, and frequently has to judge without due consideration'.[19] Most controversially, for Bellarmine it was 'the supreme Pontiff' that 'amongst Christians held first place', whereas the 'last' was reserved for 'laics, among whom kings and princes are numbered'.[20] To fortify his idea of the inferiority of temporal monarchs, Bellarmine maintained that they could not make priests conform to their will. He also indicated that in case a king acted 'unworthily', the Pope had the supreme power to 'restrain and punish' him.[21] Bellarmine was adamant about who was the highest authority in the body politic:

> the temporal and spiritual power in the Church are not two separate and distinct things, as two political kingdoms, but they are united so that they form one body; or rather they exist as the body and soul in one man [the Pope], for spiritual power is as the soul, and temporal power as the body.[22]

In tune with these considerations, in his polemical *Responce aux Principaux Articles et Chapitres de l'Apologie du Belloy* (composed in 1588)[23] Bellarmine accused the French monarchist Pierre de Belloy (1540–1612) of being a false Catholic who refused to accept the tenets established at the Council of Trent (1542–63). The most interesting part of this tract is the third in which Bellarmine addressed the question of whether kings could be dispossessed of their throne by papal decree 'because of heresy, right of succession or of command'.[24] In contradistinction to Belloy's opinion, Bellarmine pointed out that there existed several 'canonical decrees' proving that 'all heretics regardless of degree and rank, are deprived of temporal power'.[25] Likewise, numerous historical examples showed that popes had deposed heretical sovereigns: the most famous case was Pope Zachary's excommunication of Childeric and deliverance of the people 'of their oath of allegiance'.[26] The power of the Pontiff was also justified by divine right. For this reason, Bellarmine strongly rejected Belloy's claim that kings had received their authority directly from God. For the Cardinal it was indisputable that power was given to monarchs 'through human intervention'[27] and that kingdoms were established 'not directly and immediately by God, but thanks to human preservation and judgement'.[28] Moreover, the Catholic Church could command temporal authorities to punish not just blasphemous people but 'mainly heretics'. And, 'should they not abide by this order, the Pope could expel them from his company, and deprive them of all authority and dominion over Catholics'. He could also 'command the faithful populace not to obey or comply with them in any way'.[29] Equally, the Catholic Church could undo kings and, 'eventually, declare subjects delivered from the obedience due to monarchs'.[30] In such a case subjects would not sin because they acted against a king that the Church had reduced to the status of private subject.

Bellarmine underlined that, as the supreme governor of all Christians, the Pope had the 'right' to depose kings on the basis of an important and just cause.[31] Despite conceding that *'puissance Ecclesiastique'* and *'politique'* could be occasionally separated, Bellarmine underscored that in Christendom these two *'puissances'* were 'so joined and tied together, that they formed not just a commonweal, a Kingdom, or a family, but one same body'. What counted the most for Bellarmine was that *'la puissance Ecclesiastique'* was 'almost like the mind, whilst politics like the body'.[32] In his radical conclusion, the Cardinal proclaimed that *'la puissance Ecclesiastique'* led and governed *'la politique'*.[33]

The damage caused by Bellarmine's theories was not only related to his 'pestilent and dangerous conclusion' based on 'the natural liberty of the subject' that the multitude originally held power 'by the law of God' (who became thus 'author of a democratical estate').[34] It was also that his ideas threatened the cornerstone of Filmer's vision of politics: Bellarmine's 'papal monarchomachy' entrusted the Pontiff with the authority to gauge heirs to the throne of national monarchies and determine who ought to be empowered.[35] Conceding such an authority to the Bishop of Rome, Bellarmine tainted with a lethal element of uncertainty the patriarchalist process of transmission of power. In other words, the Cardinal's tenet irreparably broke the continuity of political might which Filmer saw assured by the Adamite model. For Sir Robert there was no separation between Adam's reign and national states. In contrast to Bellarmine's idea that temporal polities were the outcome of Cain's murder and of his consequent divine banishment, Filmer depicted these political entities as legitimated by the original fatherly power embodied in Adam. Whilst Bellarmine saw the fragmentation of the prime universal order caused by Cain's act as deleterious chaos afflicting nations,[36] Filmer elicited from the Adamite paradigm what he thought to be the most viable solution to govern efficiently the Augustinian city of man.[37] It followed that the fatherly authority of Adam did not die out.[38] On the contrary, it represented the continuity of political interaction and justified the superiority of secular rulers over the Pontiff.

Moreover, Filmer expressed a more utilitarian idea of national integrity than Bellarmine. Whereas for the latter the concept of *caritas* defined the duties of the king towards his subjects,[39] for Filmer *caritas* did not distinguish the good monarch from the tyrant. In Filmer's account of power there could be no deviation from allegiance to the supreme sovereign. The latter established when a state of emergency occurred and acted in an extraordinary manner. Hence the theories of Bellarmine and Filmer differed at an ontological level. Accordingly, for the former only God and, through His intervention, the Church guided by the universal power of the Pope could solve problems affecting political societies. For the latter, instead, it was the power of monarchs that, thanks to its Adamite origins, gave stability to the State. In supporting the indirect power of the Pope, Bellarmine retrieved a kind of general and universal lost harmony, whilst the layman Filmer primarily delineated the best asset for the body politic in the here and now.

Most importantly, Bellarmine's vision of politics was not the only to kindle Filmer's reaction. Undaunted by taking to task high-calibre Jesuits, Sir Robert also challenged Francisco Suarez. In *Defensio Fidei* (1613) the latter clarified that the central point to be discussed in politics was whether the Pope was spiritually above all secular sovereigns. Secondly, it was necessary to ascertain whether the Pontiff was superior not only to the person of the king but also to his power in temporals. Lastly, in the wake of the second point it was fundamental to establish whether the power in temporals thus assigned to the Pope could regulate the precepts of Christian princes to the extent that they could be deposed by papal decree. In giving a positive answer to all three questions Suarez adhered to Bellarmine's controversial doctrine of the indirect power of the Pope[40] and defended the Cardinal from James I's accusations. Suarez explained that, although 'the regal power itself is directly from God as the Author of nature', kings could not consider themselves as divinely appointed 'through special revelation or grant'. This meant that their power 'is only granted directly by God to that subject in whom by the force of natural reason alone it is found; but this subject is the people itself, and not any individual of it'.[41]

Likewise, in his influential *Tractatus De Legibus ac Deo Legislatore* (1612) Suarez had argued at length that, since the whole community had provided kings with power, the people could legally restrain monarchs. The people were indeed the ultimate repository of power since they had given it to governors.[42] Above all, in *Defensio Fidei* the Jesuit champion returned to the usual burning issue: he distinguished between the power of the king and that of the Pontiff. He did not apply the same criteria to define them because 'the reasoning is by far different'. Whereas 'the Pontifical monarchy was instituted over the Church Universal directly by God Himself and ordered under such conditions that it cannot be changed', there was no doubt that 'the method of temporal rule was not defined nor ordered by God, but this was left to the disposition of men'.[43] Moreover, Suarez dismissed conciliarist theories by declaring that

the spiritual power never was in the community of the whole Church, because Christ conferred it not on the body, but on its Head, of His Vicar, and therefore the Church cannot concur in the election of the Pontiff as giving the power but as designating the person.[44]

Again the double-standard approach to this argument was employed: Suarez was quick to point out that 'the civil power' resided 'in the community itself and through it was transferred to this or that prince by the will of the community itself'.[45] This rule did not apply to 'the supreme spiritual jurisdiction of the Pope' for it had been 'conferred by divine law that it cannot be limited, neither diminished nor increased'.[46] Suarez was convinced that 'the regal power, or that of any supreme temporal tribunal' was the product of human decision and that, as such, it 'could have been in the beginning made greater or less'. Equally, this same power could 'be changed in passage of time or diminished' depending on how 'expedient' this was 'for the common good'. The decision rested with he 'who will have the power for this purpose'.[47]

Unsurprisingly, these doctrines were badly received in monarchical circles around Europe. Suarez's ideas eroded the foundations of kingly rule from two angles. Firstly, by denying that sovereigns had been granted power directly from God but only thanks to the mediation of the people, the Jesuit polemicist undermined the theory of the divine power of kings. Secondly, he dealt another blow against the *political ego* of monarchs by showing that only the Pope had a truly divine power and as such an indisputably superior authority over temporal rulers. Whilst 'the Pope's power cannot be so altered' since 'it is not in the power of men to change the monarchical regime in the Church', 'the human community can transfer its jurisdiction to a person, or to another community'.[48] Therefore, for Suarez it followed that the temporal power of national rulers was 'not only subject to change, but also rather mutable and more dependent on the wills of men'.[49] He contended that 'the power of dominating or ruling men politically has been given to no man in particular directly by God'.[50]

De Legibus threatened patriarchalism by asserting that in Scripture hereditary succession to the throne 'is not said perpetually to have existed among men'. Adam had nothing more than 'an economic power' and certainly 'not a political one' since there was no polity at his time and, therefore, no political institution.[51] Suarez insisted that power originally 'exists in no single person, but in the collectivity of men'. In his view 'all men are born free, and therefore none has political jurisdiction over another, just as no dominion'.[52] Since their power had been delegated by the community, princes were 'ministers of the Republic'. Hence his criticism of patriarchalism pointed to the assertion that Adam from the very 'beginning of the creation' held 'the principate and consequently sovereignty over all men, and thus it could be derived from him, either through the natural origin of primogeniture, or through the will of Adam himself'.[53] Statements like this were, according to Suarez, patently wrong.

Conceding only 'domestic' power to Adam, his theory overtly collided with the configuration of the origins of political power delineated in patriarchalist treatises. Since he refused to assign any value to 'the force of creation' as a means to justify subjects' subordination to the sovereign, Suarez completely effaced any role Adam had had in the formation of political society as would later be claimed by Filmer. Drawing on Roman law, he also separated economic and political powers as different spheres of human interaction. Adam 'had power over a wife, and afterward paternal power over his sons so long as they were not emancipated' and over 'servants and a complete family'.[54] Yet 'after families began to be multiplied, and the individual men separated, they who were the heads of the individual families had the same power over their families'. Thus, political power had nothing to do with the development of early society since it 'did not begin until several families began to be gathered into one perfected community'. This also meant that 'that community did not begin through the creation of Adam, nor by the will of him, but by all who came together in it'. Therefore, there was no reason or evidence 'to say that Adam from the nature of the subject had the political primateship in that community'. Overthrown from his 'patriarchalist pedestal' of originator of politics and kingship, Adam was reduced to nothing higher than 'king of his own posterity'.[55] Suarez singled out Cain as 'the first to divide the perfect [original] community by separating himself from the paternal family; and likewise afterwards was Nimrod with respect to Noah'.[56] Accordingly, the Jesuit theorist argued that power 'has been granted to the community of men by the Author of nature, yet not without the intervention of the wills and consents of men, from whom such a perfected community has been gathered'.[57]

Furthermore, Suarez supported the controversial theory of mixed government. Relying on Bellarmine's '*The Pope*, Book I', he first declared that the three traditional forms of government could be mingled together to forge one type of political power. Following Aristotle, he then reiterated that although monarchy was normally reputed to be the best kind of polity, the 'determination' to establish who was in charge of governing was 'necessarily ... made by human decision'.[58] Drawing on the works of Cajetan and Vitoria, he finally affirmed that 'the civil power ... has emanated from the people and the community by legitimate or regular right either proximately or remotely'. Hence 'it could not be otherwise held, to be just'.[59] In tune with this, Suarez did not miss one last chance to attack the concept of hereditary monarchy. He remarked that because 'succession ... does not go on forever', it 'cannot be the first root of this power in the king'. Rather, 'the first one have the supreme power directly from the commonwealth' and this procedure extended from the first king 'to the successors'.[60]

This series of forthright anti-patriarchalist concepts provoked Filmer's strong criticism. It surely inspired one of his most vehement reactions to be found in *Patriarcha*. As he put it, 'Father Suarez the Jesuit riseth up against the royal authority of Adam in defence of the freedom and liberty of the people'.[61] Although he saw no 'reason' for not calling 'Adam's family a commonwealth, except we will wrangle about words', Filmer was prepared to 'let Father Suarez understand what he please by Adam's family'. In doing so, Suarez would find himself in the inescapable position to have to 'confess ... that Adam and the patriarchs had absolute power of life and death, of peace and war and the like, within their houses or families'. Hence the Jesuit would have to acknowledge that these were 'kings of their houses or families'. And since they were 'so by the law of nature', it was impossible not to ask 'what liberty will be left for their children to dispose of'.[62] Attacking Suarez's contention that 'community did not begin at the creation of Adam', Filmer observed:

> [i]t is true – because he had nobody to communicate with. Yet community did presently follow his creation, and that by his will alone, for it was in his power only, who was lord of all, to appoint what his sons should have in proper and what in common.

In practice, 'property and community of goods did follow originally from him' for 'it is the duty of a father to provide as well for the common good of his children as for their particular'.[63]

Filmer's priority was to reject Suarez's doctrines on Adam by showing their absurdity. Accordingly, he pointed out that Father Francisco even contradicted Bellarmine when concluding 'that "by the law of nature alone it is not due unto any progenitor to be also king of his posterit"'. In fact, '[t]his assertion is confuted point blank by Bellarmine, who expressly affirmeth that "the first parents ought to have been princes of their posterity"'. It followed that, unless Suarez or his supporters provided 'some reason' for their assertions, it was necessary to 'trust more to Bellarmine's proofs than to his [Suarez's] bare denials'.[64] Filmer dismissively invited the two Jesuits, and 'all those who place supreme power in the whole people', to prove 'that there is but one and the same power in all the people of the world, so that no power can be granted except all the people upon the earth meet and agree to choose a governor'.[65] For Filmer this clearly demonstrated the lack of truth and logic informing their doctrines.

He further struck at the heart of Jesuit thought by enquiring: '[c]an they show or prove that ever the whole multitude met and divided this power, which God gave them in gross, by breaking it into parcels and by apportioning a distinct power to each several commonwealth?' For, '[w]ithout such a compact', he went on, 'I cannot see, according to their own principles, how there can be any election of a magistrate by a commonwealth, but by a mere usurpation upon the privilege of the whole world'.[66] Not content with this attack, Filmer fired some final polemical bullets at Suarez's anti-patriarchalism. He rejected the idea that 'in each particular commonwealth there is a distinct power in the multitude'. In fact, he ironically asked: 'was a general meeting of a whole kingdom ever known for the election of a prince? Was there any example of it ever found in the whole world?' The answer was scathing: '[t]o conceit such a thing is to imagine little less than an impossibility, and so by consequence no one form of government or king was ever established according to this supposed law of nature'.[67]

This passage leaves no doubt: Filmer did not tolerate those who denied Adam's role as the *principium* of the body politic, which, in turn, could not exist without the monarch (its *salus*). More strikingly, Filmer declared that, should 'a king' be bound by 'human laws' he would be deprived of 'supreme power amongst men'. Indeed, even 'a popular government ... cannot be one minute without an arbitrary power freed from all human laws'. In a move which was unique within the monarchist galaxy, Filmer proclaimed that it would not be conceivable 'for any government at all to be in the world without an arbitrary power'. As he succinctly put it, '[i]t is not power except it be arbitrary'.[68] And this was a concept on which he did not spare emphasis: in *The Free-Holders Grand Inquest* he again stated that 'the supreme power is always arbitrary – for that is arbitrary which hath no superior on earth to control it'. For him, '[t] he last appeal in all government must still be to an arbitrary power, or else appeals will be *in infinitum*, never at an end'. To theorists like the Jesuits or like the pamphleteer William Prynne (1600–69) he laconically and trenchantly responded that '[t]he legislative power is an arbitrary power'.[69]

Against all Ultramontanist pretences to papal superiority, Filmer conceived the king as *lex loquens* and *legibus solutus*. Unrestrained by external or internal authorities, the king wielded his *ab-solute*[70] and indivisible power to guide the nation efficiently and safely. The opposite was true of democracies where 'confused multitudes, without heads or governors' controlled power.[71] This situation had caused calamitous events in ancient Rome, where the best people were forced into exile whilst '[t]he worst men sped best'. Like Athens, 'so Rome was a sanctuary for all turbulent, discontented and seditious spirits', being the populace – 'this beast of many heads' – in charge of the polity.[72] In light of these precedents, Filmer deemed it all the more urgent to fight off what he – by all means too exaggeratedly – considered the menacing proposi- tions of Bellarmine and Suarez.

To fully understand Filmer's vitriol against popular power it is necessary to approach the political and ideological landscape of the first few decades of seventeenth-century England. This leads to the question of which theoretical paradigms were then available to thinkers engaged in intellectual disputes; which philosophical languages circulated; in what ways political theory and practice were interwoven. To cast light on these points we first concentrate on opposition to the monarchy.[73]

NOTES

1 On Jesuit political ideas see e.g. T. P. Clancy, *Papist Pamphleteers. The Allen-Persons Party and the Political Thought of the Counter Reformation in England* (Chicago, 1964); R. Mousnier, *L'Assassinat d'Henry IV 14 mai 1610* (Paris, 1964); M. Turchetti, *Tyrannie et Tyrannicide de l'Antiquité à Nos Jours* (Paris, 2001); H. Höpfl, *Jesuit Political Thought. The Society of Jesus and the State, c.1540–1630* (Cambridge, 2004); S. Tutino, 'Huguenots,

Jesuits and Tyrants: Notes on the Vindiciae Contra Tyrannos in Early Modern England', *Journal of Early Modern History*, 3 (2007), pp. 175–96.

2 It is a telling anecdote that in 1601 John Dave's audience at St Paul's Cross knew they had to cheer for 'Bezen' (Bèze) and boo for 'Bellamye' (Bellarmine) (A. Milton, *Catholic and Reformed. The Roman and Protestant Churches in English Protestant Thought 1600–1640* (Cambridge, 1995), p. 543). For a complete study of Bellarmine's political ideas see S. Tutino, *Empire of Souls. Robert Bellarmine and the Christian Commonwealth* (Oxford, 2010).

3 The promoter of Bellarmine's ideas in England was Matthew Kellison (1561–1641), author of *The Right and Jurisdiction of the Prelate, and the Prince* (written in 1614 and published for the first time at Douai in 1617). Kellison claimed that, as the spiritual leader of Christendom, the Pope was empowered to intervene in secular affairs and depose monarchs (J. P. Sommerville, 'Kellison Matthew', in A. Pyle (ed.), *The Dictionary of Seventeenth Century British Philosophers* (Bristol, 2000), pp. 486–7).

4 Hélène Duccini vividly defined these Jesuits as 'a sort of world-wide mafia for parricide' (H. Duccini, *Fair Voir, Faire Croire. L'opinion publique sous Louis XIII* (Seyssel, 2003), p. 92). The term 'parricide' was first employed at the time of the Jesuits Pierre Barrière's (1593) and Jean Chastel's (1594) attempts on Henry IV's life (*ibid.*, pp. 74, 90). On these themes see also E. Nelson, *The Jesuits and the Monarchy. Catholic Reform and Political Authority in France (1590–1615)* (Aldershot, 2005), esp. pp. 130 ff.

5 Other reactions came from Lancelot Andrewes (*A Sermon Preached before His Maiestie ...*, 1610); John Buckeridge (*De Potestate Papae in Rebus Temporalibus*, 1614); Richard Mocket (*God and the King*, 1615). According to Richard Tuck, Buckeridge had set out 'a patriarchal theory of kingship' against Bellarmine's theory of the role of popular consent in monarchical government. Yet for Tuck, 'much the most famous work along these lines ... was by a layman. Sir Robert Filmer' (Tuck, *Philosophy and Government*, p. 262). It is important to note that, whilst Buckeridge was first and foremost interested in emphasising the power of God and then that of the absolute temporal ruler, Filmer focused on the absoluteness of the king's prerogative. Buckeridge underlined the respect monarchs owed the law of God and stressed the relation between 'prince' and 'priest' – 'the calling of King and Priest was united in one man: the Prince of the family was both chiefe Magistrate and Priest, & had the supremacie in both' (John Buckeridge, *A Sermon Preached at Hampton ...* (1606), p. 17). His sermon centred on the relation between the king and the Church in the body politic; on the subordination of earthly monarchs to the supreme divine power; on the metaphysical notions of submission and order. These points were not highlighted in Filmer's oeuvre.

6 King James VI and I, *The Trew Law of Free Monarchies: or the Reciprock and Mvtvall Dvetie Betwitxt a Free King, and His Naturall Subiects*, in Sommerville (ed.), *King James VI and I. Political Writings*, pp. 62–84, p. 71.

7 *Ibid.*, p. 82.

8 King James VI and I, *Triplici Nodo, Triples Cuneus. Or Apologie for the Oath of Allegiance ...*, in Sommerville (ed.), *King James VI and I. Political Writings*, pp. 85–131, pp. 111–12.

9 Mousnier, *L'Assassinat d'Henry IV*, p. 36.

10 Turchetti, *Tyrannie et Tyrannicide*, p. 477. Mariana was the author of *De Rege et Regis Institutione* (1599). On Mariana see H. E. Braun, *Juan de Mariana and Early Modern Spanish Political Thought* (Aldershot, 2007).

11 On the impact of Jesuit political thinking on early modern French and English absolutist discourse see C. Cuttica, 'Anti-Jesuit *Patriotic Absolutism*: Robert Filmer and French Ideas (c. 1580–1630)', *Renaissance Studies*, 25 (2011), pp. 559–79.

12 J. P. Sommerville, 'Papalist Political Thought and the Controversy over the Jacobean Oath of Allegiance', in E. Shagan (ed.), *Catholics and the 'Protestant Nation'. Religious Politics and Identity in Early Modern England* (Manchester, 2005), pp. 162–84, p. 180.

13 Robert Bellarmine, *De Laicis, or The Treatise on Civil Government*, ed. M. F. X. Millar and transl. E. Murphy (New York, 1928), ch. vi, p. 25.

14 *Ibid.*, ch. vi, p. 26.

15 *Ibid.*, ch. vi, p. 28.

16 *Ibid.*, ch. vi, p. 27.

17 *Ibid.*, ch. vi, p. 30.

18 *Ibid.*, ch. x, p. 42.

19 *Ibid.*, ch. x, p. 43.

20 *Ibid.*, ch. xvii, p. 77.

21 *Ibid.*, ch. xvii, pp. 77–8.

22 *Ibid.*, ch. xvii, pp. 81–2.

23 See Robert Bellarmine, *Responce aux Principaux Articles et Chapitres de l'Apologie du Belloy* ... (Paris, 1588; transl. from the Latin).

24 *Ibid.*, ch. xv, p. 56.

25 *Ibid.*, ch. xv, p. 58. This was a reference to Henry IV's Protestant faith.

26 *Ibid.*, ch. xv, p. 61.

27 *Ibid.*, ch. xv, p. 63.

28 *Ibid.*, ch. xv, pp. 67–8.

29 *Ibid.*, ch. xv, p. 74.

30 *Ibid.*, ch. xv, p. 75.

31 *Ibid.*, ch. xv, p. 94.

32 *Ibid.*, ch. xv, p. 98.

33 *Ibid.*, ch. xv, p. 100.

34 *PT*, pp. 5–6. For other criticism of Bellarmine see *ibid.*, pp. 13–14, where Filmer explained that the Cardinal contradicted himself.

35 G. Barbuto, 'Il "Principe" di Bellarmino', in R. De Maio, A. Borromeo, L. Gulia and A. Mazzacane (eds), *Bellarmino e la Controriforma* (Sora (Italy), 1990), pp. 123–89, p. 151.

36 On this point see D. Ferraro, 'Bellarmino, Suárez, Giacomo I e la Polemica sulle Origini del Potere Politico', in De Maio, Borromeo, Gulia and Mazzacane (eds), *Bellarmino e la Controriforma*, pp. 191–250, pp. 213, 234.

37 *PT*, pp. 23–4.

38 *Ibid.*, pp. 10–11.

39 On this see Barbuto, 'Il "Principe" di Bellarmino', pp. 143–5.

40   P. Mesnard, *L'Essor de la Philosophie Politique au XVI siècle* (Paris, 1969), p. 652.

41   Francisco Suarez, 'Defense of the Faith', in G. A. Moore (ed. and trans.), *Extracts on Politics and Government* (Maryland, 1910), bk iii, ch. iii, pp. 21–8, p. 27.

42   Francisco Suarez, 'Laws and God the Lawgiver', in Moore (ed. and trans.), *Extracts on Politics and Government*, esp. bk iii, ch. iv. Another edition of Suarez's *De Legibus* is in *Selections from Three Works*, ed. J. B. Scott and trans. H. Davis et al. (Oxford, 2 vols, 1944).

43   Suarez, 'Defense of the Faith', bk iii, ch. iii, p. 28.

44   *Ibid.*, bk iii, ch. iii, p. 28.

45   *Ibid.*, bk iii, ch. iii, p. 28.

46   It has to be noted that Suarez's vision of papal power was strikingly similar to that Filmer delineated with regard to the authority of the secular ruler.

47   *Ibid.*, bk iii, ch. iii, p. 28. Suarez described the right of subjects to depose a tyrannical monarch by saying that 'the realm could prosecute a just war against him' (*ibid.*, bk iii, ch. iv, p. 112). See also *ibid.*, bk vi, ch. iv.

48   Suarez, 'Laws and God the Lawgiver', bk iii, ch. iii, p. 106.

49   *Ibid.*, bk iii, ch. iii, p. 107.

50   *Ibid.*, bk iii, ch. ii, p. 101.

51   *Ibid.*, bk iii, ch. ii, pp. 99–100.

52   *Ibid.*, bk iii, ch. ii, p. 99.

53   *Ibid.*, bk iii, ch. ii, p. 100.

54   *Ibid.*, bk iii, ch. ii, p. 100.

55   *Ibid.*, bk iii, ch. ii, p. 100.

56   *Ibid.*, bk iii, ch. ii, p. 102.

57   *Ibid.*, bk iii, ch. iii, p. 105.

58   *Ibid.*, bk iii, ch. iv, p. 109.

59   *Ibid.*, bk iii, ch. iv, p. 110.

60   *Ibid.*, bk iii, ch. iv, p. 111.

61   *PT*, p. 15.

62   *Ibid.*, p. 16.

63   *Ibid.*, p. 19.

64   *Ibid.*, p. 19.

65   *Ibid.*, p. 19.

66   *Ibid.*, p. 20.

67   *Ibid.*, p. 20.

68   *OG*, p. 201.

69   *FH*, p. 100.

70   If it is true that 'absolute' meant independent from an allegedly superior authority (Pope or Emperor), it nonetheless indicated that the king was *legibus solutus* and supreme

in his command over Parliament and subjects. Whereas for historians like Jim Collins 'absolute' meant 'independent' and not 'unrestricted', I think that both these meanings have to be taken into account (see J. Collins, *The State in Early Modern France*, (Cambridge, 2nd edn, 2010), pp. ix-xxv, pp. xvii, xx).

71 *PT*, pp. 7–8.

72 *Ibid.*, pp. 27–8.

73 What follows mostly departs from Conrad Russell's positions on the absence of consti-tutional disagreement and parliamentary 'opposition' in the pre-Civil War Parliaments (see Russell, *Unrevolutionary England*, esp. 'Introduction', pp. ix-xxx, e.g. pp. xiv, xv, xvi, xviii and also e.g. pp. 21, 26, 33, 35, 48, 50 1, 54, 57). For the opposite view on the nature (and presence) of pre-Civil War ideological debates on constitutional matters see e.g. J. Davies, *The Caroline Captivity of the Church. Charles I and the Remoulding of Anglicanism 1625–1641* (Oxford, 1992), pp. 1–4, *passim*.

Chapter 4

Filmer's patriarchalism in context: 'popularity', King James VI and I, Parliament and monarchists

THE DANGER OF 'POPULARITY' IN JACOBEAN AND EARLY CAROLINE POLITICS

A s Peter Lake showed, by the end of the 1620s there existed 'two structurally similar but mutually exclusive conspiracy theories … purported to explain the political difficulties of the period'.[1] The monarchist narrative of 'popularity' focused on recurrent 'puritanical' plots threatening the existence of monarchy. By contrast, the 'anti-popery' argument insisted on popish conspiracies set up to overcome religion and polity in England.[2] Despite defending opposite political stances, these two narratives operated according to the same rationale. They de-legitimised each other as un-English; branded their adversaries as innovators and saboteurs of the body politic; warranted their own position 'as the guardian of English good government'.[3] In this context an image of Protestantism as inherently English was formed, whereas popery was always seen as foreign.[4] By and large, these two positions informed the ideological framework through which people defined their alignment within the political spectrum of the age.

Interestingly, amongst those whose opinions influenced Filmer was King James VI and I, who was one of the main propagators of the narrative of popularity.[5] Since the time he reigned over Scotland, where he had published *The Trew Law of Free Monarchies* (1598) and *Basilicon Doron* (1599), right up to when he became King of England in 1603, James was deeply affected by the language of popular conspiracy. He associated it with parliamentary attempts to limit his prerogative (especially in 1610 and 1614), which he considered an unbearable invasion of popular elements into his realm of action.[6] In *Basilicon Doron* James repeatedly attacked Puritans for their rebellious doctrines and said that he was often 'calumniated in their populare Sermons, not for any euill or vice in me, but because I was a King, which they thought the highest euill'.[7] He defined Puritans as 'verie pestes in the Church and Common-weale'

104

since they breathed 'nothing but sedition and calumnies, aspiring without measure, railing without reason and making their own imaginations ... the square of their conscience'.[8] For James hatred of monarchy was embedded in the minds of 'puritanical' as much as popular spirits. Accordingly, he warned his son, Prince Henry, not to be 'ouer prodigall in iowking or nodding at euery step: for that forme of being popular, becommeth better aspiring *Absalons*, then lawfull Kings'.[9] In a speech delivered to the two Houses on 31 March 1607 James declared that those who objected against him that the Scottish Parliament had great powers over the king, who therefore had to consult it at every occasion, were absolutely wrong. Their claim was also absurd. In fact, the king was 'the eldest Parliament man in Scotland' and – James stated – 'I can assure you, that the forme of Parliament there, is nothing inclined to popularitie'.[10] In another speech he caustically referred to 'the sharpe edge and vaine popular humour of some Lawers at the Barre, that thinke they are not eloquent and bold spirited enough, except they meddle with the Kings Prerogatiue'.[11]

As his attitude towards the Commons in the 1620s demonstrates, James was incensed by the 'fiery and popular spirits' dealing with 'matters far above their reach or capacity, tending to our high dishonour and trenching upon our prerogative royal'.[12] Criticised at home for his failure to aid the Protestant cause in Europe, James proclaimed that affairs of State ought not to be treated publicly. Addressing MPs in 1621, he declared that 'who shall hasten often grievances and desire to make himself popular, he hath the spirit of Satan'.[13] James was here reacting to what he saw as the Commons' audacity in voting supply to promote the foreign policy they thought the King should have pursued.[14] He viewed the narrative of popularity in political debates as intertwined with parliamentary policies that demagogically stirred up the multitude. Thus, in a speech to the Lords (1621) concerning the heated issue of his failed intervention in the Palatinate, the Stuart made it clear that, although he promised to consult Parliament should he decide to strike a peace agreement with Spain and the Habsburgs, he wanted them 'to understand that I must have a faithfull and secret counsell of warr that must not be ordred by a multitude for soe my designes may be discovered before hand'.[15] In particular, James stressed that he had the liberty to choose how to invest the money Parliament gave him and the power to establish how many men to deploy should he embark upon a war to help his daughter and Frederick in the Palatinate. He stated: 'whether [this would be] by sea or land? whether East or West? whether by diversion or otherwise by invasion uppon the Barbarian or Emperor you must leave that to kinge'.[16] Mysteries of State and kingly prerogative were indisputable assets of his monarchical power.

A few years later, in *Votivae Angliae* (1624) John Reynolds (writing under the fictitious initials SRNI) advised James to get over his fear of waging war against the hated Spaniards. This was a time for the accomplishment of war-plans against the enemy. Reynolds stressed that the King had to show to his potential allies in Europe 'the zeale and resolution of England' so as to prompt them to embark upon this decisive enterprise.[7] In other terms, Reynolds accused James of cowardice and unfavourably compared his negligence towards the nation with the glorious resoluteness of Queen Elizabeth of never-dying memory. Elizabeth, said Reynolds, had defeated Spain and curbed its aspirations to forge a universal monarchy.[18] Now it was James' turn. The message carried unmistakably dangerous implications for the King, who was always adamant that flattering popular expectations was risky. As he had argued in *The Trew Law*, those who sought after the consent of the middling sort acted to the detriment of monarchy and denied that the fatherly king was 'bound to care for all his subjects'.[19] Like fatherly love provided 'the nourishing, education, and vertuous gouerment of his [the father's] children', so the monarch acted to the 'profite and weale' of 'his people'.[20] Therefore, James inveighed against those who 'employ their pennes' to proclaim 'that every man is borne to carry such a naturall zeale and duety they owe to their owne natiue countrey, to put their hand to worke for freeing their common-wealth from such a pest' identified with the king.[21]

Influenced by his father's views, as early as 1621 the future Charles I had blamed those who embodied this spirit of popularity for the growing unrest in Parliament. For Charles, as much as for James, the cause of all political instability resided in the '*Puritanicall*' fomenters of popular power and liberties.[22] A similar opinion was expressed a few years later by the French ambassador Antoine Coeffier Ruzé, Marquis d'Effiat, who reported to King Louis XIII that 'the Puritan faction' was trying to 'turn the English Monarchy into a Republic'.[23] Indeed, signs of a republican wave reached Cambridge, where on 12 December 1627 the Dutch scholar Isaac Dorislaus delivered an inflammatory lecture defending republican values and praising citizens' active participation in the polity against all forms of absolute power. Referring to the *Iliad*, Dorislaus asserted that the most virtuous men had to fight for their country and had the duty to expel from it the sovereign-turned-tyrant so as to preserve their liberties.[24]

At the end of 1628, Dorchester, the new Secretary of State, considered that the Duke's murder had 'unleashed dangerous popular forces'.[25] Thus, the people were portrayed as 'a sea moved by tempest which though the wind be still doth not immediately calm'.[26] The spreading fear of a rising popular component in the country led Dorchester to declare that the best political arrangement was 'a settled and constant form of government' which would control the 'aegritudo' (sickness) affecting people's mind. In this climate, according to Cust, the patriot coalition represented a real danger to royalist eyes as its ideological mainstay was not limited to religion, but it entailed the attempt 'to establish a wide-ranging partnership with the subject'.[27]

To testify to what extent the political atmosphere had become tense, in December 1628 the Tuscan envoy Amerigo Salvetti reported that, '[i]t does not appear that the death of the Duke of Buckingham who was held to be the originator of all the evils of the State, has in the least modified their [patriots'] peccant humours or their small regard for the monarchy'.[28] Salvetti could not have been more explicit when he said that '[t]he King and his people in no way get on well together', so that – he continued

> I fear, if he [Charles I] cannot succeed in subduing them, that the affairs of this Kingdom will go very badly, seeing that the Puritans win more space to act with increasing daring against the king who unless he makes peace abroad will never know it in his home and will never be an absolute monarch.[29]

Two weeks earlier, Salvetti had maintained that the dispute between sailors and 'His Majesty's Customhouse officers' was of 'the greatest consequence' and that, 'unless a remedy is found, the royal power will suffer, as day by day there are symptoms of the growing and daring opposition of the people'.[30] It was on this heated stage that 'the powerful Puritanical faction, with the aid of Parliament' had the strength to 'throw everything into disorder'.[31]

Thus, having faced an unprecedented outburst of overt criticism regarding the Forced Loan (1626–27) and the Petition of Right (1628), in 1629 Charles suspended all parliamentary sessions and began an eleven-year period of so-called 'Personal Rule'.[32] This was the King's manifestation of his fatherly power over his immature child, Parliament, which would not be summoned until the nation had learnt how to deal with His Majesty.[33] This drastic move squared with Charles' official imposition of silence in political matters.[34] Yet a number of pamphleteers and polemicists did not keep quiet.[35] Aided by the works of George Buchanan and by monarchomachs' claims that, in case a king failed to protect the nation, it became legitimate to overthrow him, some of these *popular* theorists argued that people's allegiance to the sovereign was not absolute but could be rescinded if the latter did not respect his oath.[36]

Opposition to the Spanish Match, to the Forced Loan and to the billeting of troops in the counties became widespread and, as in the case of Thomas Scott of Canterbury,[37] sometimes very strong. His writings are 'particularly illuminating' to illustrate the 'combination of secular and religious arguments … emanating from puritan opponents of the forced loan'. In many respects, Scott was on the same ideological wavelength of the anti-absolutist Elizabethan lawyer James Morice, the tenacious Jacobean government critic Nicholas Fuller and the outspoken champion of free speech in Elizabeth's parliaments Peter Wentworth: they 'were linked by a shared moral imperative whereby conscience reinforced their interpretation of the law of the land'. They also had in common a strenuous insistence on 'the limited or mixed nature of the English monarchy'.[38] Such ideas, as we will see below, found a fertile ground in the increasingly patriotic Commons of the late 1620s.

At this point, before turning to the language used there, an important but largely unexplored question seems in order: in what respects was Filmer's thought in tune with or distinguished from that of King James VI and I's?

FILMER AND KING JAMES:
ABSOLUTISTS ON THE SAME TRAJECTORY?

According to Kevin Sharpe, from the end of the sixteenth century (and especially after 1603 because of the change in the sovereign's gender) the fatherly image of monarchy overlapped with that of the household. James I associated 'the king's personal and political families' whilst Charles I conformed to this image in the paintings of the royal family. As the ruler of the nation, the king was equalled to its political father. The analogue had its relevance in all types of political discourse.[39] In Ann Baynes Coiro's words, 'the allegory of kingship, the idea that the king is the nation's head (or husband, soul, or father) began to seem a metaphysical conceit that could be appreciated, perhaps, for its wit but not for its truth'.[40] It was 'after a fashion' that James took up the role of 'the divine-right patriarch'; and his 'position as a father was multiple'. In practice, the King had 'brought with him to England an heir, a back-up heir and a marriageable princess'. In writing *Basilicon Doron*, the advice-book dedicated to his son Henry, James 'styled himself publicly and explicitly as the father and husband of his people'.[41] Indeed, as remarked above, James' intellectual production had started with a patriarchal account of authority whose corner-stone was the trope of the king as *pater patriae.*

The Trew Law depicted the monarch as 'a louing Father, and careful watchman, caring for them [subjects] more then for himselfe'. His prime goal was to procure the weale of both soules and bodies, as farre as in him lieth, of all them that are committed to his charge'.[42] As the 'ouer-Lord of the whole land', the king was also 'Master ouer euery person that inhabiteth the same, hauing power ouer the life and death of euery one of them'.[43] James made it clear that 'the power flowes alwaies from' the absolute and free authority of the ruler and not from election as with 'the dukes of *Venice*'.[44] Likewise, twelve years later, James' chief minister Robert Cecil defined the king as 'the father and head of the commonwealth' to whom 'therefore helps, supplies, and supports are due'. In return, 'he holdeth himself bound to give his people a real and royal satisfaction by protection and defense'.[45]

James' patriarchalist construction of royal authority was not a transparent argument with which he simply responded to the doctrines of his master Buchanan or of Catholic resistance theorists. Rather, he used it flexibly and adapted the metaphor of the king-father to his new status as King of England. He altered his initial stance since it did not always appeal to the type of discourse his new role required. Thus, when confronted with the reaction of the Commons on the thorny case of John Cowell's absolutist *The Interpreter* (1607),[46] James modified his patriarchalist rhetoric to appease an increasingly indispensable parliamentary assembly, which could refuse him the money he needed. As Cyndia S. Clegg pointed out, if this signified a shift from 'father-provider into petitioner', 'a competing trope of English monarchy' was, nonetheless, present: 'the King's two bodies'.[47] This suggests that the meanings attached to James' physical body competed with the immemorial legal precedents informing the English political mind.[48] Thus, the common law became one of the main antagonists of James' fatherly figure. But these were not the only models. Other uses of the patriarchal trope gave different shapes to the image of the monarch. The family with its central relationship between husband and wife symbolised a little kingdom in which marriage recalled the political bond between king and subjects. For this reason, divorce and government of the household assumed great importance as interpretative patterns to define pressing political questions.[49] In a political scenario shaped by polemical rhetoric and metaphors, allusions and analogies, the legitimisation of marital divorce had dangerous implications for patriarchal authority.[50]

By and large, James' transition from espousing a patriarchal account of sovereignty to a more moderate configuration of it shows that in the 1620s in England patriarchalist discourse was undergoing a process of erosion engendered by the multiplicity of interpretative agencies reading the King's works.[51] Thus, whilst James conceded there was a difference between 'the state of Kings in their first originall' and 'the state of setled Kings and Monarches',[52] other monarchists were more radical in their assertions on the encompassing power of the royal prerogative. Whilst James had to take into consideration the weight of the common law, thinkers like Cowell and Filmer could (and de facto did) overtly reject all parliamentary claims based on the ancient constitutional status of the law in England.[53] This is not to say that King James was no absolutist (as some historians would like us to believe).[54] It is to suggest that James' monarchist discourse did not correspond *tout court* to Filmer's patriarchalist configuration of politics. In other terms, their differences were not merely dependent on the contrast between their being a practioner (King James) and a political theorist (Filmer), but they stemmed from divergent theoretical positions.

First of all, the two differed with regard to the question of the origins of political society. The Adamite model found in Filmer's theory of monarchical power a scope that was absent in the King's writings. Moreover, the Filmerian vision of the role of the sovereign was not only more extreme than James', but it had the fatherly image as its cornerstone, so that the interplay between domestic rule and public governance was more complex in Filmer than in James.[55] Whereas the latter stopped short of asserting that the monarch's will

109

was the principal actor within the body politic, Filmer conceived a model of *puissance* that had Bodinian traits as well as elements of Hobbesian pragmatism. In addition, whereas James admitted that subjects owed no obedience to the sovereign whose commands contradicted God's,[56] Sir Robert was adamant 'that not only in human laws, but even in divine, a thing may be commanded contrary to law, and yet obedience to such a command is necessary'.[57]

Secondly, James' absolutism differed from Filmer's in relation to the role of the tyrant in the body politic. Whilst James rejected the idea that a tyrant could act to the benefit of his subjects, Filmer conceded that even a tyrant would be aware of the advantages that could come to him by preserving people's property. James held that a tyrant would pursue only 'his chiefest particular' interest.[58] Hence he associated this figure with vice and lust. He saw tyrannical rule as inevitably leading the State to catastrophe since God was certain to inflict harsh punishment upon him. Instead, Filmer showed that there existed a mutual link between rulers and subjects regardless of the means through which the former had obtained power. He stressed this idea not just in *Patriarcha*[59] but also in *Observations Upon Aristotles Politiques Touching Forms of Government* (1652), where he openly maintained that 'under the worst of kings, though many particular men have unjustly suffered, yet the multitude or the people in general have found benefit and profit by the government'.[60] By resorting to Aristotle's notion that master and servant were mutually dependent on each other, Filmer played down the traditional argument that tyranny was the worst political degeneration. As he put it, 'all nations ... are bound as much in obedience to their lawful kings as to any conqueror or usurper whatsoever'.[61] Even more explicitly, he declared that Nimrod 'was by good right lord or king over his family'. It had been 'against right' that he had 'enlarge[d] his empire by seizing violently on the rights of other lords of families, and in this sense he may be said to be the author and first founder of monarchy'. But what counted was that 'all those that do attribute unto him the original of regal power do hold he got it by tyranny or usurpation, and not by any due election of the people or multitude, nor by any paction with them'.[62] Similarly, Sir Robert argued that 'it may be inferred that if the masterly government of tyrants cannot be safe without the preservation of them whom they govern, it will follow that a tyrant cannot govern for his own profit only'. Aristotle had failed to provide a definition of tyranny as a despotic relation where one party dominated and another succumbed: '[n]o example can be showed of any such government that ever was in the world as Aristotle describes a tyranny to be'.[63]

Furthermore, James and Filmer set forth different configurations of the sovereign's will and its scope. The former distinguished between absolute and arbitrary power: he admitted the legitimacy of the former whilst condemning the latter as despotic. He separated the necessary absolute power exercised by the Christian emperor from its illegitimate use made by tyrants.[64] By contrast, Filmer broke the convention that distinguished an absolute monarch from an arbitrary one. His configuration of the voluntarist theory of the legislative process fused the two categories of 'absolute' and 'arbitrary'. For him the ruler's will was entirely free, unlimited and inviolable. The arbitrariness of the sovereign's judgement was the utmost expression of royal will, which represented the highest guarantee of competence and efficiency in the body politic. Instead of searching for private interest like many popular and representative regimes did, an arbitrary power – Filmer radically implied – aimed to the pursuit of the public good. Tyranny – though it was often a duty to abide by it – acted in a vacuum (legal, ethical, hereditary), whilst the Filmerian notion of arbitrary was connected with the juridical sphere where the *arbitrary* sovereign mitigated the rigidity of the law and avoided injustice.[65]

If James insisted on the duties of the king by pointing out that a good ruler would not trespass the laws of the land, Sir Robert was more outspoken in conceding to the monarch complete freedom of action. His idea of political dominion recalled the model of the autocrat. This rested upon the primitive ideal of patriarchal rule whose authority was originally founded on the *one-to-one* concession of power from God to Adam. Hence the king was by no means restrained from acting according to his free will, which coincided with the law. In contrast, for James, kings had first governed arbitrarily, but once kingdoms had settled 'in ciuilitie and policie' they had begun to follow the law. They made the law 'but at the rogation of the people'.[66] Because of their coronation oath, sovereigns had to abide by the laws of the country. As Francis Oakley pointed out, James I had modified his opinions in order 'to soften for his audience the somewhat uncompromising contours of an otherwise distressingly absolutistic effusion'.[67] Thus, James distinguished two chronologically different phases in the formation of kingdoms whereby the ruler–subjects relation evolved and improved.[68] In contradistinction to this, Filmer advanced the Adamite origins of the polity, highlighting the genetic moment of the creation of the law of which the king was the exclusive artificer.

Although neither James nor Filmer subscribed to 'the vision of order expressed on the notion of the great chain of being' illustrated by William H. Greenleaf, they differed on issues such as 'will, promise and covenant'.[69] Whereas James admitted 'the *potencia absoluta/ordinata* distinction' and accented the self-binding nature of the king's will through the stipulation of oaths,[70] Filmer embraced a totally voluntarist approach to both power and law. Accordingly, Sir Robert distrusted the common law to the extent that he dismissed it as the mere product of 'common usage or custom'. Being 'unwritten, doubtful and difficult', it 'cannot but be an uncertain rule to govern by, which is against the nature of a rule – which is and ought to be certain'.[71] For Filmer the law was mute unless the acting power of a decision-maker gave reality to it and made it practical by communicating it to those who had to obey.[72] This emphasis on the king as *lex loquens* constitutes a defining feature of Filmer's idea of sovereignty. What gave certainty to the law and, consequently, to the body politic was not order but the power of the monarch from where order itself derived. In the Filmerian account of politics the sovereign became the supreme legislator whose political authority resembled the epistemological strength of the Cartesian *cogito*.

Furthermore, the Adamite model represented a form of return to the purity of the origins. It recalled the first principles of government to which it was necessary to resort in order to defeat corruption and anarchy ensuing from democratic rule. The Filmerian focus on Adam, first man and kingly father, symbolised an antidote to the increasing chaos caused by 'popular spirits' and 'Jesuitical' firebrands. Only the Adamite ruler could take the reins of the country and govern efficiently. By the same token, in *Observations Upon Aristotles* Filmer was to explain that at times of crisis the democratic government of Rome had relied on 'a dictator who ... was an absolute king' and that in such circumstances 'no appeal to the people was granted – which is the royallest evidence for monarchy in the world'.[73] It followed that no form of government other than monarchy could last long: hardships, emergencies, conflicts were better handled by a monarch than by a chaotic democratic assembly or by a quarrelling aristocratic body.[74] Transposed to the post-regicide political context in which it was delivered, this two-pronged attack targeted the new republican settlement in England and the idea that an assembly of men wielded power. Thus, departing once more from King James, Filmer maintained that the monarch did not have the duty to collaborate with Parliament.[75] Thanks to his competence and hereditary lineage, the king was the repository of all subjects' trust. Filmer had no doubt: 'the end of monarchy is for the best of the governed'.[76] The fatherly model made the sovereign supreme governor and protector of the country. Therefore, neither explicit consent nor tacit assent on the part of the subordinate entrusted the ruler with power. People were in a state of political minority over which the monarch supervised and decided.[77]

This account found an explanation through the patriarchalist paradigm in that it provided a cohesive narrative of sovereignty and national identity. Being invested with the title of father of the fatherland, the king became the mainstay of government and the symbolic focus of State unity. Unsurprisingly, at the end of the 1620s this picture ended up being strenuously contested. Parliament was no exception.

THE PARLIAMENTARY RESPONSE TO ABSOLUTISM:
PATRIOTISM IN THE HOUSE OF COMMONS

Ferment in the Commons can be captured in the discourses of early May 1628 focusing on a bill aimed to 'the confirmation of Magna Carta and the other six statutes insisted upon for the subject's liberty'.[78] Following the heated disputes on the Forced Loan and the imprisonment of the resisters,[79] the debates of Tuesday 6 May 1628 in the Committee of the Whole House centred on the Speaker's speech delivered in the Commons and on the King's answer to it. To the insistence on the rights of the subject advanced by many MPs,[80] the Speaker replied that the King feared that the Commons' request of an explanation 'will hazard an encroachment upon his prerogative'.[81] This exchange occurred just before the Petition of Right was addressed to Charles I;[82] that is, at a time when having considered 'the bleeding estate of the commonwealth' and 'the condition of the persons that sent us', Sir Roger North claimed MPs' 'freedom of speech'.[83] In the same session, Sir Nathaniel Rich admonished to 'first determine whether the satisfaction given by his Majesty be sufficient or not'. Although Charles promised to act according to 'his laws', for Rich MPs had 'nothing thereby but shells and shadows'.[84] It was vital, Rich continued, that 'the King assure us of his power what it is, and then we shall trust him'. It was also necessary 'to hear the King say he may not by law billet soldiers or lay loans'. Without 'the point of trust be but agreed on', it would be impossible to 'trust the King'.[85]

It was in this increasingly tense context that Sir Edward Coke invoked the importance of a 'petition of right':[86] 'not that I distrust the King, but because we cannot take his trust but in a parliamentary way'.[87] The latter idea was shared by Sir John Glanville who suggested to 'frame a petition of right, that without redress thereof we cannot go with comfort to our country'.[88] Sir Robert Phelips agreed: '[l]et our business be put in a petition of right. Let us not flatter ourselves. We have suffered as much violation of laws and liberties as ever'.[89] On the same day Edward Littleton asserted that he 'would not recede a tittle from' the resolutions taken on 3 April. To do so would weaken MPs' reputation 'abroad'. In fact, 'the world' would 'think we tacitly desert our former grounds'.[90] The major issues of 'imprisonment and restraint of personal liberty' occupied centre stage in the debates. According to Sir John Eliot, 'the liberty of the person is that which most I stand upon'. However, one could 'see it every day lost'. Hence he declared that it was imperative 'not [to] recede'.[91] These ideas were shared by Sir Walter Erle (one of the knights involved in the Five Knights' Case imprisoned for refusing to pay the Forced Loan),[92] who on 2 May 1628 had stated that what Parliament men

> have done is only for the liberty of the subject, and it is no new thing; and this we
> have done because it is conceived that the subject has suffered more in the violation
> of the ancient liberties within these few years than in three hundred years before.[93]

113

On his part, the ringleader in the Five Knights' Case and Loan-refuser MP William Coryton argued that '[o]ld laws' are said to be old buildings, and need underpinning', especially now, that is, at a time when there were those 'who dared violate Magna Carta'. As he put it, '[t]hough laws are made, it is said the King may be over severe; but it is not so with good kings. Law does direct king and people, and prerogative should help law'.[94] In addressing the issue of parliamentary supply, Coryton clarified that 'His Majesty does according to his greatness, we according to our duty. I am for a law, and a law explanatory'.[95]

Sir Roger North expressed his concerns by remarking that '[h]e that looks upon the bleeding estate of our commonwealth cannot but think it is cureless if this parliament relieve it not'.[96] In a quasi-apocalyptic tone he proclaimed that '[t]his day may either save or ruin' the commonwealth.[97] Although he did not think to be 'wise enough for counsel', he tellingly defined himself as '*a mere country rational man* that will speak my conscience'.[98] North was aware of his 'condition' as a representative of the freemen by whom he had been elected. These expected him to safeguard their interests and liberties, which were under threat because of oppressive royal policies. MPs had the responsibility to fulfil 'the desires of those that sent us to save the public and keep them from being slaves'. North had no illusion: '[t]hey will ask us, when we come home, what relief we have brought them'.[99]

During the session of 6 May, Coryton alluded to the King's conduct by emphatically declaring that '[t]ill of late no man dared think of violating them ['Old laws']'.[100] Although 'it was said that kings might lay grievous impositions upon their people', he thought that 'a just and religious king will not' act in this way. However, the situation in the country was not improving. As Coryton firmly remarked, '[b]illeting continues without answer to our petitions'.[101] For this reason, he showed his mistrust towards Charles by pointing out that he 'would give the King much, as a faithful man, then, when I see these things taken into consideration which are advantageous to the King and kingdom'. Finally, Coryton urged his colleagues to 'proceed according to our duty, with the law'.[102]

On his part, Roger North knew that people in the country would demand him to account for his efforts to attain a satisfactory answer from the King: 'we shall be asked whether we have done what they sent us for, we shall tell them we have a confirmation of Magna Carta'. He then gloomily added that '*Lex terrae* [was] yet an unfolded riddle'.[103] North expressed his disappointment for not having obtained 'all', but – nonethless – he had some 'satisfaction' because 'this shall speak to all England by our copies we have'.[104] Likewise, Nathaniel Rich argued that, even though '[i]t is said the King will free the billeting of subjects', it was undeniable that billeting 'is unlawful'. Rich also remarked that '[o]ur first grievance was that' the agents of the Crown 'imprisoned men without showing cause'. And this was 'notorious to the world'.[105]

In contrast to the absolutist opinion that the monarch was entirely free to give laws and sometimes bypass them without having to provide justification for it, Sir John Coke stated that 'an explanation is necessary'. In fact, it was '[u]seful to have those laws confirmed which will be useless and senseless without explanation'.[106]

These examples underscore the importance of the language of trust as a fundament on which the relationship between MPs and monarch rested.[107] They also exemplify the extent to which the gulf between Parliament men and the King had widened. Most importantly, these opinions formed in a context where '[t]he Country ... gave the notion of representative a new meaning' and where '[i]ts supporters manifested a sort of "constituency-consciousness" and set themselves against the royal will on the ground of their public trust'.[108] De facto, the MPs who presented their fellow countrymen's grievances as representatives for their constituencies 'came up via a process of shared experiences to contribute to the emergence of a national or "Country" attitude'.[109] Despite maintaining that 'before 1640 ideology was absent from the process of parliamentary selection', Mark Kishlansky recognised that 1628 signalled 'the stirrings' of the belief in Parliament as 'a political institution in which the rights and liberties of the subject were protected'.[110] The year 1628 was 'different' in that it saw the King and many MPs at odds on issues such as arbitrary arrest and imprisonment without cause shown to the extent that it is possible to speak of 'mutual distrust' between them.[111] In fact, the Commons opted for restoring trust in the common law rather than in the monarch.[112] The leaders in the Commons dismissed moderation and any offer to compromising on those matters they deemed Charles had violated.[113] According to Patrick Collinson, this general climate denotes 'the ideological capacity for resistance' in England at that time.[114] In a similar vein, Richard Cust has underlined the practical implications of the rhetoric of republican discourse and the putting into practice of Renaissance political thought in this phase of political tension between the King and the Commons.[115]

Speeches like those of Coryton and North showed that MPs wanted to consolidate the primacy of the nation against the supreme prerogative of the monarch. They contested Charles' policy of imposing taxes without consulting Parliament. They not only countered the concept of absolute prerogative, but they also resorted to historical examples in order to prove Parliament's ancient status as the fundamental constitutional organism of the country.[116] Aiming to increase the power of the parliamentary assembly, they embodied the spirit and values of the 'public man'.[117] In fulfilling their duty in office they were driven by integrity and probity. Moreover, they were aware that they had to 'speak for their country'.[118] Their rhetoric was founded on the constitutional bastion of freedom of speech in Parliament.[119] Thus, for Roger North his 'purpose' as one of the 'parliament men' was to 'speak freely'.[120] In fact, the language of the parliamentary Proclamation was informed by the neo-Roman rhetoric of freedom. In their refusal to accept the notion that freedom of speech was only granted by the King and that as such it could be taken away by his decision, MPs made it clear that they were no servants but freemen.[121] Most importantly, several amongst them – exactly like Thomas Scott of Canterbury – well understood that it was crucial to be reputed 'honest patriots' by their constituents in the country.[122] At a time when opinions were becoming increasingly polarised, these MPs promoted the image of a political type whose chief task was the patriotic consolidation of parliamentary England. In tune with this, by 1628 they also endorsed the notion that the liberties of Parliament were equal to those of the subject.[123] Obviously, these ideas did not go un-answered.

FILMER AND ENGLISH PATRIARCHALISTS:[124]
THE LANGUAGE OF THE *PATER PATRIAE* AS
A RESPONSE TO THE 'HONEST PATRIOTS'

A series of strong replies to the type of discourses presented above came from works that were neither officially commissioned by the Crown nor widely circulated.[125] Amongst the theorists who defended the absolute prerogative of kings was Sir Francis Kynaston (c. 1586–c. 1642),[126] author of *A True Presentation of forepast Parliaments* (1629). Kynaston opposed these parliamentary views by remarking that good counsellors would not seek 'for over much Freedome of Speech'.[127] According to him, it was highly inappropriate to try to attain – as the likes of Coryton and North had done – '[l]icence to speak freely and yet impertinently, and indiscreetly, unless one will say, That it is fit for a man to aske counsell or liberty to erre, and doe absurdly'.[128] For Kynaston those who had been 'chosen by their Countries and Burroughs as the fittest men' to represent them were 'not Tribuni Plebis, nor have the Sacred Tribunitiall Power, Priviledge, or Protection'. In fact, 'their Election is commaunded by the kings Writ of Summons'. Above all, their convocation as Parliament men was exclusively due to 'the kings Prerogative and gracious favours, whose will and sole Power is the Ortus and Interitus of Parliaments'.[129]

Kynaston had no doubts that it was the inadequacy of MPs to fulfil their role that had prompted the King to dissolve Parliament. The latter was replete with 'the baser universall sort of the Populace', whose irrational acts had proved 'many times fatall' in history.[130] In consequence, he thought it deplorable that they still claimed their right to speak freely instead of submitting to his majesty's will.[131] Kings could not be judged by 'the common judgement of the Vulgar'.[132] The latter's opinions were always unduly partisan: a sovereign 'is seldome or never well thought off, by the generallity of the People' even when acting well and doing good. His ill actions would be 'amplify'd and aggravated,

and so exposed to the view of all the World', especially to 'the Populace ...,
whose eyes are commonly in their eares'.[33]

Similarly concerned with the rise of opposition advocating wider political
participation for the people, in the third chapter of *Patriarcha* Filmer referred to
the question of the role of knights and burgesses in relation to their electorate.
He ruled out the validity of MPs' parliamentary arguments by saying that he
had

> not heard that the people ... did ever call to an account those whom they had elected.
> They neither give them instructions or directions what to say or do in parliament,
> therefore they cannot punish them, when they come home, for doing amiss.[34]

Only '[i]f the people had any such power over their burgesses', Filmer observed,
'then we might have some colour to call it the natural liberty of the people'.
People had to 'trust those whom they choose to do what they list, and that is as
much liberty as many of us deserve for our irregular elections of burgesses'.
Likewise, those seeking immoderate freedom of speech could be punished
'for intermeddling with parliamentary business'.[35] In contrast to all parliamentary pretences of freedom of speech, Filmer remarked that

> during the time of parliament those privileges of the House of Commons – of
> freedom of speech, power to punish their own members, to examine the proceed-
> ings and demeanour of courts of justice and officers, to have access to the king's
> person and the like – are not due by any natural right, but are derived from the
> bounty or indulgence of the king, as appears by a solemn recognition of the House.[36]

After all, as he was to remind in *The Free-Holders*, '[t]ouching freedom of
speech, the Commons were warned in Queen Elizabeth's days not to meddle
with the "queen's person, the state, or church government"'.[37] It was through
analogous arguments that Filmer dismantled the language of 'representation'
advocated by many MPs in 1628. Theoretically, this translated into his rejection
of the parliamentary constitutionalism of Cokean legacy. In devoting *Patriarcha*'s third chapter to prove that all claims of the antiquity and immemorial
origins of Parliament were totally unfounded, Sir Robert wanted to show the
indivisibility and superiority of absolute monarchy. He did so in a similar vein
to the anti-lawyers discourse articulated by Kynaston.

Both Kynaston and Filmer were well aware of the rhetorical power of the
speeches pronounced in the Commons. Encouraged by the spreading of
monarchomach literature and Dutch ideas of resistance,[38] these representatives of the 'common people' – according to monarchists – carved out an important role for themselves and, consequently, for the populace. They placed their
public conscience at the forefront of the political arena so as to guarantee the
integrity of the country against royal abuses. In so doing, they failed to discern
how 'dangerous a thing' it was 'to show favour to common people' since these
'interpret all graces and favours for their rights and just liberties'.[39] To contrast

the language of active parliamentarianism based on the republican principles of Seneca, Livy, Guicciardini and the Ciceronian model of citizenship, Filmer resorted to the patriarchalist paradigm. This provided him with a theory of sovereignty which was strongly anti-republican.[140]

Thus, when at the beginning of *Patriarcha* Sir Robert spoke of 'the whole fabric of this vast engine of popular sedition',[141] he had in mind thinkers that, by propagating factious tenets, stirred up 'the common people'.[142] As a result, many subjects had been 'fooled' to adhere to the opinion that 'a man may become a martyr for his country by being a traitor to his prince'.[143] Of all anti-monarchical ideas this was the most venomous because it mirrored those of Roman republicans whose iconic martyr was Brutus, the killer of Caesar. Grounded on Cicero's *De Officiis* and the ideal of virtuous citizenship, the patriot narrative – according to Filmer – encouraged citizens to fulfil their duty towards the *patria* by overthrowing the legitimate ruler when they thought it necessary. This political activism threatened to irreparably compromise the unity of the kingdom, which for Filmer was enshrined in the monarch. By seizing upon republican and godly patriotism, these divisive spirits made the king the mere figurehead of the English nation; replaced him with the authority of Parliament; questioned the inviolability of his prerogative.

That Filmer was responding to parliamentary arguments of the sort mentioned above is once more proved by his referring to Charles I's 'speech after his last answer to the Petition of Right' in which 'his majesty' had confirmed that 'the prerogative of a king is to be above all laws, for the good only of them that are under the laws, and to defend the people's liberties'.[144] Therefore, those sitting in the Commons, who 'say it is a slavish and a dangerous condition to be subject to the will of any one man who is not subject to the laws', were obnoxious fomenters of rebellion. Eyeing the debates of 1628, Filmer retorted that, without 'the bounty of the prerogative', the life of the subjects 'would be desperately miserable'.[145] And yet this message fell on deaf ears.

According to Sir Robert, many theorists as well as sundry MPs demagogically lured ignorant subjects into the deceptive belief that liberty (other than that provided by the king) was everything. However, what they proposed – Filmer caustically remarked – was no more than 'shows or pretexts of liberty'. Indeed, they engendered 'several degrees of slavery, and a liberty only to destroy liberty'.[146] For Filmer these '[l]ate writers' were new followers of 'the subtle schoolmen, who to be sure to thrust down the king below the pope, thought it the safest course to advance the people above the king, that so the papal power may more easily take place of the regal'.[147]

Less systematically but in tune with his goals, other English monarchists attacked the same political paradigms and accused patriots and Jesuits, 'popular' firebrands and papalists of sowing the most poisonous seeds of rebellion against monarchical government.[148] Thus, Kynaston defined the monarch, who was endowed with 'the Royall and just Prerogative ... by the Lawes of God and the Custome of Nations', as 'Pater Patriae'.[149] He claimed that there existed 'a strong Relation of Filiationis et Paternitatis between the King and the Parliament':[150] as the relationship between father and son was grounded on 'mutuall trust and Confidence', so in the polity Parliament must not 'plot' against the sovereign.[151] The echo of the events of May 1628 resonated loud and clear. Kynaston depicted two rhetorical narratives at odds at the end of the 1620s: one that supported the king as he was 'greater' than the 'Country' and another that thought the 'Country' was 'greater' than 'the King'. According to Kynaston, this second group proclaimed to have 'a neerer Relation to themselves then to the King',[152] so that they acted 'for the Country' against the service due to the sovereign. In investigating the nature of this contrast, he took into consideration the opinion of Ralph Starkey's *The Priviledges and Practice of Parliaments*[153] and explored 'what Relation of a Counsell he hath to his King; and what Relation he hath of a Patriot to his Country: and will keep him from presuming far on the first and too much for the latter'.[154]

The patriots were the most severe menace for the nation since they were flaunting their role as defenders of the homeland. In so doing, they pretended to safeguard the common good regardless of the king's commands. Therefore, Kynaston – just like Filmer – scornfully admonished:

> let no man be so uncharitable as to think, that a wise and religious king, can or will neglect the good of his Subjects and Kingdom, wch is his own estate and subsistence: or yet be arrogant as to think, that he hath a greater care of the Commonwealth then the King hath. Let no man that resists the King out of an opinion that he stands for the Country, deceive himself.[155]

Aware of the tension mounting in the late 1620s parliamentary debates and following James I, Kynaston also spoke of 'solicitous men' who 'cannot vindicate themselves, from too much affectation of Popularity (a vice condemn'd in all Subjects)'.[156] He pointed out that this harmful search for popular consent was likely to affect 'young men or unexperienc'd men, or indifferent men' with lethal consequences for the government. Therefore, he asserted that 'there is but one King of this Kingdome, and all others (how great, noble, or powerful soever) are but Subjects; that the King, as he is but one Head, so all his Subjects make but one Body'.[157] Targeting 'popularity', Kynaston maintained that it was vital

> to regard our (the) King and Soveraigns good more then our own; and if so, let no man think himself *a good Patriot*, that under a pretence of the Liberty of the Subjects or the Commonwealths Welfare stands in opposition to the Kings pleasure, or is too rigid and strict for legality in a busines, that the King directs to be done.[158]

Kynaston disparaged as unfounded the seditious patriots' 'care of the Commonwealth' and underpinned the idea that it was the king that had the greatest interest in the preservation of the public good. To deny this principle corresponded to dismantling the most stable foundations of government.[159]

Despite their justice and generosity, Kynaston claimed, monarchs were being attacked not only by the 'Practice of Parliaments, wch tacitely detracts from the power of Kings, attributing all things to Parliaments ...', but also [by] other spurious vagabond Books, wch like Rogues are to be whipt to the place of their Births if they were known'.[160] The first work in question was 'a Pamphlet intituled *Tom Tell Tro[a]th*,[161] written by one more fit to be stiled Tom of Bedham, for his base calumnies utter'd against King James of ever blessed memory, under the colour of Counsell'.[162] The second was 'a treatise call'd *The Practice of Princes* non less ignominiously written, then impertinently forc'd, wth Quotations of Holy Scripture, prophaned by the Swine that writ it'. This author could be

> iustly account[ed] a neer neighbour (if not the same) with *The Pragmaticall Practice of Parliaments*: who by his practicall lemma and title, hath some smack of a Common Layer in him, who never learn'd Civilitie, but is one of those Brutes that dare speak ill of those in Authority to himself.[163]

The most important aspect of Kynaston's argument was his attack on *Tom Tell-Troath*, for this tract voiced criticism of James' foreign policies in the Palatinate and cultivated the argument – thriving in the alehouses – of the 'cruell father' who had abandoned his offspring and the glory of England.[164] *Tom Tell-Troath* dealt thus a blow not only to the patriarchal image of the king, but – most significantly at that time – to his patriotic role and aura.

Like *Patriarcha*, *A True Presentation* confirms that two major features of political debate and theoretical dispute of the early Caroline reign were patriotism and patriarchalism. Patriotic identity based on the public man's parliamentary activity opposed all fatherly configuration of monarchical power; the Ciceronian model of liberty contrasted with absolutist ideas of supreme kingship. Most importantly, Filmer and Kynaston were not alone in elaborating this patriarchalist discourse whose richly metaphorical vocabulary informed political arguments both in the pre-Civil War period and at the time of the Exclusion Crisis (1679–81). More to the point: patriotism, fatherhood and parricide occupied a significant portion of the ideological stages on which Filmer, first, wrote and, then, was published.[165]

As for the former context,[166] we find that in the early 1630s Peter Heylyn's *Augustus*, which was conceived to advise Charles I, separated 'a cunning Sophister' from 'a faithfull Subject' on the basis that the former 'coynes distinctions betwixt the welfare of the *King*, and the weale of the *Kingdome*'.[167] In a similar vein to Kynaston, Heylyn tellingly defined the emperor as '*Guardian of Orphanes*' and 'a Father of his *Country*'.[168] Adhering to the Filmerian arguments illustrated above, Heylyn held that '[t]he treasures of kings are then greatest, not when their own Coffers are full onely, but their subjects rich'.[169] Likewise, in his early poems the Laudian champion had satirised any manifestations of 'godly patriotism', in particular targeting Puritan views.[70] Later on in life, Heylyn significantly claimed that the only form of partisanship to be found in his *Cosmographie* (1652) was that of a monarchist patriot.[71]

In using the traditional image of the king as *pater patriae*,[72] Filmer, Kynaston and Heylyn built their narrative of authority on solid foundations. They used a narrow canvas to convey wider political implications and meanings. In this sense, they continued the efforts of other English thinkers. Amongst them was the widely read historian and civil lawyer Sir John Hayward (1564?–1627), who had maintained that 'our country is dearer vnto vs then our parentes: and the Prince is *pater patriae*, the Father of our Country: and therefore more sacred and deere vnto vs, then our parentes by nature'.[73] In the virulently anti-popish climate of the early seventeenth century, Hayward deplored the 'Iesuits' because of their idea that the Pontiff held supreme authority over temporal monarchs. As he put it, authors like Robert Parsons 'do yeeld a blindfold obedience' to their superior, 'not once examining either what hee is, or what he doth command'. De facto, 'although the Pope should swarue [swerve] from iustice, yet by the canons, men are bound to performe obedience vnto him, and God only may iudge his doings'. But when it came to 'a king', Parsons justified rebellion and said that 'the Lords Lieutenant' could 'bee cast out of state' by 'the Lords annointed in the view of his subiects, nay, by the hands of his subiects'.[74] In terms that Filmer was to employ in *Patriarcha*, Hayward explained that as '[t]he law of God commandeth that the child should die, for anie contumely done vnto the Parents' even 'if the father be a robber' or 'a murtherer' for '[n]o offence is so great, as … parricide', so 'the Prince is the father of our country … and therfore he must not be violated, how impious, how imperious soeuer he be'.[75]

More important from a theoretical viewpoint was Thomas Craig's *Concerning the Right of Succession to the Kingdom of England* (published in 1703)[76] in which the erudite Scottish lawyer (1538–1608) accused Parsons of having propagated the doctrine which made it 'lawful for the People to Dethrone and Depose (to say no worse) even the persons of Kings'.[77] Defining republics as degenerations of monarchies, Craig maintained that the 'Prince' was 'the Common Father of the Country, to whom we owe our well being in Civil Society'.[78] Craig's argument was deeply patriarchalist in that he saw the bond between king (James) and subjects (Englishmen) as of a biological nature. The keynote of his 'nation-specific' and gendered reflection was the creation of a common identity between the ruler as father and his subjects as men. Common manhood and common nationhood were thus intertwined.[79] In articulating his ideas of legitimate succession and absolute monarchical power, Craig was probably following the early fifteenth-century French jurist Jean de Terre Rouge, who insisted on the 'genetic propagation' of royal qualities by means of semen.[180] Clearly, Filmer was to write in the same trajectory of thought. And this is an important point since it shows the interplay between fatherhood (down to its genetic components) and political authority conceived in relation to national unity, which Filmer revived so strongly in *Patriarcha*.

Adhering to the concept of the patriotic king, in his anti-papist *Triplici Nodo* (1608) James I too spoke of the 'fatherly care' he took of his subjects.[181] It was, indeed, this 'care' that had prompted him to implement the Oath of Allegiance in order to separate 'quietly minded Papists' from dangerous 'powder-Traitors'.[182] By the same token, in *The Trew Law* James had signed the 'Advertisement to the Reader' with the telling pen name of 'C. Φιλοπατρις', that is, 'a lover of his country'.[183] Having explained that '[t]he King towards his people is rightly compared to a father of children', James declared that 'the stile of *Pater patriae* was euer, and is commonly vsed to Kings'.[184] Likewise, in the parliamentary speech of 16 March 1610,[185] James clarified that there were 'three principall similitudes that illustrate the state of MONARCHIE': one divine, one political and one philosophical. God, father and head were thus the three cardinal images on which the role of the king was modelled. With regard to the second, James reiterated the idea that monarchs 'are also compared to Fathers of families: for a King is trewly *Parens patriae*, the politique father of his people'.[186] He then stressed that, '[f]or the King' was '*Parens Patriae*', his good 'cannot bee diuided from the generall good of the Common wealth'.[187] Hence 'if the King wants, the State wants, and therefore the strengthening of the King is the preseruation and the standing of State; And woe be to him that diuides the weale of the King from the weale of the Kingdome'.[188] Identifying absolute monarch and fatherland, James' discourse recalled the principles expounded in the 1606 Convocation Book where *potestas regia* and *potestas patria* had coincided.[189]

In the aftermath of the Oath of Allegiance, Richard Mocket's (1577–1618) *God and the King* (1615) – which was personally supported by James and which was prescribed as a 'catechism' to be read by all youth – suggested that the maxim '"Honor thy Father, and thy Mother"' pertained to the political sphere rather than to the familial one. The commandment had, in fact, more to do with political obedience than with submission within the household.[190] Mocket established that there was 'so mutual a dependance' between the society of kings and that of fathers that 'the welfare of the one is the prosperity of the other'.[191] However, bypassing the traditional line of argumentation set out in seventeenth-century Church catechisms, Mocket resorted to 'the Evidence of Reason' to stress that 'there is a stronger and higher bond of Duty between Children and the Father of their Countrey, than the Fathers of private Families'.[192] To justify this concept Mocket – in the same way as Filmer was to do – declared that fathers procure the good onely of a few, and not without the assistance and protection of the other, who are the common Foster-fathers of thousands of Families, of whole Nations and Kingdoms, that they may live under them an honest and peaceable life.[193]

Having affirmed that the duty of subjects towards their sovereign was grounded on 'the Law of Nature' and 'also enjoyed by the Moral Law, and particularly ... in the fifth Commandment', Mocket concluded that subjects were 'required to honor the *Fathers* of our Countrey and the whole Kingdom ... much more' than 'the *Fathers* of private Families'.[194]

Two years later, supporting Bishop Lancelot Andrewes (1555–1626) against the Jesuit Thomas Fitzherbert, the royal chaplain and Cambridge regius professor of divinity Samuel Collins (1576–1651) looked to 'the subiection that we owe to Princes' as having 'primacie' amongst subjects. For him the principle '*Honour thy father*' prescribed that 'much more' was due to the '*patrem patriae*' for he was 'the father of the whole Countrey'.[195] Likewise, in a response to Parsons' defence of papal authority over temporal sovereigns probably written in 1609 and not published until 1624,[196] the patriarchalist Edward Forsett (1553/4–1629/30) rhetorically asked whether Nature 'left any such law or libertie, that in any respects the childe may renounce or disclaime his parents'. To support such a view corresponded to allow people's rebellion against their king, which, in turn, was tantamount to forgetting 'that the Prince is *Pater Patriae*, the Father of the Countrey'.[197] In addition to this, the similitude of the head and the body showed 'the dutious dependancy of the Subject upon the person of the Soveraigne, with a true naturall relation and recognition of all love and obedience, having from nature (out of the resemblance of those paternes) no other law, then *parendi* & *patiendi*'.[198] In accordance with this attempt to reinforce the patriotic image of the sovereign, in 1627 Robert Sanderson (1587–1663), future Bishop of Lincoln, explained that often in history 'Iudges, and Nobles, and Princes [were] delighted to bee called by the name of *Fathers*'. This had been the case with the 'Philistims' and, especially, in Rome where

> the Senatours were of old time called *Patres, Fathers*: and it was afterwards accounted among the Romans the greatest title of honour that could bee bestowed vpon their Consuls, Generalls, Emperours, or whosoeuer had deserued best of the Commonwealth, to haue this addition to the rest of his stile *Pater patriae*, a Father to his Countrie.[199]

In consequence, for Sanderson 'all good Kings and Gouernours should haue a *fatherly care* ouer, and beare a *fatherly affection* vnto those that are vnder them'.[200]

Not limited to the pre-Civil War years, the idea of the king as the patriotic (fatherly) protector of the country was used in 1643 by the Church of Ireland Bishop of Derry Robert Mossom (d. 1679), who argued that '*jus Regium* commenth out of *jus Patrium*'.[201] Mossom maintained that 'Kings, are the Successors of the Patriarches, both in the right of their Fatherhood, as Fathers of the Country; and in the rule of their Government as Governours of the Common-wealth'. The only 'difference' was 'that the Patriarchs were Kings of their Families, and Kings are the Fathers of their Countries'.[202] Mossom opposed the notion that people had the right to rebel against the monarch precisely because the latter was *'Pater Patriae'*.[203] In tune with this view, one year later the Scottish *'jure divino* episcopalian' and privy councillor John Maxwell (d. 1647)[204] reminded that 'the obligation to *pater patriae*, to the father of the kingdom, is stronger, is straighter, than to *pater familiae*, to our naturall father'.[205] For Maxwell, '[t]he tye betwixt King and People, Prince and Subject is greater, is stricter than any betwixt man and wife, father and sonne'.[206] Hence the reference to the father in the Fifth Commandment 'principally ... meant the king'.[207] Above all, scornful of the enemies of kings, the Bodinian Maxwell caustically condemned 'the specious and spurious pretences of our glorious Reformers, and *zealous Patriots'*.[208] However, he did so without success: the father of the fatherland was to be killed by a group of parricides only five years later (1649).

These examples are important because they unveil that specific line of monarchist discourse which placed centre stage the supreme fatherly monarch by portraying him as the guardian of the nation against patriots and republican hotheads as much as fanatical Jesuits and ultramontane papalists. In order to further dissect this type of patriarchalist monarchism (of which *Patriarcha* was the quintessential expression) it is now necessary to investigate the concrete models as well as unfold the ideal references with which these political theories need to be associated.

PARALLELS AND PROBLEMS: THE MODEL OF THE FATHERLY *PATER PATRIAE* APPLIED

In seventeenth-century England the notion of the king as righteous and patriotic head of the monarchy was largely applied to Prince Henry (1594–1612), son of King James VI and I and designated to inherit the Crown as Henry IX. In the transition from the Elizabethan to the Jacobean reign, many Englishmen looked to Henry as the best future substitute for the *Scottish* sovereign. Henry represented a model of kingship more akin to that embodied by Elizabeth. In contrast to James' endeavour to establish a pacific reign, the young prince was thought to be more in favour of an aggressive military policy which matched the expectations of many subjects. However, his premature death (1612) destroyed all hopes. As a result, 'patriotic aspirations' began to be focused on his sister Elizabeth, who the following year was to marry the Elector Palatine, the Calvinist Frederick.[209] Thus far Henry's brief public-life story. Yet much more important and enduring was the symbolic role he played at diverse levels in early modern England. Henry typified the virtuous Protestant warrior engaged to fight the Antichrist of Rome. For many subjects his thirst for glory – coupled with his support of the arts, science and colonial enterprises – framed him as an ideal figure. His pedigree corresponded to a form of glorious imperialism aimed at destroying papal power and, thanks to the enforcement of God's commands, enhancing the position of the English nation in the world. Prince Henry was identified with the British-born Godly Emperor Constantine. He symbolised 'the Protestant vocation' informing the political and religious mood of many Englishmen whose dissatisfaction with the Stuart regime was steadily growing.[210] During the early Jacobean reign Henry's ghost loomed large in the collective imagery. Later on, being moved by Protestant zeal and hostile to any proposal of a peaceful settlement with Catholics (which James had been trying to accomplish with Spain), sundry subjects sustained the cause of Elizabeth and Frederick in the Palatinate. The Protestant party placed Henry's sister onto the pedestal of chivalric devotion. They turned her into the emblem of their cause, representing her as the fusion of the myths of Gloriana and the Faery Queen.

In contrast to this flourishing royal image, the policies of Charles I – and the powerful role of the grey eminence Buckingham[211] – engendered criticism soon into the new reign. Charles initially strove to play the role that his brother would have performed had he lived. However, his marriage to the Catholic Henrietta Maria and the Duke's murder (1628) prompted the King to abandon his pursuits of a Henrician policy, which was supposed to make him more acceptable to the nation.[212] This failure to embrace the political model and the spiritual legacy left unaccomplished by Henry's death signalled the beginning of a crisis affecting the Caroline reign and the Crown's vision of monarchy. The repercussions of this crisis – which was economic, political, military, moral and European in scope due to the Thirty Years War (1618–48)[213] – were to appear in their fully tragic scale in the bellicose 1640s. Haunted by his brother's ghost and attacked by radical opponents, at the start of the Personal Rule Charles saw the role of Protestant champion be taken up by the King of Sweden, Gustavus Adolphus.[214]

In fact, both Stuart kings had the 'unfortunate privilege' to experience what Queen Elizabeth had perceived only as a threat. This was the dangerous use of patriotism made by religious zealots at odds with the monarchy. Thus, the turning point in the moulding of patriotism occurred in the transition from the Tudor to the Stuart dynasty, when '[t]he triple identification of monarch, nation and church was broken'.[215] Whilst sixteenth-century theorists (except for the likes of John Ponet)[216] had not adopted patriotism as their Trojan horse to attack monarchical principles,[217] seventeenth-century writers employed it to contest the sovereign's policies and the monarchical regime. In the 1530s patriotism had played a vital role in kindling monarchical propaganda. King and country had been identified.[218] As such, to sustain the Crown had corresponded to a patriotic act: the defence of Protestantism and its highest earthly representative, Queen Elizabeth, had been framed according to the patriotic vocabulary.

By the same token, the 1584 Bond of Association concocted by Sir Francis Walsingham and Lord Burghley aimed at patriotically protecting Elizabeth's 'royal person' from all conspiracies orchestrated against her.[219] Rumours of Catholic plots widely circulated, increasing people's anxiety towards popish influence. Walsingham and Burghley drew up the document with the end of preserving the integrity of the nation by metaphorically binding it around the Queen. The Bond had to show people's loyalty to Elizabeth.[220] As Stephen Alford has recently explained, the Bond encapsulated the need felt by faithful subjects and probe councillors to 'challenge those who threatened the security of the queen's person, the stability of the kingdom and the promotion of God's truth'.[221] These causes all coexisted. Most importantly, the Bond of Association was couched in the language of patriotism. Thus, in 1584 patriots were those who stood in defence of the monarchy and not those who opposed it. In the Tudor era the appeal to patriotic vocabulary and its associated images 'was designed to unite the Protestant nation behind their undisputed monarch'.[222] However, this was to change: in the 1620s claiming to be on the patriotic side meant to manifest one's loyalty to the nation in contrast to the monarch. 'Patriot' was thus a changing word deployed to serve opposite political projects and theoretical discourses.[223]

The two Stuarts' lack of success in promoting their cause in ways that appealed to a large number of Englishmen engendered a situation that Kevin Sharpe aptly described as 'the nostalgia for lost days of harmony, unity and order [that] informed the policies of the king no less than the rhetoric of the country'.[224] At a time when James I had (unsuccessfully) tried both in his policies and in his writings to appear as the personification of English identity,[225] the keynote was the representation of strong monarchical authority. This explains why Filmer and theorists like Kynaston promoted a patriotic image of kingship. Their purpose was to regain the nation to the monarchical side. Insurgent malcontent amongst subjects, increasing opposition in Parliament and mordant criticism in political literature prompted Filmer to reshape the configuration of monarchy, rethinking the role of the ruler therein. His Adamite narrative reinforced the primary role of monarchical sovereignty. It also dismissed as an unpardonable demystification of kingly supremacy the idea that men's rational consent in the state of nature had brought about power.

In tune with this, Filmer was to effectively attack Hobbes' vision of a bellicose state of nature as the precondition of political society. Not only did Filmer

identify this scenario with the most damaging to men, but he also emphasised the nurturing role of the family. Foregrounding the pristine place of the
familial unit in the construction of the body politic was a strategic means to
depict the state of nature as subject to enduring conflict. Contract and consent
were thus portrayed on a canvas where misery and violence, individualism
and human atomism figured as the only elements of a necessarily desolate
political landscape.[226] Conversely, fatherly power governing the household
generated harmony. It epitomised the antithesis of the state of general disorder
yielded by contractarian views. Fatherly authority and paternal love became
the quintessence of monarchical superiority. Therefore, the configuration of
Adam's primacy in the divine process of creation responded to the necessity
of having an undivided and undisputed power enabled to prevent a condition
of perpetual war similar to the state of nature. For Filmer only the Adamite
solution could guarantee to 'every man to live in peace, that so he may tend
[to] the preservation of his life, which whilst he is in actual war [as in the state
of nature] he cannot do'.[227]

FILMER, ADAM AND THE SOVEREIGN

Filmer's political use of fatherhood also explains why mothers and wives were
excluded from *Patriarcha*. Since Adam conflated conjugal and paternal power
in himself, there was no need to further explore the position of Eve. Paternal
power subsumed all other relationships so as to eliminate the danger of multi-
plying and as such dispersing the *oneness* of fatherly authority. The emphasis
on Adam and his productive function as the first man from whom all others
derived indicates that Filmer was convinced of an image of power which
comprised masculine traits and patriarchal strength. By depicting Adam as
the progenitor of humankind and first monarch, he made politics the product
of generation. In his discourse this term assumed an exclusively male (and
masculine) meaning. Bestowing the role of founder of politics to Adam,
Patriarcha excluded the fertile nature of women from this realm of human
interaction. In order to place his political edifice on solid foundations, Filmer
employed the family as his forceful metaphor without taking the economic
and property-related aspects of the household into much consideration.[228]

   In *Patriarcha* the question of political authorisation found its legitimacy
in the intelligible and uninterrupted line of continuity tailored in patriarchal
fashion through the absolute fatherly rule of Adam. Despite the absence of
subjects when he was created, Adam naturally had the power to govern his
posterity. Although there were no subjects, there was a head.[229] This served
Filmer to set out his patriarchalist representation of sovereignty whereby the
only authorising agency within the body politic was the entity which preceded
political community itself and the creation of all laws: this was – and could

only be – the Adamite sovereign. As Sir Robert explicitly stated, '[c]ustoms at first became lawful only by some superior power which did either command or consent unto their beginning'.[230] This form of 'superior power' was 'kingly power ... [f]rom whence we must necessarily infer that the common law itself, or common customs of this land, were originally the laws and commands of kings at first unwritten'.[231]

On the whole, Filmer dissected the foundations of politics. He investigated the nature of power and explored the intrinsic force of political command. Like Hobbes, he advocated the idea that the will of the sovereign was the touchstone of political life in the reign. As he put it, '[t]o be governed is nothing else but to be obedient and subject to the will or command of another: it is the will in man that governs'.[232] In his account of monarchical sovereignty God certainly had a prominent position, but it was His lieutenant on earth that attracted Filmer's mind and drove his pen.[233] As he unequivocally explained, '[t]he supreme power being an indivisible beam of majesty cannot be divided among, or settled upon a multitude'. In addition, targeting parliamentary stalwarts he declared that, 'God would have it fixed in one person, not sometimes in one part of the people and sometimes in another, sometimes ... nowhere, as when the [Parliament's] assembly is dissolved it must rest in the air or in the walls of the chamber where they were assembled'.[234] Filmer embraced the Bodinian idea that sovereignty was absolute, indivisible and inalienable. He gave ample consideration to Bodin's notion of the perpetuity of sovereignty and drew upon the French's anti-Aristotelianism so as to discredit the stances of Bellarmine and Suarez on the separation of domestic and political authority.[235] Filmer's concept of sovereignty also recalled the idea of the French jurist Charles Loyseau (1564–1627), for whom sovereignty was the form that gave being to the State.[236]

Since the preservation of sovereignty was the fundamental task of the governor, Filmer advocated the *arcana imperii* as a means to rescue monarchy from decadence due to time and political turmoil.[237] Sharing King James' view that 'the mysterie of the Kings power' had to be kept away from the public and that subjects should 'incroach not upon the Prerogative of the Crowne',[238] Filmer argued that the 'vulgar' must not 'pry into' the 'arcana imperii' or 'cabinet councils'.[239] As 'it is not fit to tie the master to acquaint his servant with his secrets, counsels, or present necessity', so the same 'may be said of the king's commanding a man to serve him in the wars'.[240] Secrets of State pertained exclusively to the sovereign.[241] After all, for Filmer political decisions and actions were the affair of a highly trained minority.[242] This perspective contrasted sharply with the ideas of pamphleteers such as the well-known Thomas Scott, who in *Vox Populi* (1620) had advocated the necessity of having a public sphere at liberty to debate. As an 'honest' and 'zealous Patriot', Scott felt entitled to discuss matters of State which were vital to the preservation of the common good. As he had also explained in *Vox Regis* (1624), it was essential that monarch and subjects exchanged opinions freely so as to maintain the commonwealth in good health.[243] Equally, George Wither's *Wither's Motto* (1621) had claimed the importance of a wider collective space where to promote political participation. Infringing the royal proclamation 'Against excess of lavish and licentious speech of matters of state' issued on 24 December 1620, the poet Wither – and others like King James' critic and Inner-Temple poet William Browne and the anti-absolutist politician (MP) and poet Christopher Brooke – contributed to a new pattern of republican literary culture critical of the Jacobean monarchy and engaged in addressing an emerging politicised public.[244]

Against these oppositional forces, Filmer maintained that harmony could only be found in an absolute monarchy where political matters were left to the control of the supreme and patriotic king.[245] In carving out such an image of the ruler, Filmer attempted to revitalise the aesthetics no less than the politics of kingship. In their respective fields, Anthony van Dyck and Filmer gave of sovereignty a persuasive, effective and durable representation. It was precisely in this context that at Blackfriars van Dyck painted 'his flattering dream of a wise, sensitive, dignified monarchy'.[246] As Kevin Sharpe argued, 'in the tender and delicate portrayals of Charles with his wife and children, van Dyck complemented the representation of the "little god on earth" with that of a very human husband and father'. Charles and Henrietta Maria 'were the "first royal couple to be glorified as husband and wife"', and Charles was the first monarch in a long time to be *fit* to be father.[247] Fatherhood was essential to royal propaganda since it pictured the king as the father of the country.[248] Filmer knew it and, despite declaring to treat with great 'cautions' issues of power because he himself had 'nothing to do to meddle with mysteries of the present state',[249] he employed the patriarchalist paradigm so as to participate in this process of fortification of monarchy.

As we shall see in the next chapter, his attempt was not (fully) appreciated until much later in the century.

NOTES

1 P. Lake, 'Anti-popery: The Structure of a Prejudice', in Cust and Hughes (eds), *Conflict in Early Stuart England*, pp. 72–106, p. 91. Lake identified 'two competing sets of social and political, as well as religious, priorities and values' as major features of ideological conflict in early seventeenth-century England (*ibid.*, p. 97).

2 A well-known exponent of the idea that a 'Jesuitical' conspiracy was impending was Lewis Owen, author of *The Unmasking of All Popish Monks, Friars, and Jesuits* (1628).

3 Lake, 'Anti-popery', p. 91.

4 *Ibid.*, p. 82.

5 Pocock labelled James I and Filmer 'the twin dragons of theoretical absolutism' and highlighted the influence of the former on the latter (J. G. A. Pocock, *The Ancient Constitution and the Feudal Law* (Cambridge, 1957), p. 149).

6 For an account of James' policies and relationship with Parliament see Hirst, *England in Conflict*, pp. 79–102. The disputes that erupted in Parliament in 1614 were an anticipation of the conflicts of the 1620s (see S. Clucas and R. Davies, 'Introduction', in S. Clucas and R. Davies (eds), *The Crisis of 1614 and the Addled Parliament. Literary and Historical Perspectives* (Aldershot, 2003), pp. 1–14).

7 King James VI and I, *Basilicon Doron*, in Sommerville (ed.), *King James VI and I. Political Writings*, pp. 1–61, p. 26.

8 *Ibid.*, pp. 26–7.

9 *Ibid.*, p. 54.

10 King James VI and I, *A Speach to both the Houses of Parliament ... March 1607*, in Sommerville (ed.), *King James VI and I. Political Writings*, pp. 159–78, p. 174.

11 King James VI and I, *A Speach in the Starre-Chambe ... 1616*, in Sommerville (ed.), *King James VI and I. Political Writings*, pp. 204–28, p. 213.

12 Cited in Cust, '"Patriots" and "Popular" Spirits', p. 56.

13 Cited in M. Smuts, *Court Culture and the Origins of a Royalist Tradition in Early Stuart England* (Philadelphia, 1987), p. 45, n. 39.

14 Hirst, *England in Conflict*, pp. 9, 23. In 1621 the Commons opposed James' attempts to control open debate and challenged his belief that resorting to extraordinary measures was one of his inherent rights. This corresponded to criticising the idea that kings represented the whole body politic (*ibid.*, p. 14). According to Hirst, the outcome of the parliament of 1621 was to be the groundwork for conflict (*ibid.*, p. 106).

15 King James VI and I, *My Lords and Gent: all* (report of James I's speech accepting subsidies but refusing parliamentary supervision of foreign policy), c. 1621, Folger Shakespeare Library (Washington DC), MS X.d.150, fo. 1v.

16 *Ibid.*, fo. 1v. James concluded by expressing his desire 'that god will blesse or labour for the happy restitution of my children, And whosoever did the wrong I deserved the contrary at theur hands' (*ibid.*, fo. 1v).

17 See Cogswell, *The Blessed Revolution*, pp. 289–90. Reynolds targeted the Jesuits, whom he thought should be banished from the country.

18 *Ibid.*, p. 290.

19 King James VI and I, *The Trew Law*, p. 65.

20 *Ibid.*, p. 65.

21 *Ibid.*, p. 71.

22 Cust, 'Charles I and Popularity', p. 243.

23 B. Cottret, 'Diplomatie et Éthique de l'État: l'Ambassade d'Effiat en Angleterre et le mariage de Charles Ier d'Angleterre et d'Henriette-Marie de France (été 1624–printemps 1625)', in H. Méchoulan (ed.), *L'État Baroque 1610–1652* (Paris, 1985), pp. 221–42, p. 236.

24 M. Todd, 'Anti-Calvinists and the Republican Threat in Early Stuart Cambridge', in L. Lunger Knoppers (ed.), *Puritanism and Its Discontents* (Newark and London, 2003), pp. 85–105, p. 87. Similarly, in 1599 the English translation of Gasparo Contarini's

pro-Venetian *De Magistratibus et Republica Venetorum* (1543) had staged a defence of the government of the multitude against the idea of pure monarchy (A. Hadfield, *Shakespeare and Republicanism* (Cambridge, 2005), pp. 41–2).

25 Cust, 'Was There an Alternative to the Personal Rule?', p. 340.

26 Cited in *ibid.*, p. 340.

27 *Ibid.*, p. 342.

28 *Historical Manuscripts Commission*, Eleventh Report, Appendix, Part I, 'The Manuscripts of H. D. Skrine Esq., Salvetti Correspondence', *Letter 16th December 1628* (1887), p. 173.

29 *Ibid.*, p. 173.

30 *Ibid.*, *Letter 2nd December 1628*, p. 172.

31 *Ibid.*, *Letter 9th December 1628*, p. 172. Salvetti remarked that 'the King with a few of his councillors pursue a course devoid of decision or steadiness of purpose, when duty calls for both' (*ibid.*, p. 172). For Cust, at this time, 'there was even fresh talk of striking down evil counsellors and taking revenge on the enemies of the people' (Cust, 'Was There an Alternative to the Personal Rule?', p. 346).

32 Hirst, *England in Conflict*, p. 128. See also L. J. Reeve, *Charles I and the Road to Personal Rule* (Cambridge, 1989), *passim*.

33 Thinkers like Filmer capitalised on the Commons' failure to symbolically incorporate the kingdom (Hirst, *England in Conflict*, p. 129). Their task was now to paint a political fresco where the king was the father of the nation.

34 See Thompson, 'Licensing the Press', *passim*. This was the time (1629) when the merchant Richard Chambers was jailed for having compared English monarchy to Turkish despotism (Hirst, *England in Conflict*, p. 125).

35 E. Cope, *Politics Without Parliaments 1629–1640* (1987), pp. 27 ff.

36 See Sommerville, *Royalists and Patriots*, esp. pp. 55–104.

37 For Scott, billeting was 'against the liberty of a free Englishman and gentleman and of a parliament man' (*PP 1628*, vi, p. 220). Derek Hirst pointed to the longing for rebellion that members of the political elite such as Scott and Simonds D'Ewes expressed in their diaries in the early 1620s (Hirst, *England in Conflict*, p. 45).

38 Tyacke, 'Introduction', pp. 11–12. However, I think Scott's seeming support for a mixed monarchy should be taken with caution: his radical (quasi-)republicanism should be kept in focus.

39 Sharpe, *Remapping*, p. 105.

40 A. B. Coiro, 'A "Ball of Strife": Caroline Poetry and Royal Marriage', in T. N. Corns (ed.), *The Royal Image. Representations of Charles I* (Cambridge, 1999), pp. 26–46, p. 31.

41 *Ibid.*, p. 27.

42 King James VI and I, *The Trew Law*, p. 65.

43 *Ibid.*, p. 75.

44 *Ibid.*, p. 76.

45 *PP 1610*, i, p. 30.

46 *The Interpreter* was suppressed by proclamation in 1610 and published in 1637.

47 C. S. Clegg, *Press Censorship in Jacobean England* (Cambridge, 2001), p. 12.

48 Hirst, *England in Conflict*, pp. 22–4.

49 See M. L. Shanley, 'Marriage Contract and Social Contract in Seventeenth-Century English Political Thought', in J. B. Elshtain (ed.), *The Family in Political Thought* (Brighton, 1982), pp. 80–95; B. Roberts Peters, *Marriage in Seventeenth-Century English Political Thought* (Basingstoke, 2004), *passim*.

50 See e.g. *PP 1610*, i, p. 13.

51 Sharpe, *Remapping*, p. 150.

52 King James VI and I, *A Speach to the Lords and Commons ... 1609*, in Sommerville (ed.), *King James VI and I. Political Writings*, pp. 179–203, p. 183.

53 On these issues see Clegg, *Press Censorship in Jacobean England*, esp. p. 141.

54 For in-depth criticism of Paul Christianson's idea that James was a moderate theorist see J. P. Sommerville, 'King James VI and I and John Selden: Two Voices on History and the Constitution', in D. Fischlin and M. Fortier (eds), *Royal Subjects. Essays on the Writings of James VI and I* (Detroit, 2002), pp. 290–322. See P. Christianson, 'Royal and Parliamentary Voices on the Ancient Constitution, c. 1604–1621', in L. L. Peck (ed.), *The Mental World of the Jacobean Court* (Cambridge, 1991), pp. 71–95.

55 On this important point see esp. chapter 9 below.

56 *PP 1610*, ii, p. 103.

57 *PT*, p. 43.

58 James VI and I, *Basilicon Doron*, p. 20.

59 See chapter 2 above.

60 *OA*, pp. 253–4.

61 *PT*, p. 39.

62 *Ibid.*, p. 8. Conquest was traditionally – and certainly by Bodin – reputed to be the cause of despotism, that is, of a regime where subjects' property was entirely in the hands of the sovereign.

63 *OA*, p. 253. Filmer praised Plato and criticised Aristotle, whose doctrine he described as 'not without some folly' and imbued with 'fancy' (*PT*, p. 15). He added that 'Aristotle, in his books of *Politics*, when he comes to compare the several kinds of government, ... disputes subtly to and fro of many points, and judiciously confutes many errors, but concludes nothing himself'. Worse still, '[i]n all those books' very 'little in commendation of monarchy' could be found (*ibid.*, p. 24).

64 R. Zaller, 'The Figure of the Tyrant in English Revolutionary Thought', *Journal of the History of Ideas*, 54 (1993), pp. 585–610, p. 589.

65 See e.g. *PT*, pp. 45–6, 49; *FH*, p. 119.

66 King James VI and I, *A Speach to the Lords and Commons ... 1609*, p. 183.

67 F. Oakley, *Omnipotence, Covenant, and Order. An Excursion in the History of Ideas from Abelard to Leibniz* (Ithaca and London, 1984), p. 118.

68 This idea presented striking similarities to Sir John Fortescue's discourse on monarchy as *dominium regale* opposed to monarchy as *dominium politicum et regale*. In *De Dominio Regale et Politico* (1470s) Fortescue had argued that 'the first king may rule his people by such laws as he maketh himself [...levying] impositions ... without their consent. [Instead t]he second king may not rule his people by other laws than such as they assent

unto' (John Fortescue, *The Governance of England: otherwise called the Difference between an Absolute and a Limited Monarchy*, ed. C. Plummer (Oxford, 1885), p. 109).

69 F. Oakley, *Politics and Eternity. Studies in the History of Medieval and Early-Modern Political Thought* (Leiden, 1999), p. 327.

70 *Ibid.*, p. 327.

71 *AN*, p. 153.

72 *PT*, p. 52.

73 *OA*, p. 259.

74 See *ibid.*, pp. 264 ff.

75 In case of conquest, the conqueror had the power to govern without intermediate bodies.

76 *Ibid.*, p. 243.

77 See e.g. *PT*, pp. 30 ff.

78 *PP 1628*, iii, p. 254. See also *ibid.*, ii, p. 125; Pocock, *The Ancient Constitution*, pp. 44–5.

79 Underdown, *A Freeborn People*, p. 40. For examples of resistance to billeting of troops in the Commons see *PP 1628*, ii, pp. 127–8, 168–70, 253–5, 361–5, 383–5.

80 Kishlansky, *Parliamentary Selection*, p. 18.

81 *PP 1628*, iii, p. 254.

82 J. A. Guy, 'The Origins of the Petition of Right Reconsidered', *HJ*, 25 (1982), pp. 289–312, esp. pp. 297 ff.

83 *PP 1628*, iii, p. 269.

84 *Ibid.*, p. 270.

85 *Ibid.*, p. 270.

86 The petition was submitted to the Lords on 8 May. The Commons' decision to accept (William Coryton being an exception) a petition instead of a bill procedure represented 'a major setback in terms of what had gone before' (Guy, 'The Origins', p. 312).

87 *PP 1628*, iii, p. 272.

88 *Ibid.*, p. 272.

89 *Ibid.*, p. 273.

90 *Ibid.*, p. 275.

91 *Ibid.*, p. 278.

92 Guy, 'The Origins', p. 291. Guy defined Sir Edward Coke, Eliot and Coryton as the hardliners in the Commons (*ibid.*, p. 303, n. 62).

93 *PP 1628*, iii, p. 209.

94 *Ibid.*, p. 275. According to L. J. Reeve, Coryton did not fight a 'constitutional battle' but rather embraced both 'royalism and parliamentary power' (*ODNB*, 'Coryton, William').

95 *PP 1628*, iii, p. 275.

96 *Ibid.*, p. 275.

97 *Ibid.*, p. 275.

98 *Ibid.*, p. 275 (italics added).

99 *Ibid.*, p. 275. Already in the parliament of 1621 Edward Alford had complained that the parliamentary assembly had 'donne no good for our Countrie' (*Common Debates 1621*, eds W. Notestein, F. Relf and H. Simpson (New Haven, 7 vols, 1935), iii, p. 435). He also warned his fellow MPs to 'remember that England sent us. That must be satisfied' (*ibid.*, p. 484).

100 *PP 1628*, iii, p. 280.

101 *Ibid.*, p. 280.

102 *Ibid.*, p. 280.

103 *Ibid.*, p. 280.

104 *Ibid.*, p. 280.

105 *Ibid.*, p. 281.

106 *Ibid.*, p. 281.

107 This issue will come to the fore again in the debates of the 1680s (see Part II below).

108 Zagorin, *The Court and the Country*, p. 86.

109 R. Ashton, *The English Civil War. Conservatism and Revolution 1603–1649* (1978), p. 70.

110 Kishlansky, *Parliamentary Selection*, pp. 16, 18.

111 M. Kishlansky, 'Tyranny Denied: Charles I, Attorney General Heath, and the Five Knights' Case', *HJ*, 42 (1999), pp. 53–83, p. 83.

112 *Ibid.*, p. 82.

113 *Ibid.*, p. 79. Kishlansky, however, argued that the Commons' claims that they were defending traditional liberties 'can only be charitably interpreted as self-delusional' (*ibid.*, p. 78). The opposition to Charles I that erupted in the Commons in 1628 was the outcome of 'a conspiracy against him', the sign that his government and actions were being surreptitiously misrepresented. The Commons made it sound as if the King was suspending civil liberties as part of his deliberate policy rather than as an expedient (*ibid.*, p. 83). For Kishlansky the Commons' confrontation over the Forced Loan was driven by the attempt to obtain the dismissal of the Duke of Buckingham, who was their main target (*ibid.*, pp. 79–80).

114 P. Collinson, 'Afterword', in J. F. McDiarmid (ed.), *The Monarchical Republic of Early Modern England. Essays in Response to Patrick Collinson* (Aldershot, 2007), pp. 245–60.

115 R. Cust, 'Reading for Magistracy: The Mental World of Sir John Newdigate', in McDiarmid (ed.), *The Monarchical Republic*, pp. 181–99, pp. 198–9. On the early importance of constitutionalism see Winship, 'Freeborn (Puritan) Englishmen', esp. pp. 1071–4. Winship highlighted how under James the voices raised in favour of more parliamentary rule, law and liberty, and against the threat of tyranny, came not just from Puritans as in the 1580s but from a wider 'company' of commonwealthmen (*ibid.*, pp. 1065–6).

116 Hirst, *The Representative of the People?*, pp. 7–9, 11–12 and esp. chs 8–9, e.g. p. 188.

117 On this see Cust, 'The "Public Man"' and chapter 2 above.

118 Hirst, *England in Conflict*, p. 13.

119 On freedom of speech in early Stuart parliaments see D. Colclough, *Freedom of Speech*

in *Early Stuart England* (Cambridge, 2005), esp. pp. 120–95. On the origins of the rhetoric of freedom of speech deployed by numerous MPs in the 1620s controversies over the royal prerogative see M. Peltonen, 'Rhetoric and Citizenship in the Monarchical Republic of Queen Elizabeth I', in McDiarmid (ed.), *The Monarchical Republic*, pp. 109–27.

120 *PP 1628*, iii, p. 280.

121 Colclough, *Freedom of Speech*, pp. 184–5.

122 On the link between patriotism and office-holding see C. Condren, *Argument and Authority in Early Modern England. The Presupposition of Oaths and Offices* (Cambridge, 2006), esp. pp. 149–62.

123 Colclough, *Freedom of Speech*, pp. 194–5.

124 Civil War royalists like Dudley Digges and John Bramhall were to adopt the metaphor of the *pater patriae* to describe the king. Yet they did not make use of Filmerian patriarchalism, nor did they refer to Adam as the first parent from whom kingly authority stemmed (Daly, 'John Bramhall', p. 29, n. 10). Moreover, whereas Bramhall insisted on the law and its binding power 'quite apart from the authority of the law-giver', Filmer focused on the latter's absoluteness (on Bramhall's position see *ibid.*, p. 38, n. 47).

125 Cope, *Politics Without Parliaments*, p. 27.

126 On Kynaston see C. Cuttica, 'Sir Francis Kynaston: The Importance of the "Nation" for a Seventeenth-Century English Royalist', *History of European Ideas*, 32 (2006), pp. 139–61.

127 Francis Kynaston, *A True Presentation of forepast Parliaments to the viewe of present tymes and Posteritie*, BL, Lansdowne MS 213, fos 146a–76b, fo. 168a.

128 *Ibid.*, fo. 168a. Having denied the legislative role of the Commons, Kynaston asserted that in the Saxon era those elected to the assemblies 'did … never meddle publikely wth the Arcana imperij, or the Sacred Prerogative of kings' (*ibid.*, fos 153a–4a; see also *ibid.*, fo. 163a). Likewise, he maintained that only monarchs could 'defend, or spare whom they please' and this was so for to the king 'belongs the power of Judicature, and not to the House of Commons'. The king gave 'Parliament no account of his just reasons' (*ibid.*, fo. 161a).

129 *Ibid.*, fo. 162a. See also *ibid.*, fo. 172a.

130 *Ibid.*, fo. 171b.

131 Referring to the imprisonment of the poet, judge and vociferous MP John Hoskyns (1614), Sir Henry Wotton had declared that the former was in 'for licentiousness baptised freedom'. Wotton had interestingly remarked that 'a false or faint patriot did cover himself with the shadow of equal moderation' so as to make 'irreverent discourse' appear 'honest liberty' (cited in Colclough, *Freedom of Speech*, p. 39).

132 According to Kynaston, kings 'are in the heads of Almighty God' and 'are only directed, formed, and inclined by God himself, and by no earthly mortall Power or Policy' (Kynaston, *True Presentation*, fo. 171a).

133 *Ibid.*, fo. 172b. With the late 1620s political scenario in mind, Kynaston maintained that it was 'a deplorable thing to think that want of Money should worke such effects, as to prostrate in a sort a Sovereign to the Devotion of his Subjects and Vassals, and should expose his Ministers and Officers to the censure and mercy of a Multitude' (*ibid.*, fo. 172a). On Parliament as a political body subject to passions see *ibid.*, fos 175a–b.

134 *PT*, pp. 56–7.

135 *Ibid.*, p. 57.

136 *Ibid.*, pp. 55–6.

137 *FH*, p. 124. In 1652 Filmer mocked 'freedom of debate' in Parliament as an obstacle to all legislative procedures and, more generally, to the task of governing (see *OA*, pp. 278–9).

138 J. Scott, *Commonwealth Principles. Republican Writing of the English Revolution* (Cambridge, 2004), esp. pp. 233–7. On the circulation of resistance theories (Catholic and Puritan) in England see Burgess, *British Political Thought*, pp. 101–21. In the first two decades of the seventeenth century, Dutch republican writings such as Paulus Busius's *De republica* (1613) flourished. The same can be said of Johannes Althusius' *Politica Methodice Digesta* (first published in 1603 and revisited in 1610 and 1614); of the works of Clemens Timpler and Johann Heinrich Alsted, and of those of Spanish theorists such as Fernando Vázquez (M. van Gelderen, 'Aristotelians, Monarchomachs and Republicans: Sovereignty and *respublica mixta* in Dutch and German Political Thought, 1580–1650', in van Gelderen and Skinner (eds), *Republicanism. A Shared European Heritage*, vol. 1, pp. 195–217). As for the diffusion of republican ideals in Elizabethan and Jacobean England, both in political literature and in plays, see Hadfield, *Shakespeare and Republicanism*, esp. pp. 28, 50–3, 65–6, 95.

139 *OA*, p. 270.

140 See *ibid.*, esp. pp. 256–75. In *The Elements of Law* Hobbes accused 'moral philosophers' like Seneca and Cicero ('so greatly esteemed amongst us') of justifying the notion that 'tyrannicide is lawful, meaning by a tyrant any man in whom resideth the right of sovereignty' (Thomas Hobbes, *The Elements of Law Natural & Politic*, ed. with a preface and critical notes by F. Tönnies (Cambridge, 1928), Part II, ch. 8, p. 138; see also *ibid.*, ch. 9, pp. 145–6).

141 *PT*, p. 3.

142 *Ibid.*, pp. 2–3. In his translation of Thucydides (1628) Hobbes expressed the same opinion towards the danger of demagogues and orators swaying 'amongst the common people' (see N. Malcolm, *Reason of State, Propaganda, and the Thirty Years' War. An Unknown Translation by Thomas Hobbes* (Oxford, 2007), pp. 87–8). Hobbes also pointed out that Thucydides' writings supported the maxim whereby it was dangerous to partake secrets of State (*arcana*) with 'the common people', which was essential teaching of the *ragion di stato* theorists (*ibid.*, esp. p. 113). It is important to remember that Hobbes wrote this in the mid–late 1620s.

143 *PT*, p. 5. On this see chapter 2 above.

144 *PT*, p. 44.

145 *Ibid.*, p. 44.

146 *Ibid.*, p. 4. Filmer ironically observed that they had to 'take heed that they do not deny by retail that liberty which they affirm by wholesale' (*ibid.*, p. 4).

147 *Ibid.*, p. 5.

148 On the increasing fear that riots and tensions amongst the populace would be conducive to general revolt in the period under scrutiny see Hill, 'The Many-Headed Monster', esp. pp. 297–8, 306.

149 Kynaston, *True Presentation*, fo. 163b.

150 *Ibid.*, fo. 163b.

151 *Ibid.*, fo. 164b.

152 *Ibid.*, fos 162a–b.

153 This work was composed around 1620 but it was first published in 1628 (J. Greenberg, *The Radical Face of the Ancient Constitution. St Edward's 'Laws' in Early Modern Political Thought* (Cambridge, 2001), p. 168).

154 Kynaston, *True Presentation*, fo. 162b. Kynaston devoted a few passages to attack Starkey's views on the legislative importance of Parliament, especially in regard to religion. Whereas for Starkey Parliament was entitled to deal with religious matters such as the treatment of 'Papisticall Superstition', 'Romish Churches' and idolatry, for Kynaston such a contention was absurd since Parliament did not have the continuity necessary to deliberate on these affairs. Instead, monarchs were 'Supreme Heads of the Church and therefore instrumentall Causes of the Plantation and Conservation of Gods true Religion and Service in this Land' thanks to their 'personall capacities'. The truth was that parliaments 'more commonly follow the Religion of their King, then Kings do the Religion of their People' (*ibid.*, fos 168b–70a).

155 *Ibid.*, fo. 167b.

156 *Ibid.*, fo. 166a.

157 *Ibid.*, fo. 166b.

158 *Ibid.*, fo. 167a (italics added).

159 *Ibid.*, fo. 167b.

160 *Ibid.*, fo. 161a.

161 See Anon., *Tom Tell Troath or A free discourse touching the manners of the tyme Directed to his Majestie by way of humble advertisement* (Holland?: S. n.; although the database EEBO suggests 1630 as the possible date of publication, the pamphlet must have circulated before, given that Kynaston's writing is from 1629). According to Lord Baltimore, *Tom Tell Troath* had been written by a Dutchman called Boutefeus (see Lord Baltimore, *Answer to Tom Tell Troth* (1642)).

162 Kynaston, *True Presentation*, fo. 161a.

163 *Ibid.*, fos 161a–b.

164 Cogswell, *The Blessed Revolution*, p. 24.

165 On some of these themes see Cuttica, 'Anti-Jesuit *Patriotic Absolutism*', *passim*.

166 On the late seventeenth-century publication of Filmer's works see Part II below.

167 Peter Heylyn, *Augustus* ... (1632), p. 189.

168 *Ibid.*, p. 146.

169 *Ibid.*, p. 146.

170 A. Milton, *Laudian and Royalist Polemic in Seventeenth-Century England. The Career and Writings of Peter Heylyn* (Manchester, 2007), p. 19.

171 *Ibid.*, p. 154. Anthony Milton argued that 'Heylyn's patriotism had a Laudian inflection', especially for 'his rejection of the country's ties to the Continental Reformed tradition' (*ibid.*, p. 183, n. 44).

172 This Roman concept was used in 1571 by Andrea of Isernia in a work published in

Naples: 'we must love the Prince and the *respublica* more than our father' (cited in E. H. Kantorowicz, *The King's Two Bodies. A Study in Medieval Political Theology* (Princeton, 1957), p. 248). Kantorowicz's study provides a thorough explanation of the historical origins of the metaphor '*pater patriae*'. On the latter see also Figgis, *The Divine Right of Kings*, esp. pp. 149–52. Figgis stated that 'so widespread a metaphor as that of the King being *pater patriae* is sure to be pressed to its full extent by some writers' (*ibid.*, p. 152). *Patriarcha* was a case in point.

173 John Hayward, *The First Part of the Life and Raigne of King Henrie the III* ... (1599), p. 105.

174 John Hayward, *An Answer to the First Part of a Certaine Conference Concerning Succession, published not long since vnder the name of R. Dolman* (1603), p. 45. In this work Hayward took Pierre de Belloy's side against Parsons' *Conference about the Next Succession* (Antwerp, 1595).

175 Hayward, *An Answer*, p. 46. Filmer made use of Hayward's historical accounts and of his reply to Parsons' tract (see *PT*, pp. 34, 54).

176 Thomas Craig, *Concerning the Right of Succession to the Kingdom of England, two books; against the sophisms of one Parsons a Jesuite, who assum'd the counterfeit name of Doleman* ... (1703). The treatise was finished in 1603 to inaugurate the new reign of James I but it was not published until a century later.

177 *Ibid.*, 'To the Most Serene Prince James VI, King of Scotland, His Most Gracious Sovereign, *Edinburg, January* the First, 1603' (ii page).

178 *Ibid.*, bk 1, ch. 3, p. 15. See also *ibid.*, bk 1, ch. xx, pp. 188, 190.

179 A. McLaren, 'Challenging the Monarchical Republic: James I's Articulation of Kingship', in McDiarmid (ed.), *The Monarchical Republic*, pp. 165–80, p. 178.

180 *Ibid.*, p. 178, n. 45.

181 King James VI and I, *Triplici Nodo*, p. 87.

182 *Ibid.*, p. 86.

183 King James VI and I, *The Trew Law*, p. 62.

184 *Ibid.*, p. 76.

185 It was on this occasion that he proclaimed that '[t]he State of MONARCHIE is the supremest thing vpon earth: For Kings are not onely GODS Lieutenants vpon earth, and sit vpon GODS throne, but euen by GOD himselfe they are called Gods' (King James VI and I, *A Speach to the Lords and Commons 1609*, p. 181).

186 *Ibid.*, p. 181.

187 *Ibid.*, p. 195.

188 *Ibid.*, p. 195. John Buckeridge had declared that, 'by the necessitie of the precept, Honour thy father and mother', all monarchs were 'Fathers of Countries' (Buckeridge, *A Sermon Preached at Hampton*, p. 16).

189 According to Hirst, in 1610 James changed attitude towards Parliament. Frustrated by the latter's lack of cooperation, defeated in his project to unify England and Scotland, struggling to pursue his diplomatic goals and a successful foreign policy, James gave up hopes to govern in total agreement with the assembly (Hirst, *England in Conflict*, pp. 23–4).

190 Richard Mocket, *God and the King* ... (1615), p. 2. This was the translation of *Deus et*

Rex of the same year. Although Mocket's authorship has been cast in doubt, he is here taken as the author of *God and the King* (see *ODNB*, 'Mocket, Richard').

191 Mocket, *God and the King*, p. 2.

192 *Ibid.*, p. 3.

193 *Ibid.*, p. 3. As is well known, the idea that love of one's country came before love of one's family stemmed from republican discourse. Thus, in the preface to his translation of John XII's *Treasury of Healthe* (1550) Humphrey Lloyd had recalled Cicero's maxim according to which 'everyman is not born for himself but chiefly to benefit his native country, then his parents, afterwards his children and friends'. Lloyd had devoted his work to the profit of his 'native country' (Humphrey Lloyd, *John XII's Treasury of Healthe* (1550), 'Preface').

194 Mocket, *God and the King*, p. 77.

195 Samuel Collins, *Epphata to F.T.* (Cambridge, 1617), p. 496. In 1612 Collins had taken Andrewes' side in the latter's dispute with Bellarmine, publishing *Increpatio Andreae Eudaemono-Johannis Jesuitae* (*ODNB*, 'Collins, Samuel'). In a sermon preached at St Paul's Cross in 1607 Collins had attacked Catholics for 'treading down Kings, the deputies of God, from their throne of Maiestie to set up a foxie Intruder in their roome' (Samuel Collins, *Sermon at Paules-Crosse* (1610), p. 53).

196 See *ODNB*, 'Forsett, Edward'.

197 Edward Forsett, *A Defence of the Right of Kings* ... (1624), p. 23.

198 *Ibid.*, p. 23.

199 Robert Sanderson, *Ten Sermons Preached* ... (1627), p. 165.

200 *Ibid.*, p. 166.

201 Robert Mossom, *The King on His Throne* ... (York, 1643), p. 15. This phrase was taken from Lancelot Andrewes, according to whom 'the Kings right [derived] from the Fathers, and both hold by one Commandement' (Lancelot Andrewes, *A Sermon Preached before His Maiestie* (1610), p. 13).

202 Mossom, *The King on His Throne* ..., p. 15.

203 *Ibid.*, p. 15. See also Sommerville, *Royalists and Patriots*, p. 32.

204 *ODNB*, 'Maxwell, John'.

205 John Maxwell, *Sacro-Santa Regum Majestas: or, The Sacred and Royal Prerogative of Christian Kings* (Oxford, 1644), p. 169. Like Filmer, Maxwell saw Nimrod as the first founder of monarchy and as the embodiment of the irresistible nature of kingly power. Maxwell argued that even the most evil ruler had received divine approbation and that, therefore, a royal tyrant represented an oxymoron (Zaller, 'The Figure of the Tyrant', p. 598).

206 Maxwell, *Sacro-Santa Regum Majestas*, pp. 99–100.

207 *Ibid.*, p. 161.

208 *Ibid.*, p. 117 (italics added).

209 Smuts, *Court Culture*, p. 31.

210 W. Hunt, 'The Spectral Origins of the English Revolution: Legitimation Crisis in Early Stuart England', in G. Eley and W. Hunt (eds), *Reviving the English Revolution. Reflections and Elaborations on the Work of Christopher Hill* (London and New York, 1988), pp. 305–32, esp. pp. 317 ff.

211 Writing on 3 August 1624 to Louis XIII, the French ambassador Effiat explained that the Duke 'is so powerful ['puissant'] that it is possible to say that the King *really* loves him, allows him to do what he likes, and sees only through the favourite's eyes' (cited in Cottret, 'Diplomatie et Éthique de l'État', p. 226).

212 Hunt, 'The Spectral Origins', p. 322.

213 See J. Scott, *England's Troubles. Seventeenth-Century English Political Instability in European Context* (Cambridge, 2000).

214 For a general account of these issues see Sharpe, *Remapping, passim*.

215 G. Brennan, 'Papists and Patriotism in Elizabethan England', *Recusant History*, 19 (1988), pp. 1–15, p. 13. See also G. Brennan, *Patriotism, Power and Print. National Consciousness in Sixteenth-Century England* (Cambridge, 2003).

216 See J. W. Allen, *A History of Political Thought in the Sixteenth Century* (2nd edn, 1941), pp. 118–20. In *A Short Treatise of Politike Power* (1556) Ponet argued that '[n]ext to God men ought to love their country and the whole commonwealthe before any member of it', including the king (cited in Brennan, 'Papists and Patriotism in Elizabethan England', p. 4). According to Stephen Alford, Ponet set out a fierce 'critique of the absolute power of monarchs' (S. Alford, 'A Politics of Emergency in the Reign of Eliza-beth I', in Burgess and Festenstein (eds), *English Radicalism*, pp. 17–36, p. 20).

217 Stressing that sixteenth-century political thinking was informed by radical ideas, Alford referred to Sir Thomas Smith, John Aylmer, Christopher Goodman, Thomas Cartwright as exponents of the concept of mixed polity and to their works as containing 'republican implications' (Alford, 'A Politics of Emergency in the Reign of Elizabeth I', p. 21). In this respect, Patrick Collinson's views confirm Alford's perspective with regard to a vibrant core of sixteenth-century polemical writings questioning the extent of the royal prerogative and setting the limits of monarchical authority (*ibid.*, p. 22).

218 This idyllic picture temporarily faded when Queen Mary's marriage to the Emperor Charles V's son Philip (1554) altered the perception that English people had of their sovereign as the representative, defender and pursuer of the glory of their nation. The foreign 'contamination' the marriage brought about affected patriotic sentiments for the monarchy and left political thinkers and propagandists on the monarchical side bereft of arguments with which to face the situation (Brennan, *Patriotism, Power and Print*, p. 34).

219 Interestingly, in 1681 the patriotic Bond of Association was used against James II to exclude him from the succession and preserve 'the Elizabethan Settlement' (Condren, *Argument and Authority*, p. 152).

220 See P. Lake, '"The Monarchical Republic of Elizabeth I" Revisited (by its Victims) as a Conspiracy', in B. Coward and J. Swann (eds), *Conspiracies and Conspiracy Theory in Early Modern Europe. From the Waldensians to the French Revolution* (Aldershot, 2004), pp. 87–111.

221 Alford, 'A Politics of Emergency in the Reign of Elizabeth I', p. 32.

222 D. Cressy, 'Binding the Nation: The Bonds of Association, 1584 and 1696', in D. Cressy (ed.), *Society and Culture in Early Modern England* (Aldershot and Burlington, 2003), pp. 217–34, p. 230.

223 As Condren put it, '[t]he true patriots were on all sides' (Condren, *Argument and Authority*, p. 162).

224 K. Sharpe, *Criticism and Compliment. The Politics of Literature in the England of Charles I* (Cambridge, 1987), p. 19.

225 A fate experienced by both Charles and the Duke in the 1620s.

226 For Filmer's searing critique of Hobbes and the state of nature see *OG*, pp. 187–97.

227 *Ibid.*, p. 188.

228 According to Rachel Weil, 'Filmer was uninterested in discussing actual relationships among members of actual families', for he primarily aimed at establishing order in society (R. Weil, 'The Family in the Exclusion Crisis: Locke versus Filmer Revisited', in A. Houston and S. Pincus (eds), *A Nation Transformed. England after the Restoration* (Cambridge, 2001), pp. 100–24, p. 110). However, Filmer did deal with actual relationships within the household in *In Praise of the Vertuous Wife*.

229 *AN*, p. 145.

230 *PT*, p. 45.

231 *Ibid.*, p. 45. This idea was a direct attack on Suarez's refutation of the principle that the ruler could establish customary laws.

232 *OA*, p. 254.

233 Lee Ward argued that Filmer's theory ran the risk of making the great power of the ruler interfere with God's (Ward, *Politics of Liberty*, p. 31).

234 *OA*, p. 236.

235 See chapter 3 above.

236 Charles Loyseau, *Traité des Seigneuries* (Chasteaudun, 1610), ch. ii, pp. 14–15.

237 It has been implied that Filmer's 'patriarchal justification' of political power 'represents the development of the principles of state secrets into a political theory of "the profound secrets of government"' (J. Goldberg, *James I and the Politics of Literature. Jonson, Shakespeare, Donne, and their Contemporaries* (Baltimore and London, 1983), p. 85).

238 King James VI and I, *A Speach in the Starre-Chamber … 1616*, p. 212. James admonished his subjects that 'if there fall out a question that concernes my Prerogative or mystery of State, deale not with it'. He deemed these 'transcendent matters' and the king's 'secretest drifts' as the backbone of politics (*ibid.*, p. 212).

239 *PT*, p. 3.

240 *Ibid.*, pp. 43–4.

241 Filmer said that, since '[a]n implicit faith is given to the meanest artificer in his own craft … much more is it, then, due to a prince in the profound secrets of government' (*ibid.*, pp. 3–4).

242 *Ibid.*, p. 4. Such a vision of politics should have appealed to Charles' austere attitude towards dissent; uncompromising secrecy in his policies; control over ecclesiastical and political appointments (Hirst, *England in Conflict*, pp. 6–7). This last passage of *Patriarcha* might also indicate that Filmer was responding to a practical problem. This had to do with the increasing weakness of a king, Charles I, who had to confront subjects that told him how to run the Church; tried to dictate policies on taxation; contested his royal prerogative and, above all, did not collaborate with him.

243 Colclough, *Freedom of Speech*, p. 111. Many MPs in James' First Parliament (1604–10) remarked that the good of the country required them to 'freely and openly deliver' their opinion (*ibid.*, pp. 158–9).

244 See M. O'Callaghan, *The 'Shepheards Nation'. Jacobean Spenserians and Early Stuart Political Culture, 1612–1625* (Oxford, 2000), p. 2 and *ODNB*, 'Wither, George'. On the republican Wither see also D. Norbrook, *Writing the English Republic. Poetry, Rhetoric and Politics, 1627–1660* (Cambridge, 1999), esp. pp. 238–42 where it is underscored that in the 1650s poetry and politics were deeply intertwined.

245 See e.g. *PT*, pp. 12, 28.

246 P. Thomas, 'Two Cultures? Court and Country under Charles I', in Russell (ed.), *The Origins of the English Civil War*, pp. 168–96, p. 176.

247 Sharpe, *Remapping*, pp. 444–5.

248 One of van Dyck's earliest portraits ('the great peece') represented Charles as head of his family and head of his people, presiding over both spheres with might and confidence (R. Cust, *Charles I. A Political Life* (Harlow and New York, 2005), p. 158).

249 *PT*, p. 3.

Chapter 5

Writing in the early Caroline regime and
the issue of *Patriarcha*'s non-publication

The previous three chapters have delineated the reasons that prompted
Filmer to write *Patriarcha*, illustrated the text's content and elucidated the
ideas that informed his political context. This approach has cast new light
on the document itself; it has provided novel insights into the cauldron of
publications in which the treatise was conceived; it has also established what
other kinds of preoccupations and/or motivations besides the textual narrative in itself drove Sir Robert to compose his writing. Complementing this
trajectory of research, the present chapter explores the impact *Patriarcha* had
on the Crown and the royalist entourage in the 1630s; it pays attention to the
type of audience Filmer sought to address, impress, condition; it attempts to
establish how the treatise took part in the ideological enterprise of royal-image
construction involving different cultural codifications: political, pictorial,
theological, literary. Most of all, the following pages focus on Filmer's failed
attempt to have *Patriarcha* licensed for publication in 1632,[1] which constitutes
a turning point in the study of the work. The historical and political circumstances in which this episode[2] happened will be connected (in Part II) with
those in which the book was, eventually, published in 1680.

This chapter will thus function as a bridge between the narrative hitherto
developed, and the analysis of Filmerian patriarchalism's successful second
life in the late part of the century. In practice, the 1620s–30s and the 1680s are
here studied as emblems of ideological continuity of which *Patriarcha* is taken
as a prominent instance. More specifically, Filmer's concept of monarchical
authority is further dissected in relation to the central issue of monarchist
patriotism. The interplay of political and gendered codes informing *Patriarcha*
is then unravelled, whilst the context in which it was officially prevented from
being published will be given full and unprecedented attention. This should
thus re-write the history of the text in terms of its political use and theoretical
appeal, as well as encouraging new discussions over the philosophical nature
of early modern political ideas.

CAROLINE ROYALISM IN CONTEXT:
WHAT PLACE FOR FILMER?

In the political controversies animating the early Caroline era *Patriarcha* attacked 'that damnable conclusion which is made by too many that the multitude may correct or depose their prince if need be'.[3] This was the 'interesting' way in which Filmer depicted 'popularity' as the very opposite of what he regarded to be good and valuable.[4] For Sir Robert popular government nourished personal greed and private interest in contrast to the king's search for the public benefit. Whilst democracies lacked loyalty and obedience, kingly rule made harmony and peace thrive.[5] Linked to these issues was the question of the king's prerogative. On the one hand, monarchists asserted that the ruler owned extra-legal powers to confiscate his subjects' property in order to safeguard the public good. On the other hand, their opponents argued that such a power undermined the rule of law since it deprived people of their essential right to private property. The former placed the public interest above individual rights, whereas the latter identified the two spheres and thought that to protect the private goods of every Englishman was to preserve the general interest.

Such rival opinions were put forward in the context of the so-called Forced Loan (1626–27). This was Charles I's attempt to obtain money to undertake his wars against France and Spain. The Royal Council started to levy impositions in mid September 1626 and, despite the fact that several members of the gentry (commissioners) refused to help the Crown and that, in certain cases, they even openly resisted its decisions, the King went on to collect the loan.[6] The Crown made numerous attempts to persuade subjects of the importance and legitimacy of this levy. Charles issued a warrant in which he explicitly ordered the clergy to urge people to pay the fee. Yet a few county gentlemen refused to comply. From this imprisonment and violation of the common law followed.

Most importantly, the Forced Loan provoked a great deal of theoretical discussions that were sustained by divergent ideological stances.[7] In an increasingly heated climate, arguments such as the right to resist royal acts that had not been approved by Parliament became widely popular: treatises of both English and continental resistance theorists were placed under careful scrutiny – so much so that, as early as May 1622, Cambridge booksellers had been 'examined in consistory' concerning purchases of Calvinist works of resistance theory such as the *Vindiciae contra Tyrannos*, Bucanus's *Loci communes* and David Pareus's *Ad Romanos*.[8]

Likewise, a flurry of tracts defending the absolute prerogative of kings voiced their support for the levy of taxes as one of the monarch's powers. To advocate these positions authors often adopted the political languages of Tacitism, reason of State and the *arcana imperii*.[9] On each side, theories explored the relation between kings and subjects, marking out the distance between those who considered Parliament as the guarantor of the people's liberties and staunch partisans of absolute monarchy. Amongst the latter, the loyalist clerics Roger Maynwaring (1589/90–1653), Robert Sibthorpe (d. 1662) and Isaac Bargrave (1586–1643)[10] between February and July 1627 preached a series of sermons that inflamed the political arena. Responding to the instructions that William Laud, Archbishop of Canterbury, had sent to the clergy in order to persuade parishioners of their duty to pay the Forced Loan, these authors urged people to accept the absolute power of monarchs. Thus, expressing unwavering support for the theory of the divine right of kings,[11] Maynwaring, Sibthorpe and Bargrave maintained that kings were responsible for their decisions and actions only before God, from whom their power derived.[12] For this reason, subjects had to obey their monarch and resistance to him was regarded as a crime against divine authority. Most importantly, the political opinions of these preachers coincided with those of Charles I. As a result, they stirred up popular discontent towards the Stuart's authority and prompted discussions on whether complete obedience to kings was due in any circumstance or, instead, some form of opposition to those which were judged to be absolutist policies was justified. Despite Laud's advice to Charles 'to think better' of publishing Maynwaring's work, 'for that there were many things therein which will be very distasteful to the people',[13] the King insisted that the cleric's *Religion and Alegiance* should be printed displaying the inscription of his special command. In July 1628 he sent an order ('three times in one day') to Bishop George Mountain (Montaigne) to ensure that Maynwaring's preaching licence was fully restored after he had been impeached by Parliament because of *Religion and Alegiance*.[14]

The language of these sermons as of many pamphlets issued before the start of the Personal Rule resonated with the consequences of the Caroline disastrous military campaigns of 1625–28: the disintegration of Mansfeld troops, the defeats at Cadiz and La Rochelle.[15] They also echoed the conflict between those who thought God was punishing England because of increasing popery and corruption at court and those in the royalist camp according to whom the King was being betrayed by his subjects.[16] It was in this context[17] that, 'with Charles's government very much in mind', Filmer wrote *Patriarcha*. According to Richard Cust, his theory was part and parcel of the 'conventional' anti-popular mainstream for it employed 'the standard classical sources used by others to discuss the issue'. By identifying private interest, love of faction, innovation, disorder and disobedience with 'the very antithesis of everything he valued', Cust connected Filmer's work with 'assumptions and ideas which were entirely familiar to the king'.[18] As shown by *His Majesties Declaration* of 1640, Charles certainly shared Filmer's critical view of the parliaments of the 1620s, where 'in stead of dutifull expressions towards his person and government, they vented their own malice and disaffections to the state', endeavouring 'nothing more then to bring into contempt and disorder all government and magistracy'.[19]

However, as will be explained in chapter 6, Filmer's attitude towards the royal cause both at the beginning of the conflict and then at the time of military strife differed from what might have been expected of him in light of his political philosophy. Despite being identified as an extreme apologist for the kingly prerogative by the parliamentarians in Kent, 'from the first' – as Laslett pointed out – 'he took only slight action in support of Charles I, and that from a distance'.[20] Perhaps this was a consequence of his having been refused the licence to publish *Patriarcha* (1632). Or, instead, more decisive reasons have to be sought in Filmer's doctrines whose radical approach to politics might have made Charles uncomfortable. After all, following the King's dissolution of Parliament in March 1629 more rigid measures to control what his subjects could read were adopted.[21] Charles established that every work concerning 'matters or affaires of State' was to be published only after 'the view, appro-bation and license of my secretaries Weckherlin, who is to acquainte me of such things as he shall finde cause'.[22] In tightening up restrictions on publi-cations the Stuart wanted to prevent public opinion from tampering with governmental policies. Interestingly, censorship did not exist 'only to perse-cute radicals and separatists'. In fact, as Anthony B. Thompson underlined, '[o]n at least two occasions Weckherlin felt nervous enough about submitted manuscripts that he consulted the king'.[23] One of these occasions involved *Patriarcha*. In this respect, since Charles I's chosen rhetoric of authority was based on 'silence',[24] it is plausible to infer that the treatise did not conform to the King's strategy encapsulated in the 1628 declaration that 'the times are now for action, action I say not words'. This statement meant that it was not only unnecessary to persuade people to fulfil their duties but also dangerous, since doing so could be interpreted as evidence of royal weakness. For this reason, in insisting on the importance and superiority of absolute monarchy, *Patriarcha* reaffirmed something that, from the (early 1630s) ideological stand-point of the King, did not need to be reaffirmed: royal authority.

This would explain also why the other work submitted to Weckherlin at the same time as *Patriarcha* did not obtain the licence. This tract focused on Gustavus Adolphus, King of Sweden between 1611 and 1632. The latter represented in Europe and, especially, in England the hero of the Protestant Cause. He was also a French client and, therefore, at odds with Charles' diplo-matic policies.[25] At a moment when the Stuart King was still endeavouring to present his authority as the embodiment of virtue and stability, the emergence of the fierce young prince of Sweden and the eulogies he prompted could not but constitute a further cause of anxiety for the Crown. The image of the Protestant icon Gustavus – whose victorious enterprises in Germany in defence of Elizabeth and Frederick had raised the spirits of many enthusiastic Protestants – could only increase the gap between Charles and the nation. By electing Gustavus Adolphus to the role of defender of the interests of the anti-Catholic coalition, many works came to be seen as a form of reproach directly addressed to Charles. However, Gustavus' sudden death on the battlefield of Lutzen in November 1632 marred the expectations of many English Protestants. This prompted an array of highly commendatory poems dedicated to the heroic memory of the King of Sweden whose motivations and deeds were depicted as 'the measure of true kingship', which in the late 1620s–early 1630s in England was seen as amply neglected.[26]

In this milieu works that focused on Gustavus Adolphus or that, like *Patriarcha*, carved out a new model of kingship could be seen as daring criticism of Charles' policies and/or as not entirely in tune with his view of power. By representing the Swedish prince or the patriarchal ruler as the ideal monarch, these writings did not match the ends of the Caroline regime. In other words, to praise a ruler who had aggressively promoted the Protestant Cause against the upholders of the anti-Christ was a pungent way of remarking that both James I and his son had failed to intervene to aid Elizabeth and Frederick in the Palatinate in 1620.[27] Similarly irreconcilable to Charles' ideal of monarchy was Filmer's Adamite model. This did not include Eve and as such hindered the Stuart's attempt to propel an image of the Crown whose keynote was the happy marriage between the King and the Queen. In this respect, *Patriarcha* did not respond to the pacifying and idealised portrayal of royalty that the court had been striving to foster since the mid–late 1620s.[28]

As illustrated in chapter 2, it was only one week after Charles had decided to limit the freedom of thinkers to address political affairs that Weckherlin submitted Filmer's treatise to the King. The latter showed no hesitation in denying the licence for publication. More hesitant, by contrast, is the historian at work in finding plausible answers to clarify the monarch's decision. Amongst the very few who engaged in this task Richard Cust suggested that Charles regarded Filmer's principles as too extreme and, therefore, unsuited for an audience already hostile to the Stuart government.[29] Similarly, Anthony Milton had previously argued that the type of absolutism Filmer, Kynaston and Hobbes expounded has to be kept separate from the main current of royalist thought. As 'pure absolutists', they represented a 'small' group of thinkers whose political principles did not correspond to the model pursued by the Crown.[30] In particular, Filmer countenanced an 'extreme' form of 'absolute royal sovereignty' which distanced his work from the more 'moderate and traditional' ideas held by the King and by Thomas Wentworth. According to Milton, the royal refusal to send *Patriarcha* into print and the lack of any clear proof that Kynaston's *A True Presentation* had been 'recommended for publication' indicate that Charles intended to remove himself from the 'outspokenly public "absolutist" trends of thought' of these two theorists.[31] By the same token, at his trial Archbishop Laud told prosecutors that several absolutist treatises had been written but denied publication in the course of the Personal Rule.[32] Laud wanted to dissociate himself from the works of Filmer, Kynaston, Hobbes, Heylyn, that is, from their 'set of answers to a "crisis of the mixed constitution" – a crisis that is just as evident in the anxieties and presuppositions behind the thoughts and actions of Charles, Wentworth, Laud, Finch and others'.[33] For Anthony B. Thompson, 'Charles's unwillingness to see Filmer in print ... resulted in large part from his inability to control news pamphlets'.[34] Sir Robert's case simply 'shows that authors sometimes came to Weckherlin and by-passed the stationer, perhaps hoping that a direct approach to the Latin secretary would enhance their chances of receiving the licence'.[35]

Although accurate and persuasive, these views do not take into account that at the time of his refusal Charles had already dismissed Parliament and was trying to increase his power by removing all obstacles to his projects. This seems to be at odds with the hypothesis that the King's sole reason for not having *Patriarcha* printed was its radical absolutist language, when de facto the Stuart ruler was putting into practice policies that Filmer's theories could be employed to justify.[36] More persuasively, Cust has recently argued that the sovereign 'did not feel confident about himself as a monarch until well into the 1630s when he had made a success of being a father and found assurance in this role as leader of a nation at peace'.[37] This last aspect of Charles' personality and political conduct might indicate that the decision of preventing the publication of *Patriarcha* had something to do with the process of royal-image construction which was aimed at re-adjusting to a (*truly*) male monarchy.

THE *CUNNING* PATRIARCHALIST (RE)-APPROPRIATION OF PATRIOTISM: A THEORETICAL APPROACH

That patriarchalism was the instrument through which Filmer addressed the vital issue of the relationship between monarch and subjects might be well known. That *Patriarcha* reinvigorated the fatherly bond between king and country[38] only a few years after accusations of parricide had been laid at the door of the incumbent sovereign[39] and at a time when – despite tragically failing – Charles I himself had insisted 'on making trust the touchstone of his relations with Parliament and the political nation generally'[40] is highly significant and needs multiple considerations. Firstly, the Filmerian attempt to establish a model of polity conceived along fatherly lines drew on principles whereby kings were either natural fathers of their people, or heirs of these original fathers, or had 'to be reputed' as the legitimate heirs to the first natural fathers.[41] Secondly, *Patriarcha* was also a sign that, despite the overwhelming importance monarchy had for the great majority of English people, Filmer saw it necessary to reaffirm that this was the most historical, natural and divine polity in the world.

Confronted by what Kevin Sharpe has called the binary but intertwined processes of 'mystification' and 'demystification' of monarchy,[42] Filmer presented kingship under the de-mystified image of patriarchalist rule and its fatherly leader. Defending the process of Adamite mono-genesis, he depicted humankind as initially constituted by one family. Albeit divided into many nations as a consequence of 'the confusion of Babel', men were still descendants of Adam through Noah. For Filmer this was sufficient to guarantee '[n]ot only until the Flood, but after it, ... patriarchal power'.[43] The 'confusion of tongues' neither produced chaos, which would have implied the absence of Adam's original directing power, nor set 'multitudes ... at liberty to choose what governors and government they pleased'. Filmer held that there were 'heads' and 'fathers' ruling over 'distinct families' and that all of them derived from Adam and his immediate descendant Noah.[44] From a political standpoint, it followed that '[i]t is but the negligence or ignorance of the people to lose the knowledge of the true heir, for an heir there always is'. This was so to the extent that, '[i]f Adam himself were still living, and now ready to die, it is certain that there is one man, and but one in the world, who is next heir, although the knowledge who should be that one man be quite lost'.[45] Filmer's patriarchalist model implicitly rejected the concept of a community of natives who had the right to bypass the authority of the fatherly king. By placing Adam in the forefront of his political discourse, he depicted the sovereign as father of the fatherland and the nation as a patriarchal monarchy. The fatherly king personified the body of the nation. Conceiving the State as the emanation of a single person and his mighty will guaranteed stability. The Filmerian king embodied the inviolable nature of the temporal authority of the national sovereign.

The Adamite paradigm also consolidated the perpetuity of the *patria*. It dismissed the alternative perspective that gave primacy to the constitutional triad 'people–Parliament—law' as representatives of the country. By relying on the polycentric nature of patriotism, Filmer associated the image of the monarch with that of the father. Rhetorically forceful, his message aimed to create a mutuality of interests between ruler and nation at a historical juncture of mounting dissatisfaction with the King's policies. In practice, *Patriarcha*'s articulation of monarchy responded to the problem of situating the identity of the kingdom. If the Tudor era had 'invoked' the king 'as the guardian of the social order, but not as its creator',[46] Filmer overcame this view by identifying sovereigns with the political power of Adam – 'the father of all flesh'.[47] This step had a twofold political meaning: firstly, it solved the problem of continuity since the creation of monarchical government corresponded to the origins of political society; secondly, it interpreted the creation of laws and customs as the outcome of the supreme decision of the *lex loquens* king.[48] In this way the king was depicted not only as *father of the law* but also as *father of the land*. He was the shaper of the nation's ethos. In other words, he was the creator of a monarchically wrought national identity. The Adamite monarch became thus the creator of meaning in the whole polity: his voice validated political authority.[49] This clarifies why Filmer rejected patriotic, 'puritanical' and Jesuit doctrines: they threatened the officially legitimising political and legal agency. They challenged the word of the ruler. In fact, when at the beginning of *Patriarcha* Filmer declared that it was 'hard to say whether ... the vulgar opinion' defending popular government was 'more dangerous in divinity or dangerous in policy',[50] he had in mind active resistance to the kingly monopoly of validation in political and ecclesiastical affairs. Equally, Filmer vehemently dismantled all parliamentarian claims (sustained by the Cokean view of the common law) whereby immemorial regulations and precedents could act as bridles on the free will of the ruler. This was akin to diverting the vocal agency of legal authority from the king to the fictitious medium of the common law.[51]

According to Filmer, in creating the law the king was totally independent from any other law. The law was the result of a decision isolated from any kind of legal context. It originated in the void of pre-existing regulations.[52] The rules implemented by the monarch came into being within a total absence of legal framework or legislative control. Filmer emphasised the centrality of he who made the law; of he who gave existence to it. He fused narrative of right and narrative of might.[53] His theory of sovereignty was informed by the juxtaposition of origins and principles; by the identification of law and power; by the metaphorical overlapping of Adam and king.

Patriarcha has thus to be seen as a representation of what Sharpe has called 'the social and political structure of the Renaissance English state'.[54] It articulated a new narrative of political thought within a framework familiar to many, namely the patriarchal structure of society. Whilst scholars as ideologically different as Gordon Schochet, Glenn Burgess and Carole Pateman all argued that for Filmer 'paternal and political power were not merely analogous but *identical*',[55] it is important to highlight that his discourse did not rely exclusively on this identification. As we have seen in chapters 2 and 4, fathers and kings had clearly different roles to fulfil in the body politic. Filmer's work was not primarily dependent on patriarchal ideology and its prescriptions on the role of the father in the family. In fact, he did not expound a theory of the jurisdiction of the 'father–husband–householder'. In his political tracts he did not sketch a picture of life in the family, nor did he analyse the place of wives in the household. Rather, he was chiefly concerned with developing a political theory which made socio-political cohesion dependent upon *the word and the sword* of the absolute monarch. Most importantly, Sir Robert delineated an idea of rulership whose mainstay was the king conceived as the new Adam reigning over the fatherland.[56] He realised that the model of the king as *pater patriae*, which 'the Protestant Reformation had enormously bolstered',[57] was a powerful weapon to deploy in the battle of ideas between opposing views of government and nation.[58]

As mentioned in the previous chapter, his patriarchalist portrayal of the sovereign was the political equivalent of what van Dyck pursued at pictorial level. In transposing Adam, the first father, into the earthly political debates of early seventeenth-century England, Filmer contributed to this ongoing process of royal-image construction. If political arguments are 'words and images put together to persuade an audience of something',[59] then *Patriarcha* was an attempt to regain the fading trust in monarchy which many county gentlemen and MPs had begun to withhold. As van Dyck's representation of Charles unfolded 'three faces' of the monarch as 'the unimpeacheable enemy of corruption, the father of his country, and the leader of a polite and commercial people',[60] thus Filmer focused on the second motif to forge an image of the ruler as 'patriot king'.[61]

THE DOUBLE EDGE OF PATRIARCHALISM. KING VERSUS COUNTRY: A BATTLE OF REPRESENTATION(S)

As Glenn Burgess has persuasively pointed out, republican theorists were not unique in appropriating the notion of patriotic liberty and love of country. Monarchist thinkers did so too by associating loyalty to the king with allegiance to the nation.[62] This had illustrious sixteenth-century predecessors: in William Shakespeare's *Richard II* king and nation were patriotically identified. According to Gerald Newman, in the early modern period patriotism 'usually focused upon the king': hence Shakespeare's patriotic evocation of primitive fidelity to England as a 'royal throne of kings'.[63] However, in *Richard II* Shakespeare proved to be aware that patriotism was a double-edged political tool. On the one hand, it could mean support for the country against the king, a position embraced by Gaunt who opposed Richard II by elevating England to primary object of protection.[64] On the other hand, Shakespeare set forth the monarchical nature of English patriotism by eliciting an image of the king as interwoven to

> This blessed plot, this earth, this realm, this England,
> This nurse, this teeming womb of royal kings,
> Feared by their breed and famous by their birth
> Renowned for their deeds as far from home.[65]

In line with this view, but approximately thirty years later, Thomas Heywood's *Funeral Elegie upon King James* (1625) explicitly defined the king as 'royall Patriot'.[66] In 1630 the royal printer 'was required' to fulfil his patriotic 'services in printing ... King Iames his works ... for ye advancement of

151

our religion & honor of ye Nation'.[67] In particular, the promotion of James' *Meditations* was part of a vast ideological and political enterprise at the heart of which stood the reaffirmation of national self-interest along monarchist lines. Likewise, in the wake of the Bohemian crisis, Ben Jonson's *Pan's Anniversary* (1621) had provided a powerful image of the nation as governed by the orderly 'Royall Pan'. This presented 'a king-centered idea of nationalism to oppose the nativist and anti-courtly patriotism of the Spenserians'.[68]

Furthermore, because James I had neither deployed his army on the battlefield, nor had he joined the polemical fray sparked off by the Thirty Years War, many Protestants saw his pacifism and the decision not to help his daughter in Bohemia as evidence that he had failed to fulfil his paternal duties. Since Queen Elizabeth Tudor was a woman and had died unmarried (making it impossible to reconcile kingship and paternity), King James was expected to play the role of the caring father of the country. However, it was the Commons' policy of intervention in the Palatinate that was depicted as 'vigorous and masculine' in contrast to the *rex pacificus' effeminate* diplomatic choices.[69] In fact, James' negligence proved to have lasting consequences on the political representation of royalty during the reign of his son Charles. As Thomas Cogswell explained, the idea as well as the ideal of a pacifying reign to which James had been inclined throughout was at the end of his realm simply not viable. The voice of the people was clear: it cried 'war, war, war'. Those who did not sustain this popular refrain incurred the ire of many subjects. Above all, one acting in this way was tellingly called a 'royalist',[70] which meant to be seen as unpatriotic. To refuse war was tantamount to dismiss one's interest in safeguarding England. And the events of 1624, with the turn of fortune occurring to Buckingham and Charles as the result of their allying with the 'patriot coalition' to support war against Spain (and their consequent acquiring a positive reputation in the eyes of Parliament and the public), clearly show the prominence of patriotism in early seventeenth-century England.[71]

In this context many Protestants relied on the flourishing market of newsbooks and corantos persistently reporting on events from the continent to mount a stream of patriotic propaganda in favour of Elizabeth and Frederick. The latter were, in fact, the symbols of the holy war against the Roman anti-Christ.[72] In their quest for an alternative image of monarchy, the representatives of the 'common people' advocated the importance of constitutional guarantees to limit the arbitrariness of kingly authority. A host of parliamentary discourses used 'country' to symbolise a fatherly and protective entity acting at the collective level through its trusted representatives in Parliament to preserve the interests of freeborn Englishmen.[73] This rhetoric stemmed from civic humanist treatises like John Barston's *The Safeguard of Societie* (1576), which argued that 'our native country is the universall parente of us all, for which no good man will refuse his life'.[74]

To respond to this argument it was necessary to re-appropriate the ideas of people like Richard Morison (c. 1510–56), who was one of the first English thinkers to combine humanist values of civility with the theory of the divine rights of kings.[75] In his *Lamentation in whiche is Shewed what Ruyne and Destruction Cometh of Seditious Rebellyon*, written against the Pilgrimage of Grace (1536), Morison had conceived defence of the commonwealth and obedience to the monarch as part of the same duty. He had successfully fused loyalty to the prince and loyalty to the country by arguing that the citizen was a subject 'bound inevitably to obey the laws made by his king for the common weal'.[76] Hence rebels were depicted as unpatriotic sinners.

In the next century, monarchists like Filmer, Forsett and Kynaston continued on this theoretical route: by identifying king and nation, they rejected the opinion fostered by republican and godly patriots, public men and MPs that love of country meant primarily allegiance to Parliament.[77] Filmer argued that people had to obey the king if they truly wanted to promote the interests of their country. Therefore, being faithful to the country as claimed by the 'common people' entailed being unfaithful to the sovereign. This was so because the latter *was* the country and as such could not be dissociated from the representation of the national commonweal. The ruler was identified *tout court* with the nation, so that those who aspired to become martyrs for their native land by fighting the king (in Parliament, in the localities and in print) inevitably betrayed the kingly *pater patriae*. Whilst in the sixteenth century patriotic duties and obedience to the king had (to a large degree) coexisted,[78] *Patriarcha* showed that in the 1620s 'patriot' was no longer a neutral term:[79] defining oneself as a 'patriot' or being labelled as such meant to be a partisan of the country against absolutist kingship. It suggested allegiance to a cause that had its focal point in the protection of the liberties and rights of freeborn Englishmen against royal abuse, Catholicism and foreign cultural taste. In the domain of ideas commonwealth patriotism corresponded to the rejection of the concept of absolutist royal prerogative and unaccountable kingly power.

The outcome of this conflict at both practical and ideological level found an interesting and topical moment. This occurred at the end of the 1670s: the wheel of fortune turned full circle when the issue of the preservation of the nation came to the fore again. In consequence, *Patriarcha* was made public since it enabled monarchists to portray the king as the fatherly protector of the fatherland. At pains to strengthen the hereditary tie between the future James II and the country, royalist supporters found in *Patriarcha* the fiercest defence of monarchical legitimacy against all external pretences to obtain the English Crown.[80] Once more, in the collective imagery as much as in the more rarefied world of intellectual debates two political groups formed: courtiers, loyalists, Yorkists, on one side, and countrymen, patriots, republicans, on the other.[81]

In substance, both Filmer's attempt to publish his treatise (1632) and its actual publication (1680) remind us that the military, political, cultural crisis the monarchy faced at those two historical junctures was largely the same. His work was an attempt to respond to such a crisis. It was also a radical and distinct way of doing so. Despite Sidney's[82] and Locke's[83] opinion to the contrary, Filmer's patriarchalism did not correspond to the perspectives of Maynwaring and Sibthorpe.[84] As this book shows, *Patriarcha* was neither a propagandist piece like the sermons of these clerics, nor an occasional tract exclusively devoted to defend the idea of monarchical government. Without being celebratory of the Stuart dynasty,[85] Filmer attempted to influence the modes in which many of his contemporaries looked at the institution of monarchy.[86] His *Patriarcha* was thus much more than a tract written to justify royal attempts to impose taxes indiscriminately. With its thorough articulation of kingship it remodelled the image of the sovereign. The Filmerian account of supreme power moulded a form of 'rational authoritarianism'[87] which pointed towards the construction of the (rational) State. The same cannot be said of the Arminian political thinking of Maynwaring, Sibthorpe and Bargrave. Their discourse was still heavily couched in the language of divinity. In their works God occupied centre stage. Unlike Filmer, they equated obedience and reverence in the Church with obedience and reverence in the polity.[88] In substance, a major difference between Sir Robert's theory and the doctrines of Maynwaring, Sibthorpe and Bargrave was his systematically patriarchalist configuration of politics. And this is precisely why Filmer – rather than the other authors – left a mark on the late seventeenth-century political and ideological landscape. In fact, he set forth his patriarchalist account of sovereignty in such a stringent way that fifty years later (1680s) his words were still inflaming political debates. Above all, they led some of the most excellent minds of the century to test their philosophical acumen and political wit in lengthy replies.[89]

Before analysing in detail the context(s) in which Filmer's patriarchalism acquired its posthumous fame, we need to consider the period of his life and work following the writing of *Patriarcha*.

NOTES

1 Neither Schochet nor Daly was aware of Filmer's request for the royal licence. According to the former, '[s]ometime in the early 1640s he wrote *Patriarcha*, ... and manuscript copies circulated among the manor houses of Kent, ... [b]ut the work was apparently never intended for a larger audience, and Filmer would not agree to requests that he publish his essay. Thus, *Patriarcha* was withheld from the press during its author's life' (Schochet, *Patriarchalism in Political Thought*, p. 116). Likewise, for Daly Filmer realised that 'there was no point in publishing his first work when occasion seemed to prompt him to expand parts of it instead' (Daly, *Sir Robert Filmer*, p. 14). Daly suggested that,

although in his writings he had not made any direct reference to the contemporary political situation, Filmer had written *Patriarcha* in order to defend the monarchy in the Ship Money controversy (*ibid.*, p. 4).

2 This refers to the manuscript note that was found in the Trumbull Papers in 1989. The title of the sale catalogue is *The Trumbull Papers. Day of Sale Thursday 14th December 1989* ('Sotheby's 1989'). The relevant item is no. 44. It is described on p. 121 and illustrated on p. 122.

3 *PT*, p. 32.

4 Cust, 'Charles I and Popularity', pp. 243–4.

5 See *PT*, pp. 32 ff.

6 Cust, *The Forced Loan*, p. 3 and *passim*.

7 See *ibid.*, pp. 4 ff.

8 D. D. Brautigam, 'Prelates and Politics: Uses of "Puritan", 1625–40', in Lunger Knoppers (ed.), *Puritanism and Its Discontents*, pp. 49–66, p. 64.

9 See e.g. P. Burke, 'Tacitism, Scepticism, and Reason of State', in Burns and Goldie (eds), *The Cambridge History of Political Thought 1450–1700*, pp. 479–98; J. H. M. Salmon, 'Seneca and Tacitus in Jacobean England', in Levy Peck (ed.), *The Mental World of the Stuart Court*, pp. 169–88; Tuck, *Philosophy and Government, passim*.

10 See Roger Maynwaring, *Religion and Alegiance* (1627), esp. pp. 19–20, 26–30; Robert Sibthorpe, *Apolostike Obedience Shewing the Duty of Subjects to pay Tribute and Taxes to their Princes ...* (1627), e.g. p. 23; on Bargrave see below. To these should be added the Bishop of Ely Matthew Wren (1585–1667), author of the controversial *A Sermon Preached before the Kings Majestie* (1627).

11 Sommerville pointed out that the term 'Divine Right of Kings' is 'a misnomer, for absolutists asserted the natural right of all governments' (Sommerville, *Royalists and Patriots*, p. 13).

12 For an illustration of the variety of radically absolutist positions in early seventeenth-century England see L. Levy Peck, 'Beyond the Pale: John Cusacke and the Language of Absolutism in Early Stuart Britain', *HJ*, 41 (1998), pp. 121–49.

13 Cited in Cust, *The Forced Loan*, p. 62.

14 Davies, *The Caroline Captivity*, p. 34, n. 152.

15 In the 1620s England also experienced an economic crisis that badly affected trade (*ibid.*, pp. 52–5). In addition, the country had to confront one of the most devastating plagues since the Black Death, with the inevitable economic disaster (Hirst, *England in Conflict*, pp. 113–14).

16 *Ibid.*, pp. 77, 112–22.

17 See Cust, *The Forced Loan*, p. 67.

18 Cust, 'Charles I and Popularity', pp. 243–4.

19 Cited in C. Russell, *The Causes of the English Civil War* (Oxford, 1990), p. 205. By 1626 both Laud and Wren had identified Puritanism with 'political subversion, by which they meant the recent parliamentary opposition to Charles I' (Davies, *The Caroline Captivity*, p. 14).

20 Laslett, 'The Man', p. 533.

21 Thompson, 'Licensing the Press', pp. 662–3.

22 Cited in *ibid.*, p. 666 (for the original see BL, Trumbull MS, Misc. Corr., xviii, fo. 104).

23 Thompson, 'Licensing the Press', p. 678.

24 Sharpe, *Remapping*, pp. 143–4.

25 Hirst, *England in Conflict*, p. 146. In fact, following Buckingham's death, Charles had attempted to establish peace with France and Spain so as to appease mounting hostility towards his policies (*ibid.*, pp. 117 ff.).

26 R. Wilcher, *The Writing of Royalism 1628–1660* (Cambridge, 2001), p. 15.

27 See Hirst, *England in Conflict*, pp. 103–12.

28 See Wilcher, *The Writing of Royalism*, pp. 11–12.

29 Cust, 'Charles I and Popularity', pp. 243–4.

30 A. Milton, 'Thomas Wentworth and the Political Thought of the Personal Rule', in J. F. Merritt (ed.), *The Political World of Thomas Wentworth, Earl of Strafford, 1621–1641* (Cambridge, 1996), pp. 133–56, p. 155. According to Mark Goldie, the doctrines of Hobbes and Filmer were the exception rather than the rule in royalist political thinking. After all, James Tyrrell was to roundly observe that the Filmerian view of power 'savours of Mr Hobbes' divinity' (cited in M. Goldie, 'The Reception of Hobbes', in Burns and Goldie (eds), *The Cambridge History of Political Thought 1450–1700*, pp. 589–610, p. 610).

31 Milton, 'Thomas Wentworth', p. 155.

32 *ODNB*, 'Laud, William'. Laud was impeached by Parliament for high treason and executed in 1645.

33 Milton, 'Thomas Wentworth', p. 155.

34 Thompson, 'Licensing the Press', p. 669.

35 *Ibid.*, p. 668.

36 However, Filmer's arguments do not seem to agree *tout court* with Charles' immoderate taxation policies and with other vexatious administrative measures taken up to the 1640s.

37 Cust, 'Was There an Alternative to the Personal Rule?', pp. 350–1.

38 See e.g. *PT*, pp. 5, 12.

39 See Zaller, 'The Figure of the Tyrant', p. 602; P. Croft, *King James* (Basingstoke, 2003), pp. 127–8; S. Fang Ng, *Literature and the Politics of Family in Seventeenth-Century England* (Cambridge, 2007), p. 60.

40 Zaller, 'The Figure of the Tyrant', p. 591, n. 26.

41 *PT*, p. 10. It should not be forgotten, however, that *Patriarcha* admitted election, donation, succession and usurpation as legitimate sources of political power.

42 On this see Sharpe, *Criticism and Compliment*; Sharpe, *The Personal Rule of Charles I*; Sharpe, *Remapping*.

43 *PT*, p. 7.

44 *Ibid.*, pp. 7–8.

45 *Ibid.*, p. 10.

46 D. M. Loades, 'Literature and National Identity', in Loewenstein and Mueller (eds), *The*

Cambridge History of Early Modern English Literature, pp. 201–28, pp. 227–8.

47 *AN*, p. 139.

48 *PT*, p. 52.

49 On the function of the royal voice see H. Love, *Scribal Publication in Seventeenth Century England* (Oxford, 1993), pp. 161–2.

50 *PT*, p. 3.

51 On some of these themes see also chapter 2 above.

52 Sir Walter Raleigh had elaborated a similar idea by calling 'entire' a power not derived from other human sources, that is, not shared with anybody else but independent in its fullness (see J. H. Burns, 'The Idea of Absolutism', in J. Miller (ed.), *Absolutism in Seventeenth-Century Europe* (1990), pp. 21–42, pp. 25–6). However, this does not make Raleigh an absolutist in the same terms as Filmer since the former recognised a form of popular power in government and admitted limited rulership (*ibid.*, p. 26).

53 Susan Wiseman separated the moment of right from that of might in Filmer's political theory. According to her, 'patriarchal theory produced in the war years focuses on the intimate link between father and son in determining who is king' (S. Wiseman, "Adam, the Father of All Flesh': Porno-Political Theory in and After the English Civil War', in J. Holstun (ed.), *Pamphlet Wars. Prose in the English Revolution* (1992), pp. 134–57, p. 138). Wiseman also argued (unconvincingly) that '[i]n constantly tracing political authority back to Adam, Filmer produced a vision of the first fathers establishing something very much like colonial plantations' (*ibid.*, p. 150).

54 K. Sharpe, 'The Royal Image: An Afterword', in Corns (ed.), *The Royal Image*, pp. 288–309, p. 289.

55 C. Pateman, *The Sexual Contract* (Cambridge, 1988), p. 24. See also Schochet, *Patriarchalism in Political Thought, passim* and Burgess, *The Politics of the Ancient Constitution*, p. 134.

56 In a manuscript titled *Treatises on Rebellion* and attributed to Filmer by Schochet (Schochet, 'New Bibliographical Discoveries', pp. 135–47) the author said that, after the first phases of political society, 'at last many heads did center in one supreame, many naturall Parents chose one common parent to them all (or *Pater Patriae*) to whome they submitted the excercise of the legislative power so it was before in every father of a family, over whose children and servants he had a power over to life and death' (BDO, Tanner MS 233, *Treatise on Rebellion*, fos 75–133, fos 80–1; italics added). Whereas Laslett referred to this work and others in the same volume of the Tanner MSS as Filmer's (Laslett, 'The Man', p. 541, n. 53; for the other works see below in this note), Sommerville decided not to include them in his new edition of Sir Robert's political tracts as 'internal evidence renders Schochet's attributions doubtful' (Sommerville, 'Introduction', p. xxxvii). On his part, Daly convincingly (and *definitely*) ruled out Schochet's hypotheses with regard to Filmer's possible authorship of these manuscripts: above all, he showed the great distance separating political statements to be found in this material from Sir Robert's known absolutist principles (Daly, *Sir Robert Filmer*, Appendix B, pp. 194–8). Personally, I agree with Sommerville and Daly: I am not persuaded the tract on rebellion is Filmer's in that, despite the patriarchalist motifs punctuating the text, the language adopted does not correspond to Sir Robert's. Especially, the description of tyranny sketched in this manuscript as well as in the printed *Discourse on Government and Common Right* (where parts of the former ended up) is far from Filmer's staunch

denial that tyranny applied to monarchy. The manuscript goes as far as to advocate disobedience to a usurping or illegitimate power. Moreover, the opinions expressed here with reference to limited and mixed monarchy, popular power, election, consent, obedience, fundamental laws are largely incompatible with *Patriarcha* or any of his later tracts. In other terms, I see the author(s) of these manuscripts – mainstream royalists for Daly – as too mild in comparison with Filmer. For instance, there is too much talking of limited power and kings' duties towards their subjects (see *Treatise on Rebellion*, e.g. fo. 88). It is then argued that 'we finde no (jus) no right for tyranny and arbitrary power; which is to be esteemed a Sin' (*ibid.*, fo. 97; see as well *ibid.*, fo. 85 for un-Filmerian attacks on 'usurping tyrants' whose 'martiall sword' engendered 'the oppression of the people'). In these pages, God's role had primacy over the ruler's (see *ibid.*, e.g. fos 124, 130–3). In addition, the use of sources and metaphorical language are not those generally to be found in Sir Robert's works. Finally, there are too few references to other authors, as it was common for Filmer to do. Nor are the arguments sophisticated and elaborate enough to be his. To assign the material in Tanner 233 to him would produce a picture of a very inconsistent and contradictory Filmer. In any case, these manuscript pages would not add anything new about his thought since they expound traditional monarchist rhetoric and unyieldingly criticise all forms of popular government (see *ibid.*, fos 75–133, esp. fos 75–86). Other two pieces deal with power (fos 38–74) and with the Engagement (fos 135–47). There follows *A Discourse upon a case of conscience not mine, but by a learned Divine* (fos 148–71, ascribed to Filmer by Bancroft and titled *Of military employments, how far lawful* in the BDO Tanner catalogue); *Concerning actions in things indifferent* (fos 172–6); *Defence of the preceding treatise* (fos 177 ff.).

57 von Friedeburg, 'The Making of Patriots', p. 891.

58 Despite Filmer's infrequent adoption of the terms '*pater patriae*', 'fatherland' and '*patria*', this book shows that in many passages he was at work to elicit images of the sovereign which were akin to the meanings generally attached to these expressions.

59 R. Weil, *Political Passions. Gender, the Family and Political Argument in England 1680–1774* (Manchester, 1999), p. 13.

60 Sharpe, *Remapping*, p. 445.

61 This concept was to be elaborated by Lord Bolingbroke (1678–1751) in *The Idea of a Patriot King* (1738): see D. Armitage, 'A Patriot for Whom? The Afterlives of Boling-broke's Patriot King', *JBS*, 36 (1997), pp. 397–418, p. 406. See also Condren, *Argument and Authority*, p. 154 for the appeal to the ruler as the patriotic guardian of public care and pursuer of the nation's good whose (English) model was Queen Elizabeth.

62 G. Burgess, 'Patriotism in English Political Thought, 1530–1660', in R. von Friedeburg (ed.), *'Patria' und 'Patrioten' vor dem Patriotismus* (Wiesbaden, 2005), pp. 215–41, p. 237.

63 G. Newman, *The Rise of English Nationalism. A Cultural History 1740–1830* (1987), p. 53. See also C. McEachern, *The Poetics of English Nationhood, 1590–1612* (Cambridge, 1996), pp. 5–33.

64 Brennan, *Patriotism, Power and Print*, p. 104.

65 William Shakespeare, *King Richard II*, ed. C. R. Forker (2002), 2.1.50–3, pp. 246–7.

66 Cited in Burgess, 'Patriotism in English Political Thought', p. 230.

67 Cited in D. Fischlin, '"To Eate the Flesh of Kings": James VI and I, Apocalypse, Nation, and Sovereignty', in Fischlin and Fortier (eds), *Royal Subjects*, pp. 388–420, p. 408.

68 C. Perry, "'If Proclamations Will Not Serve": The Late Manuscript Poetry of James I and the Culture of Libel', in Fischlin and Fortier (eds), *Royal Subjects*, pp. 205–32, p. 221.

69 Underdown, *A Freeborn People*, p. 27. This aspect of James' legacy is rather paradoxical considering his deliberate rhetorical efforts to present himself as caring father of the country (see chapter 4 above).

70 Cogswell, *The Blessed Revolution*, p. 310.

71 On this see *ibid.*, pp. 84 ff.

72 Clegg, *Press Censorship in Jacobean England*, pp. 172–3.

73 See chapter 4 above.

74 Cited in Cust, 'The "Public Man"', p. 118.

75 Burgess, 'Patriotism in English Political Thought', p. 222.

76 Cited in *ibid.*, p. 222. According to Burgess, in this milieu 'royalist patriotism' had three theoretical components: liberty identified with property and its protection; the law of the land; kingship.

77 For Burgess, however, in early modern English patriotic parlance republicanism and monarchism coexisted thanks to the figure of the subject-citizen (*ibid.*, p. 228).

78 Land and monarchy were, instead, seen as 'in opposition' to each other rather than as overlapping terms in works such as John Leyland's *Itinerary* (from the years between 1535 and 1543), William Harrison's *Description of Britain* (1577) and William Camden's *Britannia* (1586). These exemplified the separation of land and king as cornerstones of England's national identity (Brennan, *Patriotism, Power and Print*, p. 121).

79 On the neutrality of meaning of 'patriot' see Burgess, 'Patriotism in English Political Thought', pp. 232, 240. Mary G. Dietz erroneously maintained that '[u]ntil near the end of the seventeenth century ... "patriot" lay relatively idle in English political discourse' (M. G. Dietz, 'Patriotism', in T. Ball, J. Farr and R. L. Hanson (eds), *Political Innovation and Conceptual Change* (Cambridge, 1989), pp. 177–93, p. 182).

80 They did this to a price. That is, they explicitly ignored Filmer's ideas of the legitimacy of conquest and usurpation to gain power. Likewise, they did not focus on his 'Cromwellian' *Directions for Obedience to Governours in Dangerous and Doubtfull Times* (1652), whose arguments were similar to Hobbes' *Leviathan*, a text much despised by Restoration royalists (see chapter 6 below).

81 J. Spurr, *The Post-Reformation. Religion, Politics and Society in Britain 1603–1714* (Harlow, 2006), p. 164.

82 According to Sidney, '[t]he production of Laud, Maynwaring, Sybthorpe, Hobbes, Filmer, and Heylyn seems to have been reserved as an additional curse to compleat the shame and misery of our age and country' (Sidney, *Discourses*, bk. i, ch. 2, p. 11).

83 Locke maintained that to grasp the scope of Filmer's dangerous theoretical novelty and its 'sad Effects' it was necessary to recall 'the Memory of those who were Contemporaries with *Sibthorp* and *Manwering*'. Locke stressed the negative impact that their theories had had on royal policies in the late 1620s and pointed out that Filmer had carried their '[a]rgument farthest, and is supposed to have brought it to perfection' (Locke, *Two Treatises of Government*, bk. i, p. 161).

84 Both Sidney and Locke read Filmer's treatise as a product of Laudian royalism (Scott, *Commonwealth Principles*, pp. 50, 87). It is, however, important to underline that, whilst

Laud's preoccupations were ecclesiastical, Filmer's were exclusively secular. On this point, I disagree with Sommerville's associating the works of the clerics William Beale, Maynwaring and Sibthorpe with those of 'the laymen' Kynaston and Filmer, 'who had little to say about church affairs' (J. P. Sommerville, 'Lofty Science and Local Politics', in T. Sorell (ed.), *The Cambridge Companion to Hobbes* (Cambridge, 1996), pp. 246–73, pp. 255, 258).

85 What Anthony Milton has recently said of Filmer's close friend Heylyn, that is, 'Heylyn had an unshakable belief in monarchy, but not necessarily in the Stuarts', can almost certainly be applied to Sir Robert as well (Milton, *Career and Writings of Peter Heylyn*, p. 226).

86 He was 'a squire who was not a regular attender at court', but one who sent out his political ideas 'in the form of scribally published essays with a fair hope of it reaching the oral decision-makers' (Love, *Scribal Publication*, p. 175).

87 P. K. Monod, *The Power of Kings. Monarchy and Religion in Europe 1589–1715* (New Haven and London, 1999), p. 109.

88 See e.g. Isaac Bargrave, *A Sermon Preached Before King Charles, March 27*[th] *1627 ...* (1627), pp. 4–5, 14.

89 Gaby Mahlberg has convincingly explained that republican texts like Sidney's *Court Maxims* (1665) and Neville's *The Isle of Pines* (1668) conveyed a strong anti-patriarchalist message in order to criticise the restored Stuart monarchy. Mahlberg has also underscored how Neville used republicanism in order to show that monarchical patriarchalism was a morally corrupt theory due to its originating through practices such as incest and polygamy. This was part of a broader attack upon Charles II whose lustful conduct turned on its head the gender image with which patriarchalism depicted the sovereign (Mahlberg, 'Republicanism as Anti-patriarchalism', esp. pp. 138, 144–5).

Chapter 6

Filmer in the 1640s and 1650s: political troubles and intellectual activism

AN IMPORTANT FRIENDSHIP

It was at Westminster that Filmer met one of his closest and most faithful friends: 'the officially accredited voice of Personal Rule policies' Peter Heylyn (1599–1662).[1] Notorious for his sharp tongue, Heylyn was not only a prolific author but was the heavyweight of the Laudian theological, ecclesiastical and ideological settlement. Once appointed to a stall at Westminster Abbey (1631), Heylyn proved to be a skilful preacher whose doctrinal views were in tune with Filmer's. As Heylyn confirmed, their friendship formed at some stage in the 1630s in London: 'my preferment in the Church of *Westminster*, ... gave me the opportunity of so dear and beloved a neighborhood' with Filmer.[2]

A letter Heylyn sent to Sir Robert on 3 July 1648 illustrates the familiarity with which they treated each other. Heylyn declared to be 'much bound to you [Filmer] for your good affections to me in preparing me your whole stock of eye-water, though I am so unfortunate as not to gain benefit of them'.[3] In a humorous tone (even though talking about his physical ailments), Heylyn said to Filmer: '[t]hat viol of you which you gave to me, I spilt in my pocket. So that I have plundered you and done no good to my selfe', but – he added – 'I will not give over the experiment of it'.[4] Heylyn also informed his friend that '[s]ome writing I received from you by my nephew, but I think not all'.[5] Heylyn was always eager to stay in contact with Sir Robert: '[b]efore your going out of Town, where I shall write unto to send it at your convenience. I hope this letter will come time enough to find you in London, or otherwise will come late to you'.[6] He also mentioned his health and his 'whole family' at the East Gates of London, and referred to some questions related to one of his tenants' rent.[7] Grounded on personal sympathy, their close friendship was, above all, based on ideological and political affinities.

A significant example of their solid bond had occurred in 1640, when Heylyn entered the dispute on the right of bishops to submit their proposals to the House of Lords and take part in any matter brought before it. In a sermon preaching the necessity of 'Peace and Unity' between 'men of different persuasions' delivered from the pulpit of Westminster Abbey on 13 December, Heylyn attacked the intransigent positions of his archenemy John Williams, Dean of Westminster (1620) and Bishop of Lincoln (1621),[8] who had just been released from the Tower.[9] Heylyn played the irenicist card and argued that different confessions had to reach peace. Instead of disputing time and again on specific theological principles, he stressed the importance of 'seeking to compose the differences' by considering that the 'diversity of opinions, if wisely managed, would rather tend to the discovery of the Truth, than the disturbance of the Church'.[10] Famously, Heylyn was publicly interrupted by an incensed Williams who cried 'No more of that point'.[11]

Once the sermon was over, Bishop Williams summoned a prebend as witness and demanded of Heylyn a copy. The latter replied that he had already given Williams 'the whole book of Sermons that he then had with him'.[12] On the very same evening, Williams asked to his lodging the sub-dean Newell, Dr Thomas Wilson and Heylyn himself, who categorically refused: he would not go to Williams' cloister but he would meet him either in Parliament or in the law courts or in the public chapter house of the Abbey so as to account for his sermon. To put it briefly, Heylyn did not intend to make this matter private since for him it had a public scope. After a bitter exchange, Heylyn disrobed and

> took Sir *Robert Filmore* his Learned Friend, with some Gentlemen of Quality that were his Auditors, out of the Church along with him to his House, where he immediately Sealed up the Book that contained this Sermon, and other Notes, to which they also set their Seals, that so there might not be the least alteration made in the Sermon.[13]

Besides Filmer, 'who had heard all that passed before',[14] that evening Heylyn was accompanied by John Towers, the royalist and Laudian Bishop of Peterborough.

Always on the front line of political disputes, in the mid–late 1640s Heylyn the political theorist[15] found in Filmer's writings a mine of absolutist stances with which to counterattack adversaries like Henry Parker. In particular, Heylyn was provided with a powerful analysis of government and a penetrating critique of the most important theorists of natural rights.[16] Moreover, the Laudian champion shared with Filmer a conciliatory approach towards the Protectorate: they both subscribed to the notion that obedience to Cromwell was necessarily due except for those acts which went to the detriment of the legitimate governor. By virtue of the fact that the usurper would protect his subjects, to respect his power corresponded – so Heylyn and Filmer argued – to safeguarding the original authority of the momentarily defeated monarch.[17]

162

Heylyn praised his friend's 'eminent abilities in these Political Disputes, exemplified in his judicious observations on *Aristotles* Politiques, as also in some passages on *Grotius, Hunton, Hobbs*, and other of our late Discourses about Formes of Government'.[18] These Filmerian works – Heylyn clarified – 'declare abundantly how fit a Man he might have been, to have dealt in this cause, which I would not willingly should be betrayed by unskilful handing'.[19] Heylyn was here asking Filmer's son for his 'equal Judgement, in whom there is so much of the Father' with regard to the controversy that had involved Heylyn with James Harrington following the publication of *The Stumbling-Block* (1658). An ironic Heylyn concluded by referring to 'those many undeserved civilities, which your Father [Robert], your self, and the rest of your Family, have been from time to time vouchsafed unto'.[20]

As a devoted follower of his political views, Heylyn found it unfortunate that Filmer had not intended to publish 'his Excellent Discourse called *Patriarcha*' for 'it would have given such satisfaction to all our great Masters in the Schools of *Politie*, that all other Tractates in that kind, had been found unnecessary'. However, since Filmer 'did not think it fit while he was alive, to gratifie the Nation in publishing that excellent Piece', his friend had 'adventured on that work'. And this Heylyn had done in spite of 'the Consciousness of my own inability might deter me from, if the desire of satisfying the expectation of such a modest and ingenious Adversary [Harrington], had not over ruled me'.[21] Together with showing that Heylyn considered Filmer an unrivalled political thinker, this passage indicates that the clergyman was not aware of Sir Robert's attempt to obtain the royal licence to publish *Patriarcha* as early as 1632. This can be explained with the fact that they probably became close towards the end of the 1630s. Although Heylyn had been appointed at Westminster in 1631, it is likely that, for a certain period after his father's death (1629), Filmer spent more time in Kent managing his household.[22]

Even though Algernon Sidney was to define Heylyn as Filmer's 'master' and as he who had 'guided' the latter,[23] Heylyn's words well illustrate that he recognised his intellectual debt towards Filmer rather than the other way round.[24] After all, Heylyn stated that *Patriarcha* 'might have served for a Catholicon or General Answer to all Discourses' supporting popular power.[25] Since 'Catholicon' commonly indicated a 'drug or medicine', which cured all diseases and provided a universal remedy, Heylyn's claim may be that *Patriarcha* was a solution and a response to faulty political reasoning of all kinds. Heylyn tailored some of Filmer's concepts to his political ends and channelled *Patriarcha* into a specific ideological framework. Hence the treatise came to be associated with the opinions of High Church clerics such as Roger Maynwaring, Robert Sibthorpe[26] and, partly, Heylyn himself.[27]

Crowning this important and intellectually fertile friendship stands the encomiastic letter of consolation that Heylyn was to send on 20 April 1659 to one of 'his ever Honoured Friend''s sons, Edward. In what can be read as an appropriate epitaph too, Heylyn tellingly wrote:

[h]ow great a loss I had in the death of my most dear and honoured Friend, your deceased Father, no man is able to conjecture, but he that hath suffered in the like. So affable was his Conversation, his Discourse so rational, his Judgement so exact in most parts of Learning, and his Affections to the Church so Exemplary in him, that I never enjoyed a greater Felicity in the company of any Man living, than I did in his. I may affirm both with safety and modesty, that we did not only take *sweet Counsel together, but walked in the House of God as Friends*.[28]

This world of erudite rapports informing Filmer's life and work – fully presented in chapter 1 – was put to the test with the opening of the new decade in 1640. The phases post-*Patriarcha* were spent between the fulfilment of some sporadic public duties and the development of both old and new ideas, which were to confirm their author's calibre as a political theorist as much as guarantee him a place in the 'pantheon' of the most targeted thinkers.

FILMER AND THE CIVIL WAR

On 8 November 1641, we find Filmer and another of his acquaintances, Sir John Culpeper,[29] present at the same parliamentary session: as reported by Simonds D'Ewes, 'after praiers upon SIR JOHN CULPEPPERS motion it was ordered that Sir Robert Philmore who had in his hands the polle-monie of the Countie of Kent received upon the review should bee paied in to the Chamberlaine of London'.[30] Filmer was here acting as a commissioner for the Poll Tax. Traces of Filmer's fulfilment of public roles emerge again for the year 1642 when, according to the *Journal of the House of Lords*, 'Sir *Edward Fish*, Baronet, and Sir *Robert Filmer*, Knight, did undertake, Body for Body, That the Bishop of *Bath* and *Wells* shall appear before the Lords in Parliament, on *Friday* come Sevennight; and in the mean Time he is to be at Liberty'.[31]

However, these were to remain isolated episodes in Sir Robert's public engagement. In fact – and quite surprisingly given his political stances – at the outbreak of the Civil War he remained neutral. This was due, partly, to his bad health and age, and, partly, to his reluctance to directly commit to political action. The same had happened during the highly tense parliamentary election of 1640 when he had declined to take sides in the contest between the two main candidates, his friends Edward Dering and Roger Twysden. When the Maidstone Assize began in March 1642, the judge of King's Bench Sir Thomas Malet summoned a grand jury formed by county gentlemen in order to draw up a petition to be presented to Parliament in defence of the royalist cause. The petition contained the invitation to the gentry of Kent to gather at Blackheath on the morning of Friday 29 April 'to accompany the petition to the house'. Seeing this as an overt challenge to their authority, the Commons called the promoters of the petition before the bar of the House. As a result, several people were imprisoned: amongst these was Twysden, for whom – as already explained – Sir Robert stood bail and paid £5000 to have him freed.

Whilst Filmer did not get involved in organising royalist resistance in Kent, his relatives in Colchester, the Argalls, tried to raise troops in support of the King in a county predominantly sided with Parliament.[32] And yet keeping quiet in his house at East Sutton did not spare him troubles: in September of the same year Filmer's estate was ransacked by parliamentarian troops. In some letters from September 1642 and July–August 1643 he gave a full account of the sack of his manor: the soldiers seized his 'horse, arms, furniture, pistol, muskets, billets, and many other things'.[33] In the course of the Civil War his house was searched and his goods sequestered nine times. As both Sir Robert's correspondence and his wife Anne's testimony show, every time bedding and linen were stolen and often money was menacingly requested. Moreover, when on his way to London in July 1643 he was stopped, searched, and his horse kept.

Some time later, Filmer incurred again the suspicions of the parliamentarian leaders in the county (almost certainly as a result of his well-known political opinions). Following some false accusations made by one of his tenants, according to whom he had concealed 'divers arms' in the church at East Sutton, in the winter of 1643 Filmer was imprisoned and, subsequently, sent to Leeds Castle.[34] With Sir Robert in prison, the bulk of the household administration fell upon his wife, Lady Anne, who undertook such a demanding task with resoluteness.[35] She proved not to fear threats like that issued by the staunch parliamentarian Richard Beale, county treasurer and committeeman, warning her of the consequences of not paying taxes.[36] And money was always an issue. Following 'an Ordinance of Parliament dated the 27th of October 1643', on 15 June 1644 Sir Robert had to pay £60 to support Scottish soldiers allied to the English Parliament. Of all those who had to give money (amongst whom was his brother Edward, who paid £9), Sir Robert was by far the most heavily charged.[37]

In the meantime, Anne had succeeded in persuading Anthony Weldon, the unpopular ringleader for the parliamentarians in Kent and, above all, chairman of the County Committee, to keep her husband at Leeds Castle, a prison near home. In a moving and firm letter Anne claimed that their family had already suffered the theft of their coach horses and of five other horses at the hands of the parliamentarian troops. Emphasising the difficult situation in which she had been forced by events, Anne appealed to Weldon to take into account Sir Robert's 'dangerous and painfull infirmity of the stone of wch his father died'.[38] She thus requested that the imprisonment

> may be to a place of wholesome and pure aire ... and that it may be at such a distance that I may be able these shortt dayes to goe and return without indangering my

owne health to give my nessisary attendance on him .... If these trew reasons may be considered you shall doe a charity wch I am confident will hereafter be pleasing to yr. Selves and oblige me to acknowledge myselfe, Sr. Yr humble servant. A. Filmer.[39]

Anne also pleaded her husband's complete innocence by assuring Weldon that he had stayed away 'from medling on either side in deed or so much as words'.[40] Whilst looking after her family, she also dealt with tax collectors and tenants, and again she did so resolutely. In light of her strong character, Anne was very likely an important source of inspiration for the little-known but highly noteworthy tract *In Praise of the Vertuous Wife* (mid 1640s) examined in chapter 1.

Equally ignored by scholars has been Filmer's excursion into theological territory.

FILMER AND THEOLOGY: A SMALL BUT SIGNIFICANT AFFAIR

During his time in prison Filmer wrote a theological tract, *Of the Blasphemie against the Holy-Ghost*, which was on sale by 9 February 1647.[41] Here he showed his erudition on theological matters; singled out Calvin whose doctrines he saw as an example of impiety towards the Holy Ghost; made clear his aversion to all forms of godly and anarchic antinomianism propagated at that time by the sects.[42] To begin with, Filmer targeted those who had followed 'onely their owne *zealous conceits*, and not the *Canon* of holy *Scripture*' in defining '*the Sinne against the Holy Ghost*'.[43] He thought that many people attributed this sin far too easily and carelessly. Amongst these were 'the Schoole-men' and the Jesuit '*Bellarmine*', who 'is so liberale in bestowing' the sin 'upon such as he calls Heretiques'.[44] Indeed, Filmer pointed out, '[n]either are the Papists the onely men that have beene mistaken about this sinne, but too many Divines of the Reformed Churches have started aside from the Scripture' too. As a result, Sir Robert retorted, they gave 'such intricate and contradictory definitions of this sinne, as tend onely to the perplexing of the tender consciences of weake Christians'.[45] Against those whom he considered fanatics intent on destroying England's peace in the mid 1640s, Filmer pleaded for moderation in doctrinal matters such as this. Most importantly, he insisted on the necessity of looking at the Scripture.[46] Following 'the *Evangelists*' Matthew, Mark and Luke, he asserted that 'the *Blasphemie against the Holy-Ghost* is not a sinne committable by any Christian that lived not in the time of our Saviour'.[47]

Despite attacking 'that Great Cardinall' Bellarmine's contradictory and erroneous arguments,[48] Filmer's most piercing criticism was devoted to demolishing 'Master Calvin' whose 'judgement' set out in the *Institutes of the Christian Religion* (1536) had dangerously 'gained the greatest reputation amongst the multitude' in England.[49] Calvin had proclaimed that sinners against the Holy Ghost were those '*who of determined malice resiste the known truth of God to the end onely to resist*'.[50] The Genevan reformer had not only failed to give a precise definition of the sin but he had also wrongly mingled 'the *Truth of God*' and 'the *Word of God*', so that blasphemy was equated to an act of apostasy.[51] Secondly, when speaking of knowledge, Calvin – Filmer continued – must have referred to faith because 'faith is properly by believing and not by knowing the truth'. Thirdly, in using the word '*Resisting*' Calvin must have meant '*unbeleeving*'.[52] In substance, Filmer opposed Calvin's rigid theory by remarking that nobody 'can force himselfe to believe what he lists or when he lists': there are circumstances under which uncertainty prevails and one does not know 'what to beleeve'. In his interesting definition, these are moments of 'suspension' of one's 'faith', of 'trepidation' of one's 'understanding'. Therefore, 'this cannot bee called a resisting of the *Knowne Truth*' since 'the truth is not knowne, but doubted of'.[53] There exists a big difference, Filmer argued, between 'truth of words or speech' and 'truth it selfe' in that the former is merely 'the signe of truth' whilst the latter lies 'in the understanding'. Thus, 'many things believed in *Deed* ... are denied in *word*': such a 'denyall' is no resisting though, but only a show of resistance of truth. From this Filmer inferred that true resistance occurs at the level of understanding, which is where truth resides, whereas 'the understanding can resist no truth, but by unbelieving onely'.[54]

To conclude, for Filmer, Calvin had articulated an impossibility in that a man could not at the same time both believe and disbelieve something. He had made resisting the truth equal to unbelieving what one believes ('to resist the truth which is knowne, which is believed by the resister himselfe, is a direct contradiction'). Hence it resulted that, following Calvin's opinion that any sin might be a sin against the Holy Ghost, this act of resistance was committed by every man on earth and, at the same time, by none at all.[55] Most importantly, Calvin's 'unbridled and unlimited proposition' unleashed 'dangerous inferences' that affected 'weake consciences'.[56] And the dire consequences of such doctrines were everywhere to be seen in the England of the self-proclaimed saints. In contrast to the reigning confusion caused by sectarian hotheads, Filmer's enquiry into 'the *Blasphemie against the Holy-Ghost*' aimed at expounding ideas which were in tune with '*the Doctrine of the* Articles *of the* Church *of* England'.[57] That he succeeded in doing so is confirmed by the fact that in *Theologia Veterum* (1654) Heylyn approvingly referred to the opinions expounded 'by my Learned Friend Sir R.[obert] F.[ilmer] in his *Tractate Of the blaspemiy of the Holy Ghost*'.[58] For in *Ecclesia Restaurata, Ecclesia Vindicata, Aerius Redivivus* and *Historia Quinquarticularis* Heylyn had addressed the main ecclesiastical questions of his time from a strongly Laudian and fiercely anti-Puritan angle, his comment on Filmer's only theological work sheds light on the latter's doctrinal inclinations.

Interestingly, Sir Robert had also shared his long days at Leeds Castle with two theologians who were probably influential in the thinking for and writing of *Of the Blasphemie*. They were the Reverend Robert Dixon (1614/15–88) and John Reading (1587/88–1667). Whilst the former was a royalist divine,[59] the latter – according to Anthony à Wood – was, instead, a '"severe Calvinist", ... a good preacher "very much resorted to for his frequent and edifying sermons, and held in great esteem by the neighbourhood, especially by the puritanical party"'.[60] Nonetheless, during the early 1640s Reading preached forcefully against rebellion and in favour of Charles I. In particular, on 23 August 1641 he had delivered an assize sermon at Maidstone (*A Sermon Delivered*, 1642), which condemned the 'state-threatening schismaticks' and which was dedicated to the royalists Sir Thomas Malet and Sir Edward Dering. Thanks to royal support, Reading gained Laud's favour and this facilitated his appointment to the rectory of Charthan (Kent) in 1643.[61] At Leeds Castle Reading composed *Guide to the Holy City* treating themes close to those of *Of the Blasphemie*.

On the whole, theology was not a subject that occupied much of Filmer's intellectual energies. Besides investigating the issue of blasphemy, at some point (probably in the 1640s) he composed an essay titled *Of the Sabeth*, which was never published. Here he maintained that, although the right form of Sabbath worship had not been established until Moses had received the Law on Mount Sinai, there had always been in place through the ages a type of 'moral Sabeth' commanded by God.[62] A further endeavour to clarify theological matters came in the form of a commentary on and an explanation of the basic precepts of Christian doctrine (the Decalogue, the Apostles's Creed, the Lord's Prayer and the Sacraments). This was the unpublished *Theologie: or Divinity*, which most likely was again a product of the 1640s. This manuscript provided definitions of essential principles of both theology ('Speach concerning god') and divinity ('the knowledge of divine thinges').[63] Often based on a question–answer structure, the work addressed the moral law as 'commanding good: and forbiddinge evill'; the nature of sin; the divinity of the Ten Commandments; the texts and the doctrines of the precepts. He also referred to 'Athiesme' as a mere impossibility ('terror of conscience') and spoke of 'hipocrisie' as detrimental to conscience.[64] By and large, Filmer proved to be a very clear and methodical exponent of the distinctions between the various parts of understanding.[65] He then set forth an analysis of passions such as love, hatred, fear, hope and trust. In particular, Filmer emphasised that the worst enemy of love was 'Self-Loue: whereby wee loue our Selves merely as our selves, not as gods images'.[66] He also discussed other affections. Amongst these he singled out desire, which was 'threefoulde' consisting in 'Admiration: Emulation, Jelousie', and anger, that is to say, 'an affection rising from the boiling of the blood about the harte'.[67] Curious details aside, *Theologie: or Divinity* offers a more traditional Filmer with regard to his opinions of witchcraft and confirms his attachment to the Church of England, to which – he implied – it was necessary to be united. It also shows that the great value of his thoughts is not to be found in his theological writings.

FILMER GOES PUBLIC: POLITICAL IDEAS AND DISPUTES

Once released from prison at some stage in 1645 (probably after the victory of the parliamentarians at Naseby in the summer of that year), Filmer commenced writing – or, in some cases, revising ideas previously elaborated in an unsystematic form[68] – a series of political works which were published by the royalist printer Richard Royston.[69] In the first of these works, *The Free-Holders Grand Inquest Touching Our Sovereaigne Lord the king and His Parliament*, which was out on 31 January 1648 without the author's name, Filmer principally focused on constitutional problems.[70] Having begun it in all probability in 1644 to respond to William Prynne's *Sovereign Power of Parliaments and Kingdoms* (1643) and very likely to criticise Hyde's official royalist stance,[71] Sir Robert showed great knowledge of legalistic affairs. *The Free-Holders* stemmed from his decision to confront the parliamentarian discourse based on the antiquity of the ancient constitution. Aware that it was necessary to meet the defenders of the common law on their ground, Filmer appealed to a series of historical arguments (including the Norman Conquest) to show that the Commons could not claim any participation in the decision-making process. He dismissed their competence[72] and placed the king above the three estates (the Lords temporal, the Lords spiritual and the Commons).[73] Whilst 'the three estates make the body', the king was *'caput, principium et finis parliamentorum'* – as maintained by Sir Edward Coke.[74] Resorting to a political language other than that adopted in *Patriarcha*, Filmer sought to demonstrate the secondary role of the Commons in both legislative and judicial matters. They could only 'consent to what is ordained' by the counselling Lords for the King.[75] He asserted that 'parliaments are the king's guests'.[76] As he put it, '[t]he votes of the Lords may serve for matter of advice; the final judgement is only the king's'.[77] From historical precedents, Filmer drew the conclusion that 'the decisive or judicial power exercised in the chamber of peers is merely derivative, and subservient to the supreme power which resides in the king'.[78] All parliamentary privileges derived from the monarch's 'grace and favour': in fact, 'the king by his writ gives the very essence and form to the parliament'.[79] In reality, Filmer continued, 'the opposition between the liberties of grace and nature' was so 'strong' that 'it had never been possible for the two houses of parliament to have stood together without mortal enmity and eternal jarring, had they been raised upon such opposite foundations'. And 'the truth' was that 'the liberties and privileges of both houses have but one and the self-same foundation, which is nothing else but the mere and sole grace of kings'.[80] He was adamant, therefore, that 'the king ordains, the Lords advise, the Commons consent'.[81] In line with these opinions, Filmer attacked the validity of the coronation oath as the instrument through which, according to Prynne, 'the just laws and customs, which the vulgar hath, or shall choose' were defended.[82]

In the meantime, Filmer had regained possession of his estates and treasured frequent contacts with neighbours and county friends. He had also kept up his correspondence, from which it emerges that he was busy with quarrels linked to manorial estates and land.[83] Yet it was the public arena of political debates that was to occupy him the most. In April 1648 Royston sent out (anonymously) one of Filmer's most powerful and subtle pieces, *The Anarchy of a Limited or Mixed Monarchy*. The latter's major target was Philip Hunton's *Treatise of Monarchie* (1643) and the parliamentarian defence of a mixed constitution. Sir Robert forcefully criticised the theory of natural rights and discounted all defences of contracts as utterly absurd.[84] In articulating his doctrine, he struck at both 'Romanists' (Jesuits and Ultramontanists) and 'plebists' (supporters of popular government) for advocating rebellion against kings.[85] Filmer then confirmed that all power was in its origins Adamite and that as such no claims of 'public consent' in conveying it to governors could be reputed legitimate.[86] The people could only be subordinate and could not choose or regulate 'any right or power of their own by nature'.[87] Should the ruler be 'no judge', anarchy would ensue.[88] As for the common law, Filmer proclaimed that it was 'an uncertain rule to govern by', which was inevitably conducive to chaos. This argument was meant to depict Hunton as somebody for whom 'every man is brought by … to be his own judge'.[89] For this and many other reasons, Hunton's book was on Filmer's account 'a better piece of poetry than policy'.[90] In addition to Hunton, *The Anarchy* criticised 'the Observator', namely Henry Parker, for overthrowing 'absolute and arbitrary government in this kingdom'.[91] Against Parker's opinions set forth in the controversial *Observations upon some of his Majesties Late Answers and Expresses* (July 1642), Sir Robert proved that neither Poland nor Sweden or Denmark were States in which the monarch did not hold absolute power. In fact, their kings were neither 'moderated' nor 'limited'.[92] That kingship was and ought to be absolute and indivisible Filmer had no doubts and he felt he needed to repeat it. In this respect, his *The Necessity of The Absolute Power of all Kings: And in particular, of the King of England* (1648) assembled numerous excerpts from Jean Bodin's *Les Six Livres de la République* (1576) in order to elucidate precisely the concept of indivisible and absolute monarchical sovereignty.

By then, the war was renewed. And in Kent things were particularly unfavourable for those who sided with the King since, following Colonel Edwyn Sandys' victorious expedition (1642) and the subsequent royalist defeat of 1645, the county had fallen under Parliament's control.[93] This situation lasted until 1648, when a large portion of the Kentish gentry prepared for an uprising to free Charles I (then a prisoner on the Isle of Wight). In fact, this rebellion engendered the Second Civil War. It was at this historical juncture of petitioning royalists and rival committeemen that in a letter dated 25 May one of Sir Robert's cousins, the staunch loyalist Anthony St Leger,[94] informed him that the day before there had been a meeting at Maidstone 'of many gentlemen of the county, where it was desired by the parliament men, Captain Lee, Mr. Westroe and Mr. Oxindin that they might enter in to a treaty to save drawinge blood'. As a result, it had been decided that

> there should be nothing of violence donne to either partie betwixt that tyme and Satterday at five of the clocke in the afternoone and in the interim it should be lawfull for anie of the gentlemen to come to Maidston to dibate and propose of what they should thinke might be for the good of the Countie.[95]

Since the goal of the meeting was to plan a royalist uprising (the outcome of which was the disastrous battle of Maidstone fought on 2 June 1648 and won by the parliamentarian troops led by Sir Thomas Fairfax), St Leger required Filmer's collaboration. He explained: 'I being there was desired to write to you that you would meete there this day, this I promised to doe who shall ever be, Sir Your friend and servant to command Anth. St. Leger'.[96] The following day, Sir Robert received another brief letter in which he was invited once more to participate at the 'counsell at Maidstone in this great concernment of the county'.[97] The letter bore the explicit words, '[m]ake hast[e] to Your Friends and servants' and was signed by 'Edward Hales, Rob. Barnham, Jo. Maplisden, Anth. St. Leger, John Lambe, John Smythe'.[98] But this was not the last letter concerning such a matter Filmer was to receive. He was again asked to sustain the King's cause in a new message sent on the same day (26 May) and this time approved by 'Edward Hales, Anth. St. Leger, Tho. Fludd, Rob. Barnham, Richard Colepepyr, and John Smythe'.[99] They all knew of his infirmity and age, but they were simply hoping he would 'make' his 'personall appearance here to consult about generall businesse now in agitation', without expecting 'any actual service from' him. Filmer's 'presence' was deemed to 'conduce to the publicke good', a cause that 'all the gentlemen of the Country both East and West are engaged in'. Thus, they concluded: 'we hope you who have been ever a well wisher to such an act, will not now draw back'.[100] Despite the pressure, it is not clear whether Filmer attended the meeting. Yet, since he constantly suffered from the stone and had previously declined to become involved, it is very likely that he did not.[101]

After the execution of Charles I in January 1649,[102] Filmer spent three years 'in silence' at work on some important political theses which he made public only in 1652 when the ambitious *Observations Concerning The Originall of Goverment, Upon Mr Hobs Leviathan, Mr Milton against* Salmasius, *H. Grotius* De Jure Belli went to print. Undaunted by the eminence of the targets chosen, he set out a series of arguments aimed at demolishing contractualist theories, the notion of the popular origins of society and republican principles.[103] Sir Robert began with a resolute attack on Thomas Hobbes' *Leviathan* (1651) for having claimed people's participation in founding government.[104] In particular, he was annoyed by Hobbes' choice of words: the title of his book should have referred to 'a weal public, or commonweal' and not, as it did, to the dangerous and misleading 'commonwealth'. The problem for Filmer was that '[m]any ignorant men are apt by the name of commonwealth to understand a popular government, wherein wealth and all things shall be common', so that a condition of general 'levelling' comparable to 'the state of pure nature' would be imposed on the community.[105] He then proceeded to defend the French – but Leiden-based – absolutist thinker Claude de Saumaise (Salmasius), author of *Defensio regia pro Carolo I* (1649), against the vitriolic reaction of John Milton's *Pro populo anglicano defensio* (1651). Filmer accused Milton of having stripped the monarch 'of all power whatsoever' and of having confined him to 'a condition below the meanest of his subjects'.[106] As for Grotius, Filmer lambasted the Dutch scholar for having glossed over the notion that 'the law ... is nothing else but the will of him that hath the power of the supreme father'.[107] On the whole, the most striking feature of this work lies in Filmer's pungent assertiveness that all power was not only supreme but also 'arbitrary'.[108]

Subsequently, on 25 May 1652 Royston published *Observations Upon Aristotles Politiques Touching Forms of Government*, which is one of the most theoretically interesting and critically sound of Filmer's works. Here he delineated a forthright absolutist vision of power and an attack on all forms of mixed government. Above all, he discredited Venice with its institutional system formed of intermediate bodies and different judicatures, which hindered direct monarchical governance. He yielded a rhetorically persuasive account of how counterproductive republican governments were to people because of high taxation, the presence of a standing army and the strictures of their legislation. Identifying 'popular' with republican, Filmer underlined how the Dutch and the Venetian republics lacked the same moral fibre to be found in monarchies.[109] The atheistic Venice and the sectarian Amsterdam were thus sanctuaries for troubles due to their oppression of the clergy and constant warfare caused by factions.[110] His criticism, however, did not stop at their internal affairs, but extended to their international policies and external relations too.[111]

Despite showing some continuity in both content and style, this series of writings did not display the same insistence on the patriarchalist language to be found in *Patriarcha*. Moreover, they often addressed specific legal or moral issues linked to the political situation in England. The latter case presented itself in 1652 when Filmer dealt with the new revolutionary scenario in the aftermath of the King's beheading. He concerned himself with the question of what attitude subjects should adopt in case an illegitimate government attained power. He put forward a range of political considerations in order to advise those who were undecided about whether to comply with Cromwell's government or refuse to do so. The result was *Directions for Obedience to Governours in Dangerous and Doubtfull Times* (1652),[112] where he embraced a stance very similar to that of the so-called de facto theorists according to whom the defeated royalists had to submit to the new regime.[113] His central argument was that resistance was never a lawful means of political action. Not even the support for the cause of a defeated party justified rebellion. Obedience had to prevail over questions of partisanship. A usurper – exactly like a legitimate ruler – had the duty of 'preservation of the subjects' and, therefore, 'to obey' him 'is properly to obey the first and right governor, who must be presumed to desire the safety of his subjects'.[114] Filmer inferred that 'so long as our obedience aims at the preservation of those in subjection and not at the destruction of the true governor', to obey was legitimate. In addition, he argued that '[t]hough a usurper can never gain a right from the true superior, yet from those that are subjects he may'. This was so especially when the people did not know anybody with 'a better title than the usurper', who had thus 'a true right'. Filmer was adamant that 'a usurped power ... may be obeyed not only in lawful things but also in things indifferent'.[115]

This interesting and perhaps unusual essay crowned a career as a political writer that had taken a decisively more public turn within the time span of four years. But publicity was not something Filmer ever lacked. In this regard, if post-mortem references to his works are more commonly acknowledged (and yet, as clarified in Part II below, this does not entail that they have been fully studied, or let alone recognised as numerous and important), by far less known is the scale of his fame as a thinker when he was still alive or before *Patriarcha* was published in 1680.

AN UNDERESTIMATED AFFAIR:
FILMER'S PRE-1680S INFLUENCE

Thomas Burton's testimony reported in chapter 1 shows the success of some of Filmer's works and the reputation he had acquired by the mid 1650s. Above all, it reveals that *Patriarcha* was read and circulated well before its eventual publication in 1680. In this respect, the general scholarly opinion is that 'Filmer received a lot of free publicity from his enemies, and this had to assist the sale of his books, to both friend and foe'.[116] Thus, if for Laslett up to 1714 'Locke was not wasting his publisher's money by including the *First Treatise* in his book' in consideration of *Patriarcha*'s editorial success,[117] Richard Ashcraft maintained that Filmer's tracts 'were not widely owned': in fact, '42% of the libraries contained a political work by Filmer, and a much smaller percentage his *Patriarcha*'.[118] Of his writings the one that was most likely to be found in library catalogues belonging to clergymen, lawyers, political office-holders, physicians, academics, merchants, gentlemen, artists across England in the second half of the seventeenth century was *Quaestio Quodlibetica*. It 'was read by at least 25% of literate society' and in all likelihood a much higher percentage owned the pamphlet. For Ashcraft this shows that the Filmerian tract on usury was 'more widely known than any of his political writings'.[119]

However, this assumption is incorrect. Written at various stages during the 1640s, Sir Roger Twysden's *Certaine Considerations upon the Government of England*[120] criticised both Coke's historical positions and *Patriarcha*. Rejecting all opinions in favour of mixed governments, which imposed too many legal fetters upon the king's power, Twysden nonetheless opposed monarchical absolutism à la Filmer. In particular, he attacked the idea that kings held supreme authority as legitimate inheritors of Adam's absolute power.[121] Likewise, targeting Filmer's *The Anarchy* Twysden argued that only a limited monarchy based on a parliamentary assembly preserved subjects' liberties and rights.[122] In contrast to his friend, Twysden also stressed that the best way to serve the sovereign was according to his laws and not according to his will.[123] In rejecting *The Anarchy*, that 'learned treatis', Twysden dismissed as false the opinion that from the original meaning of the Greek word 'monarch' it was possible to infer that 'one doth governe alone, [which] would prove every monarch illimited'. Unlike Filmer, Twysden maintained that it was not a contradiction to have a 'supream limited power' since the word 'supremus' did not mean 'without limitation'.[124] Moreover, whereas Filmer said 'that never any nation or people were governed by a limited or mixed monarchy', and that 'no auctor, auntient or moderne, can bee produced ... to prove ether the limitation or mixture of a monarchy', Sir Roger could not 'think at this day but all the christian princes in Europe are more or lesse limited or mixed'.[125]

The Kentish antiquarian's attention to Sir Robert's ideas was surely no isolated episode. Tristram Sugge, fellow of Wadham College in Oxford, was 'influenced' by both Filmer's patriarchalist views and his opinions of usury. In the late 1640s Sugge had borrowed a manuscript copy of *Patriarcha* from a member of his college, George Ashwell,[126] 'a convinced royalist' in tune with Filmer's political stances and a friend of Heylyn's.[127] Likewise, soon after appearing in 1648, Sir Robert's *The Necessity* prompted vehement reactions: in *Relations and Observations*, the Presbyterian political pamphleteer Clement Walker stated that around

> the 19 day of August ... came forth a pestilent Book entituled [*The Necessity*] concerning which, I am to admonish the Reader, that it is conceived to be a Cockatrice hatched by the Antimonarchical Faction, to envenome the people against the KING and PRINCE.[128]

It is significant that Walker – an enemy of radicals in Parliament, in the army and in the counties – saw *The Necessity* as the product of the evil machinations of anti-monarchical hotheads whose aim was to totally discredit the King. A year after Filmer's death, the future Bishop of Winchester, Brian Duppa referred to him in glowing terms.[129] In a letter sent to Sir Justinian Isham, Duppa declared:

> in the point of government, I know no man speaks more truth than the knight you mention [Filmer], who follows it to the right head and spring, from whence the great wits have wandered, and have sought for that in their own fancy which they might have found in the plain Scripture road, where God, having created our first father to be the first monarch of the world, gave him dominion over all His creatures.[130]

Interestingly, in the same year the republican John Streater had launched an anti-tyrannical journal whose title strikingly resembled the Filmerian publication: it was called *Observations Historical, Political, and Philosophical, Upon Aristotles.*[131] Still in 1654, the lawyer and parliamentary diarist Guybon Goddard (1612–71) alluded to Filmer's tracts when discussing the issue of the origins of government. He argued that, '[t]o say that there was one' ruler 'before there were many, and consequently, that the legislative power was first in that one, is vain, and of no great value'. And to refer to 'Adam is as impertinent, since Adam's right was paternal, and not despotical'. In contrast to Filmer, Goddard thought that 'when the world increased, and government, more general than that of a family, was thought necessary, the people chose that Government'.[132] In 1656 one John Hall of Richmond – talking of 'the judicious Author of a Treatise called, *The Anarchy of a limited Monarchy*' – stated that Filmer had 'founded Monarchy on Patriarchal Right' in line with 'the most general opinion of the Royalist'.[133] Two years later, in *The Divine Right and Originall of the Civill Magistrate*, the presbyterian Edward Gee criticised Filmer's idea of power.[134] Moreover, in 1660 Henry Stubbe referred to 'Tributa out of Sir Robert Filmores discourses upon Aristotles politicks',[135] published eight years earlier.

The Restoration also saw the publication of the noteworthy monarchical tract *New Atlantis* that intended to continue Francis Bacon's famous work. The author, hiding under the initials R. H.,[136] started off by declaring his monarchist patriotism: 'I were an unworthy Son of my dear Countrey, should I not endeavour with hers to promote the happinesse of him that is PATER PATRIAE [the king], since both interests are inseparable'.[137] If this first Filmerian expression of monarchical support was indirect, R. H. – addressing Charles II as 'the Fountain of all Law and chief NOMOTHETES in these your Kingdoms'[138] – explicitly quoted Sir Robert's *Anarchy* as the work to be consulted in order to see the illogicity of the arguments that the best monarchy was a mixed one.[139]

In 1673 the poet and Puritan-basher Samuel Butler approvingly referred to '*Sir R. Filmer* in his Observations, *touching Forms of Government*, speaking of the *Low-Country* Rebellion' in order to show that the 'causes of our Rebellion 'had been' the same with those for which the *Netherlanders* took up Arms against their Lawful Soveraigne'.[40] As a result, Butler continued, 'through the multitude of *Religions* as well as *Taxes* we [English people] were turn'd *Dutch*'.[41] Butler accused 'our late Commonwealths-men' for having 'made choice of' those two 'same great Enemies to Monarchy, namely *Venice* and the *Low-Countries*' as 'convenient Models for their new-fangled Government, reconciling Church and State to these disagreeable Platforms'. Accordingly, he thought 'it not impertinent to insert what a *great Wit*, the fore mention'd Sir *R. Filmer* in his *Observations* upon *Aristotles Politicks* remarks concerning them'.[42] This was that

> [t]he Religion in *Venice* and the *Low-Countries*, (saith he) is sufficiently known, much need not be said of them: they admirably agree under a seeming Contrariety, ..., that one of them hath all Religions, and the other no Religion; the Atheist of Venice may shake hands with the Sectary of *Amsterdam*. This is the Liberty that a popular State can brag of, every man may be of any Religion, or no Religion, if he please, their main Devotion is exercised only in opposing and suppressing Monarchy.[43]

By and large, these few examples should discourage scholars from giving a premature burial to Filmer's theories and from assuming they were soon ignored. Undoubtedly, for Filmer the period of greatest fame, especially for number of references to his treatises, started in 1679 and developed to a larger extent in the 1680s. Both Filmer's political tracts and the 'Excellent Rational Discourse of Usury' *Quaestio Quodlibetica* were often mentioned in catalogues and lists of books in 1678, 1680, 1681, 1682 and 1683. Above all, his patriarchalism appealed to many authors and stirred controversy for a long time to come.[44] Part II will now pay attention to the context in which *Patriarcha* was released in the public arena and to the broader political, ideological and intellectual climate in which Filmer's *posthumous* life developed.

NOTES

1 A. Milton, 'Canon Fire: Peter Heylyn at Westminster', in C. Knighton and R. Mortimer (eds), *Westminster Abbey Reformed. Nine Studies, 1540–1642* (Aldershot, 2003), pp. 207–31, p. 231. For a thorough and complete study of Heylyn's life and work see Milton, *Career and Writings of Peter Heylyn*.

2 Peter Heylyn, *Certamen Epistolare, or, The Letter Combate* ... (1659), Part iii, pp. 207–9, p. 207.

3 KAO, U120, C6, A18.

4 *Ibid.*

5 *Ibid.*

6 *Ibid.*

7 *Ibid.*

8 See Merritt, *The Social World of Early Modern Westminster*, p. 84. In his role as dean, Williams – a vehement critic of Laud – contributed to raise the Puritan presence at St Margaret's Church (see *ibid.*, pp. 341–2). On the whole, although anti-Catholicism increased considerably during the 1630s, in this parish there seems to have been none of the conflict that affected St Martin's (*ibid.*, pp. 348–50).

9 Milton, *Career and Writings of Peter Heylyn*, p. 45. According to Anthony Milton, in his attacks on Williams Heylyn was moved by long-term and 'personal animosity' towards the bishop (*ibid.*, pp. 45–8).

10 Cited in *The Historical and Miscellaneous Tracts of the Revered and Learned Peter Heylyn, D. D.* (1681), 'The Life', p. xv.

11 See Milton, *Career and Writings of Peter Heylyn*, pp. 106–11.

12 Cited in Milton, 'Canon Fire', p. 223.

13 *The Historical and Miscellaneous*, 'The Life', p. xv.

14 Heylyn, *Extraneus Vapulans ...* (1656), p. 60.

15 His most famous political work was *The Stumbling-Block of Disobedience and Rebellion*, which was published in 1658 but which had originally been written in 1644. Heylyn had also a crucial role as editor of the royalist *Mercurius Aulicus*, the first issue of which appeared on 1 January 1643.

16 See Heylyn, *Certamen Epistolare*, pp. 207–9.

17 On this point see Milton, *Career and Writings of Peter Heylyn*, p. 226; see also *DO, passim*.

18 On these writings see below in this chapter.

19 Heylyn, *Certamen Epistolare*, p. 208 (misnumbered as p. 387).

20 *Ibid.*, p. 209.

21 *Ibid.*, p. 208.

22 However, it is also possible that Heylyn had in mind Filmer's reluctance to publish *Patriarcha* after he had been refused permission. In other terms, Heylyn's words might hint at Filmer's sincere disillusionment with the government's unwillingness to see *Patriarcha* in print. Heylyn's testimony would thus count as evidence that Filmer had – so to speak – 'touchy feelings' about his failed attempt to make his treatise public.

23 Sidney, *Discourses*, bk i, ch. 1, p. 5; see also *ibid.*, pp. 14, 37, 45.

24 This is confirmed by as unsympathetic a commentator as William Atwood, who in 1694 declared: '[y]et I cannot but observe, that tho' the Notions are adopted by *Church-men*, they had a *Lay*-Father, which was that man of immortal memory, Sir *Robert Filmer*; of whom the great Dr. *Heylin* did not blush to learn Politicks' (William Atwood, *The Antiquity and Justice ...* (1694), p. 49).

25 Heylyn, *Certamen Epistolare*, p. 208.

26 On these two clerics see chapter 5 above.

27 See Laslett, 'The Gentry of Kent', p. 155, n. 21.

28 Heylyn, *Certamen Epistolare*, p. 207.

29 Sir John Culpeper (d. 1660) was an influential member of the Privy Council and Chancellor of the Exchequer, whose advice was highly reputed by Charles I. Culpeper also collaborated with Hyde and Falkland to draw up the King's *Answer to the Nineteen Propositions* written in response to parliamentarian claims to power after Charles

had fled from London in June 1642. However, in November 1640 (in the Long Parliament) Culpeper had been a fierce critic of Charles I's policies of high taxation and had contested the legitimacy of Ship Money for it was a way for the King to bypass the law (Eales, 'The Rise of Ideological Politics in Kent', pp. 310–11).

30 *The Journal of Sir Simonds D'Ewes from the first recess of the Long Parliament to the withdrawal of King Charles from London*, ed. W. H. Coates (New Haven, 1942), p. 102.

31 'House of Lords Journal Volume 4: 15 February 1642', in *Journal of the House of Lords 1629–1642* (1802), vol. 4, pp. 585–7, p. 585. The Bishop of Bath and Wells from 1632 to 1670 was William Piers (also spelt Peirs). Following a dispute with Sir Francis Popham, patron of the parish of Buckland St Mary, in 1640 Piers had been impeached and imprisoned in the Tower (*ODNB*, 'Piers, William').

32 Cleggett, *The Filmer and Wilson Families*, ch. 4.

33 KAO, U120, C6, A7 (7 August 1643), A8 (14 August 1643).

34 Filmer's imprisonment represents evidence that from 1643 the County Committee had become dominated by the extremist party for which sequestration and imprisonment had to fall not just on outright royalists but also on 'neuters' ('the king's inactive sympathizers') like Filmer (Everitt, *The Community of Kent*, p. 147).

35 In a letter written from Leeds Castle (1644) to Anthony Weldon and to the Committee at Knole, Filmer recognised that he had 'to leave the attendance of all my business to my wife' (KAO, U120, C4/4). In their reply the members of the committee inflexibly demanded a horse and more arms.

36 'Letter of Warning from Richard Beale ...', KAO, U120, C4/3. In another letter, Anne appealed against over-assessment for taxes (see KAO, U120, C4/6).

37 See *Receipts of the money for our brethren of Scotland by vertue of an Ordinance of Parliament dated the 27ᵗʰ of October 1643*, PRO, SP 28/158, 'Commonwealth Exchequer Papers', Part 1. Laslett referred to this document but mistakenly maintained that Sir Robert paid £18, which was, instead, the amount given by one Richard Webb of Barming, near Maidstone, whose name on the list comes immediately after Sir Robert's (Laslett, 'The Man', p. 537). Although throughout the period further strains were put on his family, Filmer never had to compound for his estates and East Sutton remained free of debt until the 1680s (see *ibid.*, p. 541).

38 KAO, U120, C6, A9. In prison Filmer received a letter from the parliamentarian Augustine Skynner (the knight of the shire who had replaced Dering in 1642) demanding that he provide a horse for a muster on Offham Green (KAO, U120, C4-2, 'Letter from Augustine Skynner summoning him to provide a horse for a muster on Offham Green, 1643').

39 KAO, U120, C6, A9–10.

40 KAO, U120, C6, A9.

41 In the seventeenth century the work was wrongly attributed to the scholar of ancient Greece and Sir Thomas Bodley's protégé John Hales (1584–1656) and was reprinted in the edition of Hales' complete works (1677). The latter attribution is still applied in the database EEBO. For a convincing explanation of why *Of the Blasphemie* is Filmer's see Schochet, 'New Bibliographical Discoveries', pp. 145–6. The original draft manuscript of this work is in BDO, being part of the uncatalogued material which used to belong to the late Peter Laslett. The text (item e on the list) consists of 7 fos, quarto.

42 Bostridge, *Witchcraft and its Transformations*, p. 14. Sutton Valence, near Filmer's home, was one of the places in Kent where groups of Independents operated. They rejected the authority of bishops, for it was a human invention, and insisted on the elective nature of pastors, which had serious political implications (Eales, 'The Rise of Ideological Politics in Kent', pp. 301–2).

43 *BHG*, p. 1.

44 *Ibid.*, p. 1.

45 *Ibid.*, pp. 1–2.

46 *Ibid.*, p. 3.

47 *Ibid.*, p. 7.

48 *Ibid.*, p. 8.

49 *Ibid.*, pp. 11, 14–15.

50 *Ibid.*, p. 15.

51 *Ibid.*, pp. 15–16.

52 *Ibid.*, p. 16.

53 *Ibid.*, p. 17.

54 *Ibid.*, pp. 17–18.

55 *Ibid.*, p. 18.

56 *Ibid.*, p. 19. See also Bostridge, *Witchcraft and its Transformations*, p. 14.

57 *BHG*, p. 21. Filmer might have been the author of some manuscript notes on theological issues such as things indifferent, the nefarious role of sects as violators of God's laws and the necessity to oppose the Independents (see BDO, Tanner MS 233, fos 172–6 (on things indifferent), 177–82 (a defence of the preceding treatise)). However, these attributions are uncertain (Schochet, 'New Bibliographical Discoveries', pp. 153–4).

58 Peter Heylyn, *Theologia Veterum* ... (1673, i ed. 1654), p. 378.

59 See *ODNB*, 'Dixon, Robert'.

60 Cited in *ODNB*, 'Reading, John'.

61 *Ibid.*

62 Filmer gave four main reasons for the existence and implementation of this moral Sabbath (see *Of the Sabeth*, BL, Harley 4685, fos 59, 64, esp. fos 59r–9v).

63 See *Theologie: or Divinity*, BDO, uncatalogued MS, part of the late Peter Laslett's library papers, item c (in three books, foliated), fo. 1.

64 *Ibid.*, fo. 4.

65 See *ibid.*, fos 2–4.

66 *Ibid.*, fos 4–5.

67 *Ibid.*, fo. 7.

68 It belongs to this phase a brief but interesting manuscript piece in Filmer's hand titled *Discussion of the point concerning the extent of royal authority* in which it is said that '[t]he question is not whether kings be limited, for it is not to be denied but that kings are greatly limited'. Rather, 'the question is whether man or any humane laws can do it'. Filmer underlined that human laws differed from divine ones. He argued that, '[i]t is

not said that kings should not exalt themselves above their brethren, for then no king could governe or command his people ouer whom God hath set him, but it is said that his hart be not lifted up above his brethren which is that he should not be proved in hand of his exaltation' (see BL, Harley MS 6867, fo. 251a).

69 Whilst chapter 1 has paid much attention to Filmer's non-political works, my accounts of his post-*Patriarcha* political tracts are succinct. This is due to the fact that the main focus of the book is on *Patriarcha* and patriarchalist ideas (thereby, his writings on usury, the household and witchcraft are given more space as they unveil important and hitherto neglected features of Filmer's patriarchalism). In any case, the other political writings receive detailed coverage throughout the book when their content is relevant to the elucidation of Filmer's theories here pursued.

70 *The Free-Holders* was republished in 1679 with other Filmerian works. It was attributed to him in an anonymous preface added to *The Necessity of The Absolute Power of all Kings*. However, Anthony à Wood ascribed it to Sir Robert Holbourne, a royalist lawyer at Oxford. Some modern scholars embraced the latter opinion (see C. Weston, 'The Authorship of the Freeholders Grand Inquest', *EHR*, 95 (1980), pp. 74–98 and C. Weston, 'The Case of Sir Robert Holbourne Reasserted', *HPT*, 8 (1987), pp. 435–60). In favour of the attribution of *The Free-Holders* to Filmer were Laslett (see the brief editorial preface to *The Free-Holders* in *Patriarcha and Other Political Works*, p. 218); Greenleaf, *Order, Empiricism and Politics*, p. 81; Sommerville, 'Introduction', p. xxxvii. Interestingly, in the papers of one Sir Alexander Malet it is stated: 'the Freeholders grand inquest is writ by Holburne, but according to Harbin [1665–1744] it is by Sir R. Filmer' (*Several Reports of the Royal Commission on Historical Manuscripts* (2 parts, 1879), 'Report and Appendix', vol. 1, p. 433a).

71 See *FH*, p. 103.

72 See *ibid.*, pp. 76–7, 80–1, 96.

73 *Ibid.*, p. 88.

74 *Ibid.*, p. 89.

75 *Ibid.*, p. 94. Here Filmer explained the difference between a judge and a counsellor.

76 *Ibid.*, p. 95. See also *ibid.*, pp. 120, 129–30.

77 *Ibid.*, p. 96.

78 *Ibid.*, p. 98.

79 *Ibid.*, pp. 99, 130.

80 *Ibid.*, p. 99.

81 *Ibid.*, p. 100.

82 *Ibid.*, p. 115.

83 On 7 April 1647 he received a harsh letter from one Thomas Diggs concerning landownership (see KAO, U120, C6, A14). Even during his imprisonment Filmer had maintained a close eye on his financial affairs: on 9 May 1645 from Leeds Castle he had addressed a bitter letter of complaint to one of his tenants, the esquire Richard Porter of Lamberhurst. Filmer talked about the value of his estate and mentioned the question of the estates for life. He then broached the issue of fault and negligence in which his property had been plunged. On 4 July 1645 Porter – a relative of Roger Twysden – replied using strong words and declaring that, as a tenant for life, he did not have to pay anything to Filmer and that he was not compelled to do so by any law. If Filmer was not satisfied

with it, Porter petulantly added, then they would have 'to make choice of one lawyer' (KAO, U120, C6, A13).

84 *AN*, p. 140.

85 *Ibid.*, p. 132.

86 *Ibid.*, p. 138.

87 *Ibid.*, p. 146.

88 *Ibid.*, p. 151.

89 *Ibid.*, pp. 153–4.

90 *Ibid.*, p. 157.

91 *Ibid.*, p. 163. Filmer pointed out the contradictory nature of Parker's arguments (see *ibid.*, p. 165).

92 *Ibid.*, p. 167. For the general discussion of these countries' government see *ibid.*, pp. 167–71.

93 Everitt, *The Community of Kent*, p. 116.

94 In 1642 St Leger had joined the King. Like the Filmers, the St Legers were a family of knights with a long tradition of service to the Crown (see *ibid.*, pp. 101–2, 107, 109, 118).

95 KAO, U120, C5/3.

96 *Ibid.*

97 *Ibid.*

98 *Ibid.* None of the signatories has an entry in the *ODNB*. The most important of them was Hales who, like other members of his family, had a political as well as a financial leading role in the rebellion of 1648. Interestingly, given that a young Sir Roger L'Estrange (see chapter 7) participated in the uprising and was on close terms with Hales (Everitt, *The Community of Kent*, p. 238, n. 1), it is likely that he knew of Filmer and the high esteem in which he was held in Kent amongst royalists. Maplisden and Hales are mentioned in *ibid.*, p. 180 and *passim* (respectively).

99 KAO, U120, C5/3. Again, no *ODNB* entry exists for any of these men. Fludd was a well-known royalist who served as sheriff during the Interregnum.

100 *Ibid.*

101 According to Richard Tuck, it is 'striking' that Filmer joined the late 1640s public pamphlet-war only 'when the royalist cause seemed substantially lost' (Tuck, *Philosophy and Government*, p. 269). This could be a sign that Filmer's ideas displeased the royalist intellectual milieu because of their extremism. Yet it could also be taken as evidence of his lack of personal esteem for Charles I and the Stuart government. In this respect, one could speculate that Filmer belonged to a sort of 'country royalism' and not to the 'court royalism' (Everitt, *The Community of Kent*, p. 230; Everitt named the Filmers as stalwart 'Cavaliers' at the head of Kentish royalism during the Cromwellian period: *ibid.*, p. 279). After the royalist defeat in 1648, Filmer apparently helped some kingly soldiers to immigrate to Virginia, where members of his family had settled (B. J. Filmer, *The Filmer Family of Kent* (Maidstone, 1964), p. 17).

102 It has to be noted that Filmer never referred to the regicide.

103 On Filmer's anti-republicanism see C. Cuttica, 'Anti-republican Cries under Cromwell: The Vehement Attacks of Robert Filmer against Republican Practice and Republican

Theory in the Early 1650s', in D. Wiemann and G. Mahlberg (eds), *Perspectives on English Revolutionary Republicanism* (Farnham, forthcoming), chapter 8.

104 Filmer, however, praised Hobbes' theory of 'the rights of sovereignty' and agreed with him on 'the rights of exercising government' (*OG*, 'The Preface', pp. 184–6, p. 184; see esp. *ibid.*, 'Observations on Mr Hobbes' *Leviathan*: or his Artificial Man a Commonwealth', pp. 187–97).

105 *OG*, 'The Preface', p. 186.

106 *Ibid.*, p. 198.

107 *Ibid.*, p. 226.

108 See e.g. *ibid.*, p. 201.

109 See *OA*, 'The Preface', pp. 235–6.

110 *Ibid.*, p. 257. Their main goal was to suppress monarchy.

111 *Ibid.*, p. 258.

112 The essay, which was appended to *Observations Upon Aristotles*, came out in May 1652, that is, the same month when Cromwell twice visited Kent (see *ODNB*, 'Cromwell, Oliver').

113 See E. Vallance, 'Protestation, Vow, Covenant and Engagement: Swearing Allegiance in the English Civil War', *Historical Research*, 75 (2002), pp. 408–24.

114 *DO*, p. 283.

115 *Ibid.*, p. 285. Some of Filmer's views recall Anthony Ascham's *What is Lawful During Confusions and Revolutions of Government* (1648), where the ways in which obedience had to be transferred from the legitimate sovereign to a usurper in case of conquest had been addressed.

116 Daly, *Sir Robert Filmer*, p. 146.

117 P. Laslett, 'The English Revolution and Locke's "Two Treatises of Government"', *Cambridge Historical Journal*, 12 (1956), pp. 40–55, p. 46.

118 R. Ashcraft, 'John Locke's Library: Portrait of an Intellectual', *Transactions of the Cambridge Bibliographical Society*, 5 (1969), pp. 47–60, p. 58, n. 31.

119 *Ibid.*, p. 58, n. 31.

120 See Roger Twysden, *Certaine Considerations upon the Government of England*, ed. from the unpublished manuscript by J. M. Kemble (1849).

121 This critical refutation of Filmer's work has been considered far more original than Locke's since it was 'more effectively' posed (F. Jessup, *Sir Roger Twysden, 1597–1672* (1965), pp. 188–9).

122 Twysden, *Certaine Considerations*, p. 94.

123 *Ibid.*, pp. 180–1.

124 *Ibid.*, p. 17.

125 *Ibid.*, pp. 17–18.

126 N. Tyacke, *Aspects of English Protestantism, c. 1530–1700* (Manchester and New York, 2001), pp. 286–7.

127 *ODNB*, 'Ashwell, George'. This also proves that *Patriarcha* circulated in manuscript outside Filmer's circle of Kentish gentlemen.

128 Clement Walker, *Relations and Observations Historical and Politick* ... (1648), p. 135.

129 Sommerville, 'Introduction', p. xiv.

130 Cited in *ibid.*, p. xiv. See 'The Correspondence of Bishop Brian Duppa and Sir Justinian Isham', ed. Sir Gyles Isham, Bart., *Northamptonshire Record Society*, 17 (1951), p. 91.

131 See Scott, *Commonwealth Principles*, esp. pp. 116, 138, 158.

132 'Guibon Goddard's Journal: November 1654', in *Diary of Thomas Burton esq.*, vol. 1, Saturday 11 November 1654, pp. lx–cii, pp. lxix–lxx. The editor John Tovill Rutt commented that '[h]ere is probably a design of controverting the following monarchical doctrines of Sir Robert Filmer [the passage referred to is in the 1680 edition of *Patriarcha, or the Natural Power of Kings*, p. 12], since so ably exposed and refuted by *Sidney*, in those *Discourses*, for which the restored Stuart, the hero of Filmer, perpetrated the judicial murder of the patriot; and afterwards by *Locke*, in his "Treatise on Government"' ('Guibon Goddard's Journal', p. lxx, n. 25).

133 John Hall of Richmond, *The True Cavalier Examined by his Principles and Found not Guilty of Schism or Sedition* (1656), p. 126 ('founded' was misspelled as 'sounded'). See also Sommerville, 'Introduction', p. xiv.

134 Sommerville, 'Introduction', p. xiv. In 1652 Filmer had attacked Gee (nicknamed 'the exercitator' after his *An Exercitation Concerning Usurped Powers*, 1650) for failing to explain the various ways in which the much in vogue consent of the people was transmitted from them to those in power as well as for not clarifying what was needed in order to have 'a right or title' from the people (*OA*, pp. 277–8).

135 See the part titled 'Miscellaneous Positions concerning Government' in H. Stubbe, *A Letter to an Officer of the Army Concerning a Select Senate* ... (1660), p. 49.

136 See J. C. Davis, *Utopia and the Ideal Society. A Study of English Utopian Writing 1516–1700* (Cambridge, 1981), p. 280, n. 4. Davis quoted R. H.'s *New Atlantis* and the anonymous *Antiquity Reviv'd* (1693) as two 'royalist utopia[s]' which were heavily influenced by Filmer's absolutist thought (Davis, *Utopia*, pp. 279–96).

137 R. H., *New Atlantis. Begun by the Lord Verulam, Viscount St. Albans: and continued by R.H. Esquire. Wherein is set forth a platform of monarchical government* ... (1660), 'Dedicatory Epistle', a4 ff.

138 *Ibid.*, 'Dedicatory Epistle', a4.

139 *Ibid.*, 'The Preface', b3 (the reference is in a footnote).

140 Samuel Butler, *The Transproser Rehears'd*, ... (1673), pp. 73, 72. This work has been erroneously attributed – and often still is (as in EEBO) – to Richard Leigh (see N. von Maltzahn, 'Samuel Butler's Milton', *Studies in Philology*, 92 (1995), pp. 482–95, esp. pp. 483–4). I thank Martin Dzelzainis for help on this issue.

141 Butler, *The Transproser Rehears'd*, p. 74.

142 *Ibid.*, p. 90.

143 *Ibid.*, p. 91.

144 See e.g. the numerous 'hits' to 'Filmer' found in the database EEBO and recorded between 1679 and 1690. The number of references to Filmer's political ideas becomes too vast between 1692 and 1700 to be recorded here. Different spellings have been tried, including 'Filmore' and 'Filmar', this latter being the way in which Sir Robert was sometimes called in the late seventeenth century.

Part II

Chapter 7

———◆———

Publishing in the Exclusion Crisis (1679–81): *Patriarcha* between fatherhood and fatherland

The chapters which form Part II deal, firstly, with the ideological context of the 1670s; with the publication and currency of Filmerian ideas in the 1680s; and, more generally, with the wide acceptance and traction of patri-archalist arguments, themes and images from the Exclusion Crisis onwards (chapter 7). Secondly, they consider the writings of the most systematic of Sir Robert's supporters, Edmund Bohun; the immediate reactions of Tyrrell, Locke and Sidney to Filmerian ideas as well as the critical response to *Patriarcha* pursued by Whigs; and, in turn, the response to their criticism of patri-archalism (chapter 8). Thirdly, they look at the 'post-plots season' of the early 1680s where the vocabulary of patriotism and parricide occupied a prominent place in debates which did not concern only the upper echelons of the republic of letters but the world of polemics and petitions in the country at large; and, to conclude, at the role of Filmerism in the cauldron of the Glorious Revolution (chapter 9).

A LONG SEVENTEENTH CENTURY: ANALOGIES AND CRISIS

Historians like Jonathan Scott have thoroughly analysed the continuities between the political and religious controversies of the early seventeenth century and those of the post-Restoration era, especially in relation to the so-called Exclusion Crisis (1679–81).[1] The past had a significant impact on the ways in which contemporaries in the 1678–81 period perceived their situation, that of the monarchy, of its adversaries and, above all, that of Parliament. Moreover, analogies between the two junctures in English history have to be connected to similar problems; crises; reactions to diplomatic moves; allegiances and military strategies occurring in Europe.[2] The mounting anxiety towards the policies of the early Stuarts resurfaced in the late part of the century with its burden of examples, warnings and advice. The thoughts and the actions of Charles II and those of his opponents in Parliament and in the country were seen through the heavily ideologically charged prism of the pre-Civil War era.[3] Thus, the same lack of trust in Charles I manifested by many MPs and pamphleteers in the late 1620s-early 1630s re-emerged during the reign of his son. Petitioning for parliaments to be summoned and rendered regular occurred with similar force and frequency in both historical phases.[4] This was so to the extent that those opposing the conduct of the two Stuarts employed the same language to set out their parliamentary agenda. The same attitude, in turn, informed the reaction of the Crown. In fact, in 1680 confronted by petitioners demanding the convocation of Parliament and rejecting some of the royal prerogative powers, Charles II scathingly dismissed these rebellious 'Gentlemen' as 'Impertinent' fools meddling in affairs of State that did not concern them. In so doing, the King attacked their idea that they had been sent by 'the County' to fulfil their duty as representatives of the people. He branded them as the mouthpieces of 'a company of late and disaffected people, who would faine sett us in troubles'.[5] These were motifs very much resonant of the controversies of Charles I's reign.[6]

Likewise, the crucial *political* issue of arbitrary government – that is, the monarch's prerogative powers to call, adjourn, prorogue and dissolve parliaments according to his will – invested with equal vehemence the discourses of petitioners and loyalists and caused the same kind of debates under Charles II's government as much as they had under that of his father. The spectre of the 1629 dissolution of Parliament with the ensuing start of an eleven-year Personal Rule on the part of Charles I reappeared in all its ominous force fifty years later.[7] Most significantly, as William Jones' *Just and Modest Vindication of the Proceedings of the Two Last Parliaments* (1681)[8] made clear, past experience showed all too well that a ruler misleading his people – 'through defect of age, experience, or understanding ... or by passion [and] private interest' – inevitably ended up in troubled waters. This happened, above all, when the monarch did not assemble parliaments, even though the public interest required it, or when he dissolved them prematurely. For many, this situation recalled Charles I's 'misled' dismissal of Parliament, which 'was one of the first sad causes of the ensuing unhappy war'.[9] References to past historical events showed that crises throughout the century occurred (largely) because of the same issues: fear of popery and arbitrary government. The characters might change – Charles II took up his father's role, whilst France that of Spain in both diplomatic affairs and popular imagery – but the plot remained unaltered.

Two major developments in the battle of ideas on popery and arbitrary government happened in 1679:[10] firstly, the re-publication of Henry Parker's *Political Catechism* (1643) that – for defending limited monarchy – had raised the ire of Peter Heylyn in *The Rebells Cathechisme* (1643); secondly, the issuing of *An Appeal from the Country to the City* (attributed to Charles Blount), which attacked popish positions and to which Roger L'Estrange replied with *An Answer to the Appeal from the Country to the City* (1679). The latter tellingly observed that the kingdom 'is again split into two parties; the one consisting of mutineers and schismatiques, the other of loyal servants and subjects of the Crown'.[11] Centred as they were on issues regarding the nature of government and subjects' obedience to the King, these disputes brought the clock back to the atmosphere of the 1640s – and, in some respects, even earlier to that of the late 1620s. The reaction of L'Estrange and other monarchist thinkers – elaborated through patriarchalist arguments[12] – targeted those for whom monarchies were the product of popular decision; the people the ultimate holders of power thanks to their representatives in Parliament; divine right succession and all claims of hereditary right to power an utter absurdity.[13] In particular, L'Estrange – in a climate of widespread petitioning in which he questioned who had the authority to establish whether the sovereign had not fulfilled his duties – argued that the principle of popular sovereignty led to the overthrowing of government.[14] In substance, for thinkers like L'Estrange the major problem was that the discourses of the good old cause were back.[15] Exactly as MPs and pamphleteers from the 1620s and 1630s questioning the relations between the king's prerogative and his subjects' rights had been accused of endangering peace and safety, so in the late 1670s and early 1680s those who made the same observations were held responsible for stirring up rebellion. In this context, as much as in the early and then late Caroline era, MPs played a pivotal role as active guardians of the country's freedom against 'Romish' threats and arbitrary rule. Their 'counsel' was seen as essential to the preservation of the nation.[16]

Together with the constitutional role of Parliament, the central issue in political literature concerned 'the nature of political allegiance' (and not just that of resistance). This proves that *Patriarcha* 'was chosen as a target' because it had developed arguments that were voiced in print in the framework of the disputes over succession and petitioning.[17] The treatise served well the cause of those who contested the active role of parliaments and their defence of people's rights. *Patriarcha* provided a fierce reaction to the theories (and practices) of those who saw in Charles II a monarch that had separated himself from his *raison d'être* (the pursuit of the public interest) and that could, therefore, be forcibly removed from power.[18] According to this argument, the King had to be forced to act in the way for which he had been instituted, since at stake were the liberties, rights and properties of the English people. This was the message 'rebels' sent out loud and clear to the ears of the monarch. The antecedent could hardly be missed: stubbornly clinging to the defence at all costs of his royal prerogative, Charles I had in the end lost his head. The same fatal scenario could once again occur in the political arena of the 1680s.[19] Unsurprisingly then, opposition to the succession of James Duke of York was seen by loyalists as a smokescreen for a more radical attempt to get rid of monarchy altogether. Those defending the ruler feared that the principles advanced by their adversaries led to the extreme conclusion that 'an actual Prince may be depos'd with as much Justice as an Heir can be excluded [from] the succession'. In this the implication was that the same procedure could be applied to dethrone 'His Majesty'.[20]

To counterattack this argument *Patriarcha* was pulled out as it constituted the most forceful defence of indefeasible hereditary government through the Adamite model.[21] For Mark Knights *Patriarcha* was 'the embodiment' of the loyalist rejection of theories of popular sovereignty and the right to resist the tyrannical ruler, which were again set forth in the autumn and winter of 1679–80.[22] The Adamite paradigm equipped defenders of monarchical absolute power with a valid alternative to the concept that government was the artificial product of a free people. Thus, the Restoration (above all, the period subsequent to 1673) saw the Stuart monarchy become increasingly committed to 'absolutism'. In this climate the role of Parliament was often dismissed. After an eighteen-year-long Cavalier Parliament (1661–79), Charles II resorted to prorogations and, eventually, to dissolutions. Of these, one occurred in 1681 at Oxford with the 'dismissal' of the Exclusion Parliament.[23] It was thus in a political context similar to that in which Filmer had composed *Patriarcha* that the treatise was published in January 1680.[24] Both situations presented a scenario in which the King had launched on a path of personal rule after having renounced to deal with Parliament and govern with it.[25]

As is well known, the publication of *Patriarcha* provoked the vehement reaction of John Locke. In his *Two Treatises on Government* (1689) Locke declared that he intended to attack 'a generation of men' that had argued for the divine origins of princes' absolute power. Locke maintained that Filmer's resumed theories had made their author the 'Idol' of all absolutists.[26] Leaving 'to historians' the task 'to relate' '[b]y whom this doctrine [of the legitimacy of absolute power] came at first to be broached, and brought in fashion amongst us, and what sad effects it gave rise to', Locke stated that his 'business' was 'only to consider what Sir *Robert Filmer* ... has said' in *Patriarcha* from which 'every one, who would be as fashionable as *French* was at court, has learned, and runs away with' the notion that '*Men are not born free, and therefore could never have the liberty to choose either Governors, or Forms of Government*'. Locke primarily aimed at dismantling the Filmerian theory that '*Adam was an absolute Monarch, and so are all Princes ever since*',[27] which had obtained considerable fame and support amongst royalists. Indeed, this was the principal reason that had prompted Locke to reply to *Patriarcha*.[28] Locke's response entailed the 'recognition of the centrality of this [Filmer's] resurrected Caroline theory to what was a resurrected Caroline crisis'.[29]

And recognition certainly came to Filmer and his theories as soon as *Patri-*

archa was published, and his other tracts republished (as advertised in the *London Gazette*[30] in April 1680).[31] In fact, patriarchalist political views found much fertile ground. In 1679 the loyalist pamphleteer author of *Truth and Honesty in Plain English* declared that monarchy was 'founded in paternity'. In a similar vein, *A Letter to a Friend, Shewing from Scripture* (1679) made use of patriarchalist arguments to attack the false principles of those who believed authority stemmed from the consent of the people. Thus, it declared that 'God did fix government in Adam'.[32] The year after, Sir John Monson's *Discourse Concerning Supreme Power and Common Right* maintained that God had assigned original power to Adam and as such it derived 'its pedigree from paternal'.[33] Likewise, Robert Constable's *God and the King* (1680);[34] the anonymous (M. R.) *Three Great Questions Concerning the Succession* (1680); Matthew Rider's *The Power of Parliaments in Case of Succession* (1680); the anonymous *Protestant Loyalty Fairly Drawn* (1681);[35] the anonymous (T. L., Gentleman) *The True Notion of Government* (1681)[36] all expounded patriarchalist opinions that had been formulated in *Patriarcha*.[37]

Furthermore, a fundamental portion of political parlance in the years leading up to the Exclusion Crisis and afterwards centred on strong criticism of Catholic doctrines concerning the authority of kings. This is to say that the highly disputed question of the deposing power of the Pope and the even more heated issue of the legitimacy of tyrannicide assumed new prominence in the 1670s. Jesuit political ideas regained the same momentum that had seen them become widespread in the late sixteenth and early seventeenth centuries with the writings of Robert Parsons (especially the much read and most furiously rejected *A Conference About the Next Succession to the Crown of England*, 1595) and of other important authors such as Bellarmine, Jean Boucher, Mariana, Suarez.[38] In the aftermath of the killings of two French kings and of the Gunpowder Plot,[39] the Jesuits – as seen in chapter 3 – had been accused of fomenting rebellion in the body politic. Not only had they argued that the Pontiff possessed the supreme authority to depose secular sovereigns in case of their heresy, schismatic acts or tyrannical conduct. They had, most of all, maintained that in some cases it was vital to act urgently and that, therefore, it was not necessary to wait for any papal approval prior to deposition: people could proceed to take up arms against their ruler.[40]

Another major aspect of the polemics being carried out in the literature of the 1670s and 1680s concerned the monarchist association of Catholic theory with Calvinist radicalism.[41] In practice, both groups were depicted as propagators of the doctrine of tyrannicide. As Filmer had done in *Patriarcha* in the 1620s, so his fellow monarchist writers a few decades later pointed out that there was no difference in the teaching of people like the sixteenth-century Parisian Catholic theologian John Major and the Protestant monarchomach Buchanan. In this respect, David Owen's *Herod and Pilate Reconciled: or The concord of papist and puritan ... for the coercion, deposition, and killing of king* (1610)[42] had been one of the first writings[43] to state that Jesuits and Puritans were firebrands whose political principles equalled each other.[44] This served Filmer's late seventeenth-century counterparts to connect popish and Whig thinking. The latter's borrowing from the former was all the more evident in that the exclusionists denied all rights of hereditary succession in favour of the community's power to decide which form of government they preferred. Parsons' arguments (his book was reprinted in 1681) were now expressed by Whig polemicists, with such a leading figure as John Somers deeply relying on *A Conference About the Next Succession* for his *A Brief History of the Succession* (1682). Thomas Hunt's *Great and Weighty Considerations* (1680) did the same and Samuel Johnson followed suit.[45] Mariana and Suarez were portrayed by royalist authors as the idols of the Whigs, who were labelled 'new Ultramontanists'. In their critiques monarchists referred to Thomas Bilson's *Christian Subjection* (1585) and to Bishop Richard Bancroft's virulently anti-Presbyterian *Dangerous Positions and Proceedings* (1593) as model-texts which had been pioneering in unmasking the political similarities between Jesuitism and Calvinism.[46]

In targeting these doctrines monarchists had a twofold goal. Firstly, they wanted to dismiss all notions of popular power.[47] Secondly, the strategic decision to adopt patriarchalism as a response to contractualists and natural rights theorists stemmed from the need to portray Whigs as unpatriotic and unfaithful subjects. Like the 'Jesuitical' fifth column that had instigated the murders of kings across Europe and like rebellious Calvinists à la Bèze whose maxims had led to the atrocious killing of Charles I, so Whigs – their adversaries' argument went – were now plotting to act in the same nefarious manner.

The controversies of the Exclusion Crisis also prove that Filmer had singled out the right target. In fact, in 1681 the royalist historian Robert Brady (and many others with him)[48] used words reminiscent of *Patriarcha* when holding that 'the Doctrine of disinheriting and deposing Kings, and of the *Natural* freedom of the People, is rank Popery: first broached and introduced by the Schoolmen, and since zealously maintained by the Jesuits and other great Men of the Papal Faction'.[49] Most revealingly, it was the Whigs who – despite their attacks on the Jesuits – in 1688 adopted the very same theory Sir Robert had strenuously rejected throughout his treatise: this was Parsons' principle[50] that it was legitimate to get rid of a sovereign whose religious opinions were not in tune with those of his subjects.[51] As Filmer had forcefully remarked in *The Anarchy*, 'the only point of popery is the alienating and withdrawing of subjects from their obedience to their prince, to raise sedition and rebellion'. In fact, since 'popery and popularity agree in this point', it followed that 'the kings of Christendom that have shaken off the power of the pope have made no great bargain of it, if in place of one lord abroad, they get many lords at home within their own kingdoms'.[52] Patriarchal naturalism provided a forceful antidote against precisely this kind of 'disease'.

At times where the hereditary principle was cast in doubt and where the legislative and executive agency in the body politic was contested (as in the 1620s and 1680s in England), the Adamite paradigm became a source of useful concepts and metaphors about parricide; of analogies illustrating husband–wife relationships; of gender-related images. Most importantly, the patriarchalist reaction to concepts of resistance and popular government, parliamentary representation and people's rights was also accompanied by the Filmerian effort to depict the monarch as father of the fatherland.[53] It was such a configuration of sovereignty that generated (and that explains) what Locke called 'the Applause that followed' *Patriarcha*'s publication.[54]

PATRIARCHA, TORY PROPAGANDA AND THE EARLY 1680s IDEOLOGICAL BATTLES

With the late 1670s a second phase in Filmer's posthumous career began.[55] In 1680 *Patriarcha* was published for the first time,[56] fuelling the well-documented reactions of Tyrrell, Sidney and Locke (the latter apparently purchased a copy on 22 January 1680).[57] These adversaries are generally regarded by scholars as the sole source of notoriety for Filmer.[58] However, this book proves that his revival was also – and greatly – due to theorists who supported and shared his doctrines. Besides the Filmerian champions Roger L'Estrange and Edmund Bohun,[59] we have John Nalson (bap. 1637–86), John Northleigh (1656/57–1705), George Hickes (1642–1715) and others.[60]

That Tyrrell, Sidney and Locke decided to dismantle patriarchalism so promptly and took their task so seriously reminds us that the patriarchalist paradigm was both an attack on 'popular' spirits *and* a forceful account of monarchical power. This is evident throughout the 1680s: John Dryden's masterly satire *Absalom and Achitophel* (1681) was published precisely with the aim of defending the monarchical cause by showing its greater appeal to people. Interestingly, Dryden discredited Monmouth by running a parallel between him and Absalom, who had rebelled against his father, King David of Israel, and was killed during the Battle of Ephraim Wood.[61] Associating political rebellion and opposition to fatherly authority was a commonplace throughout the seventeenth century, but certainly one with special meanings and metaphorical significance at this time. For monarchists like Dryden those opposing the legitimate heir (and the reign of Charles II too) acted exactly like ungrateful sons.[62]

By contrast, the latter depicted themselves as patriots. Indicative of the agenda of the period, in 1682 the explicitly self-styled 'Philopatris', literally 'lover of the country' (probably Charles Blount, 1654–93), released *A Satyrick Poem against those mercenary wretches and troublers of Englands tranquility* Thomas Flatman (1635–88) and Sir Roger L'Estrange (1616–1704).[63] In his aggressively pungent and sarcastically irreverent tone, the author of *A Satyrick Poem* attacked Flatman and L'Estrange as hacks writing 'for Bread' and printing to 'serve the Pope', their 'dearest Friend'.[64] Their aim, Philopatris charged, was to 'Blow Parliaments and all things down' so as to make 'all Dissenters drown'.[65] The likes of Flatman and L'Estrange manifested their truly dangerous nature by

> Affirming things nere [never] heard before
> That Parliaments should be no more
> But little Fingers of the State,
> And things that all men ought to hate.[66]

Popish fomenters like '*Heraclitus*' (Flatman) and the '*Observator*' (L'Estrange) accused people who were 'guilty of no fault';

> Unless it is Crime to be
> Constant and firm to Loyaltie.

Being 'men of little brains or reason', they 'transform'd' 'Loyalty' into 'Treason'.[67] Given his opinions, Philopatris predicted that he will surely be labelled a

> ... Rogue, Raskal, and Traytor,
> Because in truth I am a hater
> Of those that truly love the King.[68]

Interestingly, the same argument was put forward at the other end of the political spectrum in exactly the same terms: as Filmer's supporter Edward Pelling said, 'true loyalty has been ... reproached for a *Crime*, and esteemed a kind of *Treason* against the *People* to be Dutiful to the *king*'.[69]

The first number of L'Estrange's *The Observator, in Dialogue* had appeared on 13 April 1681. It was issued three times a week over six years (until 9 March 1687) and became the most powerful organ of Tory propaganda. *The Observator* was conceived as a dialogue between two speakers, A (later Tory, Observator and, briefly, Courantier) and Q (later Whig, then Trimmer).[70] Although James Daly maintained that L'Estrange did not refer to nor make use of Filmer's works,[71] the Tory propagandist defended Filmer against Thomas Hunt[72] (1626/27–88)[73] and used his patriarchalist ideas to attack the latter's 'popular' principles.[74] According to L'Estrange (in this case, the Tory character in the dialogue), Hunt had argued that '*[i]f the Royall Family be Extinct, it belongs to the People to make a New King under what Limitations they please*' and that '*in case of ... Discontinuance, there may be Treason committed against the People: By all which it is Evident that the Succession to the Crown is the People's Right*'.[75] As

Filmer had done in *Patriarcha* when dealing with the representatives of 'the common people', thus L'Estrange accused Hunt of not specifying '*Who*, or *What* are they, which he calls the *People*'.[76] The Tory writer was most concerned about the opinion of 'the Bare *Supposall* of [kingly] *Treason* against the *People*' because this was 'an unseasonable Revivall of that *Impious Position*, whereupon the *Last King* was *murder'd*'.[77] This dangerous doctrine was connected to Hunt's theory of 'the Originall of Government' for which the latter had – according to L'Estrange, unconvincingly – set out a series of 'Reasonings against *Sir Robert Filmore*; then under the pretence of Asserting *Liberty* against *Tyranny*, to give the *People a Disgust* even against *Monarchy it self*. By contrast, L'Estrange adhered to the Filmerian principle that 'the *Government* which *Adam* Exercised was ... of *Divine Right*' and asked: 'why may not both *Politicall*, and *Paternal Power* meet in the same Person?'[78] This first sample of L'Estrange's defence of Filmer shows how Sir Robert's patriarchalist paradigm was employed not only to oppose Whig polemicists, but also to construct a political model whereby allegiance to government was guaranteed; treason averted; peace preserved.

This was not the first time that L'Estrange had pictured Filmer in a positive light.[79] In mid December 1681 he had attacked those thinkers who defended resistance theory and claimed the right to deal with princes as they pleased by resorting to the works of '*Knox, Buchanan, Goodman*'.[80] L'Estrange focused on the 'very *zealous*' who 'for *Purity of Religion*' acted in 'the way of *Clement*, *Ravillac*, and our *Late Regicides*'. These murderers of kings made 'Subjects ... be so Busy and so Familiar with the *Guts*, the *Hearts*, and with the *Throats* of *Princes*'.[81] L'Estrange had no doubts: those who in the early 1680s in England conspired against the monarch, and the rabid Jesuits who had killed Henry III and Henry IV, all belonged to the same group of fanatics. Amongst them was 'a man that calls himself *T.H.* [Thomas Hunt]' who – besides many other nefarious things – 'throws off *Sr Rob Filmor*, and *Dr. Brady* with as much Contempt and Indignation as a *Game-Bull* would do a Couple of *Whelps*'.[82] Despite being 'a little Civiller ... to *Thomas Hobbes*', this '*T.H.*' was so impudent as to label '*FELLOWS*, and KNAVES the *Heraclitus'es* and the *Observators*', whilst he also 'Smiles upon the Clergy with one side of his Mouth, and shews his Teeth at them on the Other'. More dangerously still, such a conspirator '*Says Grace to a Sedition*; *Complements Dr. Oates*: Denies the *King* to be *Sole Governor*'.[83] Hunt propagated papist tenets: he was an instigator of rebellion exactly like the mastermind of the Popish Plot. Like a Jesuit, he also justified the killing of kings, claiming that they did not rule the country because they were under the external command of the Pope.[84]

Thus, for people like L'Estrange Filmer's patriarchalism served as an effective antidote to the spreading cancer of popular views of politics which invited men not to 'keep to their own businesse' and made 'every *Tom Fool* set up for an *Implement* of *State*; and Cry, *The King can't do* This, *and the King can't do* That'.[85] In rejecting all notions of popularity whereby '[e]very *Jack Straw* Carves the King out his *Prerogative* as he pleases',[86] L'Estrange ruled out the same language that Filmer had targeted for pleading the cause of 'the meanest artificer'.[87] This was an idea that, as Filmer had pointed out, in the late 1620s *'the common people everywhere* tenderly embrace ... as being most plausible to flesh and blood, for that it prodigally distributes a portion of liberty to the meanest of the multitude'.[88]

In the context of the Exclusion Crisis these words had a strong echo. Exactly two years later, in December 1683, when referring to Sidney's trial and the papers he had produced then, L'Estrange mentioned that the republican thinker '[c]harges Sr Robert Filmer's *Patriarcha* with wicked *Principles*, and makes them in some Measure to appear So, by *Misrepresenting* them'.[89] Connecting Sidney's '*Republican Theses*' with those of 'the *Jesuites Themselves*', L'Estrange encomiastically referred to 'the Bus'ness of *Sir Robert Filmer's Book*' which 'is *Open* for Every man to *Examine*'. Subsequently, accusing the traitor Sidney of conspiracy, L'Estrange once again defended Filmer's theory.[90] In particular, the character called 'Observator' was prompted by the character named 'Trimmer' to now dedicate 'a Few Words' to Bohun's '*Defence of Sr Robert Filmer's*'.[91] The maxim under scrutiny was that which prescribed people's submission '*unto an Absolute Kingly Government, which can be restrained by no Law, or Oath*'. In response, the 'Observator' produced a strenuous defence of Filmer's opinions (taken not only from *Patriarcha* but also from *Directions for Obedience*).[92] This defence centred on fatherly power and the superiority of 'Absolute' sovereignty deriving from it, so that '*All Other Forms*, and *Qualifications*, have Undoubtedly, been *Impos'd* upon us, by *Fraud*, and *Usurpation*'.[93] In addition, L'Estrange adhered to the Filmerian view that to consider 'the *Laws* ... *above* the *Kings*' was to give 'a *Handle* for the *Common People* to lay *hold* of; that the *King* may *Forfeit*, and Become *Accountable* to the *Multitude*'. This was conspicuously '*False*' because all laws 'are the *Kings Laws*; and 'tis *Ridiculous* to Imagine the *Laws above* him that *Made* them'.[94] Unsurprisingly, given the circumstances under which they emerged in the 1620s and then in the 1680s, the ideas of Sir Robert Filmer and Sir Roger L'Estrange coincided, testifying to the enduring presence of themes and rhetorical images throughout the century.

To fully understand the impact of these arguments in relation to the central problem of the Stuart dynasty, the next paragraph further concentrates on the early 1680s and the vexed issue of succession that generated so many heated disputes (both practically and on paper). The fundamental point was one which had concerned Charles II's predecessors, James I and Charles I: fatherhood. The virile Charles II had not fathered a *legitimate* heir, leaving the door open to a deep crisis. In this milieu Filmer's ideas set the tone of political debates by influencing monarchists as well as raising the ire of anti-patriarchalists.

FILMERIAN RECEPTIONS

In 1680 William Petyt (1640/41–1707), the propagandist of ancient consti-tutionalism and fierce adversary of the Tory historian Robert Brady (c. 1627–1700), released his *Miscellanea Parliamentaria*. In two notes Petyt distorted the meaning of Filmer's *The Power of Kings* to prove that Saxon rulers had made laws 'by the *advice* of the *Bishops*, and Wise men'.[95] Besides, whilst giving an account of Charles I's answer to the Petition of Right, Petyt mislead-ingly claimed that 'the good King condemns the Law and Doctrine of Dr. *Cowell, Blackwood, Manwaring, Fulbeck, Sibthorpe, Alablaster, Filmer,* and their Transcribers and Disciples'.[96]

Petyt's hostile reception of Filmer's doctrines was by no means unani-mously shared. In fact, a large portion of writings adopted the Filmerian association of kingship with fatherhood. Thus, in the same year William Temple (1628–99) – famous royal ambassador to the Netherlands and highly skilled statesman – praised 'a great paternal Authority' and gave a description of monarchical power where patriotic element and paternal images merged. He explained that

> the Father, by a natural Right as well as Authority, becomes a Governour in this little State: and if his life be long, and his generations many ... [h]e grows the Governour or King of a Nation, and is indeed a *Pater patriae,* as the best Kings are, and as all should be.

Temple went on to reflect that the king 'in *France,* is by the name of *Sire,* which in their ancient language is nothing else but Father, and denotes the Prince to be the Father of the Nation'. Put it succinctly, '[a]s *Patria* does the land of our Father; and so the *Dutch* by expressions of deerness, instead of our Countrey, say our *Father-land*'.[97] Temple's image of the *pater patriae* was not at all unusual in the early 1680s,[98] especially in the wake of the Popish Plot (1678–81). In 1681 the clergyman and Charles II supporter Samuel Crossman (d. 1684) – speaking of the mutuality of interests between 'the Princes Soveraignty and the Subjects Safety, his Augustness & their happiness' – described the ruler as '*Pater patriae, Medicus, Maritus regni*'. For Crossman '[t]he Soveraign is the common Father of the Country: He the Physician, we the weak Patients; he the Husband, the Kingdom his Spouse'. In Crossman's familial–medical analogy, the monarch's 'absence makes us a Family of desolate Orphans, an Hospital of languishing Patients, and the whole Kingdom a solitary helpless Widow expos'd to endless Oppressions'.[99]

Other authors were then more directly Filmerian. Firstly, in *A Letter from a Student at Oxford to a Friend in the Country* ... (1681), the then undergraduate White Kennett (1660–1728, future historian and Bishop of Peterborough) announced that, having 'read (but only to know how the better to confute) those grand Patriots of Rebellion and Confusion: *Hobbs, Milton, Hunton,* and others', he had found 'their fallacies so well discovered in the incomparable Treatises of *W.ldon, Filmer, Diggs* and *Falkner'*.[100] Secondly, in 1682 the patriarchalist, king's scholar at Westminster School and High Churchman Edward Pelling (d. 1718) – targeting the 'Jesuitical' Henry Neville and other republicans – declared that

> the ashes of that Learned, Loyal, and Honourable Person, Sir *Robert Filmir*, have been of late polluted with a great deal of dirt ... because he was such a Fatal Enemy to that Jesuitical Principle, that the Original of all Power and Government is in the People.[101]

From the opposite side of the ideological spectrum, the writer on horticulture Samuel Gilbert (d. 1692?) pointed out – with much hostility to Filmer's ideas – that Tyrrell's *'Patriarcha non Monarcha, the Patriarch unmonarch'd'* constituted

> observations on a late Treatise, and other Miscellanies, Published under the name of Sir *Robert Filmer* Baronet, in which the falseness of those opinions, that would prove *Monarchy Jure divino*, are laid open: and the true principles of Government, and property especially in our Kingdom asserted, by a Lover of Truth and of his Country.[102]

In this tense context, Filmerian opinions were so divisive as to cause the expulsion of a fellow from Lincoln College (1683) for having prompted his students to read Milton against that 'valiant tory thinker Sir Robert Filmer'.[103]

Giving a perfect illustration of the texture of the ideological debates and the type of rhetorical appeals widespread in the anti-popish climate of the 1680s, the mathematician and theologian Isaac Barrow (1630–77) – drawing on Bodin's work – attacked the papist theory of the superiority of spiritual power over temporal. In so doing, he argued that, being 'thwarted ... in the exercise of their power', '[m]any good Princes' such 'as *Henry* the Second of *England*, King *Lewis* the Twelfth of *France*, (that Just Prince, *Pater Patriae*)' had been 'forced to oppose ... the Popes'.[104] Likewise, the anti-Presbyterian Church of England clergyman Thomas Gipps (d. 1709) asserted that '[w]hat the *Pater familias* is in the Œconomy of the House, the same is *Pater Patriae* in the Polity of the State'. And '[t]o uncover the Nakedness of the Father of thy Countrey' was not only 'inconsistent with all those foresaid Duties of Fearing and Honouring him',[105] but it led – in the words of the prolific L'Estrange – to the killing of martyr-kings like Charles I, 'a known *Pater Patriae, & Defensor s[f]idei*, a true nursing Father to the Church, and Indulgent Parent to his People'.[106]

The Rye House Plot (1683)[107] prompted many works that defended – through patriarchalism – the supreme power of the monarch against all rebellious spirits. As the anti-Whig *The Arraignment of Rebellion* (1684) maintained, 'a Family becomes a Kingdom: and the King, or *Pater patriae* Father of the Countrey, is the very *Paterfamilias* Master of the Family'. Its author, the Kentish clergyman

John Aucher (d. 1701), described the origins of sovereignty in common patriarchalist fashion. Relying on the analogy between families and polities, Aucher gave a detailed account of biblical transmissions of paternal power through the ages since Adam.[108] This process had culminated in individual 'Fathers of Families' gathering together to 'give up this their absolute power ... into the hands of some one person, incorporating themselves, and their Families into his Family'. As a result, 'their several paternal powers' had been concentrated 'in him alone', who was thereby acknowledged 'the common Father of them all'.[109] In order to prevent 'the same inconveniences as before', that is, of having – at his death – to return the power of the king to each family-father, such a power was extended to and fixed in 'his Heirs after him'. This made 'his Family to be a Family of Fathers in their several generations to them, and their Families for ever'. And for Aucher this was 'indeed the true original of Kings, and Monarchs', to whom 'all particular paternal powers' were 'really transferr'd, and united in them'.[110] More to the point (and recalling some of the thinkers encountered in chapter 4), Aucher made it clear that allegiance to the sovereign had priority over obedience to the father because 'the King is more our Father, than our Father that does beget us'. He was adamant that, since '[n]o man is so much our Father, as the King', all 'the honour' was 'most eminently, and in the first place' due to the latter.[111]

The message was obvious and its purposes unmistakably enunciated. Nobody, especially in the mid 1680s when confusion and rebellion seemed to people like Aucher to be gaining the upper hand, could have any doubts about who the supreme governor was and why obedience was due to him. This was not lost on John Walker (1650–1730), who defended 'the necessity and reasonableness of subjection to the higher powers'. Above all, Walker argued that people had to do good 'more especially to the *Pater Patriae*, the publick Parent or Father of the Countrey or Kingdom, in that the Good of the whole Community or Body is involv'd in his, and his Happiness and Welfare doth derive and extend unto all'.[112] On his part, James II's royalist propagandist John Wilson (1626–96) resorted to Roman history to attack his republican adversaries: although Caesar had been welcomed 'with the supernumerary Titles of *Pater Patriae*', he had been 'murder'd in the Senate' by some 'deprav'd natures' 'upon a Conspiracy of *Brutus*, and *Cassius*, and other Senators'. According to Wilson, those who had killed Caesar were guilty of the most heinous of crimes: 'Parricide'.[113] The hint to the English scenario was not difficult to spot.

In 1684 the non-juror Filmerian apologist John Nalson – anti-Catholic and anti-Presbyterian as well as a self-styled 'true Church of England King's Protestant'[114] – attacked Sidney's ideas by declaring that the republican firebrand had made

> a mighty flutter about those Treasonable Papers found in his Study, as being only some private things written in Answer to Sr. *Robert Filmer's* Book, which yet remains

unanswerable, and lays down that wild Position of the Soveraignty of the People, as the Foundation of all Governments, which is not only in it's own Nature perfect Non-sense, but destructive of all Government.[115]

In the same year, the former Whig propagandist, Shaftesbury's protégé and virulent anti-Catholic (now turned Tory polemicist) Elkanah Settle (1648–1724)[116] significantly identified 'the very *Loyallest* of all our late Members of *Parliament*' with those who

> were not all *Shaftsburys* nor all *Sidneys*; neither such that were for *Associating* to *Kill-Kings*, to *keep out Popes*, nor answering of *Filmers* out of *Buchanans* and *Miltons*, nor seating the *Good Old Cause* at the *Right Hand of GOD*. Not those that made *popery* the *pretence* alone to manage their own *Hellish Republick Machinations*.[117]

With the death of Charles II (February 1685), monarchists often gave standard hagiographic pictures of the deceased King. Conforming to such a trend, Henry Anderson (b. 1651/52) portrayed a deeply loyalist account of that 'Patron of Christianity' who was also 'a most tender *Nursing Father* of the Church and People of *England*' as well as '*Pater Patriae*, Father of Gods *Israel*, and Defender of the Faith'.[118]

Less generically pro-monarchy but forthrightly patriarchalist in tone and Filmerian in content was the lengthy *The Triumph of our Monarchy* (1685), composed by the prominent Tory pamphleteer (and Dryden's close friend) John Northleigh (1656/57–1705). Northleigh targeted Sidney, Neville and Hunt (the latter was accused of having derided the monarchy by 'calling it the Court of *King* Adam, and *King Father*', which again testified to the relevance of the vocabulary of fatherhood)[119] and defended the idea of the indivisibility of sovereignty as 'all the Dominion and Power' had been conferred on 'a *single* Person'.[120] He insisted on the falsity of republican claims that the first government to be instituted was 'a Republick', so that the 'paternal Power of these Patriarchal Kings was no more than that of a Burgher in the Town of *Amsterdam*' and that the 'Cities' over which 'Kings and Princes Reign'd ... were nothing else, but as perfect Republicks, as *Venice, Genove*, or the united Provinces in the *Netherlands*'.[121] Such 'Seditious Souls' as Sidney, Neville and Hunt could not be 'convinc'd' that 'Patriarchal Power was Monarchical, unless we can prove every patriarch a Crown'd King'.[122] Stating that kings were 'the very Fountain of Power it self', Northleigh targeted *Plato Redivivus* by using Filmer's Platonic concept that 'those that beget' had the right 'to Rule over what they have begotten'.[123] Northleigh pointed to the 'Impertinent fury' and 'insignificant Folly' with which Neville 'lay out his Lungs against Sir Robert Filmer' in order to deny all '*Paternal* Right'.[124]

Sharpening his rhetorical knife, Northleigh maintained that 'all the Venom and Poyson of Mr *Hobs*', that is, his dangerous doctrines of the 'Origination of Society out of Fear, his definition of Right to Conflict in Power, his Community in Nature, his Equality in persons, ..., the Pest and Plague of the People' were highly 'priz'd with our Republicans'. However, whilst for the author of *Leviathan* equality exclusively applied to the state of nature, these new 'Levellers' made 'all' people 'Common, under the Inclosures of a Society, and the several restrictions of so many Civil Laws'.[125] The antidote to this Hobbesian disease could only be found in a polity[126] where '[p]aternal Power' had been 'patriarchal, and Absolute' in the family, but had subsequently become subordinate to 'a Supream Sovereignty Paramount' that had been established by 'Civil constitutions'.[127] Most importantly, for Northleigh those who opposed this government were culpable of 'Parricide'.[128]

Northleigh also accused the republican 'Rebels' of denying the divinity of kings, a tenet they used as 'their Trojan Horse' to 'introduce Popery' and an oppressive government. In tune with these treacherous manoeuvrings, the republican fifth column libelled 'the works of that Learned Person' and 'Loyal Subject' Filmer and misrepresented his 'very principles and positions about' monarchical power.[129] Northleigh argued that Sidney had completely distorted Filmer's ideas of necessary submission to 'an absolute Kingly Government, not restrainable by Law, or Oath'.[130] In reality, people like Sidney were hypocrites wanting to install a 'Monster with many Heads' as supreme guide of the country. They covered their true intentions by crying against the '*Arbitrary Power of Kings*' when, in fact, they 'themselves would make the *People as Arbitrary*'.[131] Like Filmer, Northleigh was trenchant: '[t]he Question is not, whether there shall *be an Arbitrary Power*, but the Dispute is who shall *have* it'. The people had to be governed by 'a Power of making Laws, and that Power (so long as consonant with reason) must be *Arbitrary* for' – as *Patriarcha* had so forcefully explained – 'to make *Laws*, by *Laws*, is Nonsense'. The conclusion Northleigh drew was straightforward and left no doubts about the fact that republicans 'would fix' such a power 'in *many*, and the *Multitude*', an 'Aristocracy' would have it 'in a *few*, and therefore in a Monarchy must be setl'd in ONE'.[132]

Like the opinions of the thinkers hitherto examined, Northleigh's strongly Filmerian arguments were no isolated manifestation. It was in the same period that the viscerally anti-republican works of one of the authors who contributed the most to perpetuate Filmer's fame appeared.

NOTES

1 Scott prefers to speak of 'succession crisis' (see Scott, *England's Troubles, passim*). He has argued throughout that the central problem in the 1670s and 1680s was not 'exclusion' (of James Duke of York and from 1685 King James II) but 'succession' and the issue of the twin dragons 'popery' and 'arbitrary government'. Amongst the vast literature on the Restoration period see e.g. J. Spurr, *England in the 1670s: 'This Masquerading Age'* (Oxford, 2000); T. Harris, *Restoration: Charles II and His Kingdoms, 1660–1685*

(2005); G. S. De Krey, *Restoration and Revolution in Britain: A Political History of the Era of Charles II and the Glorious Revolution* (Basingstoke, 2007).

2 See Scott, *England's Troubles, passim.*

3 This is one of the main arguments of J. Scott, *Algernon Sidney and the Restoration Crisis: 1677–1683* (Cambridge, 1991).

4 One famous example was the so-called 'monster petition of 1679–80' presented to Charles II on 13 January 1680 by the inhabitants of London, Westminster and Southwark and signed by over 16,000 people (for other petitions in the following two years see T. Harris, *Politics under the Later Stuarts. Party Conflict in a Divided Society 1660–1715* (Harlow, 1993), esp. pp. 102–8 and for the role of crowds in London see T. Harris, *London Crowds in the Reign of Charles II: Propaganda and Politics from the Restoration until the Exclusion Crisis* (Cambridge, 1987)).

5 Cited in M. Knights, *Politics and Opinion in Crisis, 1678–81* (Cambridge, 1994), p. 236.

6 See e.g. *PP 1628*, esp. vol. vi.

7 Scott, *Algernon Sidney and the Restoration Crisis*, p. 75.

8 This work denied that the powers of prorogation and dissolution resided solely in the king (*ibid.*, p. 75).

9 *Ibid.*, p. 76.

10 This was the year when the Licensing Act was lapsed, generating 'an explosion of political pamphleteering' (Harris, *Politics under the Later Stuarts*, p. 20).

11 Cited in Knights, *Politics and Opinion in Crisis*, p. 243.

12 *Ibid.*, p. 246.

13 According to Daly, the late seventeenth-century Whigs – unlike their predecessors in the 1640s who focused on rebellion – wanted to alter the succession to the monarchy and 'cut down its legal powers' (J. Daly, 'The Idea of Absolute Monarchy in Seventeenth-Century England', *HJ*, 21 (1978), pp. 227–50, p. 244).

14 Knights, *Politics and Opinion in Crisis*, p. 245. Amongst vehement critics of popular stances in this period was David Jenkins, author of *The King's Prerogative* that came out nine days before the 31st anniversary of Charles I's beheading (Knights, *Politics and Opinion in Crisis*, p. 246). L'Estrange displayed the same criticism in his *Citt and Bumpkin* (1680).

15 Knights, *Politics and Opinion in Crisis*, pp. 249–50.

16 For Mark Knights the language adopted in the pamphlets of this phase was couched in a 'religiously apocalyptic' vocabulary (*ibid.*, p. 254).

17 *Ibid.*, pp. 255–6. Petitioning represented (and was perceived as) an attempt to oust the legitimate ruler and invade his prerogative with the aim of installing a new political agency/agent: the representatives of the country.

18 Scott, *Algernon Sidney and the Restoration Crisis*, p. 76.

19 *Ibid.*, pp. 76–7.

20 Cited in Knights, *Politics and Opinion in Crisis*, p. 240.

21 Yet elsewhere Filmer observed that divine providence could alter the succession and allow the takeover of a usurper. As he put it, '[m]any times by the act either of an usurper himself, or of those that set him up, the true heir of a crown is dispossessed, God using

the ministry of the wickedest men for the removing and setting up of kings. In such cases the subjects' obedience to the fatherly power must go along and wait upon God's providence, who only hath right to give and take away kingdoms, and thereby to adopt subjects into the obedience of another fatherly power' (*AN*, p. 144).

22 Knights, *Politics and Opinion in Crisis*, p. 249. Knights added that *Patriarcha* 'was also part of a re-examination of material written in the 1640s that was relevant to the current crisis' (*ibid.*, p. 249).

23 M. Goldie, 'John Locke and Anglican Royalism', *Political Studies*, 31 (1983), pp. 61–85, p. 62.

24 See Laslett, 'Introduction', p. 57. Filmer's other tracts were out by the middle of 1679, but they too were republished as soon as January 1680.

25 For a clear account of the Exclusion Crisis see, amongst several others, Harris, *Politics under the Later Stuarts*, pp. 80–116.

26 Locke, *Two Treatises of Government*, bk i, ch. 1, § 2, p. 160.

27 *Ibid.*, bk i, ch. 1, § 5, p. 161.

28 On Locke's attack see my introduction. When addressing the issue of the ideological separation between late seventeenth-century Tories and Whigs, it is important to remember that the former were not 'soft on either popery or arbitrary government', but that they defended – as much as their adversaries – Church and State from the internal and external threats they perceived. In fact, this attitude had characterised Filmer and his political views: popery was as much a danger for him as it was for those whom he repeatedly attacked because of their doctrines of popular government. Likewise, parliamentary rule was seen by Filmer as oppressive and as fatal to the well-being of the nation, as well as the Crown was held to be the cradle of the forces of popery and arbitrary authority by its opponents.

29 Scott, *Algernon Sidney and the Restoration Crisis*, p. 208. For Jonathan Scott 'the ideological polarities' of eighteenth-century political thinking derived from the opposing theories of Filmer, on one side, and Sidney and Locke, on the other. Their controversy 'set the terms' for eighteenth-century debates not only in England but also in Europe and America (*ibid.*, p. 210).

30 For details on the *London Gazette* see chapter 9 below.

31 *The London Gazette*, no. 1503, 12–15 April 1680, p. 2 ('Advertisements'). Scorn was not spared either: as Narcissus Luttrell reported, Filmer's *The Power of Kings* had come out by 13 April and had been condemned as 'a piece highly advancing the king's prerogative to the perfect abridging the subjects liberties' (Narcissus Luttrell, *Narcissus Luttrell's Popish Plots Catalogues*, ed. Luttrell Society, with an introduction by F. C. Francis (Oxford, 1956), p. 10). See also Knights, *Politics and Opinion in Crisis*, p. 249, n. 112.

32 Cited in Knights, *Politics and Opinion in Crisis*, p. 246. In the mid 1670s, none other than Marchamont Nedham had asserted that the English king held 'a Paternal, absolute Divine Right' (Marchamont Nedham, *A Pacquet of Advices and Animadversions Sent for London to the Men of Shaftesbury* (1676), p. 43).

33 John Monson, *Discourse Concerning Supreme Power and Common Right* (1680), pp. 2–8 (this had been composed in 1641). Schochet challenged this attribution and maintained that the work was Filmer's (see Schochet, 'New Bibliographical Discoveries', esp. pp. 135 ff.). Evidence to support the Monson attribution remains very uncertain.

34 For specific passages in which the doctrine of paternal power was claimed see Robert Constable, *God and the King* (1680), pp. 3–4.

35 This work was vehemently anti-popish and strongly critical of Jesuit political ideas.

36 As the title announced, this tract had been written 'in vindication of kingly-prerogative'.

37 References to these works as 'expressions of Filmerianism' can be found in Knights, *Politics and Opinion in Crisis*, p. 249, n. 112. However, Knights only gave the titles with no authors' name or any further details. These works were all published in London.

38 Suarez's *De Legibus* was republished in 1679 whilst the Protestant George Buchanan's *De Iure Regni* was reprinted one year later (see J. Rose, 'Robert Brady's Intellectual History and Antipopery in Restoration England', *EHR*, 122 (2007), pp. 1287–317, p. 1288).

39 The Restoration divine George Hickes composed an account of the trial and execution of the covenanter James Mitchell, who had been accused of having attempted to murder James Sharpe, Archbishop of St Andrews. The outcome was the tellingly titled *Ravillac Redivivus* (1678; Ravaillac being Henry IV's murderer). Two years later, Hickes also wrote *The Spirit of Popery speaking out of the Mouths of Phanatical Protestants* about the prosecution of the Presbyterian ministers John Kid and John King for high treason and rebellion.

40 See chapter 3 above and Goldie, 'John Locke and Anglican Royalism', p. 72.

41 According to John Miller, this royalist conflation of Jesuits and Puritans as hotheads holding the same anti-monarchical doctrines was 'in no way a coherent ideology' (J. Miller, *Popery and Politics in England, 1660–1688* (Cambridge, 1973), p. 71; Miller's position is criticised by Rose, 'Robert Brady's Intellectual History', p. 1289).

42 The last chapter was titled 'Puritan-Iesuitisme' (see David Owen, *Herod and Pilate Reconciled* ... (Cambridge, 1610), ch. 9, pp. 46–75). This work was reprinted in 1643 with the telling title of *Puritano-Iesuitismus, the Puritan turn'd Jesuite*.

43 An earlier instance seems to have been Oliver Ormerod's *The Picture of a Puritane* (1605), where the author referred to '*Puritano Papismus: or a Discoverie of Puritan Papisme*' (see Collinson, 'Antipuritanism', p. 28).

44 Filmer owned Owen's work (for the copy of the 1729 inventory of *Catalogue of Printed Books* sold from East Sutton Park by Arthur Wilson Filmer at Sotheby's, London, on 1 October 1945 see Appendix 1 below). On Bancroft, Owen and other English anti-resistance theorists see Sommerville, *Royalists and Patriots*, esp. pp. 187–91.

45 Goldie, 'John Locke and Anglican Royalism', p. 73.

46 *Ibid.*, pp. 73–4. Goldie used the term 'Catholic' to define what was mainly 'Jesuit' thinking. It was, in fact, common amongst Catholic authors to reject theories of tyrannicide; embrace conciliarist principles; support absolutism (French political reflection and the Appellants case being good examples of many of these tendencies). Goldie pointed out that '[f]ear of Popery' overcame 'hatred of Nonconformity' in two occasions, one of which was the Exclusion Crisis period (*ibid.*, p. 76).

47 *Ibid.*, p. 74.

48 See Rose, 'Robert Brady's Intellectual History', pp. 1287–317.

49 Robert Brady, *The Great Point of Succession* ... (1681), p. 38. As for Filmer, see *PT*, p. 2. Interestingly, Mary Astell followed the same trajectory to reconstruct the origins of the ideas of resistance amongst both Catholic and Protestant writers (see Mary Astell, *An Impartial Enquiry into the Causes of Rebellion and Civil War*, in Springborg (ed.),

Mary Astell. Political Writings, pp. 129–97). See also Pocock, *The Ancient Constitution*, pp. 213–17.

50 Notorious adherents of this theory were the sixteenth-century Leaguers Louis Dorléans, Jean Boucher and Gulielmus Rossaeus (William Reynolds or Rainolds).

51 See Clancy, *Papist Pamphleteers*, p. 198 and Sommerville, *Royalists and Patriots, passim*. To further prove how widespread the opinion that Jesuits and Puritans (read: Whigs and republican patriots) held the same rebellious views be it sufficient to remember that John Nalson's major work, *Impartial Collection of the Great Affairs of State* ... (1682–83), carried on its cover 'the Janus-faced puritan-cum-Jesuit' (Rose, 'Robert Brady's Intellectual History', p. 1296).

52 *AN*, 'The Preface', pp. 132–3.

53 Gooch observed that 'it was Filmer's task to translate the metaphor [which described the king as the father of his people] into an argument for absolutism' (Gooch, *Political Thought in England*, p. 162).

54 Locke, *Two Treatises of Government*, bk i, ch. 1, § 1, p. 159.

55 Of Filmer's political writings only *Patriarcha* and *The Necessity* were not issued in 1679.

56 See Robert Filmer *Patriarcha, or, The natural power of Kings by the learned Sir Robert Filmer* (printed and are to be sold by Walter Davis, 1680) and Robert Filmer, *Patriarcha, or, The natural power of kings by the learned Sir Robert Filmer, Baronet* (printed for Ric. Chiswell, Matthew Gillyflower and William Henchman, 1680).

57 J. R. Milton, 'Dating Locke's "Second Treatise"', *HPT*, 16 (1995), pp. 356–90, p. 363.

58 For an account of this historiographical trend see my introduction. To contradict this view be it sufficient to consider the following sample of references to Filmer's writings throughout the 1680s: Lancelot Addison's *The Moores Baffled being a Discourse Concerning Tanger* (1681), referring to *Quaestio*; Gilbert Burnet's *The Letter Writ by the Last Assembly General of the Clergy of France to the Protestants* (1683) and William Cave's *A Dissertation Concerning the Government of the Ancient Church by bishops, metropolitans, and patriarchs* (1683), both referring to *Patriarcha*; Edmund Elys's *Justifying faith: or, That faith by which the just do live briefly describ'd in a discourse on 1 Joh. 5.12.* (1679), referring to *Quaestio*; four biographical Hobbesian volumes, three of which mention *Quaestio* and one *Observations Concerning Hobs, Milton, Grotius* (written between 1678 and 1682, two in Latin and two in English, and published by William Crook(e)); William Hughes' *The Spirit of Prophecy* (1679), mentioning *Quaestio*; Henry Killigrew's *Sermons* (1685), in which a catalogue from 'The Works of Doctor *Hammond*' referred to *The Free-Holders Grand Inquest, touching our Sovereign Lord the King and His Parliament. To which are added Observations upon Forms of Government. Together with Directions for Obedience to Governours in dangerous and doubtful Times* By the Learned Sir *Robert Filmer*, Knight; John Lightfoot's *The works of the Reverend and learned John Lightfoot D. D., late Master of Katherine Hall in Cambridge* (1684), listing *Patriarcha*; George Mackenzie's *A Defence of the Antiquity of the Royal Line of Scotland* (1685), listing *Patriarcha*; Richard Smith's *A Letter from Mr. Richard Smith to Dr. Henry Hammond* (1684), Thomas Tanner's *Primordia* (1683), Richard Cumberland's *An Essay towards the Recovery of the Jewish Measures & Weights* (1686) and Henry Wharton's *The Enthusiasm of the Church of Rome* (1688) all listing the – by then – amply read *Patriarcha*. It is significant that, with the exception of William Atwood (see chapter 9), there are almost no references to Filmer and his writings in the year 1690.

59 See below in this chapter and chapter 8, respectively.

60 See Daly, *Sir Robert Filmer*, p. 181. As highlighted by Jacqueline Rose (Rose, 'Robert Brady's Intellectual History', p. 1291, n. 18; p. 1306, n. 110), two useful studies on some of these royalist polemicists and on Whig–Tory caricatured images of one another are S. Randall, 'Roger L'Estrange, John Nalson and "Proto-Tory" Ideas, 1677–1680' (M.Phil. thesis, University of Cambridge, 2003) and G. Tapsell, 'Politics and Political Discourse in the British Monarchies, 1680–1685' (Ph.D. thesis, University of Cambridge, 2003), respectively.

61 See John Dryden, *Absalom and Achitophel A Poem* (1681).

62 In *The Second Part of Absalom and Achitophel* (1682, line 749) the author (most probably Hahum Tate) attacked 'Dissembl'd patriots, brib'd with Egypt's gold' (cited in Rose, 'Robert Brady's Intellectual History', p. 1311). According to Annabel Patterson, Dryden expressed a form of Filmerian 'Adamic kingship' (A. M. Patterson, *Fables of Power: Aesopian Writing and Political History* (Durham and London, 1991), p. 101).

63 Philopatris, *A Satyrick Poem* ... (1682). Flatman was the anonymous author of eighty-two weekly numbers of the pro-government pamphlet *Heraclitus ridens, or, A discourse between jest and earnest ... in opposition to all libellers against the government*, which was published from February 1681 to August 1682 (*ODNB*, 'Flatman, Thomas'). L'Estrange was the well-known author, Tory champion and licenser of the press about whom I will talk below. On L'Estrange see A. Dunan-Page and B. Lynch (eds), *Roger L'Estrange and the Making of Restoration Culture* (Aldershot and Burlington, 2008).

64 Philopatris, *A Satyrick Poem*, p. 2.

65 *Ibid.*, p. 6.

66 *Ibid.*, p. 12.

67 *Ibid.*, p. 12.

68 *Ibid.*, p. 15.

69 Edward Pelling, *Sermon Preached at St. Mary Le Bow. Novemb. 27, 1682* (1683), p. 4.

70 *ODNB*, 'L'Estrange, Sir Robert'.

71 Daly, *Sir Robert Filmer*, p. 181. According to Daly, the same was true of John Nalson and Laurence Womock, who showed 'no traces of Filmerism or of anything related to it' (*ibid.*, p. 181). On the whole, Daly did not see any '[e]vidence of Filmerian ideas in royalist writers' throughout the seventeenth century, and certainly not in the post-Restoration period (see esp. *ibid.*, 'Appendix A', pp. 173–93; but for very different conclusions on Filmer's influence see Schochet, *Patriarchalism in Political Thought*, esp. pp. 185–8, 214–15). For Daly even the deeply Filmerian Robert Brady 'had not read Filmer' and never mentioned him directly, but only through Whig critics such as John Somers (Daly, *Sir Robert Filmer*, pp. 183–5). Likewise, neither Thomas Goddard nor Sir George Mackenzie mentioned Filmer (*ibid.*, pp. 185–6). Daly paid more attention to Nathaniel Johnston, but only to conclude that he 'was in some ways the compleat royalist political thinker' whose sources were 'Digges, Sheringham, Nalson and Mackenzie' and not the upholder of 'legal patriarchalism' à la Filmer (*ibid.*, pp. 187–90). According to Daly, these authors and Sir Robert at most shared an idea of the origins of government based on Adam's power and some generic royalist statements about politics. Filmer was unique throughout the century and remained so in the panorama of post-revolutionary England when he was 'mentioned specifically but seldom and in terms which re-emphasize the puzzling problem of his influence on royalists' (*ibid.*, p. 191). Moreover, as proved by

Jeremy Collier's case, the Jacobites were not familiar with Filmer either (*ibid.*, p. 192). The present chapter and the two following ones will prove these conclusions far-fetched.

72 Hunt was the author of the strongly exclusionist *Great and Weighty Considerations Relating to the Duke of York* (1680) and of *Postscript for Rectifying some Mistakes in some of the Inferior Clergy, Mischievous to our Government and Religion* (1682) where he attacked parish divines for propagating tenets such as the divine right of kings and passive obedience. The *Postscript* turned Hunt into a Whig hero and earned him the epithet 'Postscript Hunt' (*ODNB*, 'Hunt, Thomas').

73 Sir Roger L'Estrange, *Observator in Dialogue* (1681–87), 'Saturday, December 24, 1681; Issue 83', p. 2.

74 Rejecting the idea of the unalterable hereditary succession of kings, Hunt targeted *Patriarcha* and its Adamite theories. Hunt also sustained a contractual view of the origins of society and supported the right of resistance against unlawful governors.

75 L'Estrange, *Observator*, 'Issue 83', p. 1. With the *Observator* L'Estrange represented the opinions of the provincial Tories in contrast to the urban setting of Whiggery (M. Goldie, 'Roger L'Estrange's *Observator* and the Exorcism of the Plot', in Dunan-Page and Lynch (eds), *Roger L'Estrange*, pp. 67–88, p. 74). *Patriarcha* was, after all, the product of a Kentish gentleman. For possible Kent-based connections between L'Estrange and Filmer see chapter 6 above.

76 L'Estrange, *Observator*, 'Issue 83', p. 2.

77 *Ibid.*, p. 2.

78 *Ibid.*, p. 2.

79 Considering that the *Observator* had in the clergy its principal audience, L'Estrange's encomiastic words about Filmer must have had an impact on them (Goldie, 'Roger L'Estrange's *Observator*', p. 75). For Goldie, L'Estrange was 'Filmerian' *and* 'Hobbesian' in that he embraced both patriarchalism and Hobbes' positions on religious affairs. L'Estrange was undoubtedly 'crystalline about one doctrine': sovereignty was 'univocal and absolute, and cannot be divided or shared'. He also rejected the theory of mixed monarchy that had been so caustically criticised by Filmer and Hobbes (*ibid.*, pp. 82–3). Goldie, however, underlined that 'L'Estrange is arguably more persistently Cicerorian than Filmerian or Hobbesian' in that he espoused 'a doctrine of the middle way in politics' defending those who held office and whose values rested on responsibility, self-abnegation, public duties, moral discipline (*ibid.*, p. 85). And yet it cannot be neglected that the three thinkers all converged on the issue of popular power as the cradle of instability and, worse, anarchy. Annabel Patterson argued that 'L'Estrange had established a reputation ... for that extreme form of theoretical royalism known as Filmerism' (Patterson, *Fables of Power*, p. 139). In a similar vein, whilst referring to his *Fables of Aesop and Other Eminent Mythologists ...* (1692), Mark Loveridge spoke of 'L'Estrange's Filmerite pitch' (M. Loveridge, *A History of Augustan Fable* (Cambridge, 1998), p. 157).

80 L'Estrange, *Observator*, 'Wednesday, December 14, 1681; Issue 80', p. 1.

81 *Ibid.*, 'Wednesday, December 14, 1681; Issue 80', p. 1.

82 *Ibid.*, 'Wednesday, December 14, 1681; Issue 80', p. 1.

83 *Ibid.*, 'Wednesday, December 14, 1681; Issue 80', p. 1.

84 *Ibid.*, 'Wednesday, December 14, 1681; Issue 80', p. 1.

85 *Ibid.*, 'Wednesday, December 14, 1681; Issue 80', p. 2.

86 *Ibid.*, 'Wednesday, December 14, 1681; Issue 80', p. 2.

87 *PT*, pp. 3–4.

88 *Ibid.*, p. 2 (italics added). John Nalson had vented his scorn for the common people by equating rebellions with 'Popular Insurrections of the Mind', which occurred 'when the misled Passions (those Common People of the Soul) usurp the Sovereignty' (John Nalson, *The Common Interest of King and People* ... (1677), ch. i, p. 3). Nalson had also compared '[t]he Members or Representatives of a Republick', who 'stil'd themselves' as '*Custodes Libertatis Patriae*' with kings and had concluded that, whilst these republican patriots were 'but the Guardians, and as such, many times commit great Wastes', 'a *Monarch* is truly *Pater Patriae*, the Father of his Country' (*ibid.*, ch. iv, p. 112).

89 L'Estrange, *Observator*, 'Monday, December 24, 1683; Issue 461', p. 1.

90 *Ibid.*, 'Saturday, January 5, 1684; Issue 468', p. 1.

91 *Ibid.*, 'Saturday, January 5, 1684; Issue 468', p. 1.

92 In his last political tract, Filmer had reiterated that '[a]ll power on earth is either derived or usurped from the fatherly power, there being no other original to be found of any power whatsoever' (*DO*, p. 284).

93 L'Estrange, *Observator*, 'Saturday, January 5, 1684; Issue 468', p. 1.

94 *Ibid.*, 'Saturday, January 5, 1684; Issue 468', p. 2.

95 William Petyt, *Miscellanea Parliamentaria* (1680), p. 67.

96 *Ibid.*, p. 136.

97 William Temple, *Miscellanea ... by a person of honour* (1680), pp. 65–6.

98 Interestingly, during the period 1660–78 the expression '*pater patriae*' was often found in re-publications of works originally printed a few decades earlier (such as those of Francis Bacon, William Prynne, Sir Henry Wotton). The majority of references to the phrase come from the time around the beginning of the Restoration with only a few from the 1670s (the database EEBO shows that for the years 1660–78 out of forty-nine records only fourteen containing *pater patriae* are post-1670). With regard to the image of the *pater patriae* in Edward Bagshaw, Bishop Sanderson and William Falkner see Daly, *Sir Robert Filmer*, pp. 179–81.

99 Samuel Crossman, *Two Sermons preached in the cathedral-church of Bristol* ... (1681), p. 24. In the same year, Sir William Dugdale and Thomas Frankland resorted to the metaphor of the king as *pater patriae* when describing the reigns of James I and Charles I (see Sir William Dugdale, *A Short View of the Late Troubles in England* ... (Oxford, 1681), p. 267 and Thomas Frankland, *The Annals of King James and King Charles the First* ... (1681), *passim*). The playwright Elkanah Settle, instead, used the expression '*pater patriae*' to show that Charles II was not fulfilling his paternal role: he asserted that 'when a Popish *Monarch* shall subvert all Right, and violate all Laws, till oppressing a wretched Nation, more like a *Lupus Agri* than *Pater Patriae*, he so wholly perverts the Duty of his great Office, and defaces in himself the nearest Image of a Deity, by so falsly representing his Vice-gerent' (Elkanah Settle, *The Character of a Popish Successour* ... (1681), pp. 21–2). Settle wanted to influence the outcome of the forthcoming parliament by demonstrating the necessity of legislation that banned a Catholic succession. He accused the Duke of York of trying to alienate English people from their king. *The Character* provoked a number of replies from Tory propagandists, to which Settle in turn responded later on in 1681 with *A Vindication of 'The Character of a Popish Successor'*. Surely at odds with Settle's views was the sharp-tongue L'Estrange for whom

the king – in the context of the '*Privileges*' of 'a *City*' – 'is Ty'd by evident *Reason of State*, and by *Political Equity*; both as a *Wise Prince*, and as a *Pater Patriae*, a Father of his Country' 'to *Resume*, for the *Safety* of the *whole*, such Indulgences as were only *Granted* for the *behoof* of a *Part*' (Sir Roger L'Estrange, *A Memento Treating of the Rise, Progress, and Remedies of Seditions* ... (Printed in the year 1642, and now reprinted, 1682), p. 83). For the use of the phrase *pater patriae* see also Bulstrode Whitlocke, *Memorials of the English affairs* ... (1682), p. 279.

100 White Kennett, *A Letter from a Student at Oxford to a Friend in the Country Concerning the Approaching Parliament* ... (1681), p. 14. '*W.ldon*' is most likely Robert Weldon, rector of Stony Stanton in Leicestershire, and author of *The Doctrine of the Scriptures concerning the Originall of Dominion* published in 1648 by Richard Royston (I thank Johann Sommerville for help on this point).

101 Edward Pelling, *The Apostate Protestant a Letter to a Friend* ... (1682), p. 58. This was also the year when the commemoration of 'Gunpowder Treason Day' in London was marred by troubles amongst the mob. In the same year, whilst addressing the important issue of the legitimacy of 'conquest', Denzil Holles clarified that '[f]or the first, Sir *Robert Filmer* will tell you, *No Man can bind himself in a matter depending of his own Will, there can be no Obligation which taketh State from the meer Will of him that bindeth himself*'. Discussing the value of grants and charters, Holles quoted Filmer as his guide: 'yet Sir *Robert Filmer* tells us expresly; *The Laws, Ordinances, Letters, Patents, Priviledges, and Grants of Princes, have no Force but during their Life, if they be not ratified by the express Consent, or at least by the sufferance of the Prince following, who had knowledg thereof*' (Denzil Holles, *Lord Hollis, his Remains Being a Second Letter to a Friend* ... (1682), pp. 296, 299).

102 Samuel Gilbert, *The Florists Vade-Mecum* ... (1682), 'A Catalogue of some Books lately Printed for, and sold by *Thomas Simmons*, at the *Princes Arms* in *Ludgate-street*'.

103 Cited in R. Ashcraft, *Revolutionary Politics and Locke's Two Treatises of Government* (Princeton, 1986), p. 187.

104 Isaac Barrow, *A Treatise of the Pope's Supremacy* ... (1683), pp. 145–6.

105 Thomas Gipps, *Three Sermons preached in Lent* ... (1683), p. 12. In the same year, John Hayward's *The Right of Succession asserted against the false reasonings and seditious insinuations of R. Dolman alias Parsons and others* was republished for his strong opposition to Jesuit political doctrines.

106 Sir Roger L'Estrange, *Theosebia*, ... (1683), p. 11.

107 See chapter 9 below.

108 John Aucher, *The Arraignment of Rebellion* ... (1684), pp. 95–6.

109 *Ibid.*, p. 97.

110 *Ibid.*, p. 97.

111 *Ibid.*, pp. 97–8.

112 John Walker, *The Antidote:* ... (1684), p. 113.

113 John Wilson, *A Discourse of Monarchy* ... (1684), pp. 52–3. According to Schochet, two Filmerian authors writing in 1684 were Thomas Goddard and Sir George Mackenzie (d. 1691). The former argued that between the Flood and the creation of the Greek states absolute authority had been in the hands of fathers due to their superiority over the rest of humankind. The royalist Scots George Mackenzie published his *Jus*

Regium where he criticised the idea of a state of nature in which men were originally free. Above all, he embraced a version of the patriarchalist doctrine which, despite not coinciding with Filmer's, certainly recognised the importance of the paternal right to describe sovereignty. Likewise, Nathaniel Johnston (d. 1705) referred to *Patriarcha* as a repository of arguments with which to reject both the notion of popular authority and the theory of consent (Schochet, *Patriarchalism in Political Thought*, pp. 208–9). However, it should be noted that a theorist like Mackenzie made explicit use of *Patriarcha* when attacking 'Jesuitical and Fanatical Principles': 'that every man is born free, and at Liberty to choose what form of government he pleaseth' was for him 'most false, for every man is born a Subject to his own Parents, who ... do all other things that a King could do, as we see the Patriarches did in their own Families' (George Mackenzie, *Jus Regium* ... (1684) p. 24). The phrasing in the two texts is almost exactly identical.

114 *ODNB*, 'Nalson, John'.

115 John Nalson, *Reflections upon Coll. Sidney's Arcadia* ... (1684), p. 10.

116 See *ODNB*, 'Settle, Elkanah'. Settle's allegiance to the Whig cause lasted up until 1682. However, Shaftesbury's departure for the Netherlands and the failure of the exclusionist project at the end of the same year changed Settle's political militancy, as a result of which he began writing Tory propaganda.

117 Elkanah Settle, *The Present State of England in relation to popery manifesting the absolute impossibility of introducing popery and arbitrary power into this kingdom* ... (1684), p. 22. In this work, which was both a recantation and a confutation of his own previous views from 1681 (see above in this chapter), Settle also criticised the author of *The Character of the Popish Successour* (namely, himself) for, 'instead of *Pater patriae*', he had made the king 'nothing but a downright *Lupus Agri*' (Settle, *The Present State* ..., p. 24).

118 Henry Anderson, *A Loyal Tear Dropt on the vault of the High and Mighty Prince, Charles II, of glorious and happy memory* (1685), p. 13.

119 John Northleigh, *The Triumph of our Monarchy, over the plots and principles of our rebels and republicans being remarks on their most eminent libels* (1685), p. 623 (misprinted as p. 523).

120 *Ibid.*, p. 624.

121 *Ibid.*, p. 627. For Filmer's severe criticism of these republics see *OA, passim.*

122 Northleigh, *The Triumph of our Monarchy*, p. 627.

123 *Ibid.*, p. 633.

124 *Ibid.*, pp. 637–8.

125 *Ibid.*, p. 639 (misprinted as p. 638). This argument on the 'levelling' pursued by '[m]any ignorant men' who 'are apt by the name of commonwealth to understand a popular government, wherein wealth and all things shall be common' came straight from *OG*, 'The Preface', p. 186. As for Filmer's similar criticism of Hobbes see *ibid.*, pp. 187–97.

126 See Northleigh, *The Triumph of our Monarchy*, pp. 641–5.

127 *Ibid.*, p. 653.

128 *Ibid.*, pp. 646 ff.

129 *Ibid.*, pp. 653–4.

130 *Ibid.*, p. 655 (since after this point there are gaps in the pagination, I refer to the pages as they appear in the printed edition, without necessarily taking into account the consequential order).

131 *Ibid.*, pp. 670–1.

132 *Ibid.*, p. 671. In 1686 Fabian Philipps, apologist of the regime of the 'martyr' Charles I, praised 'the Learned Collections of Sir *Robert Filmer*' with regard to the Norman Conquest. He then remarked that 'when men are, (saith the Learned *Sr Robert Filmer*) Assembled by an humane power, the authority that doth assemble them, Can also limit and direct the execution of that Power' (Fabian Philipps, *Investigatio jurium antiquorum et rationalium Regni* ... (1686), pp. 173, 382). In a note Phillips also referred to 'Sir *Robert Filmers* Patriarcha or the natural power of Kings. p. 60' (*ibid.*, p. 382).

Chapter 8

Much ado about nothing? Edmund Bohun's
rehabilitation of *Patriarcha*, the issue of
allegiance and Adamite anti-republicanism

The fatherly care of the sovereign for his subjects was a cardinal theme
in the work of Filmer's strenuous defender[1] Edmund Bohun (1645–99).[2]
In 1684 the deeply unpopular Williamite Tory writer – who was a strong
opponent of dissenters too – issued *A defence of Sir Robert Filmer* against
Sidney's scaffold speech, whilst the following year he published and prefaced
an edition of Filmer's *Patriarcha*.[3] Bohun emphasised that kings 'could feel
for their people the same "natural affection of a father" for his children' to the
extent that princes loved not only their people in general, but each particular
individual.[4] Throwing a few critical remarks at Sidney's treacherous conduct,
Bohun started off *A defence* by describing Filmer as 'a Gentleman, who was
known to me by his Learned, and Ingenious Works, and in all probability died
when I was an infant'.[5] By contrast, Sidney was a hothead whose standpoints
'will be accounted Treasons in all Goverments, but Pure Democracies': so
much so that even 'the Pretended Common-Wealth of *England* would hardly
have endured such Doctrines' because they were 'contrary to their Interest'.[6]

Having dismissed the republican thinker, Bohun employed the same
language used by King James VI and I in the 1610s to charge that only those
who had '*itching* Fingers to be plucking down their Princes, and calling them
to account, and revenging their own supposed Wrongs on them' would be so
wicked as to attack Filmer's ideas.[7] The latter had proved that the sole 'fear
of Punishment' as a 'motive' to obey 'Princes' was not enough to guarantee
stability in the polity for, in this case, 'the Obedience is weak, irregular,
unsteady'.[8] Similarly, Bohun argued that subjects had to show their attachment to 'the Lawful Heir' by resisting any 'Usurper' without 'just Title'. Yet 'if
the Right Heir, or Family fail, or is extinguished; then that Obligation fails' too,
so that subjects 'have no right to Usurp upon them ['the Heirs of the Usurper']
because their Ancestors did so upon another preceding Family'.[9] Otherwise,
by leaving 'Eternal Liberty to Subjects ... to revenge from one Generation to

another, one Usurpation with another, the World would be turned into ... a Field of Blood'.[10] This view implied that men were safe only in a patriarchal monarchy where they 'can assure' themselves 'of more Justice ... from a Prince, or single Person'.[11] Resorting to the Adamite paradigm,[12] Bohun declared that 'an Hereditary Monarchy' had been 'setled by God himself in the very infancy of Mankind', as Filmer had so eloquently proved.[13] Bohun elucidated his notion of sovereignty by distinguishing between a 'Magistrate', a term denoting 'a Subordinate Governour', and 'a Soveraign Prince'.[14] The latter was the creator of all laws to which people submitted out of their 'Allegiance' to his Adamite aura.

It is important to notice that, whilst 'allegiance' denoted a personal and unconditioned bond towards those in power (often expressed through an oath of fidelity to the monarch), the term 'trust' (employed by Locke in the *Two Treatises*) referred to an impersonal and formal mechanism based on the social contract. It is thus plausible to maintain that in stressing the argument of allegiance to the king monarchists like Bohun delineated a type of patriotic allegiance, whereas the model set forth by their opponents entailed a form of trust in the law, in its formality and impartiality. In this respect, Filmer and Locke produced diametrically opposite theories of 'trust'. Whereas the patriarchalist saw trust as the outcome of fatherly care, Locke theorised that trust was reposed in the hands of governors by the people, who could – when they reputed the action necessary following violations and abuses of such a trust – dissolve government and re-appropriate their original power.

For Bohun the 'highest' divinely sanctioned and most original power was '[p]aternal'. Drawing on Seneca, he underscored the intertwined relation between 'the Duty of a Prince' and that of 'kind Parents': '[t]hat which becomes a Parent, becomes a Prince: Who is stiled THE FATHER OF HIS COUNTRY, without flattery'.[15] The image of the king as *pater patriae* was here employed with rhetorical vigour: despite being called 'the Great, the Happy, the August', the 'highest' title was that which 'styled him the Father of his Country', so that 'the Prince might consider the power of a Father was given him'. This was 'the most Temperate of all Powers' because it took great care of 'the Welfare of the Children' placing 'their Good before its own'. Endowed with 'Clemency', kings treated 'the meanest of their Subjects as their Children, and all Subjects' looked 'upon their Prince, as their common Father'.[16] For Bohun such a mutuality of interests had fundamental consequences in that it created a condition where 'there could be no Tyrants' nor 'Traytors and Rebels' since 'both Prince and People would strive to out do each other in the Offices of Love and Duty'.[17] As shown in *Patriarcha*, this harmony could only be found in a patriarchal monarchy where the fatherly care of the prince informed ruler-ship over subjects. Likewise, Bohun thought that only a persuasive account of the advantages provided by a fatherly monarchy prompted people to see the superior guardianship and effective authority of kings. This position also helped Bohun when rejecting the ruinous doctrine that since the 'Multitude (*Plebs*) makes a King', it 'may DEPOSE him'. As Filmer had explained, this creed came from the deadly arsenal of popish theories, 'imbraced by the School-men, and after them by the Presbyterians'.[18] Against it, *A defence* drew the very Filmerian conclusion that 'many a Child, by succeeding a King, hath the right of a Father, over many a Gray-headed Multitude, and hath the Title of *Pater Patriae*'.[19] By the same token, it was against the *dead* old cause 'Clamour' of 'Mr. *Sidney*' and against the still very much *alive* noise of republican theorists that Bohun put forward the Adamite paradigm whereby the monarch was father of the fatherland.[20]

BOHUN AND *PATRIARCHA*

In his longer writings defending Filmer's theories,[21] Bohun argued that *Patriarcha* was the result of Sir Robert's courage to maintain

> the Antiquity and Excellence of *Monarchy* against the Pretences of the *Republican* Writers of those times, with such strength of Argument and variety both of Ancient and Modern Learning that he baffl'd all the shews of Reason they were able to produce against this first and best form of Government.[22]

Bohun clarified that 'this Piece (which was one of the best he wrote on this subject) was never published in his life time, but passed from hand to hand in Manuscript till the year 1680'. Despite 'all these injuries' (such as mistranscriptions), 'it met with a general esteem amongst Learned and Loyal men'.[23] Bohun observed that, besides content (which 'no sooner did it appear in the World ... gave such an Alarm to our Loyal Commonwealthsmen' sending 'several Pens at work to traduce and defame both the Author (though dead) and the Book too'),[24] 'Stile' and format of the book, *Patriarcha*'s 'timing' had done much to enrage Filmer's adversaries. This was so because 1680 'was a year that could least brook this sort of Tractates of all other'.[25] In fact, 'this Piece was not to be indured in such a Crisis of Affairs', so that his enemies tried at all costs 'to cry it down, and make the people believe Sir *Robert Filmar* was for an *Absolute Monarchy* Jure divino'.[26] Amongst the guilty ones was Tyrrell, who had claimed that for Filmer the only legitimate form of government was an unlimited monarchy[27] and had unfairly concluded that Sir Robert's monarch '*can ever be obliged by any Fundamental*' laws or '*any Coronation Oaths, to abstain from the Lives, Liberties and Properties of their Subjects farther than they themselves shall think it convenient*'.[28]

If this attempt at tuning down some of Filmer's radical principles was no doubt part and parcel of Bohun's polemically driven attack on Tyrrell's 'Cavils and Misconstructions', it can also be seen as an expression of some differences between Sir Robert and his advocate.[29] In this respect, Bohun expounded more standard monarchist views on the origins of government and obedience; rejected the idea of popular sovereignty and scathingly discounted the notion of the 'Election' of monarchs.[30] He displayed a traditional representation of the Adam and Eve story;[31] assigned considerable weight to divine Providence as a factor determining political life;[32] made primogeniture one of the assets of both political and societal organisation;[33] gave great importance to social hierarchy.[34]

Despite these more mainstream positions, Bohun was *tout court* in tune with Filmer with regard to power and governance. Thus, he pragmatically declared that 'no Prince' would attack 'any Man' so brutally 'whom he believed able (if willing) to revenge the wrong'. Hence 'all this discontented fretful [republican] Rhetorick' set out by 'the Enemies of Monarchy' was 'of no use'.[35] In fact, worse than tyrants were '[a]mbitious and factious' men 'left at liberty to insinuate into the Rabble and the Great and little Vulgar' dangerous opinions legitimating the punishment of princes *'when they do amiss'*.[36] Contrary to Tyrrell's distorting accusations that Filmer had turned subjects into *'Slaves'* as *'in all Absolute Monarchies from France to China'*,[37] Bohun claimed that those who maintained that kings were *'bound to Act according to Laws, and to their Oaths'* defended rebellion. They were extremely nefarious people since they thought it *'lawful for a Man to defend himself against the injustice and oppression of his Prince'*.[38] But despite being blatantly 'false', their view of political affairs was proving influential. As Bohun said, 'there were more Clamors of Arbitrary Government, Tyranny and Slavery here in *England*, between 78 and 82. and between 38. and 48. than in all the absolute Monarchies between *France* and *China*, and the South and North Pole'.[39]

Bohun's main goal was, therefore, to show that Filmer had employed the patriarchalist paradigm in order to depict sovereigns as deriving their power from 'the Fountain head' and prove 'that *Adam* who was the Father of Mankind was a Prince'.[40] Bohun remarked that Tyrrell had attacked Filmer by arguing that patriarchalist 'Treatises' said 'little or nothing of the Rights of Children in the state of Nature towards their Parents'. This argument revealed that the author of *Patriarcha non Monarcha* had failed to see the dangers ensuing from having children who might disobey their parents. Politically, this was tantamount to legitimate subjects' rebellion to the ruler.[41] Instead, Bohun maintained that 'a Son is subject to his Father, and most of all in a state of Nature'.[42] He spoke of 'a priority of Being': if this 'gave *Adam* a power over his Wife, it gave him much more so over his Children'.[43] In fact, '*Adam* had a full and Princely Power over all his descendants'.[44] Like Filmer, Bohun stressed that only fatherly kings 'willingly bear so great a burthen' as to look after and guide their people.[45] Hence he rejected Tyrrell's accusation that it was 'incon-venient to give the Right of a Supreme Father, to one who because he is not the natural Father, may possibly want the Natural affection of a Father'. To this Bohun responded that God had made 'all Governments ... spring from Paternal Power' because this was 'the mildest of all Powers' passed on 'to Hereditary Monarchies, which are the Divinest, the most Natural and the best of all Governments, and in which the People have the least hand'.[46] In his attack on 'the Republicans'[47] Bohun reiterated that 'the Original of all these Ancient Monarchies was founded in Paternity'. Most important of all for our discourse, he asserted that 'the Nation' took 'a Name from their Founder or Father' and the people 'were call'd the Children of their Founder, Father, and first King'.[48] The latter was *pater patriae*.[49]

Thanks to 'the easie and sweet Methods of a *Paternal Monarchy*', achieved 'with much simplicity, integrity and justice, and with as little oppression as State and Magnificence',[50] '[p]eople' clung 'stifly to' fatherly rulers 'when they are once setled' and averted that great 'Calamity' of having 'the Title of their Prince disputable by the Sword'.[51] If usurpation occurred, 'Subjects' would always be 'bound to serve and defend' their usurping prince 'as if he could derive his pedigree from the Eldest Son of *Noah*'.[52] Obedience was owed to him unconditionally, otherwise 'there would be no end of Usurpations, but Mankind would be exposed to eternal Confusions, Wars and Devastations'.[53] In fact, being 'Paternal Government' divinely sanctioned, it followed that 'not one title of Popular Elections' existed 'in those Earlydays':[54] Adam and Noah 'were Sovereign Princes as they were the Fathers of Mankind', which confirmed that God was 'the Author of Monarchical Government, and not any Pacts or Elections of the People'. Since God had begun 'this Government twice in the World', there was no 'need ... of a whimsical popular Election of the immediate Successors of these two Patriarchs'.[55] Bohun drew his argument nearer to the original Filmerian doctrine by establishing that, even when due to 'the failure of a Line or Race of Kings' a king was nominated by 'the prime Heads and Fathers of Families', monarchical (fatherly) power was never 'a Donative from the people'. Rather, the 'Consent' of 'the Heads of the People' was only a 'substituted' testimony of God's proper power.[56]

For Bohun the superiority of patriarchal monarchies was further demon-strated by the fact that 'the [republican] Commonwealths that have so arisen in the World are as rare as a *Phenix*'. The example of '*Rome*' so often brought up by republican thinkers only showed that '[i]t was a Cup too much of Sedition, disloyalty and ingratitude to the best form of Government in the World'.[57] Exactly like Filmer, Bohun compared Rome with England. In both cases, 'the care and kindness of their Princes' had given people wealth until 'discontented Demagones' [*sic*] had 'put a Cup of seditious Principles into their Hands' prompting people to seek 'after more liberty than they knew how to use, and so indeed intoxicated them'. The latter ended up 'like drunken Men' who 'staggered and reeled from one Form of Government to another, till at last in spight of all their aversions, they fell all under absolute Monarchies again'. In his vivid prose and with an eye to events around him, Bohun – for whom 'this was the fate of all the Old Commonwealths' – remarked that 'what fortune attends the New Edition [of a commonwealth], God only knows'.[58] The real danger stemmed from 'the rage and disingenuity of our Republicans',[59] who – exactly like the Jesuits – propagated lethal doctrines based on the idea that subjects could 'take Arms to revenge their quarrel' against 'Princes' who 'abuse their power'. In fact, by acting in this way, subjects turned into 'Rebels'. After all, Bohun categorically maintained, God had 'never vested the Populace, nor any Subject upon earth with a power of judging the Supreme Powers under which they live'.[60]

Bohun addressed further important political points in 'A Conclusion or Postscript' added to his edition of *Patriarcha*. Here he clarified that Filmer had been '[o]verwhelmed with the Confusions and Disorders of the Times in which he lived, and died'.[61] As such the publication of *Patriarcha* was made all the more 'necessary' because of the 'late too near approaches to' England's 'former state of misery and disorder'.[62] In this respect, Bohun interestingly saw *Patriarcha* 'as Practical' in that its 'main end is to make men better Subjects to their Prince, better Neighbours to each other in the State', expunging all divisions between royalists and patriots, court and country[63] and adopting, instead, the monogenetic principle whereby mankind had derived from 'one common Father'.[64] The indisputable fatherly origin of political power prevented monarchies from falling prey to 'Confusion, distrust, and Cruelty', which was the norm in 'Republicks, or Many Headed Governments'.[65] For Bohun the antithesis of Adamite monarchies were 'pure despotick and absolute Tyrannies', which 'had they proceeded from Pacts and Agreements they would in all probability have been at least Elective Monarchies, which is next the despotick, the worst and most uncertain and weak form of Monarchies'.[66] In his ranking of different governments, Bohun significantly placed the elective type just above the despotic form. At the opposite end of the spectrum stood 'Paternal Monarchy, Successive and Hereditary, which is the very best Form of Government'.[67] The latter was the most apt to prevent 'all violent and undutiful resistance' since '[t]he People' could be 'thoroughly convinced that their Prince' was not only 'the Minister of God', but also 'the Father of their Country'.[68] As a result, Bohun concluded, '[t]his aws and appeaseth them [subjects], keeps them quiet, and safe too'.[69]

In his analysis of Filmerian ideas Bohun picked up the one which could most fruitfully serve the monarchist cause in the disputes of the mid 1680s. This concerned *Patriarcha*'s image of the monarch as caring fatherly authority. In contrast to republican views, Filmer's patriarchalism fostered 'Mutual Trust and Confidence betwixt the Prince and People'. This type of polity was the best because it possessed 'the very Soul of all Government', that is, 'fatherly love and filial duty and reverence'. It followed that 'when the Prince is once secure of the duty and affection of his Subjects, not only his, but their lives will be the more easie and pleasant'.[70] Most importantly, Bohun pointed out that 'a distrust of their Subjects Loyalty' had 'made Princes place their security in standing Armies and Guards of Foreigners'[71] (which for Filmer was a feature of popular states),[72] with 'destructive' consequences for them and 'miserable' results for the people. Relying on Aristotle, Bohun specified that the 'difference betwixt a Despotick and a Paternal Monarchy' was 'that the Guards of the former are Foreigners, and of the latter, Natives'.[73] This was a clear rejection of the traditional (Machiavellian) republican trope of a militia formed of native citizens as opposed to mercenaries or foreign troops generally employed by monarchs. The patriarchalist Bohun – like Filmer before and Jeremy Collier after him[74] – wanted to put the record straight by showing that patriotic commitment was not an exclusive feature of republics. Rather, it primarily pertained to fatherly monarchies where the paternal role of the prince stimulated feelings of unselfish dedication to public causes such as the protection of the kingdom.

In light of how crucial the debate on the much dreaded 'standing army' had been in English political parlance throughout the century,[75] it is evident that Bohun targeted his adversaries by striking a highly sensitive chord. Without a patriarchal monarchy, the nation would inevitably plunge into a state of constant warfare due to a menacing foreign military presence. By contrast, the propagation of 'this Paternal Power' in many different parts 'round the Globe of the Earth' ultimately confirmed that monarchy was the best form of government. It also proved that the patriarchalist 'Doctrine' did not – as its enemies charged – defend tyranny in princes 'by setting them out of the reach of violence from their Subjects, and making them accountable to none but God'. Rather, Bohun explained, it prompted sovereigns to 'consider' that 'they must know that they are the Fathers of their People, and ought to treat them [subjects] accordingly'.[76] Indeed, this scenario was what made fatherly monarchies peaceful and more successful. 'And surely' – Bohun emphasised – 'there is no nation under Heaven [which] has more reason ['to be very thankful'] than the English who are under a Paternal Monarchy, which has taken the best care that is possible to secure them, not only from oppression and wrong, but from the very fear of it'.[77] Besides referring to contemporary controversies on hereditary right, this argument reconciled in Filmerian fashion defence of patriarchalism and patriotic sentiments: kingship and fatherland were conjoined against republican patriots. To further show that that of the 'patriotic monarch' was the model to be adopted in England Bohun tellingly reminded his readers that 'when of late years the People were Cajoled into a Rebellion against' their prince 'upon a Pretence that their Liberties were in danger of being taken from them', 'an Arbitrary Government' – 'which had no right, nor shewed them any Mercy' – had been 'set up with a standing Army'.[78] It had thus been 'their deliverers, and their Army, their Representatives, whom they [had] set up against their King', that had 'enslaved them'. Only 'his late Majesties Restauration' had brought back England's 'former state of Liberty' and one which – Bohun warned – could be lost again 'by another Rebellion' or destroyed 'by our folly'.[79]

Bohun manifested with regard to the 1680s the same fears that had informed Filmer's anti-patriots discourse in the 1620s. Most of all, as Sir Robert had targeted 'the common people' and their mouthpieces, so his disciple deployed a similar attack upon the self-styled 'Representatives' of the people who had ruined the country in the 1640s, had tyrannically ruled in the 1650s and who were once again ready to strike against the monarchy in the 1680s.

THE THEORETICAL APPEAL OF *PATRIARCHA*: PATRIARCHALISM AND PATRIOTISM REUNITED

The analysis hitherto conducted helps us understand that *Patriarcha* needs to be interpreted as a *work of crisis*, that is to say, as a text connected to the Caroline crisis of the late 1620s and to the exclusion–succession crisis of the 1680s. In the former context, conflicting political views of liberty and sovereignty had mirrored the works of patriots and monarchists. Equally, the publication of *Patriarcha* occurred at a time when the monarchy was severely attacked and justification for political obligation questioned.[80] Distinguishing between *kingship by invitation* and *kingship by hereditary right*, the exclusionists rejected not only the succession of James Duke of York, but also Charles II's claims to be the legitimate royal heir as Charles I's son. Whigs argued that Charles II had attained power thanks to the parliamentary appointment of 1660, which entailed the right to deprive him of his mandate in case of his tyrannical conduct.[81] Like Filmer in the Caroline era, the Tories now knew that their task was to win back those (moderates) who, as a consequence of the Popish Plot, had decided to support the rebellious opposition.[82]

In this climate, terms like 'Martyrs' and 'Traytors' became (once again) central. In the battle of ideas as much as in the political arena of party-conflict people strove to be depicted as 'Martyrs' to the country and its cause, whilst labelling their adversaries as 'Traytors' to the nation and to King and/or Parliament. This was the language Filmer had adopted at the beginning of *Patriarcha* when addressing vital questions about monarchical government and obedience. As such in 1680 the treatise was unearthed precisely because of the message it conveyed with regard to the issue of 'a man' who 'may become a martyr for his country by being a traitor to his prince'.[83] Patriarchalism offered a powerful answer to the humanist and republican contention that *amor patriae* was intertwined with *caritas*, as this tenet implied the dangerous (because sacred) equation of the self-sacrifice of the citizen dying *pro patria* with Christ's death for the salvation of humankind.

This explains why patriarchalist writers like Filmer and Bohun articulated a narrative of kingship whereby kings had to be benevolent towards each particular subject, act for the *communis patria* ('the new *corpus mysticum*', namely 'the national territorial monarchy')[84] and pursue the general interest in a fatherly manner. In so doing, they defused the explosive device of martyrdom, both in its original Christian component and in its newly tailored republican fabric of Ciceronian, Stoic and humanist brand. This is also why Filmer, Bohun, Northleigh and others insisted on the notion of 'parricide' as the worst crime subjects could commit against their king. Their identification of the supreme ruler with '*Patria ipsa*'[85] was a forthright attempt to rule out the doctrine for which 'in defence of the fatherland it was a merit rather than a crime if a man killed his own father'.[86] Patriarchalist discourse neutralised the dangers of parricide by adopting (somehow modified) the medieval formula *pro rege et patria*, making in this way obedience to the fatherly ruler coincide with love of and respect for the fatherland. Finally, the juxtaposition of king and fatherland gave a more immortal aura to the former, whose death would not alter the continuity of the royal dynasty: in fact, rulership was now embodied in that collective and everlasting entity called *patria*. The physical death of the sovereign only constituted an individual–personal separation from the fatherland, which lived on unmodified through the Adamite and hereditary continuity of the Crown.[87]

By identifying monarchy *tout court* with the State, the patriarchalist Filmer re-appropriated the powerful republican motif of the good citizen's public self-sacrifice and deprived it of its dangerous contents. He turned it to the advantage of the supreme monarch to whom the people's sacrifice was now due as towards a father. The rhetorical apparatus of paternal images provided by his patriarchalist discourse rendered such an act less violent and more acceptable (more plausible and more appealing) in that it belonged to the emotionally, culturally and socially safer sphere of the family. In contrast to the concept of the 'commonweal'[88] as *res publica*, Filmer shaped the kingdom as *res patrum*. As a result, his patriarchalist narrative of politics transposed the republican virtues of *pietas* and *caritas* from the family into the realm of the monarch.[89] This type of king aimed to mould a new people. The patriotic *cultus* for the commonweal(th) in the Filmerian account became the sovereign's 'public cares'[90] for the kingdom. Conversely, democracies lacked the fatherly care of the king, which was the sole agent capable of keeping them together. In fact, they could be preserved only by having

> some powerful enemy near, who may serve instead of a king to govern it, that so, though they have not a king among them, yet they may have as good as a king over them, for the common danger of an enemy keeps them in better unity than the laws they make themselves.[91]

Filmer remarked that fatherly rule had come to the fore in ancient Rome. At the apex of 'her chief popularity' Rome 'was oft[en] beholding for her preservation to the monarchical power of the father over the children'.[92] Similarly to Bodin, he saw in 'the fatherly power' the cardinal reason why 'the Romans flourished in all honour and virtue, and oftentimes was their commonweal thereby delivered from most imminent destruction'. This had occurred when 'the fathers' had acted against their sons' reforms in order to prevent sedition and fulfil their public duty towards the State.[93] By means of an astute rhetorical move, Filmer considered fatherly action at the time of the Romans as the quintessential example of patriotic virtue devoted to the public good. Hence he showed that patriotism and royal prerogative were compatible. Their fusion in the person of the absolute monarch created powerful government from which nations greatly benefited.

By and large, these considerations help us recognise that some ideological motifs, elements of political parlance, objects of discursive interest run through the decades from the Jacobean era to the 1680s as central loci of debate. One of these concerned the patriotic configuration of the representative of the country. Who was more entitled to well govern the nation; guarantee national interests (and, most importantly, promote the international Protestant cause); preserve harmony in the body politic? What type of power suited these goals best? Which body exercised authority in such a manner to keep people of different religious creeds together? At the level of collective imagery, people asked who embodied the general spirit of the nation: king or countrymen? Monarch or Parliament?[94]

It was in this milieu that *Patriarcha* responded to opinions like those of the Earl of Shaftesbury (1679): '[t]he Parliament of England is that Supreme and absolute Power, which gives Life and Motion to the English Government'.[95] Contentions such as this implied the role of Parliament as the kernel of popular consent through free elections and contested the legal monopoly of the king as *lex loquens*. Centred on alternative views of the English nation, these tensions shaped opposite rhetorics of government and allegiance. Thus, for some, hereditary monarchies were more suited to guarantee public interest. By contrast, Whig pamphleteers claimed – exactly like their counterparts in the patriotic parliaments of the 1610s and 1620s – that subjects were entitled whether through their representatives in Parliament, through petitioning or through demonstrations to tell their rulers how to act. As the patriotic pamphlet *A Speech made by a True Protestant English Gentleman* (1679) put it, it was their 'Birth-right' and 'Privilege' to be able to petition, whilst for the sovereign this practice constituted an 'Honour'.[96]

In line with these perspectives, the frontispiece of Tyrrell's *Patriarcha non Monarcha* made it clear that its author was '*a Lover of Truth and of his Country*', defending '[t]he true Principles of Government and Property (especially in our Kingdom)' against '[t]he Falseness of those Opinions that would make Monarchy Jure Divino'.[97] Tyrrell remarked that all of Filmer's writings '(*except the* Patriarcha)' had been published '*at first in single Tracts without Name*' and were now bound together '*in defence of Kingly Government*' and also '*to confute divers levelling Notions then too much in fashion*'.[98] Tyrrell could not figure out who might have wanted the publication of *Patriarcha*[99] and of the other tracts '*at such a* Time *as they did*'. The only explanation must be that '*the Publishers thought these Pieces, which printed apart could onely serve to ensnare the Under-standings of some unthinking Country-Gentlemen or Windblown-Theologue*', would now – '*twisted into one Volume*' – successfully '*bind the Consciences, and enslave the Reasons of all his unwary Readers*'.[100] And yet in 1680 *Patriarcha* was printed on its own[101] and in 1685 reprinted again on its own in the 'improved' edition by Bohun. Was this evidence that the treatise did not need to be issued with other writings as it was powerful enough to capture people's attention and provide readers with forceful arguments? That Tyrrell wrote *Patriarcha non Monarcha* would confirm the truth of such a hypothesis.[102]

On his part, Locke explained:

> I should not speak so plainly of a Gentleman, long since past answering, had not the Pulpit, of late Years, publickly owed his Doctrine, and made it the Current Divinity of the Times. ... For I should not have writ against Sir Robert, or taken the pains to shew his mistakes, Inconsistencies, and want of (what he so much boasts of, and pretends wholly to build on) Scripture-proofs, were there not Men among us, who, by crying up his Books, and espousing his Doctrine, save me from the Reproach of Writing against a dead Adversary. They have been so zealous in this Point, that if I have done him any wrong; I cannot hope they should spare me.[103]

Of all Filmerian notions that which caused Locke's vehement reaction was the notion of the king-patriarch. Locke disparagingly branded it as 'this strange kind of domineering Phantom, called the Fatherhood, which whoever could catch, presently got Empire, and unlimited absolute Power'.[104] Defining the Adamite paradigm as 'true in no Sense', Locke clarified that he had dealt with Filmer's arguments 'to let the World see, how Incoherencies in Matter, and Suppositions without Proofs put handsomely together in good Words and a plausible Style, are apt to pass for strong Reason and good Sense'.[105]

Like Locke, Sidney considered Filmer a dangerous innovator, a destroyer of peace and a denier of people's original freedom from which Parliament derived its authority.[106] In *Plato Redivivus* (1681) the republican Henry Neville declared that he 'did not think it worth the taking notice of' patriarchalism.[107] And yet, as Gaby Mahlberg has persuasively explained, Neville did engage with the claims of a patriarchal monarchy in many ways.[108] One of his arguments – and one which much resembled the Lockean perspective – was that patriarchalism was just a 'fancy' that had been 'first started, not by the solid judgement of any man, but to flatter some prince; and to assert, for want of better arguments, the divine right of monarchy'.[109] Therefore, it could not be taken seriously. This opinion was not shared by the Whig leader John Somers, who in 1680 took patriarchalism to be one of the four chief arguments deployed to sustain monarchical government.[110] In line with this, Tyrrell admitted that patriarchalism was spreading like 'Poyson', not only amongst the gentry and the clergy but also – and much more dangerously for the long-term consequences – at the universities.[111]

In substance: what do these anti-patriarchalist opinions tell us about the reception of Filmer's theories? Certainly that many thinkers realised the force of the patriarchalist paradigm in dismissing all claims of an originally free state of humankind. For Filmer the 'fiction' was that set up by contractualists and natural rights theorists, who argued that such an anarchic and confusion-ridden state like the state of nature had once existed and, above all, that political society had stemmed from it. In addition, Filmer – and others with him – viewed the idea that Parliament represented the people as a mere legal fantasy. That the principle of representation was the best way to protect subjects and open up participation in the political sphere was for Filmer both absurd and lethal. Indeed it was a fictional mechanism devised to mislead people in making them believe what was not and could not be: that power originally belonged to them. The reality was quite different in that it showed the king as the lawgiver in the body politic with Parliament as his assisting organ.[112]

It was precisely to this vein of monarchist thinking that during and after the Exclusion Crisis many theorists subscribed.[113] Besides Bohun, amongst these was a host of anti-republican, anti-resistance and pro-hereditary monarchy theorists and clergymen: William Falkner (*Christian Loyalty*, 1679); the non-juror George Hickes (*The Spirit of Popery*, 1680 and *The Harmony of Divinity and Law*, 1684); William Sherlock (*The Case of Resistance to the Supreme Powers*, 1684); Sir George Mackenzie (*Jus Regium*, 1684); Thomas Goddard (*Plato's Demon*, 1684); John Northleigh (*The Triumph of Our Monarchy*, 1685 [114]); the influential absolutist political writer Nathaniel Johnston (*The Excellency of Monarchical Government*, 1686).[115] Many of them made use of Bodin's concept of sovereignty in order to prove that the monarch 'was the sole, omnicompetent and illimitable source of law'.[116] Besides depicting Presbyterians as Jesuits in disguise who advocated resistance theory and accusing the Whigs of wanting to impose the same form of arbitrary government experienced under Cromwell, these *Filmerian* monarchists delineated a strong patriotic image of the king through the Adamite paradigm.

This is to say that in the succession context Filmer was used and attacked not just for his ideas of absolute and arbitrary power, but also because his patriarchalism made the ruler father of the nation in contrast to country patriotism; parliamentary accounts of people's rights and liberties; Whig notions of the ancient constitution. As a political model, the Adamite prince provided the national narrative of the body politic with an alternative image to that of Parliament men and patriotic stalwarts posing as martyrs to the cause of England. These two ideological perspectives entailed and promoted different loci of political authority.[117] They justified the right to govern the commonweal on the basis of this representational function with which either King or Parliament was invested. In this respect, *Patriarcha* participated in the post-Restoration disputes largely by means of its *fictional* configuration of political authority grounded on the Adamite role of the fatherly sovereign.

As earlier on in the century, conflict largely centred on the opposite languages of patriarchalists and patriots. No other moment illustrates the tension between these polarities better than the phase around 1683.

NOTES

1 Another forthright supporter of Filmer's theories was Charles Leslie (1650–1722). However, I do not analyse his works as they belong to the early eighteenth-century and to a different context from that here studied.

2 Bohun became press licenser for a few months in the early 1690s and remained a controversial figure throughout his life (hostility against him came from Jacobites and Whigs alike). This was due to both his political and religious positions as well as 'his abrasive personality' (*ODNB*, 'Bohun, Edmund'). On Bohun see [C. Blount], *Reasons Humbly Offered for the Liberty of Unlicens'd Printing, to which is subjoin'd, The just and true character of Edmund Bohun* (1693); *The Diary and Autobiography of Edmund Bohun, esq.*, ed. S. Wilton Rix (New York, 1975); M. Goldie, 'Edmund Bohun and "Jus Gentium" in the Revolution Debate', *HJ*, 20 (1977), pp. 569–86; Daly, *Sir Robert Filmer*, pp. 128–33.

3 Archbishop Sancroft had revised a Filmerian manuscript which he had received from one of Sir Robert's sons. Sancroft, in turn, had lent it to Bohun, who used it for his 1685 edition (Laslett, 'Introduction', p. 45). The Bohun edition is a version of one of the 1680 printings, but with additions and corrections that are derived from the Cambridge manuscript (or from a manuscript close to the Cambridge version but no longer extant: see chapter 2 above and Sommerville's notes in *PT*, pp. 1–2). The Cambridge manuscript contains three chapters – on Grotius, Selden and the civil law – which are neither in the Chicago manuscript nor in the 1680 printings. Bohun printed the chapter on the civil law, and some shorter passages that are also in the Cambridge manuscript but not in the printings of 1680 (see Sommerville's Appendix in *PT*, pp. 64–8). Bohun did not print the parts on Grotius and Selden, presumably because he knew they were in Filmer's *Observations Concerning The Originall of Government* (see *OG*, pp. 216–27). In the textual notes to Sommerville's edition, 'D' indicates the Bohun version, though readings from it are only occasionally recorded (I would like to thank Johann Sommerville for his help on these editorial and philological matters). According to Schochet, Sancroft's numerous efforts to ensure that a correct edition of *Patriarcha* was published testify to Filmer's importance within High Church circles (Schochet, 'New Bibliographical Discoveries', p. 159).

4 Weil, *Political Passions*, p. 41.

5 Edmund Bohun, *A defence of Sir Robert Filmer, against the mistakes and misrepresentations of Algernon Sidney, esq. ...* (1684), p. 2.

6 *Ibid.*, p. 3.

7 *Ibid.*, p. 4 (italics added).

8 *Ibid.*, p. 6.

9 *Ibid.*, p. 8. His idea that subjects could not take up arms against their prince did not mean that for Bohun others were barred to do so. By using Grotius' theory of 'just war', in *The History of the Desertion* (1690) Bohun admitted that, in some cases, an external prince could intervene and free a people from tyranny – as it had happened with James II who had not been usurped but conquered and whose rights had passed on to William of Orange on the basis of hereditary rights and because of James' destructive conduct towards England and its liberties (Goldie, 'Edmund Bohun and "Jus Gentium"', pp. 580–1, 584). Thus, Bohun saw the Glorious Revolution as the result of the military invasion of a foreign power and not as the act of popular forces endowed with the right to limit the monarchy (*ibid.*, p. 586).

10 Bohun, *A defence*, p. 8. Bohun thought it 'better for Subjects to suffer patiently, than to resist rebelliously, to be Martyrs than Traytors' (*ibid.*, p. 9). Despite this insistence on passive obedience, his abhorrence of rebellion and the importance of hereditary right, Mark Goldie argued that Bohun 'was never an absolutist' (Goldie, 'Edmund Bohun and "Jus Gentium"', p. 576).

11 Bohun, *A defence*, p. 9.

12 However, he differed from Filmer in that he used Eve's submission to Adam to justify political obedience to princes (*ibid.*, p. 9).

13 *Ibid.*, p. 10.

14 *Ibid.*, p. 11.

15 *Ibid.*, p. 13.

16 *Ibid.*, pp. 13–14.

17 *Ibid.*, p. 14.

18 *Ibid.*, p. 15.

19 *Ibid.*, p. 15. See *PT*, p. 10.

20 Bohun, *A defence*, p. 16.

21 These are Bohun's introduction and postscript to Filmer's 1685 (second and corrected) edition of *Patriarcha*. Here Bohun proved to be more acquainted with Sir Robert's works and also with Tyrrell's *Patriarcha non Monarcha* (composed in 1680, revised and published in 1681), which he had in the meantime read (Daly, *Sir Robert Filmer*, p. 131).

22 Edmund Bohun, 'The Epistle Dedicatory', in *Patriarcha ... to which is added a preface to the reader in which this piece is vindicated from the cavils and misconstructions of the author of a book stiled Patriarcha non monarcha, and also a conclusion or postscript ...* (1685). This edition was dedicated to Henry Duke of Beaufort, a member of the House of Lords and the Privy Council. Bohun said that, whilst some had defended 'that most illustrious Martyr Charles the First' with 'their Swords', Filmer 'with no less Danger' had written about political matters (*ibid.*, 'The Epistle Dedicatory').

23 *Ibid.*, 'The Epistle Dedicatory'.

24 *Ibid.*, 'The Preface to the Reader', ch. 1, § 3 (in the original only paragraph numbers are given).

25 *Ibid.*, ch. 1, § 4–5.

26 *Ibid.*, ch. 1, § 5.

27 *Ibid.*, ch. 1, § 5.

28 *Ibid.*, ch. 1, § 6.

29 According to Daly, Bohun was a bad and uninformed reader of *Patriarcha* who wanted 'to assimilate Filmer to widely held royalist opinions'. Indeed, 'the spirit of Bohun's monarchy' was 'fundamentally different from Filmer's love of pure will'. In resorting to 'the motif of fatherly love as the perfect bond in political life', Bohun reasserted a 'very common royalist psychological appeal' (see Daly, *Sir Robert Filmer*, pp. 128–33). As this chapter shows, Daly's opinion needs to be, partly, revised.

30 Bohun, 'The Preface to the Reader', § 57 and *passim*.

31 See e.g. *ibid.*, ch. 1, §§ 24 ff. For Bohun's approach to issues of gender and marital relationships in the household and in public see *ibid.*, ch. 2, §§ 41ff.

32 As he put it, 'no usurpation can succeed without God's permission' (*ibid.*, ch. 2, § 2).

33 *Ibid.*, ch. 1, §§ 31–9, 50. Bohun said that Tyrrell's 'Aversion for Primogeniture' was due to his being 'a younger Brother' (*ibid.*, ch. 1, § 64).

34 *Ibid.*, ch. 1, §§ 51, 66.

35 *Ibid.*, ch. 1, § 9.

36 *Ibid.*, ch. 1, § 10.

37 *Ibid.*, ch. 1, § 12. It is interesting that China was referred to as an instance of a despotic state. Bohun added the Asian country to the common black list including France, Turkey and Muscovy.

38 *Ibid.*, ch. 1, § 10.

39 *Ibid.*, ch. 1, § 12.

40 *Ibid.*, ch. 1, § 15. This was part of the attack on Bellarmine (see also *ibid.*, ch. 1, § 19).

41 *Ibid.*, ch. 1, §§ 33–4.

42 *Ibid.*, ch. 1, § 35.

43 *Ibid.*, ch. 1, § 37.

44 *Ibid.*, ch. 1, § 49.

45 *Ibid.*, ch. 1, § 44. One of Bohun's sources was Sallust (*ibid.*, ch. 1, § 45).

46 *Ibid.*, ch. 1, § 51. See also *ibid.*, ch. 1, § 72.

47 *Ibid.*, ch. 1, § 61.

48 *Ibid.*, ch. 1, § 57.

49 On the connection between fatherhood and kingship see *ibid.*, ch. 1, § 62; ch. 1, § 68.

50 *Ibid.*, ch. 1, § 46.

51 *Ibid.*, ch. 1, § 73.

52 *Ibid.*, ch. 2, § 2.

53 *Ibid.*, ch. 2, § 3.

54 *Ibid.*, ch. 2, §§ 10, 12.

55 *Ibid.*, ch. 2, §§ 15–16.

56 *Ibid.*, ch. 2, § 23.

57 *Ibid.*, ch. 2, § 28.

58 *Ibid.*, ch. 2, § 28.

59 *Ibid.*, ch. 2, § 38.

60 *Ibid.*, ch. 2, § 52.

61 *Ibid.*, 'The Conclusion by the Publisher of this Edition', pp. 153–78, p. 153 (the text is interrupted on p. 176 by an interpolation of about fourteen pages before resuming on p. 177).

62 *Ibid.*, p. 153.

63 *Ibid.*, p. 154. In 1682 Bohun had declared that the House of Commons was unfortunately 'divided into two Great Parties', one being 'the Court-Party' and the other 'the Country-Party' (Edmund Bohun, *An Address to the Free-men and Free-holders of the Nation* (1682), p. 64).

64 Bohun, 'The Conclusion by the Publisher of this Edition', p. 162.

65 *Ibid.*, p. 163.

66 *Ibid.*, p. 165.

67 *Ibid.*, p. 165.

68 This prince was 'the only unaccountable Person, to any but God' (*ibid.*, p. 168).

69 *Ibid.*, pp. 168–9.

70 *Ibid.*, p. 171.

71 *Ibid.*, pp. 171–2.

72 As he put it, 'if unity in government, which is only found in monarchy, be once broken, there is no stay or bounds, until it come to a constant standing army. For "the people or multitude", as Aristotle teacheth us, "can excel in no virtue but military", and that "that is natural to them", and therefore in a popular estate "the sovereign power is in the sword and those that are possessed of the arms" .... So that any nation or kingdom that is not charged with the keeping of a king must perpetually be at the charge of paying and keeping of an army' (*OA*, pp. 247–8).

73 Bohun, 'The Conclusion by the Publisher of this Edition', p. 172.

74 See chapter 9 below.

75 It was certainly an issue from around 1628: see L. Schwoerer, *No Standing Armies!: The Antiarmy Ideology in Seventeenth-Century England* (Baltimore and London, 1974), *passim*; Scott, *England's Troubles*, p. 166. It is worth remembering that in April 1675 the Earl of Danby had passed the Test Bill that imposed on all MPs and office-holders to declare the unlawfulness of taking up arms against the King under all circumstances and swear that they would never attempt to alter the structure of government in both Church and State. To such a manoeuvre Shaftesbury (in this representing the opposition) reacted by accusing the government of pursuing a path whose ultimate goal was to become 'absolute and Arbitrary' and of trying to enforce laws by way of a standing army, which constituted the most severe menace to Parliament's independence (Harris, *Politics under the Later Stuarts*, pp. 58–9). As seen above, for Filmer an absolute and arbitrary power was legitimate, one to be sought after and one that had nothing to do with the defence and presence of a standing army.

76 Bohun, 'The Conclusion by the Publisher of this Edition', p. 176. See also *PT*, p. 31.

77 Bohun, 'The Conclusion by the Publisher of this Edition', p. 177.

78 *Ibid.*, pp. 177–8.

79 *Ibid.*, p. 178.

80 Laslett, 'Introduction', p. 35.

81 On these issues see Harris, *Politics under the Later Stuarts*; Knights, *Politics and Opinion in Crisis*; Scott, *England's Troubles*.

82 Harris, *Politics under the Later Stuarts*, p. 95.

83 *PT*, p. 5.

84 Kantorowicz, *The King's Two Bodies*, pp. 248–9.

85 See King James VI and I, *A Speach to the Lords and Commons 1609*, p. 181.

86 Kantorowicz, *The King's Two Bodies*, p. 250.

87 On some of these concepts see *ibid.*, pp. 267–72.

88 Although Filmer began to replace 'commonwealth' with 'commonweal' in the works written after the abolition of monarchy in England (1649), he had already made use of the latter phrase in *Patriarcha* when referring to the State (see *OG*, e.g. 'The Preface', p. 186 and *OA, passim*, and *PT*, p. 19, respectively).

89 See Viroli, *For Love of Country*, pp. 19–20.

90 *PT*, p. 41.

91 *Ibid.*, p. 29.

92 *OA*, p. 260.

93 *Ibid.*, p. 260.

94 As for practical politics, historians Corinne Weston and Janelle Greenberg argued that the main conflict was between the advocates of the King as the sole governor in the realm and those who thought he had to partake his power with Parliament (C. Weston and J. Greenberg, *Subjects and Sovereigns. The Grand Controversy over Legal Sovereignty in Stuart England* (Cambridge, 1981)). This perspective has been contested, above all, by Tim Harris, who insisted on the centrality of the issue of 'Dissent' for the disputes going on throughout Charles II's reign (Harris, *Politics under the Later Stuarts*, pp. 53 ff.). In particular, for Harris, 'what is certain, is that this [earlier] Court–Country conflict did not anticipate the later split between Tories and Whigs'. This is so because the issues at stake were not the same in the two controversies. In fact, the latter divide differed from the tensions of the 1660s and 1670s in that it centred on 'the religious conflict between Church and Dissent' (*ibid.*, p. 74). Thus, for Harris Tories and Whigs were the parties of 'intolerant Anglicanism' and 'Dissent', respectively (*ibid.*, p. 82).

95 Earl of Shaftesbury, *Some Observations Concerning the Regulating of Elections for Parliament ...* (1689), p. 5. See also Harris, *Politics under the Later Stuarts*, pp. 89–90, where we are reminded that people like Shaftesbury often put aside questions of principle for more pragmatic motives (this occurred with the enlargement of the franchise, which the Earl opposed). Many an exclusionist aligned 'with either Court or Country, King or Parliament, in order to achieve their political ends' (*ibid.*, p. 89).

96 Cited in *ibid.*, p. 91.

97 Tyrrell, *Patriarcha non Monarcha*, 'Frontispiece'. For Tyrrell's attack on Filmer see J. Rudolph, *Revolution by Degrees. James Tyrrell and Whig Political Thought in the Late Seventeenth Century* (Basingstoke, 2002), esp. pp. 20 ff.

98 Tyrrell, *Patriarcha non Monarcha*, 'The Preface'.

99 However, he declared that Filmer's '*Notion of the Divine and Patriarchal Right of absolute Monarchy*' had become common amongst '*some modern Church-men, who cry it up as their* Diana' (*ibid.*, 'The Preface').

100 *Ibid.*, 'The Preface'.

101 In the same year, Filmer's *The Necessity of The Absolute Power of all Kings* had had a new edition under the title *The Power of Kings*, without it being added to *Patriarcha*.

102 Styling himself as '*being far from a Commonwealths-man*' and in favour of '*Monarchy above all other forms of Government*', Tyrrell argued that the reader '*may also consider whether most of the Arguments this Author* [Filmer] *makes use of for absolute Obedience to Usurpers, as representing the lawful Prince and Father of the People, might not serve for the establishing of Oliver and the Rump-Parliament, as well as a lawful Soveraign*'. Milton had employed '*the same places of Scripture for this purpose*', which both Filmer and Salmasius did '*for another*' (*ibid.*, 'The Preface').

103 Locke, *Two Teatises of Government*, bk i, 'The Preface', p. 156.

104 *Ibid.*, bk i, ch. ii, § 6, p. 163.

105 *Ibid.*, bk i, ch. iii, § 20, p. 173.

106 Scott, *Commonwealth Principles*, pp. 124, 334.

107 In *Court Maxims* (mid 1660s) Sidney had held the same opinion (Houston, *Algernon Sidney*, p. 97, n. 121).

108 See G. Mahlberg, *Henry Neville and English Republican Culture in the Seventeenth Century. Dreaming of Another Game* (Manchester, 2009), esp. pp. 83–138.

109 Cited in *ibid.*, p. 119.

110 John Somers, *A Brief History of the Succession* (1680), pp. 15–17.

111 Tyrrell, *Patriarcha non Monarcha*, 'The Preface'.

112 On the popularity of such a view in the period 1675–85 see Houston, *Algernon Sidney*, pp. 69–78.

113 According to Harris, 'the fiercest opponents of Exclusion' were High Church clergymen (Harris, *Politics under the Later Stuarts*, p. 94).

114 A reprint of this work came out in 1699 with the title *Remarks upon the Most Eminent of our Antimonarchical Authors and Their Writings*. Here were numerous references to Filmer's ideas and to Sidney's reaction against them (see *Remarks upon the Most Eminent of our Antimonarchical Authors and Their Writings* ... (Westminster, 1699), e.g. pp. 19, 352, 502–3, 568, 654, 656).

115 Goldie, 'John Locke and Anglican Royalism', p. 67. By contrast, for Daly none of these writers was as *absolutist* as Filmer. If Johnston was one of those whom Daly labelled 'anti-absolutist royalists', Mackenzie, Hickes and Goddard described the English monarchy as both absolute and limited (Daly, 'The Idea of Absolute Monarchy', pp. 241, 242–3). The term 'absolute' was and remained a problematic and divisive one throughout the seventeenth century (*ibid.*, p. 243).

116 Goldie, 'John Locke and Anglican Royalism', p. 69. Locke's work was, therefore, not only a refutation of Filmer's principles but also a rejection of the Bodinian reasoning of a consistent group of theorists (*ibid.*, p. 71). For Goldie this endorsement of Bodin's work made post-Restoration Tories 'unequivocally absolutist' (*ibid.*, p. 75).

117 It is worth remembering that in a short paper composed in April 1690 Locke was to call for a public repudiation of the theory of kingly divine right because it divided the nation (J. Farr and C. Roberts, 'John Locke and the Glorious Revolution: A Rediscovered Document', *HJ*, 28 (1985), pp. 385–98, esp. pp. 392–3). The exact same accusation had been laid throughout the 1680s at the Whigs' door by patriarchalists following Filmer's doctrines.

Chapter 9

◆

Patriarchalism versus patriotism in practice: *Patriarcha* from the Rye House Plot (1683) to the Glorious Revolution (1688–89)

Considered rebellious and unfaithful subjects, patriots were under heavy fire in the wake of the Rye House Plot, which cost Algernon Sidney his life (he was executed in December 1683). Planned for April when Charles II and his brother were expected to pass through Newmarket – having been largely destroyed in a fire on 22 March, the races were cancelled prompting the King and the Duke to return to London – the attack never took place. Yet news of the plot leaked with the result that it was made public on 12 June 1683.[1]

A few weeks later in *The London Gazette*,[2] the 'Society of the Middle-Temple' addressed a letter 'To the King's Most Excellent Majesty' in which they let out their 'unspeakable Joy … for the wonderful discovery of the late hellish Conspiracy, begun and carried by Desperate Persons of Fanatical, Atheistical, and Republican Principles'. The latter had 'impudently' assumed 'to themselves the name of True-Protestants and Patriots' with the aim of 'undermining the best Religion and Government in the World'. Moreover, they had contrived 'the horrid Parricide' of the King's 'Sacred Person' and 'the Barbarous Assassination' of his 'Royal Brother' James, causing in this way 'Confusion, and utter Destruction of this Monarchy'.[3]

At the end of the same month (28 July) it was King Charles himself that released a *Declaration to all His Loving Subjects, concerning the Treasonable Conspiracy against His Sacred Person and Government, lately Discovered*. The King was adamant that 'for Several Years last past, a Malevolent Party' had constantly sought 'to Promote Sedition by False News, Libellous Pamphlets and other wicked Arts'. Although His Majesty had applied all his 'utmost Care … to Govern according to Law' and shown to his subjects all his 'Zeal' in order to preserve 'the Protestant Religion', some 'Evil Persons' had misrepresented those 'Actions to the People', especially 'the weaker Sort'.[4] The latter dangerously 'looked upon Them [the plotters] as the only Patriots and Assertors of their Religion and Liberties, and gave themselves up entirely to their Conduct'.

The real watershed in the development of the events surrounding the Rye House Plot – Charles stressed – lay not only in the loyal subjects' realisation that the adversaries of the monarchy were fomenters of sedition, but chiefly in their succeeding to 'Convince the Common People of the Villanous Designs of their Factious Leaders and the Miseries that would befal them in pursuing such Courses'.[5] Once again the patriots were targeted as untrustworthy masterminds of conspiracies, whose ultimate goal was to overthrow the monarchical institution under the pretence of defending the common people.

This anti-patriots rhetoric was spread at different levels. It was employed by Charles II; by the Crown entourage; by various public figures in the localities; in political literature. As such it had been articulated in mid July 1683 when the 'Mayor, Bayliffs, and Burgesses of the Town and Country of Southampton' sent their '*humble Address*' to His Majesty. These local authorities (including the '*Justices of the Peace*') expressed their hope that the discovery of 'the late Abhorrency ... had sufficiently discouraged that Treasonable Project, and deterred the Conspirators from any further Machinations'. However, to their 'Astonishment', they had found 'that those pretended Patriots of their Country' were 'still plotting the Ruine of it'.[6] These rebellious firebrands 'stile[d] themselves True Protestants, and Zealots for Religion, ... contriving what no Turk or Jew, or any, but the most profligate Atheists, possessed with Ambition, Malice, and Revenge, durst Attempt'.[7] Since the objective of 'the Authors and Abettors of this or any other Rebellious Designs' was 'the Massacre of all good Subjects, as well as of their Prince', the participants in the 'Quarter Sessions' at Southampton proclaimed to 'always be ready' to give their 'Lives and Fortunes to oppose all Such Treasonable Practises'.[8]

On 27 July, the 'High Sheriff, the Deputy Lieutenants, Justices of the Peace, and Grand Juries for the County of Suffolk' outspokenly condemned 'the Barbarity of such ingrateful men, as have entred into this last Conspiracy'.[9] Those who had attempted to murder the monarch were unfaithful 'Phanatick[s]' who had acted like ungrateful children towards their father (the implication being that, by contrast, the drawers of this address had their 'hearts full of Duty and Care for your [Charles'] Safety'). The document argued that the problem was that 'too many Corporations' had promoted 'patriots' of the 'pretended Religion' of 'brutish' zealots intent on destroying the King's 'Sacred Majesty, the Church of England, and the Government established'.[10] Therefore, they hoped that Charles would 'hinder' these conventicles and prevent them from being 'Receptacles of bad Men, or Engines to play Republican Zealots' amongst the English people. In fact, only the monarch acted 'for the best of' his 'Subjects'.[11]

In another address to the King, reported in *The London Gazette* at the end of August 1683, after the usual series of attacks on those who had organised 'the Popish Plot' ('Devils in Flesh' devoted 'to raise a horrible Rebellion'; 'Bloodthirsty and Deceitful Men'), the 'Loyal Subjects' amongst the 'Inhabitants of the Borough of Aylesbury' located the cause of all 'Hell-plotted Machinations' in 'Seditious Conventicles' whose 'influence' had spread widely. As a consequence, they thought it pivotal to 'assure' Charles of their 'Loyal Hearts'. Most of all, they would not let any 'Factious Insinuations of causeless Fears and Jealousies, by pretended Patriots or others' remove them 'from these fixed and sincere Resolutions' of 'Obedient and Loyal Subjects'.[12]

Playing exactly the same tune, the 'Mayor, Aldermen, and Citizens of the City of Hereford' declared themselves ready to protect their King from 'the Treasonable Designs of Celebrated and pretended Patriots' whose goal was 'to bring in Confusion and Anarchy'. Having singled out 'the Conventicles' of 'miscall'd Protestants' as 'Hives of Faction', the address underlined that the danger stemming from these treacherous 'Monsters' was 'still' impending 'since in them Divisions are made and Fomented, and a Disaffection to' the 'Person' of the King 'and Government taught'.[13] Likewise, the 'Loyal Young Men and Apprentices of the City of Bristol' had their say in the aftermath of the plot by addressing to His Majesty a brief document in which they accused 'desperate Schismaticks, and practical Atheists, the Gyants of this Age, in Villany and Rebellion' to have 'carried' out 'the horrid Conspiracy'. This group of faithful subjects was certain that 'those Execrable and damnable Designs' had been 'contrived by Republicans and Conventicles' as it could be proved through their 'own Observations made on those Conspirators of this City' of Bristol. They went as far as to personally name some of their fellow-citizens as responsible for having plotted the 'Assassination' of the King. Most importantly, they tellingly defined these rebellious spirits as 'the beloved Patriots of the Dissenting Tribes'. Such a situation had 'begotten' in these loyal men 'an utter Detestation of all those Atheists and Separatists who compass the Ruine of King and Kingdoms, under the Cloak of a Pretended Tender-Conscience'.[14]

These addresses are extremely interesting in that they further show the continuity of themes and languages informing political debates in the 1620s and in the 1680s. In both historical phases, monarchists depicted patriots as traitors and malicious fomenters who pretentiously portrayed themselves as true lovers of their country against the sovereign. If the image of patriotic and republican hotheads at work to sabotage State and Church under the false pretence of being nation-lovers persisted throughout the century, the picture of loyal monarchist stalwarts with which the supporters of the King characterised themselves remained no less a constant. Moreover, *The London Gazette* illustrates that those sending their 'humble' addresses to Charles II came from different places and occupied different positions on the social ladder. From Southampton to Suffolk, from Herefordshire to Buckinghamshire their geographical provenance varied too. Equally, from mayors and aldermen to sheriffs, from simple inhabitants of a borough to apprentices, their social status was also composite. Yet what in both cases – regional and social – did not change was a crucial part of their rhetoric in defence of the monarchy: this always targeted the 'pretended Patriots' by associating their actions with 'parricide'.

Thus, addressing 'the King's Most Excellent Majesty' the 'Master, Governors, and Assistants of the Scots Corporation in London and Westminster' had described the enemies of the monarch as 'ill men ... who have shaken off their Duty and Allegiance to the King of Kings, as well as to' Charles II, God's 'Vicegerent'. Of all 'Contrivances' set out 'to destroy' the 'Life' and the 'Government' of the King, the most terrible was 'the damnable Conspiracy lately discovered' because it 'was designed for the most barbarous and cruel Parricide and murther of' the 'Sacred Majesty'.[15] The same accusations of parricide had been laid by the 'Bailiffs, Burgesses, and Commonalty of the King's Corporation of Ipswich' at the door of 'that Party, and sort of Men amongst whom' were 'such Villains and Miscreants' who 'could not be satisfied with the Blood and Gore of one King, of Blessed Memory, but were proceeding ... to gorge their Cannibal Appetites upon a Second'.[16] Explicitly comparing the situation in which the Stuart monarchy found itself in the 1680s with that of the 1640s and associating the incumbent Charles II with the martyr Charles I, this address saw '[t]he natural Consequences of this Hideous Parricide' in 'the spoiling' His 'Majesty's Three Kingdoms, of their present Tranquility, Plenty, easie Government, and Excellent Religion, and turning them into so many great Shambles land Scenes of utmost Ruine and Confusion'.[17] As confirmed by another address presented to the King on 1 August of the same decisive year, 1683, by the 'Grand Jury, at the Assizes for the County of Cornwall', the three kingdoms were replete with disobedient and ungrateful 'Men' who were 'guilty of such horrid Designs and Practises ... endeavouring by the Parricide of' the sovereign prince 'to embrew the Nation in Blood, dissolve the best constitution of Government in the World, and destroy the soundest and most Primitive Church at this time professing Christianity'.[18] As a result, this parricide would inevitably put an end to the 'happiness' enjoyed by Charles II's subjects since his 'Restauration'. What was a nation endowed with 'a long and secure Peace, and abundant plenty of all things' – thanks to the 'most wise and gracious Government' – would be soon turned into an 'Estate' marred by the same 'miserable Calamities' which had 'afflicted' it 'in the time of the late unnatural Rebellion'.[19]

In summary, the examples taken from L'Estrange's *Observator* and from *The London Gazette*, from Bohun's writings as well as from the various treatises, tracts, pamphlets and sermons so far analysed in Part II, display a great variety of mediums through which similar messages were conveyed and ideas transmitted. Such a variety also comprised different genres and arenas of discourse, including newspapers and political works, propagandist journals and official publications. What remained stable throughout were the political issues at stake and the ideological preoccupations of the contending parties involved in heated disputes on liberty and sovereignty, popular authority and monarchical power.

No less persistent was hostility to Filmerian contentions. It is now time to briefly consider the era of the Glorious Revolution (1688–89).

PATRIARCHA AND FILMER IN THE GLORIOUS REVOLUTION

In the euphoric Williamite climate of post-1688 Filmer was selected as one of – in the words of the judge and outspoken Whig politician Sir Robert Atkyns (d. 1710) – 'some Unquiet Innovating Writers, ... who would destroy Foundations, and remove our Ancient Land-marks, and the Ancient and Just Limits and Boundaries of Power and Authority'.[20] To respond to what he called 'these new and upstart Opinions', Atkyns relied on the 'contrary Judgment' of Matthew Hales and Richard Hooker, according to whom polities were the result of men's deliberation. As such, *'the Power of making Laws'* belonged to the whole society and not exclusively to the monarch. This was so obvious that, according to Atkyns, nothing more could 'be said ... in confutation of the Book that goes by the Name of Sir *Rob. Filmers'*.[21] Whilst further criticising 'these new Authors' who argued that 'the Commons had no Place, nor Votes by Election in Parliament, before the End of the Reign of *H.* 3.', Atkyns did not miss the chance to directly attack 'Sir *Robert Filmer*' for being 'in like manner positive in it in his Book call'd The *Freeholders Grand Enquest, fol.* 18'.[22] Despite hiding behind the authority of Selden, Camden 'and other Learned Authors', Atkyns continued, the likes of Filmer 'propagate that Error' which consisted in leaving 'it to K. *H.* 3. or his Son E. 1. or to any other King at any time, to send his special Writ of Summons to such of the Barons only'. Thus, Atkyns could write, 'this new fancy is wholly grounded upon the Credit of that uncertain Writer [Filmer], whom Mr. *Selden* could never meet with, and to whom he gave no credit'.[23] Most importantly, Atkyns targeted 'Innovators' à la Filmer for considering the people's power of election 'meerly as a Boon from the King'. 'Whereas', Atkyns rebutted,

> there is nothing more certain and clear than that the Freeholders (who are often call'd the People, and are the true Proprietors of the Nation and Land) had originally and from the very first Constitution of the Nation, the *Election* not only of all *Sheriffs*, but of all other Magistrates Civil or Military that had any Authority over them under the King; so that they had a mighty Freedom in the very Constitution of the Nation.[24]

For Atkyns – whose opinions confirmed the backbone of parliamentary and country ideology against which Filmer had engaged in the 1620s – 'this overthrows all the wild Fancies of Sir *Robert Filmer*, and Dr. *Heylin*, and some later Doctors' too.[25]

In the same crucial 1689, the Whig lawyer and anti-absolutist political writer William Atwood (d. 1712) tackled succession by referring to historical precedents and scornfully pointed to the 'usual suspects': 'Dr. *Brady* and his Set of Men'.[26] Atwood's stance in the debate surrounding the Glorious Revolution was clear: William and Mary had obtained *'the crown of England'* thanks to *'the people of this ancient monarchy'* reunited *'in the present assembly of Lords and Commons, notwithstanding the objections of men and different extremes'*.[27] For Atwood this meant that the people 'have yet as arbitrary a Power in this Matter, as Sir *Robert* [Filmer] and his Followers contend that the Prince has, whatever Promises or Agreements he has entred into'.[28] Insisting on the 'necessity' that 'the People must have had Power of Chusing, or there could have been no lawful Government since Queen *Elizabeth*'s time', Atwood dismissed all Filmerian principles for which hereditary monarchy was the sole form of government that guaranteed peaceful political transitions.[29]

Atwood's anti-Filmerism – influenced by Petyt's ancient constitutionalism – reached its peak in his *The Fundamental Constitution of the English Government* (1690).[30] Punctuated with constant snaps at Filmer's tenets, this work reiterated that cardinal motif whereby freeborn Englishmen held ancient liberties and privileges which had been passed down to them and restated since by each successive nation. These fundamental liberties belonged to the people as a form of protection. They moulded their identity as subjects of a monarchy where the ruler had vowed to uphold those laws by means of a coronation oath. This being the bulwark of English constitutional life, Atwood could easily explain what had happened to James II when he had violated England's most important political asset. After all, as he straightforwardly argued, mainly against Brady, the body politic was the outcome of contracts. Therefore, the king who broke them lost people's trust and as such faced dire consequences: rebellion of the subjects and his defeat as ruler. According to Atwood's Lockean view, this scenario entailed the return of power to the people, that is, to its original shrine. Such a transition, however, did not imply a dissolution of government since the ancient constitution guaranteed the necessary continuity. In being devolved to the people – to whom was entrusted the choice of a successor – power ended up in the hands of Parliament.

Whilst defining those who had *'ventur'd everything dear to them, in the same Cause with himself* [King William], *while Success was doubtful'* and who had *'facilitated that* Revolution' as *'noble* Patriots',[31] Atwood regarded those who had defended (and still did) the theory of non-resistance as well as that of the absolute sovereignty of kings as traitors.[32] Attacking *'Passive-Obedience*-Men who believe that *Monarchy* is the only Government of *Divine Right*, or that human Choice or Constitutions cannot intervene in the disposal of the *Soveraignty*', Atwood praised 'the immortal Memory of the Lord *Russel*, and other inferior *Patriots*'.[33] Most importantly, he ridiculed 'the fond Notion of an absolute *Patriarchal*

Power descending from *Adam* to our Kings in an unaccountable way', which reduced to nothing the idea of a 'Compact between Princes and their People'. Atwood did so by resorting to 'the difference between a *Patriarchal* and *Monarchical* Authority ... so well stated and prov'd by my Learned Friend Mr. *Tyrril*'.[34] The latter's refutation of Filmerian arguments was so compelling that 'few besides the unknown *Author* of the two late *Treatises* of *Government* [Locke], could have gained Reputation after him, in exposing the false *Principles* and Foundation of Sir *Robert Filmer* and his Admirers'. Amongst the latter, 'Dr *Heylyn*, in his Letter to Sir *Edward Filmer* the Son' had extolled the patriarchalist thinker as 'eminent' in the arts of politics where his *Patriarcha* 'might have serv'd for a *Catholicon*', that is, a medicine against all '*Discourses*' in favour of popular government.[35] With polemical wit Atwood added that, '[s]ince Sir *Robert Filmer* and Dr. *Heylyn* were our late *Observator*'s [L'Estrange's] Predecessors in guiding the *Inferior Clergy*', it was no surprise that the latter did not dare to criticise 'their Leaders'. Yet it was to be hoped that Heylyn's 'scandalous Reflections upon' religion and politics, 'in some measure at least occasion'd by the Countenance given to *Sybthorpism*, *Manwarism*, and *Filmerism*, may rightly raise a Prejudice against these Men and their Doctrines in the thinking Laity'.[36] Therefore, as Atwood affirmed in a passage emblematic of the extent to which late seventeenth-century ideological tensions were defined by opposite readings of Filmer's works, 'those who are not able to think of themselves, may take every Morning some Pages of the two *Treatises* of Government, for an effectual *Catholicon* against Nonsense and Absurdities'.[37] Atwood thought the *Treatises of Government* was 'the best Treatises of Civil Polity which I have met with in the *English* Tongue' because, after having confuted 'Sir *Robert Filmer*'s absurd Notions of Government, establishes it upon the only true Foundation, the Choice of the People'.[38]

Atwood's anti-Filmerism was so sedulous that he even composed an 'Appendix' to make '*Sir* Robert Filmer, *and some of our Divines, plaid against one another, in relation to Ecclesiastical and Civil Power, and Sir* Robert *against Himself*'. Again, Atwood ironically referred to 'the *Elogium* of the infallible Dr. *Heylyn*' advising 'the World' to read the 'Writings' of Filmer, that 'Wonder of his and following Ages' whose 'early Death' Heylyn 'could not reckon' with.[39] In light of this friendship, one would expect Filmer – Heylyn's 'Monarch in Politicks'[40] – to be faithful to the Church and recognise its superiority as 'his Books have manifested' him 'to be to the State'. Yet 'by subscribing to Sir *Robert*'s Judgement in Politiques, and consequently to his *Anarchy of a mixt Monarchy*', 'Dr. *Heylin*' – Atwood continued – was forced to 'confess that the Church is wholly subject to the Law of the State; and that the Civil Power is comprehensive of the Ecclesiastical'.[41] From this it followed that *Patriarcha* – 'which the Doctor by way of Prophesy ... tells us would, when publish'd', make all other political works '*unnecessary*' – sanctioned 'the Divine Right of all

Rulers' not just in temporals but 'even in Ecclesiastical Affairs'. Filmer (sarcastically dubbed 'our Prince of Politicians') had the audacity to invest monarchs 'with all that Power that the Patriarchs had' as if, '*by Right in Nature, and God's special Ordinance, were absolute Priests and Princes*'.[42] In brief, Atwood's words showed that Filmer was considered a more dangerously Erastian thinker than many of his contemporaries.

To further contest Sir Robert's oeuvre, Atwood maintained that, as the representative organ of the people, Parliament constituted the enduring thread uniting the body politic through time. Such an opinion was deeply antithetical to the Filmerian configuration of power.[43] Thus, despite writing at different times in the seventeenth century, both Atwood and Filmer knew that to win the battle of representations of sovereignty it was indispensable to identify the body which guaranteed stability and uninterrupted authority in the realm. For the ancient constitutionalist this body had the immemorial shape of the common law, whilst for the patriarchalist theorist it had the more human appearance of the absolute monarch. Patriarchalism was thus a forceful response not only to the idea that, since the ultimate repository and original source of sovereignty rested with the people, the power to choose and elect kings belonged to them, but also to that whereby every time the succession was in doubt or the royal family became extinct it was the people's task to give new shape to the State.[44] Against those who deemed that James II's escape absolved the nation from allegiance to him, the fatherly model discounted precisely this occurrence by showing its impossibility in that a father never ceased to be a father. Fatherhood was not negotiable; as such, sons/subjects had always the duty to support their parent(s)/kings.

In the landmark year of 1689, Filmer also had the dubious privilege to be referred to in a collection titled *The Dying Speeches of several excellent persons, who suffered for their zeal against popery, and arbitrary government ...*[45] Amongst these was a copy of a paper 'delivered to the Sheriffs' on the scaffold 'on *Friday December 7. 1683*. By *Algernon Sidney*', where the latter was reported to have said that the 'Papers' for which he was being tried 'plainly appear to relate unto a large Treatise written long since in answer to *Filmer's* Book, which by all Intelligent Men is thought to be grounded upon wicked Principles, equally pernicious unto Magistrates and People'.[46] At odds with such a hostile image of Filmer's principles was the controversial anti-Catholic clergyman William Sherlock (1639/40–1707). Highly criticised for taking the oaths after his initial refusal, Sherlock entered the polemical fray of 1689 by accusing the already mentioned Johnson's *Julian the Apostate* of being one of those 'Miscreant Persecutors of Crowns' spreading 'such Doctrins' that made 'Religion and Kings suffer'.[47] Instead of acting in this cowardly way, Johnson – Sherlock continued – 'should answer Bishop *Usher, Sanderson, Hammond ...*' and, above all, '*Dr. Falkner*, Sir *Robert Filmer*, the Learned and Brave Judge *Jenkins*, Dr.

Hick's Jovian' as well as 'all the Acts of Parliament that lodge the Supremacy and *Militia* in the King alone'.[48]

Sherlock's de facto obedience argument[49] prompted the staunch Jacobite bishop of the non-juring Church of England, Jeremy Collier (1650–1726) to compose *Dr. Sherlock's Case of Allegiance considered with some remarks upon his vindication* (1691),[50] where 'the Substance of Sir *Robert Filmer's* Opinion' on '*Paternal or Patriarchal Authority*' was summarised. However, Collier added, 'because the Doctor [Sherlock] has said nothing to confute it, I shall vindicate it no further'.[51] Collier's was a response to Sherlock's decision to abandon the nonjuror stance and swear allegiance to William and Mary (1690). Significantly, in replying to Sherlock's separation between 'a Subject and a Soldier', Collier resorted to the Filmerian argument that 'though every Subject needs not be a Soldier by Profession, yet whenever his Prince is in danger, and requires his Service, he is bound by the Laws of God and Man to fight for him'. This was undoubtedly so because '*the Duty of the Fifth Commandment extends to the King*, who is *Pater Patriae* ..., who has the Jurisdiction over all private Families, and from whom both our selves and our Parents have received Protection'. Moreover, being all subjects 'born equally Subjects', it followed that 'the essential Duties of Subjection ... must necessarily extend to them all'. In the end, Collier patriotically declared that 'all Persons are obliged to venture their Lives for the publick Safety, and to appear against the Enemies of their Country'.[52]

Whilst Collier's words testify to Filmer's importance, no better example confirms his notoriety than the anonymous poem in which he was labelled as the head of a 'Tribe' of patriarchalist thinkers. According to the witty *Ad Populum Phalerae, or, The Twinn-Shams* (1692),

> The *Filmer's* Tribe, with their Paternal Farse
> Into one House shall cramp the Universe:
> That *Noah's* Heirs despoticly might rule,
> Although a Cobler, Mad-man, Knave or Fool:
> When *Hodge* and *Parker's* Doctrines do revive,
> Which God Almighty's Pow'r to Monarchs give,
> To rule the World with such a perfect Sway,
> That they the *Potters* are, and we the *Clay*:
> We rub our Eyes, and quickly are aware
> What the Result of such wild Maxims are.[53]

WHAT OF FILMERISM THEN?

Regardless of the compelling evidence that Filmerian principles did matter a great deal in the contexts of the late 1670s and 1680s (a view which flatly contradicts Daly's idea that 'Filmerism' counted nothing 'for the majority of royalist and Tory writers'[54]), for historians like Alan Craig Houston it is still unclear 'who decided to publish Filmer's writings or why they did so'.[55] As 'both a traditionalist and an innovator', Filmer 'streamlined and radicalized orthodox royalist arguments'. The most evident example of this concerns the way in which he addressed the question of the 'absolute' and/or 'arbitrary' power of the monarch. In fusing the two, so Houston argued, Filmer proved to be too 'extreme' even within the royalist mainstream. And yet his doctrines fixed and reinforced opinions which were gaining importance in England during the Exclusion Crisis, so that 'their publication coincided with the discovery of the absolutist pretensions of Charles and James Stuart'.[56]

Accurate as Houston's hypothesis is, it needs to be enhanced in two regards. Firstly, I suggest that Filmer's principles had been thriving since their initial circulation in manuscript in the 1630s. As such they were chosen not only because they crystallised ideological views that were holding sway in the country, but because they also influenced monarchist theorists in the heated controversies concerning succession; hereditary rights; notions of fatherhood; national identity; political representations of kingship. Secondly, to maintain that Filmer's conclusions were issued at a time when the policies of the Stuarts shifted towards absolutism is to underestimate that absolutist methods had been adopted well before and that the publication of Filmer's writings, especially *Patriarcha*, was no coincidence. Rather, it was the result of a conscious and well-thought attempt to present the monarchy under a more credible and stronger light in the midst of the crisis of the 1680s.

It could also be advanced that what might have made Filmer's works appealing to a certain audience at this historical juncture was both the absence from them of any theory of Church affairs and the fact that Filmer was *no Hobbes*. This is to say that his writings could be safely employed as Tory political propaganda because they ignored religiously and doctrinally burning issues (toleration, dissent, heresy, sects). Since Filmer's doctrines did not inspire thoughts of toleration towards dissenting minds, they fitted the agenda of people like L'Estrange whose ideological 'goodies' were Filmerian authors such as King James, Maxwell, Heylyn, Falkner, Hickes, Sherlock, Brady and Dryden.[57] Moreover, whilst in the Restoration period Hobbes was anathematised 'as popish' and even 'as republican', the same could obviously not be said of Filmer.[58] In this respect, the latter's winning move had been to point out the numerous similarities between Jesuit and Calvinist principles. Likewise, his forthright criticism of Hobbes' state of nature[59] gave him an air of respectability, which the Tories found indispensable to hold on to so as not to be associated with the atheistic creator of the Leviathan. In practice, his absolutism was more palatable because it was not Hobbesian.[60] At the same time, it made Filmer's theory more attractive to those at work to *resolve* the dynastic problems affecting the Stuart reign in the phases pre- (but also post-) 1685.[61]

In summary, Filmer provided a significant number of late seventeenth-century thinkers with a powerful arsenal of explosive political notions with which to mine the territory where Whig armies moved. His configuration of sovereignty served to reject Whig accusations that Charles II was an invader and/or a usurper.[62] Filmer re-stated the legitimacy of the king in an unequivocal manner: he associated him with the nation and depicted him as *tout court* in tune with the ethos of the country. In other terms, patriarchalism made him the father of the land. It claimed that the ruler's fatherly care and his subjects' interest were interwoven because in a hereditary monarchy public and private benefit belonged to the same sphere. This meant that only a fatherly monarchy guaranteed that most beneficial juxtaposition of '*Salus Regis*' and '*Salus Populi*'.[63] From this account were expelled both Jesuit and godly claims that religious rectitude and political prosperity coincided. Instead, for authors like Filmer '*Cultus Dei*' and '*Salus Populi*' pertained to separate fields of action and thought.[64] Perhaps surprisingly (and no less ironically), some of these Filmerian ideas turned out to be not too distant from the (modern) trends that were to succeed in the realms of political practice and political theory during the next century.

This chapter has unveiled the forceful influence that – at times directly and at times indirectly[65] – Filmerian patriarchalism had on late seventeenth-century theorists and debates. If this occurred more evidently in the 1680s and 1690s than in the previous decades, it is not just because *Patriarcha* was published in 1680. This change was also the result of the experience of the Civil War, and the widened ideological divisions created thereby, as well as of various retrospective explanations of that event. These factors rendered the central insights of Filmer's great work more persuasive, more politically and polemically effective. In one word, by 1680 his ideas had become more 'mainstream' than they had been in the early 1630s, or indeed even in the 1640s, because they proved to be more consonant with the types of political languages and polemical goals that shaped the ideological landscape of the final phases of the Stuart regimes.

NOTES

1 On the hysteria created by the plot and the circulation of news at that time see P. Hinds, *'The Horrid Popish Plot': Roger L'Estrange and the Circulation of Political Discourse in Late-Seventeenth-Century London* (London and Oxford, 2008).

2 *The London Gazette* was first published as *The Oxford Gazette* on 7 November 1665. Once Charles II and the Royal Court had returned to London – having moved to Oxford to escape the Great Plague in the capital – the *Gazette* began to be 'Published by Authority' by Henry Muddiman. Its first issue came out on 5 February 1666. The *Gazette* was sent by post to subscribers, not printed for sale to the general public.

3 *The London Gazette*, no. 1840, 5–9 July 1683, p. 1.

4 *The London Gazette*, no. 1848, 2–6 August 1683, p. 1.

5 *Ibid.*, p. 1.

6 *The London Gazette*, no. 1849, 6–9 August 1683, p. 2.

7 *Ibid.*, pp. 2–3.

8 *Ibid.*, p. 3.

9 *The London Gazette*, no. 1852, 16–20 August 1683, p. 1.

10 *Ibid.*, p. 1.

11 *Ibid.*, p. 1.

12 *The London Gazette*, no. 1855, 27–30 August 1683, p. 1.

13 *Ibid.*, p. 1.

14 *The London Gazette*, no. 1863, 24–27 September 1683, p. 1.

15 *The London Gazette*, no. 1841, 9–12 July 1683, p. 2.

16 *The London Gazette*, no. 1848, 2–6 August 1683, p. 2.

17 *Ibid.*, pp. 2–3.

18 *The London Gazette*, no. 1864, 27 September–1 October 1683, p. 2.

19 *Ibid.*, p. 2.

20 Robert Atkyns, *The Power, Jurisdiction and Priviledge of Parliament and the Antiquity of the House of Commons* ... (1689), p. 14 (the reference to Filmer is in a note). See also Robert Atkyns, *An Enquiry into the Jurisdiction of the Chancery in causes of equity* (1695), p. 7 (where Filmer was said to have 'weakly, or rather wilfully, tho groundlesly infer[red]' that the laws of England were 'the King's Laws') and Robert Atkyns, *A Treatise of the true and ancient jurisdiction of the House of Peers* (1699), p. 13.

21 Atkyns, *The Power*, p. 15.

22 *Ibid.*, p. 25.

23 *Ibid.*, pp. 26–7.

24 *Ibid.*, pp. 31–2.

25 *Ibid.*, p. 32. Like Filmer, 'Doctor *Heylin*, in his Life of Arch-Bishop *Laud, fol.* 91. denies the Priviledges of Parliament to be the Peoples Birth-Right, but holds them not otherwise exercis'd, than by the Grace and Goodness of the King' (*ibid.*, p. 27). For attacks on Heylyn see *ibid.*, pp. 33, 55. In general, criticism of Filmer's (and Heylyn's) ideas run through the book (with regard to the Filmerian view of the place of Lords and Commons see *ibid.*, pp. 27, 31; to Saxon and Norman political organisation as described by 'New Writers, as Mr *Pryn*, and *Sir Robert Filmer*, and several others' see *ibid.*, p. 30; again to the Commons see *ibid.*, pp. 33, 40).

26 William Atwood, *Wonderful Predictions of Nostredamus, Grebner, David Pareus* ... (1689), 'The Preface'.

27 *Ibid.*, 'The Preface'.

28 *Ibid.*, 'The Preface'. Atwood even resorted to 'Sir *Robert Filmer*'s Authority' to demonstrate that '"[t]here can be no Obligation which taketh State from the meer Will of him that promises the same"' (*ibid.*, 'The Preface').

29 In a series of anonymous pamphlets published in the early 1680s Atwood had targeted

both Robert Brady and Filmer. Moreover, in *Letter of Remarks upon Jovian* (1683) Atwood had defended the Whig divine Samuel Johnson (1649–1703) whose 'antipapist, pro-exclusion tract, *Julian the Apostate*' (1682) had prompted George Hickes' (1642–1715) strongly Tory *Jovian, or, An Answer to Julian the Apostate* (1683). In this work, Hickes delivered 'an extreme Filmerian political statement in which he declared that kings alone made law and that the succession was divine and unalterable' (*ODNB*, 'Atwood, William'). Atwood was to criticise Filmer also in *The Antiquity and Justice of an Oath of Abjuration ...* (1694), p. 49 and in *The Rights and Authority of the Commons of the City of London ...* (1695), p. 15.

30 William Atwood, *The Fundamental Constitution of the English Government ...* (1690), *passim*.

31 *Ibid.*, 'The Epistle Dedicatory'.

32 *Ibid.*, 'Preface', pp. i–xxxiv.

33 *Ibid.*, 'Preface', pp. xxv, xxxi.

34 *Ibid.*, ch. 1, pp. 3–4.

35 *Ibid.*, ch.1, p. 4.

36 *Ibid.*, ch.1, p. 4.

37 *Ibid.*, ch. 1, p. 4.

38 *Ibid.*, ch. 10, p. 101.

39 *Ibid.*, 'Appendix', p. 1.

40 This confirms that seventeenth-century polemicists considered Filmer as Heylyn's master and not vice versa as sometimes wrongly implied in the historiography.

41 *Ibid.*, 'Appendix', p. 1.

42 *Ibid.*, 'Appendix', pp. 1–2. In spite of his declaration of loyalty to the Church of England expounded in *A Seasonable Vindication of the Truly Catholic Doctrine of the Church of England* published in 1683, Atwood did not hesitate to target 'the Anglican hierarchy'. In particular, he scorned 'the lower clergy' as a consequence of their 'incessant preaching of passive obedience and divine kingship'. Atwood was also a defender of Protestant nonconformity (see *ODNB*, 'Atwood, William').

43 Atwood, *The Fundamental Constitution of the English Government*, ch. viii, pp. 74 ff.

44 For the legal and political debates focused on the ancient constitution and order theory in the 1680s and 1690s see Weston and Greenberg, *Subjects and Sovereigns* and Greenberg, *The Radical Face of the Ancient Constitution*.

45 *The Dying Speeches of several excellent persons, who suffered for their zeal against popery, and arbitrary government ...* (1689).

46 'The very Copy of a Paper delivered to the Sheriffs ... By Algernon Sidney ...', in *The Dying Speeches*, pp. 18–22, p. 19.

47 William Sherlock, *Observations upon Mr. Johnson's Remarks, upon Dr. Sherlock's Book of Non-Resistance* (1689), p. 20.

48 *Ibid.*, p. 20.

49 See William Sherlock, *The Case of the Allegiance due to Sovereign Powers* (1690).

50 In the same year Gerard Langbaine remarked that 'Sr. *Robert Filmer* (if I mistake not) writ against him [John Milton], in his Observations concerning the Original of Government, printed 4°. *Lond.* 1652' (Gerard Langbaine, *An Account of the English Dramatick Poets* ... (1691), p. 377).

51 Jeremy Collier, *Dr. Sherlock's Case of Allegiance considered with some remarks upon his vindication* (1691), p. 91.

52 *Ibid.*, pp. 97–8. According to Tania Boster, 'the argument that subjects should die for the king if necessity requires it does not align with Collier's views. Yet Collier's beliefs are easily lost in the subtleties of his polemical style'. Boster proposed two hypotheses to explain the passages quoted above. Firstly, either *Dr. Sherlock's Case* was not Collier's (in fact, even though the text has been attributed to him, it is amongst his unsigned publications) or, perhaps, it 'was written in collaboration with another nonjuror, or was modified when it went to press'. Secondly, Boster suggested that 'as in a Platonic dialogue (a form Collier adopts in his moral essays), Collier manipulates the reader to come to the desired conclusion, often by presenting contrary evidence to expose logical contradictions' (I am grateful to Tania Boster for sharing her ideas on Collier in private correspondence from where the quotations above are taken). On Collier see T. Boster, *"Better To Be Alone Than In Ill Company' Jeremy Collier The Younger: Life And Works, 1650–1726'*, PhD Thesis, University of Pittsburgh, 2006.

53 Anon., *Ad Populum Phalerae, or, The Twinn-Shams* (1692), pp. 2–3.

54 Daly, *Sir Robert Filmer*, p. 124.

55 Houston, *Algernon Sidney*, p. 96. Few scholars have paid attention to this issue. An exception, but one which does not alter the usual picture, is Goldie, 'John Locke and Anglican Royalism'. Generally, the most accepted answer points to the Anglican Church. Laslett proposed the following 'candidates' as possibly responsible for the reprinting of Filmer's tracts: Archbishop Sancroft; one of Sir Robert's relatives; Royston, who was still bookseller to the King and who had a hand in the 1684 Filmerian collection (Laslett, 'Introduction', p. 36).

56 Houston, *Algernon Sidney*, pp. 94–6.

57 Goldie, 'Roger L'Estrange's *Observator'*, p. 81. In fact, for L'Estrange the regime of Charles II had been too lenient with dissenters, and with its enemies more generally (*ibid.*, p. 70). In this sense, *Patriarcha* responded to a need felt by sundry frustrated monarchists.

58 As for this criticism of Hobbes see Rose, 'Robert Brady's Intellectual History', p. 1310.

59 Hobbes' model was also worryingly anti-patriarchalist in that it underscored first and foremost the role of the mother with regard to hereditary rights and transmission of power since the mother was always certain, whilst the father was not (see Hobbes, *Leviathan*, Part 2, ch. 20).

60 This book does not examine in detail the more specific differences informing the works of Filmer and Hobbes. See C. Cuttica, 'An Absolutist Trio in the Early 1630s: Sir Robert Filmer, Jean-Louis Guez de Balzac, Cardin Le Bret and their Models of Monarchical Power', in Cuttica and Burgess (eds), *Monarchism and Absolutism*, pp. 131–45.

61 I would like to thank Tania Boster, Alan Cromartie, Gaby Mahlberg and Rachel Weil for their insightful comments on some of these points.

62 Ashcraft, *Revolutionary Politics*, p. 395; Houston, *Algernon Sidney*, p. 80, n. 53.

63 On these two definitions see Houston, *Algernon Sidney*, p. 81.

64 On this issue in relation to Parsons see M. L. Carrafiello, *Robert Parsons and English Catholicism, 1580–1610* (Selinsgrove (PA) and London, 1993).

65 This re-appropriation of Filmer was not immune to selective manipulation and to the cutting of parts of his oeuvre whose theoretical fabric did not suit specific polemical purposes. Tailoring of Filmer's works was thus pursued regularly and unreservedly.

Conclusion

This book has cast new light on many overlooked aspects of Sir Robert Filmer's biography and intellectual activity. It has abandoned mainstream interpretations of his political ideas and rethought the definition of a patriarchalist canon. More specifically, overdue attention has been paid to his most important writing, *Patriarcha* (1620s–30s). The latter – a much vituperated text whose name has historically been associated with oppressive and backward political thinking – has been examined as a powerful and radical expression of the theory here labelled *political patriarchalism*.

Thanks to a contextual approach aimed at unveiling the treatise's goals and language, this study has reconsidered the intellectual achievements of a neglected and often misunderstood thinker. Instead of placing Filmer's opinions in isolation or, at best, exclusively in relation to the posthumous criticism they underwent, they have been interpreted in concert with questions and debates informing the milieu in which he wrote his work(s). This has meant concentrating on politics and government in the Jacobean and early Stuart era; on the role metaphors, various traditions of thought, historical, biblical and philosophical sources as well as rhetorical images played in the configuration of early seventeenth-century political discourse; on controversies regarding the issues of liberty and sovereignty, monarchical allegiance and parliamentary authority, popery and popularity; on cultural and social aspects of the early modern period in England and Europe (e.g. the family, the place of women in the household, fatherhood, hierarchy). The interplay of text and context has also been applied to the historical phase when *Patriarcha* was first published (1680). The analysis of language and backdrop has helped to unfold not only the texture of his theories, but also how they were received and employed at the time of the Exclusion Crisis and afterwards. Furthermore, *Patriarcha* has been used as a thread leading us into early modern political thought and culture. In particular, it has served as a prism through which to see the lasting importance of the paradigms of patriarchalism and patriotism during the long seventeenth century in England.

By way of an informative and newly documented account of his life, education, public career, circles of friends and cultural environment, the biographical Sir Robert has emerged more clearly. This contextual narrative has established how he first formed as a thinker and how he then participated in the political and intellectual debates of early modern England and Europe. Subsequently, *Patriarcha* has been carefully dissected so as to highlight the great significance of its configuration of patriarchalist sovereignty in relation to competing visions of power and government at the end of the 1620s. On this stage rival actors shared (to a large extent) the same script. This is to say that, despite expounding opposite views of the polity, both country patriots and monarchists appropriated the patriotic rhetoric whose language focused on the defence of the nation.[1] In political literature this was reflected in the contrast between the parliamentary paradigm advocating the superior status of the country and the absolutist concept of kingly power embodied by the father of the fatherland.

Shaped by this wave of political feelings, *Patriarcha* had two main targets: patriots and Jesuits. As for the former, Filmer's cousin Thomas Scott of Canterbury has been taken as a radical mouthpiece of that cluster of ideological opposition to royal absolutism and Arminian policies that became more extreme in the shift from the Jacobean era to the Caroline reign. As for the Jesuits, Robert Bellarmine and Francisco Suarez represent two of the most intellectually compelling adversaries Filmer singled out. Their works put forward theories that were at loggerheads with his absolute and Adamite vision of power and authority. Thus, patriarchalism served Sir Robert to contest patriotic contentions on Parliament as the cornerstone of the kingdom's political identity, and dismantled popish arguments whereby the Pope controlled monarchs and was above them. The fatherly account of politics delineated in *Patriarcha* was a response to those two discourses and, above all, a statement or a re-assertion on who held ultimate power. In order to avoid the lethal political scenario in which patriots and Jesuits had the upper hand, Filmer saw it necessary to reconsider the role of the fatherly sovereign and foster his patriotic aura. *Patriarcha* was his important attempt to do so; patriarchalism his weapon. Put briefly, through patriarchalism, Filmer left no cornerstone of his opponents' theories untouched.

Patriarcha has also been studied in conjunction with a process of image-construction of monarchical authority that took place in the 1620s and 1630s in Stuart England. Most importantly, a manifold examination of the circumstances that in 1632 prompted Filmer to try to publish the treatise has enabled us to reconsider the latter's scope and place on the dynamic stage of European intellectual history from novel political and cultural perspectives. This approach has opened up new ground for a thorough discussion of patriarchalism as a political category whose impact on early modern political thought was highly significant. It has also permitted to deconstruct Filmer's vision of politics according to a wider spectrum of factors than that generally considered in the scholarship. *Patriarcha*'s analysis of power has been explored against the cultural, aesthetic, ethical background of the early Caroline era as well as the political panorama of the 1680s. In the former instance, the use of

Kevin Sharpe's work on the visual culture of Charles I's court has stimulated a broader understanding of the text and its connections to central aspects of Stuart absolutism. In the second, this way of proceeding has not only shown the importance of *Patriarcha* as an ideological manifesto serving a specific cause at a specific time, but has enabled the political thought of the period to be recast into a more coherent and genuinely European narrative.

From a theoretical viewpoint, Filmer's patriarchalism has been depicted as a forceful attempt at rethinking the nature of power. As a result of its making Adam's fatherly might the essential model of kingship, *Patriarcha* has been described as a rich account of statecraft whose fundament was the principle of the Adamite sovereign as the father of the fatherland; the founder of the State; the creator of the law. And this, in turn, has been interpreted as a move to make the ruler coincide *tout court* with the polity and to represent the will of the king as the supreme authorising political and legal voice in the body politic.

These concepts have not been read simply as a form of royal/monarchist propaganda at a historical juncture of increasing tension between the Jacobean and then Caroline regimes and their critics. They have been explained as strategic devices used to counterattack – as already mentioned – patriotism and Jesuitism. In the former case, the rich and flexible language of patriotism has been mapped out through the study of vociferous patriots and MPs claiming to be the true defenders of the country. As for Jesuitism, the tenet of the Pope's power of interference in the temporal sphere has been evaluated as a central and enduring source of fear affecting much of seventeenth-century intellectual life in England and Europe.

These controversies were also interwoven with the debate on legitimate resistance to tyrannical kings. In this respect, *Patriarcha* identified the theories of both Catholic and Calvinist monarchomachs with a cancer rapidly spreading within the body politic. Their advocating the lawfulness of parricide as a means to defend the nation prompted Filmer's patriarchalist configuration of the monarch as fatherly and patriotic head of the nation. By carving out an alternative account of what it meant to be a patriot, he strengthened a sense of national consciousness amongst disillusioned English subjects. Playing with the richly allusive discourses of fatherhood and parricide as much as with the practical issues of people's allegiance to a fatherly (masculine) king and with increasingly oppositional patriotic claims, Filmer intended to provide a persuasive image of monarchical sovereignty and remind that only by promoting Adamite monarchical government could the much coveted stability of the country be achieved. Both considerations – as amply detailed in Part II – were taken on board in the unsettled 1680s, where purchase of patriarchal ideas became widespread, and where the Exclusion Crisis debates and Tory–Whig reactions put Filmer front and centre in ways that explain just why John Locke wanted to refute him so directly.

In contrast to traditional views of patriarchalism, the present study has shown that the theoretical medium of the family as the entity where social life had at first originated epitomised the antithesis of the bellicose primitive condition of total anarchic freedom to be found in the state of nature. The Adamite narrative of the origins guaranteed a safe platform from which man's polity had stemmed and developed. Above all, it articulated a model of kingship where the ruler was the true and only protector of the subjects against those divisive spirits who claimed that Parliament was the kernel of political life. Confronted by the murders of Henry III (1589) and Henry IV (1610) in France and by the Gunpowder Plot (1605) in England, monarchists knew that words could catastrophically turn into actions, indeed murderous actions. Since the latter were (often) sustained by a discourse that centred on the formula *pro rege et patria*, which contemplated the killing of evil fathers in order to protect the fatherland, a host of thinkers re-appropriated this powerful language and deprived it of its potential dangers. They turned it to the advantage of monarchy and its supreme representative. They made obedience to the fatherly ruler coincide with love of and respect for the fatherland. In the war of images and metaphors, this corresponded to reject Théodore de Bèze's opinion that filial loyalty came second to patriotic allegiance to one's country.[2] It also amounted to rejecting Ultramontanist and papalist positions whereby people's foremost allegiance was due to the external and supranational authority of the Pope.

In substance, Filmer provided a solution to the fundamental question formulated by the French historian Bernard de Girard du Haillan in *Histoire Generale des Rois de France* (1576). Reflecting on the origins of monarchy, especially on the prime causes which had established kings' sovereignty, Haillan had complained that theories of monarchical authority discussed the subject in unconvincing terms or avoided to do so altogether. In fact, they reasoned 'as if kings fell off the sky or the clouds on earth without any first cause'.[3] Taking on this challenge, Filmer delineated one of the most fully fledged theoretical justifications of the reasons why hereditary monarchies were the sole government capable of preserving stability in the State as well as giving continuity to the political process. This patriarchalist fresco at the centre of which stood out the figure of the Adamite ruler was the strong absolutist elaboration of a unique 'English patriarchalist *politique*'. The sharpness of his discourse lay in the way that he employed the language of patriarchalism as a means of remapping the archaeology of power through the role of Adam. This effort had multiple ramifications, the most important of which reached the political and ideological scenario of the 1680s. Thus, in writing *Patriarcha* Filmer placed himself at the forefront of salient debates thriving in the republic of letters as much as in the world of early *and* late Stuart politics.

Conclusions

By pursuing these trajectories of research through the methodology of intellectual history, the foregoing pages draw thus a new picture of Filmer's patriarchalism and address – hoping to bring them closer – various audiences engaged in the study of political thought.

This book is shaped by the idea that to study Filmer, the man and the thinker, means to approach his biography and oeuvre contextually, by illuminating the relationships between his ideas and those of his contemporaries. It is also based on the conviction that even the most apparently abstruse of his concepts can be better understood if historically connected with a specific milieu of political discourses and actions. Therefore, having shown how Filmer's writings have been conventionally read as if they had been produced in the empyrean realm of eternal philosophical problems, this book has situated his patriarchalism where it belongs: at the heart of early modern political discussions and cultural debates. In this respect, this study calls into question the still much-too-common opinion that Sir Robert's theories did not succeed in the theatre of ideas and were, instead, defeated by the modern vision of politics and society ushered in by Locke's 'progressive pen'. Thus, en route to display a richer narrative of early modern intellectual history, the nine chapters explain why Filmer wrote at a specific historical juncture; for whom; against which targets; by using what type of political languages. If anything, this way of proceeding should give us a more humble but less distorted image of the value of *Patriarcha* and its doctrines both throughout the great part of the seventeenth century and in the pantheon of European political reflection.

Aware of the ever present difficulty of dealing with thoughts and events far away in time, this book hopes to have enabled readers to better grasp what Filmer *was all about*.

NOTES

1 In the words of Johann Sommerville, 'a strong sense of nationhood was a major theme in the literature of all three kingdoms which James and Charles tried to rule' (Sommerville, 'An Emergent Britain?', p. 461).

2 J. H. M. Salmon, 'France', in H. A. Lloyd, G. Burgess and S. Hodson (eds), *European Political Thought 1450–1700. Religion, Law and Philosophy* (New Haven and London, 2007), pp. 458–97, p. 472.

3 Bernard de Girard du Haillan, *Histoire Generale des Rois de France* (Paris, 1627), vol. ii, p. 11.

Appendix 1
The treasury of the scholar: Filmer's library

James Daly aptly defined Filmer as 'a very literate man indeed' who mastered Latin, Greek and French, and whose vast interests extended to scientific subjects.[1] Filmer's library shows the vast scope of his knowledge and unveils what a seventeenth-century man of letters purchased for his edification and polemical goals. In fact, delving in Sir Robert's 'bookish closet' helps to reconstruct his cultural backdrop, scholarly toolbox, erudite passions.

A list of books belonging to Sir Edward Filmer and found at East Sutton in 1729 indicates that – besides classics like Homer, Cicero, Livy, Ovid, Sallust and Tacitus – Filmer owned works by Bellarmine, Copernicus, Davila, Erasmus, Knolles, Pufendorf, Raleigh; books on cosmography and exploration (like those by Edward Grimestone and Fynes Moryson); the major texts of the time on European history; French, Latin and Greek grammar books.[2] Some of the items on the list were probably acquired after Sir Robert's death and some of his own works are included. Amongst these it is interesting to find *The Free-Holders Grand Inquest*, which is here definitely ascribed to Filmer. His other writings on the list are *Patriarcha* and *Quaestio Quodlibetica*.

Consultation of a copy of the 1729 inventory of books from East Sutton Park sold by Arthur Wilson Filmer at Sotheby's (London) on 1 October 1945[3] shows that Filmer also owned the following works: Cotton's *The Troublesome Life and Raigne of King Henry the Third* (1642); Sir Henry Wotton's *A Short View of the Life and Death of George Villiers, Duke of Buckingham* (1642); Ben Jonson's *Bartholomew Fayre: A Comedie*, *The Staple of Newes: A Comedie* and *The Divell is an Asse: A Comedie*; Selden's *Titles of Honor* (1631); Shakespeare's *Comedies, Histories and Tragedies*; two copies of Edmund Spencer's *The Faerie Queene*; various herbaria; Sir Robert Brook's *Ascuns Nouell cases de les ans et temps le Roy* (1578); Richard Cary's *Le Necessarie use & Fruit de les Pleadings, conteine en le bein de le tresreverend Edward Coke* (1601); Sir John Doddridge's *The Lawyers Light: or, A due direction for the study of the Law* (1629); Du Bartas's *His Devine Weekes and Workes* (1608, translated by Joshua Sylvester); one E. T.'s *The Lawes Resolutions of Womens Rights: or, the Lawes Provision for Woemen* (1632, which Filmer must have consulted when he wrote *In Praise of the Vertuous Wife*); Henrie Finch's *Law: or, a Discourse thereof in four Bookes* (1627); Fletwood's *Annalium* (1597) and Fortescue's *A Learned Commendation of the politique Lawes of England* (1599, translated into English by Robert Mulcaster); manuals on the function and role of the Justice of the Peace (1574), including some of Lambarde's works (*A Perambulation of Kent* and *Eirenarcha*); Thomas Lupton's *A thousand Notable Things of sundrie sorts* (1631); a copy of *Magna Charta* (1556); books on court affairs and other original things; a copy of Virgil's *The Thirteene Bookes of Aeneidos* (1596, translated into English verse by Thomas Phaer and

Thomas Twyne); diverse tracts of Sir Francis Bacon amongst which *Three Spechees of the Right Honorable Sir Francis Bacon ... concerning the Post-Nati* (1641), *Certain Miscellany Works ... published by William Rawley* (1629) and *Certaine Considerations touching the Church of England* which bore on the cover the inscription *For Mr. Robert Filmer;* David Owen's *Herod and Pilate Reconciled: or, the concord of papist and puritan* (1610); Leonard Digges' *A Prognostication everlasting of right good effect* (1605); Gervase Markham's work on horsemanship; Pliny's *Epistolarum Libri X* and his *The Historie of the World;* Bacon's *Instauratio Magna [Novum Organum]*, first edition (1620) and his *Sylva Sylvarum: or, a Naturall Historie*, first edition (1627); an English version of the Geneva Bible (1577); Robert Burton's *The Anathomy of Melancholy ... by Democritus Junior* (1632); one edition of Dante's *Divina Commedia* (with the commentary of Cristoforo Landino); the first edition of Donne's *LXXX Sermons* (1640); the first edition of Hobbes' *Leviathan* (1651); Thomas Muffet's book on insects and Aaron Rathborne's *The Surveyor;* Suetonius's *The Historie of Twelve Caesars Emperours of Rome* (1606) and Tacitus' *Annales (the Description of Germaine,* 1604–5); Girard Thiebault's *Academie de l'Espée* (1628).

Amongst the documents belonging to the Filmers is another list containing several books for sale that were published mainly in the first half of the seventeenth century, the last one being Heylyn's *Extraneus Vapulans* (1656). It includes works by Arminius, Bodin, Calvin, Charron, Du Bartas, Heylyn, Machiavelli, Melanchthon and Saravia, as well as numerous Italian, French and Spanish books. In addition, a manuscript titled *Catalogue of Bookes from the Library at Sutton Place, Sir Edmund Filmer's, December 1849 (E2–18)*, which is now held at Ham House (Surrey), contains a very long list of items purchased by the Filmers at various times. It presents its books in alphabetical order with the year of publication. Listing the items published before Filmer's death should give an idea of the readings he likely pursued.[4] Amongst these can be found Andreus' *Moral Law* (1642) and *Sermons* (1632); an edition of Ariosto's works of 1584; *An Assertion for true and Christian Policie* (1604); Bacon's *Historia* (1623); *Baronage of England* (1642); the works of Ben Johnson (1616); Bentivoglio's *Delle guerre di Fiandra* (1637); the works of Boetius (1556); Bibbia Hebraica (1647); Chillingworth's *Religion of Protestants* (1638); Coke upon Littleton (1633 and 1629); *Collection of Parliamentary Speeches* (1640); Cotton's *Concordance* (1627); Crookes's *Microcosmograph* (1615); *Dialogue on the Laws of England 13th letter* (1638); Diodoro Siculus (1604); *Discorsi Sopra Cornelio Tacito* (1635); Donne's *Sermons* (1644); Florus (1638); Finch's *Discourses* (1627); Fortescue on the *Laws of England* (1599); *Geographia Sacra* (1646); Grimstone's *History of the World* (1615); Greek Testament (1632); Hammonds' *Practicall Catechisme* (1646); Davila's *Historiae di Francia* (1642); Hobbes' *Leviathan* (1651); Hooker's *Ecclesiastical Politie* (1617); Horatius (1608); Insectarum (no date); Jewell's *Works* (1631); Joannis Seldeni (1617); Lambarde's *Eirenarcha* (1610); *Les Reports de Edward Coke* (1600); Livius' *Romana Historia* (1600); a copy of *Magna Charta;* Guarini's *Pastor Fido* (1621); Peacham's *Complete Gentleman* (1634); Polydori Vergillii's *Historia* (1651); *Sir Walter Raleighs Sceptick* (1651); *The Historie of Tithes by J. Selden* (1618); *The Annales of Cornelius Tacitus* (1604); *Theatrum Botanicum* (1640); *Treatise of the Nobilitie* (1642); Twysden on *Government of England* (no date); *Utopiae Mori* (1631); Wentworth's *Speeches* (1641); *Woman's Lawyer* (1632). This list also contains works by Lucretius, Lucanus and Sallust, and a series of unspecified *Pamphlets* from the 1640s. In addition, the following items are referred to: Filmer's *Tracts* (1647); Filmer's *Treatise of Usury Pub. By Sir Roger Twysden* (1678); Filmer's *Freeholders' Grand Inquest* (1679); Filmer's *Tracts* (1679); Filmer's *Tracts* (1684); Filmer's *Unnatural Brother* (1697); Filmer's *Defence of Plays* (3 copies, 1707).

Dry as these lists might appear,[5] they are nonetheless meaningful in that they testify to the great variety of interests to which Filmer's curious mind was attracted. Indeed, they are in line with the vast scope of his intellectual oeuvre delineated in this book.

NOTES

1 Daly, *Sir Robert Filmer*, p. 15.

2 KAO, U120/Z4.

3 See *Catalogue of Printed Books ... Sold by Order of the Trustees of the late Sir Robert Filmer* (available at the discretion of the Filmer Wilson family. I am grateful to Mr David Cleggett for having given me a copy of the catalogue). My attempt at Sotheby's to establish whether the whole stock was sold together and who or which institution bought the library proved fruitless. However, it is certain that in 1952 Peter Laslett acquired 'eleven of the remaining East Sutton Park manuscripts from the dealer Alan Keen' to which he added a further volume purchased in another occasion. These manuscripts formed Laslett's library until 2006 when they were given to the Bodleian Library where I consulted them (they remain uncatalogued). Of the twelve items, six 'are apparently in the hand of Robert Filmer', whilst both the identity of the other hands and their authorship remain uncertain – although Laslett attributed some of them to various later members of the Filmer family. I owe this information to the courtesy of Mr Michael Webb, Head of Cataloguing, Department of Special Collections and Western Manuscripts, BDO. Mr Webb provided me with the sale catalogue description 'From the Library of the Late Peter Laslett: A) Manuscripts from East Sutton Park', where a list of items by Sir Robert or belonging to the Filmers appears. Amongst them are two autograph copies of *Theologie: or Divinity* (in one case spelt *Theologie or Divinitie*); a copy of the manuscript on the 'vertuous woman'; part of an autograph draft manuscript of *Of the Blasphemie against the Holy-Ghost*; an autograph copy of some annotations on the Old Testament in Latin; an incomplete exercise/commonplace book, which is probably in Filmer's own hand.

4 In some cases the manuscript gives only the name of the author without specifying their works. Filmer's own tracts on this list are also quoted regardless of their publication date. The attribution to Sir Robert of *The Free-Holders Grand Inquest* is here once more confirmed.

5 For books Filmer could find at the parochial library at East Sutton see KAO, U120 Z7–8, *Catalogue of Books Belonging to East Sutton Parochial Lending Library*.

Select bibliography

FILMER'S PRINTED WORKS

Political writings

Directions for Obedience to Governours in Dangerous and Doubtfull Times, in Sommerville (ed.), *Patriarcha*, pp. 281–6.

Observations Concerning The Originall of Government. Upon Mr Hobs Leviathan. Mr Milton against Salmasius, *H. Grotius* De Jure Belli, in Sommerville (ed.), *Patriarcha*, pp. 184–234.

Observations Upon Aristotles Politiques Touching Forms of Government, in Sommerville (ed.), *Patriarcha*, pp. 235–81.

Patriarcha or The Naturall Power of Kinges Defended against the Unnatural Liberty of the People, in J. P. Sommerville (ed.), *Robert Filmer. Patriarcha and Other Political Writings* (Cambridge, 1991), pp. 1–68.

The Anarchy of a Limited or Mixed Monarchy, in Sommerville (ed.), *Patriarcha*, pp. 131–71.

The Free-Holders Grand Inquest Touching Our Sovereraigne Lord the king and His Parliament, in Sommerville (ed.), *Patriarcha*, pp. 69–130.

The Necessity of The Absolute Power of all Kings: And in particular, of the King of England, in Sommerville (ed.), *Patriarcha*, pp. 172–83.

Other writings

An Advertisement to the Jurymen of England, Touching Witches. Together with A Difference between An English and Hebrew Witch (1653).

'In Praise of the Vertuous Wife', in M. Ezell, *The Patriarch's Wife. Literary Evidence and the History of the Family* (Chapel Hill and London, 1987).

Of the Blasphemie against the Holy-Ghost (1647).

Quaestio Quodlibetica, or A Discourse, Whether it may bee Lawfull to take Use For Money (1653).

FILMERIAN MANUSCRIPTS

'A Defence of Sir Robert Filmer', KAO U120 Z16/4.

'An Inventory of the Goods & Chattels of Sir Robert Filmer Bar.', KAO U120 T200/19.

'Catalogue of Books Belonging to East Sutton Parochial Lending Library', KAO U120 Z7–8.

'Civil War Papers', KAO U120 C4.

'Draft of letter from Lady Filmer to Sir Anthony Weldon appealing against her husband's imprisonment', N. D. ?, KAO U120 C4/5.

'Draft of letter in Lady Filmer's name appealing against over assessment for tax referred to in C4/3', N. D. ?, KAO U120 C4/6.

Filmer MSS KAO U120; U 1870; U120, F7; U120, T171; C12/2; C12/3; C12/4; C12/6.

Filmer, Robert, *Discussion of the point concerning the extent of royal authority*, BL, Harley MS 6867, fo. 251a.

— *In praematuram Mortem, Epitaph on G. Wyatt*, BL, Additional MS 62135, fos 68–9.

— *Of the Sabeth*, BL, Harley 4685, fos 59, 64.

— *Theologie: or Divinity* (uncatalogued MS from the late Prof. Peter Laslett's library, BDO, item c).

— *Touching Marriage and Adultery*, BL, Harley MS 6866, fos 514r–22r.

'Letter from Augustine Skynner summoning him to provide a horse for a muster on Offham Green', 1643, KAO U120 C4/2.

'Letter from Sir Robert in Leeds Castle to Sir Anthony Weldon and the Committee at Knole and the latter's reply, as to a further demand for a horse and arms', 1644, KAO U120 C4/4.

'Letter of Warning from Richard Beale about consequences of non payment of taxes by Lady Filmer, with drafts of two replies one in his own name and one in his wife's', 1644, KAO U120 C4/3.

'Letters', KAO U120 C6 1634, 1636; A1 31 Oct. 1632, A2 c. 1634, A3 7 Dec. 1636, A4 16 Dec. 1638, A5 24 Oct. 1639, A6 20 Dec. 1642, A7 7 Aug. 1643, A8 14 Aug. 1643, A9 (Autumn) 1643, A10, A11 c. 1644, A12 5–6 Sep. 1644, A13 9 May 1645, A14 7 Apr. 1647, A15 20 May 1648, A16 26 May 1648.

'Loose Sheets Containing Lists of Books', KAO U120 Z6–8.

'Miscellaneous Items probably of Filmer correspondence, but often not or not fully addressed (8 docs.)', c. 1625–1786, KAO U120 C82.

'Notes by Sir Robert about the exactions made upon East Sutton Place by the Parliamentary forces', 1642, and 'the sack of East Sutton church and Place in July 1643', 1643, KAO U120 C4/1.

'Printed Pamphlets, 17th century', KAO U120 Z16 (a list).

'Sir Robert Filmer, d. 1653', East Sutton Papers, KAO File A.

'Sir Robert Filmer's Will', 1651, KAO U120 T200/12–19.

WRITINGS ATTRIBUTED TO FILMER

Treatise on Rebellion, BDO, Tanner MS 233, fos 75–133.

Various Other Works, BDO, Tanner MS 233, fos 38–74, 135–47, 148–71, 172–6, 177 ff.

OTHER MANUSCRIPT SOURCES

BL, Additional MS 72439, fo. 8. 'Reasons for refusing a licence to Sir Robert Filmer's Patriarcha of G. R. Weckherlin' (London, February 1632).

BL, Harley MS 6867, fos 251a–2b.

BL, Stowe MS 743, fos 132–3, 'Letter to the right honourable my ever honest Lord the Earl of Thanet, Surrenden-Dering 7 March 1638'.

BL, Trumbull MS, Misc. Corr., XIX, fo. 16.

KAO, U269/F35, Coll. 16 'Curious Citations'.

King James VI and I, *My Lords and Gent: all* (Report of James I's speech accepting subsidies but refusing parliamentary supervision of foreign policy), c. 1621, Folger Shakespeare Library (Washington DC), MS X.d.150.

Kynaston, Francis, *A True Presentation of forepast Parliaments, to the viewe of present tymes and posteritie* (1629), BL, Lansdowne MS 213, fos 146a–76b.

PRO, SP 28/158, 'Commonwealth Exchequer Papers', Part 1.

Scott, Thomas, KAO U951/Z/9, U951/Z/10, U951/Z16, U951/Z17 (Knatchbull Papers).

— BL, Ballard MS 61.

— BL, Harley 7018, Additonal MS 62135, n. 31.

— CCL Urry MS 66 (*Thomas Scott's Papers on the Elections to the Parliament of 1626*).

— 'Miscellaneous', BDO, Rawlinson MS A 346, fos 224a–34b, 285a–97b.

PRINTED PRIMARY SOURCES

A Sale Catalogue of the Collections of Sir Edward Dering, 1st Bart., and his son, and Sir Roger Twysden: sold by auction by Puttick and Simpson on Tuesday, June 8, 1858 and the following four days (1858).

A Treatise of the true and ancient jurisdiction of the House of Peers (1699).

An Enquiry into the Jurisdiction of the Chancery in causes of equity (1695).

Anderson, Henry, *A Loyal Tear Dropt on the vault of the High and Mighty Prince, Charles II, of glorious and happy memory* (1685).

Andrewes, Lancelot, *A Sermon Preached before His Maiestie, on Sunday the fifth of August last* (1610).

Anon., *Ad Populum Phalerae, or, The Twinn-Shams* (1692).

Astell, Mary, *Some Reflections upon Marriage. Occasioned by the Duke and Dutchess of Mazarine's Case; Which is Also Considered* (1700).

— 'An Impartial Enquiry into the Causes of Rebellion and Civil War', in *Mary Astell. Political Writings*, ed. P. Springborg (Cambridge, 1996), pp. 129–97.

Atkyns, Robert, *The Power, Jurisdiction and Priviledge of Parliament and the Antiquity of the House of Commons ...* (1689).

Atwood, William, *Wonderful Predictions of Nostredamus, Grebner, David Pareus ...* (1689).

— *The Fundamental Constitution of the English Government proving King William and Queen Mary our lawful and rightful king and queen* (1690).

— *The Antiquity and Justice of an oath of abjuration ...* (1694).

— *The Rights and Authority of the Commons of the City of London ...* (1695).

Aucher, John, *The Arraignment of Rebellion, or, The Irresistibility of Sovereign Powers Vindicated and Maintain'd in a reply to a letter* (1684).

Barbeyrac, Jean, 'Notes', in Samuel Pufendorf, *Of the Law of Nature and Nations* (8 books written in Latin by the Baron Pufendorf ... done into English by Basil Kennett ... to which are added all the large notes of Mr. Barbeyrac, 1729).

Bargrave, Isaac, *A Sermon Preached Before King Charles, March 27th 1627 ...* (1627).

Barrow, Isaac, *A Treatise of the Pope's Supremacy to which is added A discourse concerning the unity of the church* (1683).

Bellarmine, Robert, *Responce aux Principaux Articles et Chapitres de l'Apologie du Belloy, faulsement & à faux tiltre inscrite Apologie Catholique, pour la succession de Henry Roy de Nauarre à la couronne de France* (Paris, 1588).

— *De Laicis, or The Treatise on Civil Government*, ed. M. F. X. Millar and transl. E. Murphy (New York, 1928).

Bohun, Edmund, *An Address to the Free-men and Free-holders of the Nation* (1682).

— *A defence of Sir Robert Filmer against the mistakes and misrepresentations of Algernon Sidney, esq.; in a paper delivered by him to the Sheriffs upon the Scaffold on Tower-Hill, on Friday December the seventh 1683 before his Execution there* (1684).

— *Patriarcha, or, The natural power of kings by the learned Sir Robert Filmer, Baronet; to which is added a preface to the reader in which this piece is vindicated from the cavils and misconstructions of the author of a book stiled Patriarcha non monarcha, and also a conclusion or postscript/by Edmund Bohun, esq.* (1685).

Bolton, Edmund, *Nero Caesar, or Monarchie Depraved* (1624).

Brady, Robert, *The Great Point of Succession ...* (1681).

Brathwaite, Richard, *The English Gentleman Containing Sundry Excellent Rules or Exquisite Observations ...* (1630).

Buckeridge, John, *A Sermon Preached at Hampton Court before the Kings Maiestie, on Tuesday the 23. of September, anno 1606* (1606).

Burton, Henry, *Truth's Triumph* (1629).

Butler, Samuel, *The Transproser Rehears'd, ... shewing what grounds there are of fears and jealousies of popery* (1673).

Calendar of State Papers Domestic, Series of the Reign of: Charles I 1629–31, ed. J. Bruce (1860), vol. 178, undated 1630, pp. 423–30.

Calendar of State Papers and Manuscripts relating to English Affairs, existing in the archives and collections of Venice, and in other libraries of Northern Italy, ed. Brown (1864), vol. xxi, 1628–29, pp. 21–2.

Catalogue of Printed Books comprising Drama; Travel; Botany; Tracts; and General Literature (including Shakespeare, second folio, 1632), Sold by Order of the Trustees of the late Sir Robert Filmer (1945).

Collier, Jeremy, *Dr. Sherlock's Case of Allegiance considered with some remarks upon his vindication* (1691).

Collins, Samuel, *Sermon at Paules-Crosse* (1610).

— *Epphata to F.T.* (Cambridge, 1617).

Common Debates 1621, eds W. Notestein, F. Relf and H. Simpson (New Haven, 7 vols, 1935), iii.

Constable, Robert, *God and the King* (1680).

Cotgrave, Randle, *A Dictionarie of the French and English Tongues* (1611).

Craig, Thomas, *Concerning the Right of Succession to the Kingdom of England, two books; against the sophisms of one Parsons a Jesuite, who assum'd the counterfeit name of Doleman ...* (written originally in Latin ... and now faithfully translated into English, 1703).

Crossman, Samuel, *Two Sermons preached in the cathedral-church of Bristol ...* (1681).

Curll, Walter, *A Sermon preached at White-Hall on the 28. of April in 1622* (1622).

Del Rio, Martin, *Investigations into Magic*, ed. and trans. P. G. Maxwell-Stuart (Manchester and New York, 2000).

Dering, Edward, *A Collection of Speeches Made by Sir Edward Dering Knight and Baronet, in matter of Religion.* ... (1642).

Diary of Thomas Burton esq., July 1653–April 1657 (1828), vol. 1.

Dryden, John, *Absalom and Achitophel A Poem* (1681).

Dugdale, Sir William, *A Short View of the Late Troubles in England* ... (Oxford, 1681).

Earl of Shaftesbury, *Some Observations Concerning the Regulating of Elections for Parliament* ... (1689).

Fenton, Roger, *A Treatise of Usurie* (1611).

Fisher, Ambrose, *A Defence of the Liturgie of the Church of England or Book of Common Prayer, Dedicated to His Much Honoured Friend Sir Robert Filmer* (1630).

Forsett, Edward, *A Defence of the Right of Kings; wherein the power of the papacie over princes is refuted, and the oath of allegeance iustified* ... (1624).

Fortescue, John, *The Governance of England: otherwise called the Difference between an Absolute and a Limited Monarchy*, ed. C. Plummer (Oxford, 1885).

Frankland, Thomas, *The Annals of King James and King Charles the First* ... (1681).

Gilbert, Samuel, *The Florists Vade-Mecum ... together with The gardiners almanack* ... (1682).

Gipps, Thomas, *Three Sermons preached in Lent* ... (1683).

H. R., *New Atlantis. Begun by the Lord Verulam, Viscount St. Albans: and continued by R.H. Esquire. Wherein is set forth a platform of monarchical government* ... (1660).

Haillan, Bernard de Girard du, *Histoire Generale des Rois de France* (Paris, 1627).

Hall, John of Richmond, *The True Cavalier Examined by his Principles and Found not Guilty of Schism or Sedition* (1656).

Hayward, John, *The First Part of the Life and Raigne of King Henrie the III* ... (1599).

— *An Answer to the First Part of a Certaine Conference Concerning Succession, published not long since vnder the name of R. Dolman* (1603).

Heylyn, Peter, *Augustus, or An Essay of those Meanes and Counsels, whereby the Commonwealth of Rome was altered, and reduced unto a Monarchy* (1632).

— *Theologia Veterum* ... (1673, i ed. 1654).

— *Extraneus Vapulans: or the Observator Rescued from The violent but vaine Assaults of Hamon L'Estrange, Esq. and The Black-blows of Dr. Bernard, an Irish-Deane* (1656).

— *The Stumbling-Block of Disobedience* (1658).

— *Certamen Epistolare, or, The Letter Combate* ... (1659).

— *The Historical and Miscellaneous Tracts of the Revered and Learned Peter Heylyn, D. D.* (1681).

Historical Manuscripts Commission, Third Report, Appendix, 'The Manuscripts of Sir Edmund Filmer, Bart., at East Sutton Park, Co. Kent' (1872).

Historical Manuscripts Commission, Eleventh Report, Appendix, Part I, 'The Manuscripts of H. D. Skrine Esq., Salvetti Correspondence' (1887).

Hobbes, Thomas, *The Elements of Law Natural & Politic*, ed. with a preface and critical notes by F. Tönnies (Cambridge, 1928).

— *Leviathan*, ed. C. B. Macpherson (Harmondsworth, 1968).

Holles, Denzil, *Lord Hollis, his Remains Being a Second Letter to a Friend, concerning the judicature of the bishops in Parliament ...* (1682).

Jonson, Ben, *Ben: Ionson his Volpone, or, the Foxe* (1607).

— 'To My Worthy Friend, Master Edward Filmer', in *Ben Jonson, The Complete Poems*, ed. G. Parfitt (1996, repr.), Miscellanous Poems.

Journal of the House of Commons 1640–1643 (1802), vol. 2.

Journal of the House of Lords 1629–1642 (1802), vol. 4.

Kennett, White, *A Letter from a Student at Oxford to a Friend in the Country Concerning the Approaching Parliament ...* (1681).

King James VI and I, *A Speach in the Starre-Chamber, the XX. Of June Anno 1616*, in J. P. Sommerville (ed.), *King James VI and I. Political Writings* (Cambridge, 1994), pp. 204–28.

— *A Speach to both the Houses of Parliament ... March 1607*, in Sommerville (ed.), *King James VI and I. Political Writings*, pp. 159–78.

— *A Speach to the Lords and Commons ...1609*, in Sommerville (ed.), *King James VI and I. Political Writings*, pp. 179–203.

— *Basilicon Doron*, in Sommerville (ed.), *King James VI and I. Political Writings*, pp. 1–61.

— *The Trew Law of Free Monarchies: or the Reciprock and Mvtvall Dvetie Betwitxt a Free King, and His Naturall Subiects*, in Sommerville (ed.), *King James VI and I. Political Writings*, pp. 62–84.

— *Triplici Nodo, Triples Cuneus. Or Apologie for the Oath of Allegiance ...* , in Sommerville (ed.), *King James VI and I. Political Writings*, pp. 85–131.

Langbaine, Gerard, *An Account of the English Dramatick Poets ...* (1691).

Leibniz, Gottfried Wilhelm, 'Meditation on the Common Concept of Justice', in *Leibniz. Political Writings*, ed. and trans. P. Riley (Cambridge, 2nd edn, 1988), pp. 45–64.

Leighton, Alexander, *An Appeal to the Parliament; or Sions Plea against the Prelacie ...* (Amsterdam?, 1628).

L'Estrange, Sir Roger, *Observator in Dialogue* (1681–87).

— *A Memento Treating of the Rise, Progress, and Remedies of Seditions with some Historical Reflections upon the series of our late troubles* (printed 1642; reprinted, 1682).

— *Theosebia, or, The churches advocate endeavouring the promotion of loyalty to our king, and fidelity to the Episcopal Church, by describing the rebellious principles of the enemies thereof* (1683).

Lloyd, Humphrey, *John XII's Treasury of Healthe* (1550).

Locke, John, *Two Treatises of Government*, a critical edition with an introduction and apparatus criticus by P. Laslett (Cambridge, 1960).

Loyseau, Charles, *Traité des Seigneuries* (Chasteaudun, 1610).

Luttrell, Narcissus, *Narcissus Luttrell's Popish Plots Catalogues*, ed. Luttrell Society, with an introduction by F. C. Francis (Oxford, 1956).

Machiavelli, Niccolò, *History of Florence and of the Affairs of Italy from the Earliest Times to the Death of Lorenzo the Magnificent*, ed. F. Gilbert (New York, 1960).

Mackenzie, George, *Jus Regium ...* (1684).

Maxwell, John, *Sacro-Santa Regum Majestas: or, The Sacred and Royal Prerogative of Christian Kings* (Oxford, 1644).

May, Thomas, *M. A. Lucan, Pharsalia: or the civill warres of Rome, between Pompey the Great, and Iulius Caesar: then bookes* (trans., 1627).

Maynwaring, Roger, *Religion and Alegiance* (1627).

Mocket, Richard, *God and the King ...* (1615).

Monson, John, *Discourse Concerning Supreme Power and Common Right* (1680).

Mossom, Robert, *The King on His Throne ...* (York, 1643).

Nalson, John, *The Common Interest of King and People ...* (1677).

— *Reflections upon Coll. Sidney's Arcadia, the old cause being some observations upon his last paper, given to the sheriffs at his execution* (1684).

Nedham, Marchamont, *A Pacquet of Advices and Animadversions Sent for London to the Men of Shaftesbury* (1676).

Northleigh, John, *The Triumph of our Monarchy, over the plots and principles of our rebels and republicans being remarks on their most eminent libels* (1685).

Owen, David, *Herod and Pilate Reconciled ...* (Cambridge, 1610).

Pelling, Edward, *The Apostate Protestant a Letter to a Friend, occasioned by the late reprinting of a Jesuites book about succession to the crown of England, pretended to have been written by R. Doleman* (1682).

— *Sermon Preached at St. Mary Le Bow. Novemb. 27, 1682* (1683).

Perkins, William, *A Discourse of the Damned Art of Witchcraft, so farre forth as it is revealed in the scriptures and manifest by true experience* (1608).

Petyt, William, *Miscellanea Parliamentaria* (1680).

Philipps, Fabian, *Investigatio jurium antiquorum et rationalium Regni, sive, Monarchiae Angliae in magnis suis conciliis seu Parliamentis ...* (1686).

Philopatris, *A Satyrick Poem against those mercenary wretches and troublers of Englands tranquility, the authors of Heraclitus and Observator, infamous for their scribling throughout England* (1682).

Proceedings in Parliament 1610, ed. E. Read Foster (New Haven and London, 2 vols, 1966), vols i, ii.

Proceedings in Parliament 1628, ed. R. C. Johnson et al. (New Haven and London, 6 vols, 1977–83), vols ii, iii, vi.

Reports and Calendars issued by the Royal Commission on Historical Manuscripts, Buccleuch (1899), vol. i.

Rousseau, Jean-Jacques, *Oeuvres Completes* (Paris, 1964), vol. iii.

Russell, John, *The Spy Discovering the Danger of Arminian Heresie and Spanish Trecherie* (Strasbourg (i.e. Amsterdam), 1628).

Sanderson, Robert, *Ten Sermons Preached I. Ad clerum. 3. II. Ad magistratum. 3. III. Ad populum. 4. By Robert Saunderson Bachellor in Diuinitie, sometimes fellow of Lincolne Colledge in Oxford* (1627).

Scott, Thomas, 'A Discourse of Polletique and Civell Honor', in *Dorothea Scott, otherwise Gotherson and Hogben, of Egerton House, Kent, 1611–1680*, A New and Enlarged Edition by G. D. Scull (Oxford, 1883), pp. 145–98.

— 'Journal', in *Proceedings in Parliament 1628. Appendixes and Indexes*, ed. M. F. Keeler, M. J. Cole, and W. B. Bidwell (New Haven and London, 6 vols, 1977–83), vol. vi, pp. 127–37.

— 'Letters and Miscellanous Documents', in *Proceedings in Parliament 1628. Appendixes and Indexes*, ed. M. F. Keeler, M. J. Cole, and W. B. Bidwell (New Haven and London, 6 vols, 1977–83), vol. vi, pp. 218–43.

Settle, Elkanah, *The Character of a Popish Successour* ... (1681).

— *The Present State of England in relation to popery manifesting the absolute impossibility of introducing popery and arbitrary power into this kingdom* ... (1684).

Several Reports of the Royal Commission on Historical Manuscripts (2 parts, 1879), vol. i.

Sherlock, William, *Observations upon Mr. Johnson's Remarks, upon Dr. Sherlock's Book of Non-Resistance* (1689).

— *The Case of the Allegiance due to Sovereign Powers* (1690).

Sibthorpe, Robert, *Apolostike Obedience Shewing the Duty of Subjects to pay Tribute and Taxes to their Princes, according to the Word of God* (1627).

Sidney, Algernon, *Discourses Concerning Government*, ed. T. G. West (Indianapolis, 1990).

Somers, John, *A Brief History of the Succession* (1680).

Stubbe, H., *A Letter to an Officer of the Army Concerning a Select Senate* ... (1660).

Suarez, Francisco, 'Defense of the Faith', in G. A. Moore (ed. and trans.), *Extracts on Politics and Government* (Maryland, 1910).

— 'Laws and God the Lawgiver', in G. A. Moore (ed. and trans.), *Extracts on Politics and Government* (Maryland, 1910).

Temple, William, *Miscellanea ... by a person of honour* (1680).

'The Correspondence of Bishop Brian Duppa and Sir Justinian Isham', ed. Sir Gyles Isham, Bart., *Northamptonshire Record Society*, 17 (1951).

The Dying Speeches of several excellent persons, who suffered for their zeal against popery, and arbitrary government ... (1689).

The Journal of Sir Simonds D'Ewes from the first recess of the Long Parliament to the withdrawal of King Charles from London, ed. W. H. Coates (New Haven, 1942).

The London Gazette (1680).

The Poems of Richard Lovelace, ed. C. H. Wilkinson (Oxford, 1930).

Twysden, Roger, *Certaine Considerations upon the Government of England*, ed. from the unpublished manuscript by J. M. Kemble (1849).

— *The Journal of Sir Roger Twysden. From the Roydon Hall MSS.*, 'Archaeologia Cantiana', vols i–iv (1858–61).

Tyrrell, James, *Patriarcha non Monarcha. The Patriarch Unmonarch'd* (1681).

Walker, Clement, *Relations and Observations Historical and Politick, upon the Parliament Begun anno Dom. 1640* (1648).

Walker, John, *The Antidote: or, a Seasonable Discourse on Rom. 13. 1* ... (1684).

Whitlocke, Bulstrode, *Memorials of the English affairs* ... (1682).

Wilson, John, *A Discourse of Monarchy* ... (1684).

SECONDARY SOURCES

Alford, S., 'A Politics of Emergency in the Reign of Elizabeth I', in G. Burgess and M. Festenstein (eds), *English Radicalism, 1550–1850* (Cambridge, 2007), pp. 17–36.

Allen, J. W., 'Sir Robert Filmer', in F. J. C. Hearnshaw (ed.), *The Social and Political Ideas of Some English Thinkers of the Augustan Age A.D. 1650–1750. A Series*

261

of *Lectures Delivered at King's College, University of London During the Session 1927–1928* (1928), pp. 27–46.

— *A History of Political Thought in the Sixteenth Century* (2nd edn, 1941).

Amussen, S. D., *An Ordered Society. Gender and Class in Early Modern England* (Oxford, 1988).

Anglo, S., 'Reginald Scot's *Discoverie of Witchcraft*: Scepticism and Sadduceeism', in S. Anglo (ed.), *The Damned Art. Essays in the Literature of Witchcraft* (1977), pp. 106–39.

Armitage, D., 'A Patriot for Whom? The Afterlives of Bolingbroke's Patriot King, *JBS*, 36 (1997), pp. 397–418.

Ashcraft, R., 'John Locke's Library: Portrait of an Intellectual', *Transactions of the Cambridge Bibliographical Society*, 5 (1969), pp. 47–60.

— *Revolutionary Politics and Locke's Two Treatises of Government* (Princeton, 1986).

Ashton, R., *The English Civil War. Conservatism and Revolution 1603–1649* (1978).

Ball, J. N., 'Sir John Eliot and Parliament, 1624–1629', in K. Sharpe (ed.), *Faction and Parliament. Essays on Early Stuart History* (Oxford, 1978), pp. 173–207.

Barbuto, G., 'Il "Principe" di Bellarmino', in R. De Maio, A. Borromeo, L. Gulia and A. Mazzacane (eds), *Bellarmino e la Controriforma* (Sora (Italy), 1990), pp. 123–89.

Bast, R., *Honor Your Fathers. Catechisms and the Emergence of a Patriarchal Ideology in Germany 1400–1600* (Leiden, New York and Köln, 1997).

Baumgartner, F. J., *Radical Reactionaries: The Political Thought of the French Catholic League* (Geneva, 1975).

Bellany, A., '"The Brightnes of the Noble Leiutenants Action": An Intellectual Ponders Buckingham's Assassination', *EHR*, 118 (2003), pp. 1242–63.

Bostridge, I., *Witchcraft and Its Transformations c. 1650–c. 1750* (Oxford, 1997).

Bradburn, D., 'The Origin of a Species: The Making of Whig Political Thought', *Book Review*, H-Atlantic@h-net.msu.edu (May 2005; accessed 1 December 2009).

Bradshaw, D., 'Lonely Royalists: T. S. Eliot and Sir Robert Filmer', *The Review of English Studies*, 46 (1995), pp. 375–9.

Brautigam, D. D., 'Prelates and Politics: Uses of "Puritan", 1625–40', in L. Lunger Knoppers (ed.), *Puritanism and Its Discontents* (Newark and London, 2003), pp. 49–66.

Brennan, G., 'Papists and Patriotism in Elizabethan England', *Recusant History*, 19 (1988), pp. 1–15.

— *Patriotism, Power and Print. National Consciousness in Sixteenth-Century England* (Cambridge, 2003).

Burgess, G., *The Politics of the Ancient Constitution. An Introduction to English Political Thought, 1603–1642* (University Park (Pennsylvania), 1992).

— *Absolute Monarchy and the Stuart Constitution* (New Haven and London, 1996).

— 'Patriotism in English Political Thought, 1530–1660', in R. von Friedeburg (ed.), *'Patria' und 'Patrioten' vor dem Patriotismus* (Wiesbaden, 2005), pp. 215–41.

— 'Introduction', in G. Burgess and M. Festenstein (eds), *English Radicalism, 1550–1850* (Cambridge, 2007), pp. 1–16.

— 'A Matter of Context: "Radicalism" and the English Revolution', in M. Caricchio and G. Tarantino (eds), *Cromohs Virtual Seminars. Recent Historiographical Trends* of the British Studies (17th-18th Centuries), 2006–7, pp. 1–4, www.cromohs.unifi. it/seminari/burgess_radicalism.html (accessed 1 December 2009).

— British Political Thought, 1500–1600. The Politics of the Post-Reformation (Basingstoke, 2009).

Burke, P., 'Tacitism, Scepticism, and Reason of State', in J. H. Burns and M. Goldie (eds), The Cambridge History of Political Thought 1450–1700 (Cambridge, 1991), pp. 479–98.

Burns, J. H., 'The Idea of Absolutism', in J. Miller (ed.), Absolutism in Seventeenth-Century Europe (1990), pp. 21–42.

Butler, M., Theatre and Crisis 1632–1642 (Cambridge, 1984).

Christianson, P., 'Royal and Parliamentary Voices on the Ancient Constitution, c. 1604–1621', in L. L. Peck (ed.), The Mental World of the Jacobean Court (Cambridge, 1991), pp. 71–95.

Clancy, T. P., Papist Pamphleteers. The Allen-Persons Party and the Political Thought of the Counter Reformation in England (Chicago, 1964).

Clark, P., English Provincial Society from the Reformation to the Revolution. Religion, Politics and Society in Kent 1500–1640 (Hassocks (Sussex), 1977).

— 'Thomas Scott and the Growth of Urban Opposition to the Early Stuart Regime', HJ, 21 (1978), pp. 1–26.

Clark, S., 'King James's Daemonologie: Witchcraft and Kingship', in S. Anglo (ed.), The Damned Art. Essays in the Literature of Witchcraft (1977), pp. 156–81.

— 'Inversion, Misrule and the Meaning of Witchcraft', Past & Present, 87 (1980), pp. 98–127.

— Thinking with Demons. The Idea of Witchcraft in Early Modern Europe (Oxford, 1997, repr. 2005).

Clegg, C. S., Press Censorship in Jacobean England (Cambridge, 2001).

Cleggett, D. A. H., The Filmer and Wilson Families, Leeds Castle Foundation (Maidstone, 2003).

Cliffe, J. T., The World of the Country House in Seventeenth-Century England (New Haven and London, 1999).

Clucas, S. and Davies, R., 'Introduction', in S. Clucas and R. Davies (eds), The Crisis of 1614 and the Addled Parliament. Literary and Historical Perspectives (Aldershot, 2003), pp. 1–14.

Coffey, J. and Lim, P. C. H., 'Introduction', in J. Coffey and P. C. H. Lim (eds), The Cambridge Companion to Puritanism (Cambridge, 2008), pp. 1–15.

Cogswell, T., The Blessed Revolution. English Politics and the Coming of War, 1621–1624 (Cambridge, 1989).

— 'The People's Love: The Duke of Buckingham and Popularity', in T. Cogswell, R. Cust and P. Lake (eds), Politics, Religion and Popularity in Early Stuart Britain. Essays in Honour of Conrad Russell (Cambridge, 2002), pp. 211–54.

Coiro, A. B., 'A "Ball of Strife": Caroline Poetry and Royal Marriage', in T. N. Corns (ed.), The Royal Image. Representations of Charles I (Cambridge, 1999), pp. 26–46.

Colclough, D., Freedom of Speech in Early Stuart England (Cambridge, 2005).

Collins, J. B., The State in Early Modern France (Cambridge, 2nd edn, 2010).

Collinson, P., De Republica Anglorum or History with the Politics Put Back (Cambridge, 1990).

— 'Afterword', in J. F. McDiarmid (ed.), *The Monarchical Republic of Early Modern England. Essays in Response to Patrick Collinson* (Aldershot, 2007), pp. 245–60.

— 'Antipuritanism', in J. Coffey and P. C. H. Lim (eds), *The Cambridge Companion to Puritanism* (Cambridge, 2008), pp. 19–33.

Condren, C., *Argument and Authority in Early Modern England. The Presupposition of Oaths and Offices* (Cambridge, 2006).

— 'Afterword: Radicalism Revisited', in G. Burgess and M. Festenstein (eds), *English Radicalism, 1550–1850* (Cambridge, 2007), pp. 311–37.

Cope, E., *Politics Without Parliaments 1629–1640* (1987).

Cottret, B., 'Diplomatie et Éthique de l'État: l'Ambassade d'Effiat en Angleterre et le mariage de Charles Ier d'Angleterre et d'Henriette-Marie de France (été 1624–printemps 1625)', in H. Méchoulan (ed.), *L'État Baroque 1610–1652* (Paris, 1985), pp. 221–42.

Cressy, D., 'Binding the Nation: the Bonds of Association, 1584 and 1696', in D. Cressy (ed.), *Society and Culture in Early Modern England* (Aldershot and Burlington, 2003), pp. 217–34.

Croft, P., *King James* (Basingstoke, 2003).

Cust, R., *The Forced Loan and English Politics 1626–1628* (Oxford, 1987).

— 'Politics and the Electorate in the 1620s', in R. Cust and A. Hughes (eds), *Conflict in Early Stuart England. Studies in Religion and Politics, 1605–1642* (London and New York, 1989), pp. 134–67.

— 'Charles I and Popularity', in T. Cogswell, R. Cust and P. Lake (eds), *Politics, Religion and Popularity in Early Stuart Britain. Essays in Honour of Conrad Russell* (Cambridge, 2002), pp. 235–58.

— *Charles I: A Political Life* (Harlow and New York, 2005).

— 'Was There an Alternative to the Personal Rule? Charles I, the Privy Council and the Parliament of 1629', *History*, 90 (2005), pp. 330–52.

— '"Patriots" and "Popular" Spirits: Narratives of Conflict in Early Stuart Politics', in N. Tyacke (ed.), *The English Revolution c.1590–1720. Politics, Religion and Communities* (Manchester, 2007), pp. 43–61.

— 'Reading for Magistracy: The Mental World of Sir John Newdigate', in J. F. McDiarmid (ed.), *The Monarchical Republic of Early Modern England. Essays in Response to Patrick Collinson* (Aldershot, 2007), pp. 181–99.

— 'The "Public Man" in Late Tudor and Early Stuart England', in S. Pincus and P. Lake (eds), *The Politics of the Public Sphere in Early Modern England* (Manchester, 2007), pp. 116–43.

Cust, R. and Hughes, A., 'Introduction: After Revisionism', in R. Cust and A. Hughes (eds), *Conflict in Early Stuart England. Studies in Religion and Politics 1603–1642* (London and New York, 1989), pp. 1–46.

Cust, R. and Lake, P., 'Sir Richard Grosvenor and the Rhetoric of Magistrates', *Bulletin of the Institute of Historical Research*, 54 (1981), pp. 40–53.

Cuttica, C., 'Sir Francis Kynaston: The Importance of the "Nation" for a Seventeenth-Century English Royalist', *History of European Ideas*, 32 (2006), pp. 139–61.

— 'Kentish Cousins at Odds: Filmer's *Patriarcha* and Thomas Scott's Defence of Freeborn Englishmen', *HPT*, 28 (2007), pp. 599–616.

— 'Thomas Scott of Canterbury (1566–1635): Patriot, Civic Radical, Puritan', *History of European Ideas*, 34 (2008), pp. 475–89.

— 'Anti-Jesuit *Patriotic Absolutism*: Robert Filmer and French Ideas (c. 1580–1630)', *Renaissance Studies*, 25 (2011), pp. 559–79.

— 'Sir Robert Filmer (1588–1653) and the Condescension of Posterity: Historiographical Interpretations', *Intellectual History Review*, 21 (2011), pp. 195–208.

— 'An Absolutist Trio in the Early 1630s: Sir Robert Filmer, Jean-Louis Guez de Balzac, Cardin Le Bret and their Models of Monarchical Power', in C. Cuttica and G. Burgess (eds), *Monarchism and Absolutism in Early Modern Europe* (2012), pp. 131–45.

— 'Anti-republican Cries under Cromwell: The Vehement Attacks of Robert Filmer against Republican Practice and Republican Theory in the Early 1650s', in D. Wiemann and G. Mahlberg (eds), *Perspectives on English Revolutionary Republicanism* (Farnham, forthcoming).

Cuttica, C. and Burgess, G. (eds), *Monarchism and Absolutism in Early Modern Europe* (2012).

Daly, J., 'John Bramhall and the Theoretical Problems of Royalist Moderation', *JBS*, 11 (1971), pp. 26–44.

— 'The Idea of Absolute Monarchy in Seventeenth-Century England', *HJ*, 21 (1978), pp. 227–50.

— *Sir Robert Filmer and English Political Thought* (Toronto, 1979).

— 'Some Problems in the Authorship of Sir Robert Filmer's Works', *EHR*, 98 (1983), pp. 737–62.

Davies, J., *The Caroline Captivity of the Church. Charles I and the Remoulding of Anglicanism 1625–1641* (Oxford, 1992).

Davis, J. C., *Utopia and the Ideal Society. A Study of English Utopian Writing 1516–1700* (Cambridge, 1981).

— 'Afterword: Reassessing Radicalism in a Traditional Society: Two Questions', in G. Burgess and M. Festenstein (eds), *English Radicalism, 1550–1850* (Cambridge, 2007), pp. 338–72.

De Mattei, R., *Il Problema della 'Ragion di Stato' nell'Età della Controriforma* (Milan and Naples, 1979).

Dietz, M. G., 'Patriotism', in T. Ball, J. Farr and R. L. Hanson (eds), *Political Innovation and Conceptual Change* (Cambridge, 1989), pp. 177–93.

Duccini, H., *Fair Voir, Faire Croire. L'opinion publique sous Louis XIII* (Seyssel, 2003).

Dunn, J., *The Political Thought of John Locke. An Historical Account of the Argument of the Two Treatises of Government* (Cambridge, 1969).

Eales, J., 'The Rise of Ideological Politics in Kent, 1558–1640', in M. Zell (ed.), *Early Modern Kent, 1540–1640* (Woodbridge, 2000), pp. 279–313.

Eley, G., 'Is All the World a Text? From Social History to the History of Society Two Decades Later', in G. M. Spiegel (ed.), *Practicing History. New Directions in Historical Writing after the Linguistic Turn* (New York and London, 2005), pp. 35–61.

Elton, G. R., 'A High Road to Civil War?', in C. H. Carter (ed.), *From the Renaissance to the Counter-Reformation* (1966), pp. 325–47.

Everitt, A., *The Community of Kent and the Great Rebellion 1640–60* (Leicester, 1966).

265

Ezell, M., *The Patriarch's Wife. Literary Evidence and the History of the Family* (Chapel Hill and London, 1987).

Fang Ng, S., *Literature and the Politics of Family in Seventeenth-Century England* (Cambridge, 2007).

Farr, J. and Roberts, C., 'John Locke and the Glorious Revolution: A Rediscovered Document', *HJ*, 28 (1985), pp. 385–98.

Ferraro, D., 'Bellarmino, Suárez, Giacomo I e la Polemica sulle Origini del Potere Politico', in R. De Maio, A. Borromeo, L. Gulia and A. Mazzacane (eds), *Bellarmino e la Controriforma* (Sora (Italy), 1990), pp. 191–250.

Figgis, J. N., *The Divine Right of Kings* (Cambridge, 2nd edn, 1914).

Filmer, B. J., *The Filmer Family of Kent* (Maidstone, 1964).

— *Filmer Family Notes. Part One* (1984).

— *Filmer Family Notes. Part Three* (1992).

Filmer, R. M., *Deep-Rooted in Kent. An Account of the Filmer Family* (1977).

Fischlin, D., '"To Eate the Flesh of Kings": James VI and I, Apocalypse, Nation, and Sovereignty', in D. Fischlin and M. Fortier (eds), *Royal Subjects. Essays on the Writings of James VI and I* (Detroit, 2002), pp. 388–420.

Ford, R., 'The Filmer Manuscripts: A Handlist', Notes, *The Quarterly Journal of the Music Library Association*, 34 (1978), pp. 814–25.

Foster, J. (ed.), *London Marriage Licences, 1521–1889* (1887).

Friedeburg, von R., 'Civic Humanism and Republican Citizenship in Early Modern Germany', in M. van Gelderen and Q. Skinner (eds), *Republicanism. A Shared European Heritage* (Cambridge, 2 vols, 2002), vol. 1, pp. 127–45.

— 'The Making of Patriots: Love of Fatherland and Negotiating Monarchy in Seventeenth-Century Germany', *The Journal of Modern History*, 77 (2005), pp. 881–916.

Goldberg, J., *James I and the Politics of Literature. Jonson, Shakespeare, Donne, and their Contemporaries* (Baltimore and London, 1983).

Goldie, M., 'Edmund Bohun and "Jus Gentium" in the Revolution Debate', *HJ*, 20 (1977), pp. 569–86.

— 'John Locke and Anglican Royalism', *Political Studies*, 31 (1983), pp. 61–85.

— 'The Reception of Hobbes', in J. H. Burns and M. Goldie (eds), *The Cambridge History of Political Thought 1450–1700* (Cambridge, 1991), pp. 589–610.

— 'Roger L'Estrange's *Observator* and the Exorcism of the Plot', in A. Dunan-Page and B. Lynch (eds), *Roger L'Estrange and the Making of Restoration Culture* (Aldershot and Burlington, 2008), pp. 67–88.

Gooch, G. P., *Political Thought in England. From Bacon to Halifax* (1915).

Greenberg, J., *The Radical Face of the Ancient Constitution. St Edward's 'Laws' in Early Modern Political Thought* (Cambridge, 2001).

Greenleaf, W. H., *Order, Empiricism and Politics* (1964).

— 'Filmer's Patriarchal History', *HJ*, 9 (1966), pp. 157–71.

Guy, J. A., 'The Origins of the Petition of Right Reconsidered', *HJ*, 25 (1982), pp. 289–312.

Hadfield, A., *Shakespeare and Republicanism* (Cambridge, 2005).

Harris, T., *Politics under the Later Stuarts. Party Conflict in a Divided Society 1660–1715* (Harlow, 1993).

Hart, V., *Art and Magic in the Court of the Stuarts* (1994).

Hill, C., 'The Many-Headed Monster in Late Tudor and Early Stuart Political Thinking', in C. H. Carter (ed.), *From the Renaissance to the Counter-Reformation* (1966), pp. 296–324.

Hirst, D., *The Representative of the People? Voters and Voting in England under the Early Stuarts* (Cambridge, 1975).

— 'Court, Country, and Politics before 1629', in K. Sharpe (ed.), *Faction and Parliament. Essays on Early Stuart History* (Oxford, 1978), pp. 105–37.

— *England in Conflict 1603–1660. Kingdom, Community, Commonwealth* (1999).

Houston, A. C., *Algernon Sidney and the Republican Heritage in England and America* (Princeton, 1991).

Hunt, W., 'The Spectral Origins of the English Revolution: Legitimation Crisis in Early Stuart England', in G. Eley and W. Hunt (eds), *Reviving the English Revolution. Reflections and Elaborations on the Work of Christopher Hill* (London and New York, 1988), pp. 305–32.

Jessup, F., *Sir Roger Twysden, 1597–1672* (1965).

Kantorowicz, E. H., *The King's Two Bodies. A Study in Medieval Political Theology* (Princeton, 1957).

Kenny, A. and Pinborg, J., 'Medieval Philosophical Literature', in N. Kretzmann, A. Kenny and J. Pinborg (eds), *The Cambridge History of Later Medieval Philosophy from the Rediscovery of Aristotle to the Disintegration of Scholasticism, 1100–1600* (Cambridge and New York, 1982), pp. 11–42.

Kishlansky, M., *Parliamentary Selection. Social and Political Choice in Early Modern England* (Cambridge, 1986).

— 'Tyranny Denied: Charles I, Attorney General Heath, and the Five Knights' Case', *HJ*, 42 (1999), pp. 53–83.

Knights, M., *Politics and Opinion in Crisis, 1678–81* (Cambridge, 1994).

Krivatsy, N. H. and Yeandle, L., 'Sir Edward Dering', in R. J. Fehrenbach and E. S. Leedham-Green (eds), *Private Libraries in Renaissance England. A Collection and Catalogue of Tudor and Early Stuart Book-Lists* (Binghamton (New York), 2 vols, 1992), vol. i, pp. 137–63.

LaCapra, D., *Rethinking Intellectual History. Texts, Contexts, Language* (Ithaca, 1983).

Lake, P., 'Constitutional Consensus and Puritan Opposition in the 1620s: Thomas Scott and the Spanish Match', *HJ*, 25 (1982), pp. 805–25.

— 'Anti-popery: The Structure of a Prejudice', in R. Cust and A. Hughes (eds), *Conflict in Early Stuart England. Studies in Religion and Politics 1603–1642* (London and New York, 1989), pp. 72–106.

— '"The Monarchical Republic of Elizabeth I" Revisited (by its Victims) as a Conspiracy', in B. Coward and J. Swann (eds), *Conspiracies and Conspiracy Theory in Early Modern Europe. From the Waldensians to the French Revolution* (Aldershot, 2004), pp. 87–111.

— 'The Historiography of Puritanism', in J. Coffey and P. C. H. Lim (eds), *The Cambridge Companion to Puritanism* (Cambridge, 2008), pp. 346–71.

Laski, H., *Political Thought in England from Locke to Bentham* (1920).

Laslett, P., 'Sir Robert Filmer: The Man versus the Whig Myth', *The William and Mary Quarterly*, 5 (1948), pp. 523–46.

— 'The Gentry of Kent in 1640', *Cambridge Historical Journal*, 9 (1948), pp. 148–64.
— 'Introduction', in *Patriarcha and Other Political Works*, ed. P. Laslett (Oxford, 1949), pp. 1–43.
— 'The English Revolution and Locke's "Two Treatises of Government"', *Cambridge Historical Journal*, 12 (1956), pp. 40–55.
— *The World We Have Lost* (1965).
Latt, D. J., 'Praising Virtuous Ladies: The Literary Image and Historical Reality of Women in Seventeenth-Century England', in M. Springer (ed.), *What Manner of Woman. Essays on English and American Life and Literature* (Oxford, 1977), pp, 39–64.
Lawson Dick, O. (ed.), *Aubrey's Brief Lives* (1960).
Levy Peck, L., 'Kingship, Counsel and Law in Early Stuart Britain', in J. G. A. Pocock, G. Schochet and L. Schwoerer (eds), *The Varieties of British Political Thought, 1500–1800* (Cambridge, 1993), pp. 80–115.
— 'Beyond the Pale: John Cusacke and the Language of Absolutism in Early Stuart Britain', *HJ*, 41 (1998), pp. 121–49.
Lievsay, J. L., *Venetian Phoenix. Paolo Sarpi and Some of His English Friends (1606–1700)* (Lawrence, Manhattan and Wichita (Kansas), 1973).
Lindsay, P., *For King or Parliament* (1949).
Loades, D. M., 'Literature and National Identity', in D. Loewenstein and J. Mueller (eds), *The Cambridge History of Early Modern English Literature* (Cambridge, 2002), pp. 201–28.
Love, H., *Scribal Publication in Seventeenth-Century England* (Oxford, 1993).
Loveridge, M., *A History of Augustan Fable* (Cambridge, 1998).
McEachern, C., *The Poetics of English Nationhood, 1590–1612* (Cambridge, 1996).
McElligott, J. and Smith, D. L., 'Introduction: Rethinking Royalists and Royalism', in J. McElligott and D. L. Smith (eds), *Royalists and Royalism during the English Civil Wars* (Cambridge, 2007), pp. 1–15.
McLaren, A., 'Challenging the Monarchical Republic: James I's Articulation of Kingship', in J. F. McDiarmid (ed.), *The Monarchical Republic of Early Modern England. Essays in Response to Patrick Collinson* (Aldershot, 2007), pp. 165–80.
Mahlberg, G., 'Republicanism as Anti-patriarchalism in Henry Neville's *The Isle of Pines* (1668)', in J. Morrow and J. Scott (eds), *Liberty, Authority, Formality. Political Ideas and Culture, 1600–1900. Essays in Honour of Colin Davis* (Exeter, 2008), pp. 131–52.
— *Henry Neville and English Republican Culture in the Seventeenth Century. Dreaming of Another Game* (Manchester, 2009).
Malcolm, N., 'Hobbes, Sandys, and the Virginia Company', *HJ*, 24 (1981), pp. 297–321.
— *Reason of State, Propaganda, and the Thirty Years' War. An Unknown Translation by Thomas Hobbes* (Oxford, 2007).
Matteucci, N.,'Paternalismo', in N. Bobbio, N. Matteucci and G. Pasquino (eds), *Dizionario di Politica* (Turin, 1983), pp. 804–5.
Merritt, J. F., *The Social World of Early Modern Westminster. Abbey, Court and Community, 1525–1640* (Manchester, 2005).

Mesnard, P., *L'Essor de la Philosophie Politique au XVI siècle* (Paris, 1969).

Miller, J., *Popery and Politics in England, 1660–1688* (Cambridge, 1973).

Milton, A., *Catholic and Reformed. The Roman and Protestant Churches in English Protestant Thought 1600–1640* (Cambridge, 1995).

— 'Thomas Wentworth and the Political Thought of the Personal Rule', in J. F. Merritt (ed.), *The Political World of Thomas Wentworth, Earl of Strafford, 1621–1641* (Cambridge, 1996), pp. 133–56.

— 'Canon Fire: Peter Heylyn at Westminster', in C. Knighton and R. Mortimer (eds), *Westminster Abbey Reformed. Nine Studies, 1540–1642* (Aldershot, 2003), pp. 207–31.

— *Laudian and Royalist Polemic in Seventeenth-Century England. The Career and Writings of Peter Heylyn* (Manchester, 2007).

Milton, J. R., 'Dating Locke's "Second Treatise"', *HPT*, 16 (1995), pp. 356–90.

Monod, P. K., *The Power of Kings. Monarchy and Religion in Europe 1589–1715* (New Haven and London, 1999).

Morrill, J., *The Revolt of the Provinces. Conservatives and Radicals in the English Civil War, 1630–1650* (1976).

Mousnier, R., *L'Assassinat d'Henry IV 14 mai 1610* (Paris, 1964).

Nelson, E., *The Jesuits and the Monarchy. Catholic Reform and Political Authority in France (1590–1615)* (Aldershot, 2005).

Newman, G., *The Rise of English Nationalism. A Cultural History 1740–1830* (1987).

Norbrook, D., *Writing the English Republic. Poetry, Rhetoric and Politics, 1627–1660* (Cambridge, 1999).

Oakley, F., *Omnipotence, Covenant, and Order. An Excursion in the History of Ideas from Abelard to Leibniz* (Ithaca and London, 1984).

— *Politics and Eternity. Studies in the History of Medieval and Early-Modern Political Thought* (Leiden, 1999).

O'Callaghan, M., *The 'Shepheards Nation'. Jacobean Spenserians and Early Stuart Political Culture, 1612–1625* (Oxford, 2000).

'On the Surrenden Charters', *Archaeologia Cantiana*, vol. 1 (1858), pp. 50–65.

Pateman, C., *The Sexual Contract* (Cambridge, 1988).

Patterson, A. M., *Fables of Power: Aesopian Writing and Political History* (Durham and London, 1991).

Peltonen, M., *Classical Humanism and Republicanism in English Political Thought, 1570–1640* (Cambridge, 1995).

— 'Rhetoric and Citizenship in the Monarchical Republic of Queen Elizabeth I', in J. F. McDiarmid (ed.), *The Monarchical Republic of Early Modern England. Essays in Response to Patrick Collinson* (Aldershot, 2007), pp. 109–27.

Perry, C., '"If Proclamations Will Not Serve": The Late Manuscript Poetry of James I and the Culture of Libel', in D. Fischlin and M. Fortier (eds), *Royal Subjects. Essays on the Writings of James VI and I* (Detroit, 2002), pp. 205–32.

Pesante, M. L., 'L'Usura degli Inglesi: Lessico del Peccato e Lessico della Corruzione Politica alla Fine del Seicento', in G. Boschiero and B. Molina (eds), *Politiche del Credito. Investimento Consumo Solidarietà*, Atti del Congresso Internazionale Cassa di Risparmio di Asti, (Asti (Italy), 20–22 March 2004), pp. 113–38.

Petrie, S., 'The Religion of Sir Roger Twysden (1597–1672): A Case Study in Gentry

Piety in Seventeenth-Century England', *Archaeologia Cantiana*, 124 (2004), pp. 137–62.

Plamenatz, J., *Man and Society. A Critical Examination of Some Important Social and Political Theories from Machiavelli to Marx* (2 vols, 1963).

Pocock, J. G. A., *The Ancient Constitution and the Feudal Law* (Cambridge, 1957).

— *The Machiavellian Moment. Florentine Political Thought and the Atlantic Republican Tradition* (Princeton, 1975).

— 'Quentin Skinner: The History of Politics and the Politics of History', *Common Knowledge*, 10 (2004), pp. 532–50.

Reeve, L. J., *Charles I and the Road to Personal Rule* (Cambridge, 1989).

Roberts, Peters B., *Marriage in Seventeenth-Century English Political Thought* (Basingstoke, 2004).

Rose, J., 'Robert Brady's Intellectual History and Antipopery in Restoration England', *EHR*, 122 (2007), pp. 1287–317.

Roy, I., 'Royalist Reputations: The Cavalier Ideal and the Reality', in J. McElligott and D. L. Smith (eds), *Royalists and Royalism during the English Civil Wars* (Cambridge, 2007), pp. 89–111.

Rudolph, J., *Revolution by Degrees. James Tyrrell and Whig Political Thought in the Late Seventeenth Century* (Basingstoke, 2002).

Russell, C. (ed.), *The Origins of the English Civil War* (1973).

— *The Causes of the English Civil War* (Oxford, 1990).

— *Unrevolutionary England, 1603–1642* (London and Ronceverte, 1990).

Sabine, G. H., *A History of Political Theory* (1937).

Salmon, J. H. M., *The French Religious Wars in English Political Thought* (Oxford, 1959).

— 'Seneca and Tacitus in Jacobean England', in L. Levy Peck (ed.), *The Mental World of the Stuart Court* (Cambridge, 1991), pp. 169–88.

— 'France', in H. A. Lloyd, G. Burgess and S. Hodson (eds), *European Political Thought 1450–1700. Religion, Law and Philosophy* (New Haven and London, 2007), pp. 458–97.

Schochet, G., 'Patriarchalism, Politics and Mass Attitudes in Stuart England', *HJ*, 12 (1969), pp. 413–41.

— 'The Family and the Origins of the State in Locke's Political Philosophy', in J. W. Yolton (ed.), *John Locke: Problems and Perspectives* (Cambridge, 1969), pp. 81–98.

— 'Sir Robert Filmer: Some New Bibliographical Discoveries', *The Library. The Transactions of the Bibliographical Society*, 5th series, 26 (1971), pp. 135–60.

— *Patriarchalism in Political Thought. The Authoritarian Family and Political Speculation and Attitudes Especially in Seventeenth-Century England* (Oxford, 1975).

— 'Patriarchalism, Naturalism and the Rise of the "Conventional State"', in F. Fagiani and G. Valera (eds), *Categorie del Reale e Storiografia* (Milan, 1986), pp. 111–27.

Schwoerer, L., *No Standing Armies!: The Antiarmy Ideology in Seventeenth-Century England* (Baltimore and London, 1974).

Scott, J., *Algernon Sidney and the Restoration Crisis: 1677–1683* (Cambridge, 1991).

— *England's Troubles. Seventeenth-Century English Political Instability in European Context* (Cambridge, 2000).

— *Commonwealth Principles. Republican Writing of the English Revolution* (Cambridge, 2004).

Sharpe, K., *Criticism and Compliment. The Politics of Literature in the England of Charles I* (Cambridge, 1987).

— *The Personal Rule of Charles I* (New Haven and London, 1992).

— 'The Royal Image: An Afterword', in T. N. Corns (ed.), *The Royal Image. Representations of Charles I* (Cambridge, 1999), pp. 288–309.

— *Remapping Early Modern England. The Culture of Seventeenth-Century Politics* (Cambridge, 2000).

Shepard, A., *Meanings of Manhood in Early Modern England* (Oxford, 2003).

Skinner, Q., *Liberty before Liberalism* (Cambridge, 1998).

— *Visions of Politics. Volume I. Regarding Method* (Cambridge, 2002).

— *Visions of Politics. Volume II. Renaissance Virtues* (Cambridge, 2002).

Smuts, M., *Court Culture and the Origins of a Royalist Tradition in Early Stuart England* (Philadelphia, 1987).

Sommerville, J. P., 'Richard Hooker, Hadrian Saravia and the Divine Right of Kings', *HPT*, 4 (1983), pp. 225–9.

— 'Absolutism and Royalism', in J. H. Burns and M. Goldie (eds), *The Cambridge History of Political Thought 1450–1700* (Cambridge, 1991), pp. 347–73.

— 'Introduction', in *Robert Filmer. Patriarcha and Other Political Writings*, ed. J. P. Sommerville (Cambridge, 1991), pp. vii–xxxvii.

— 'English and European Political Ideas in the Early Seventeenth Century: Revisionism and the Case of Absolutism', *JBS*, 35 (1996), pp. 168–94.

— 'Lofty Science and Local Politics', in T. Sorell (ed.), *The Cambridge Companion to Hobbes* (Cambridge, 1996), pp. 246–73.

— *Royalists and Patriots. Politics and Ideology in England 1603–1640* (London and New York, 2nd edn rev., 1999).

— 'Kellison Matthew', in A. Pyle (ed.), *The Dictionary of Seventeenth Century British Philosophers* (Bristol, 2000), pp. 486–7.

— 'King James VI and I and John Selden: Two Voices on History and the Constitution', in D. Fischlin and M. Fortier (eds), *Royal Subjects. Essays on the Writings of James VI and I* (Detroit, 2002), pp. 290–322.

— 'An Emergent Britain? Literature and National Identity in Early Stuart England', in D. Loewenstein and J. Mueller (eds), *The Cambridge History of Early Modern English Literature* (Cambridge, 2003), pp. 459–86.

— 'Papalist Political Thought and the Controversy over the Jacobean Oath of Allegiance', in E. Shagan (ed.), *Catholics and the 'Protestant Nation'. Religious Politics and Identity in Early Modern England* (Manchester, 2005), pp. 162–84.

— 'Sir Robert Filmer, Usury and the Ideology of Order', in D. Carey (ed.), *Money and the Enlightenment* (Oxford, 2007), pp. 1–37.

Sommerville, M. R., *Sex and Subjection. Attitudes to Women in Early-Modern Society* (1995).

Spurr, J., *The Post-Reformation. Religion, Politics and Society in Britain 1603–1714* (Harlow, 2006).

Stedman Jones, G., 'The Determinist Fix: Some Obstacles to the Further Development of the Linguistic Approach to History in the 1990s', in G. M. Spiegel (ed.),

Practicing History. New Directions in Historical Writing after the Linguistic Turn (New York and London, 2005), pp. 62–75.

Stuurman, S., 'The Canon of the History of Political Thought: Its Critique and a Proposed Alternative', *History and Theory*, 39 (2000), pp. 147–66.

Tadmor, N., 'Women and Wives: The Language of Marriage in Early Modern English Biblical Translations', *History Workshop Journal*, 62 (2006), pp. 1–27.

Thomas, P., 'Two Cultures? Court and Country under Charles I', in C. Russell (ed.), *The Origins of the English Civil War* (1973), pp. 168–96.

Thompson, A. B., 'Licensing the Press: The Career of G. R. Weckherlin during the Personal Rule of Charles I', *HJ*, 41 (1998), pp. 653–78.

Thorp, M. R., 'Religion and the Wyatt Rebellion of 1554', *Church History*, 47 (1978), pp. 363–80.

Todd, M., 'Anti-Calvinists and the Republican Threat in Early Stuart Cambridge', in L. Lunger Knoppers (ed.), *Puritanism and Its Discontents* (Newark and London, 2003), pp. 85–105.

Tuck, R., 'A New Date for Filmer's Patriarcha', *HJ*, 29 (1986), pp. 183–6.

— *Philosophy and Government, 1572–1651* (Cambridge, 1993).

Tully, J. (ed.), *Meaning and Context. Quentin Skinner and His Critics* (Cambridge, 1988).

Turchetti, M., *Tyrannie et Tyrannicide de l'Antiquité à Nos Jours* (Paris 2001).

Tutino, S., *Empire of Souls. Robert Bellarmine and the Christian Commonwealth* (Oxford, 2010).

Tyacke, N., *Anti-Calvinists. The Rise of English Arminianism c. 1590–1640* (Oxford, 1987).

— *Aspects of English Protestantism, c. 1530–1700* (Manchester and New York, 2001).

— 'Introduction', in N. Tyacke (ed.), *The English Revolution c.1590–1720. Politics, Religion and Communities* (Manchester, 2007), pp. 1–26.

Underdown, D., 'The Taming of the Scold: The Enforcement of Patriarchal Authority in Early Modern England', in A. Fletcher and J. Stevenson (eds), *Order and Disorder in Early Modern England* (Cambridge, 2nd edn, 1987), pp. 116–36.

— *A Freeborn People. Politics and the Nation in Seventeenth-Century England* (Oxford, 1996).

Vallance, E., 'Protestation, Vow, Covenant and Engagement: Swearing Allegiance in the English Civil War', *Historical Research*, 75 (2002), pp. 408–24.

Van Gelderen, M., 'Aristotelians, Monarchomachs and Republicans: Sovereignty and *respublica mixta* in Dutch and German Political Thought, 1580–1650', in M. van Gelderen and Q. Skinner (eds), *Republicanism. A Shared European Heritage* (Cambridge, 2 vols, 2002), vol. 1, pp. 195–217.

Viroli, M., *For Love of Country. An Essay on Patriotism and Nationalism* (Oxford, 1995).

Von Maltzahn, N., 'Samuel Butler's Milton', *Studies in Philology*, 92 (1995), pp. 482–95.

Waldron, J., *God, Locke, and Equality. Christian Foundations in Locke's Political Thought* (Cambridge, 2002).

Wallace, J. M., 'The Date of Sir Robert's Patriarcha', *HJ*, 23 (1980), pp. 155–65.

Ward, L., *The Politics of Liberty in England and Revolutionary America* (Cambridge, 2004).

Weekley, E., 'The Etymology of "Roister"', *The Modern Language Review*, 7 (1912), pp. 518–19.

Weil, R., *Political Passions. Gender, the Family and Political Argument in England 1680–1714* (Manchester, 1999).

— 'The Family in the Exclusion Crisis: Locke versus Filmer Revisited', in A. Houston and S. Pincus (eds), *A Nation Transformed. England after the Restoration* (Cambridge, 2001), pp. 100–24.

Weston, C., 'The Authorship of the Freeholders Grand Inquest', *EHR*, 95 (1980), pp. 74–98.

— 'The Case of Sir Robert Holbourne Reasserted', *HPT*, 8 (1987), pp. 435–60.

Weston, C. and Greenberg, J., *Subjects and Sovereigns. The Grand Controversy over Legal Sovereignty in Stuart England* (Cambridge, 1981).

Wilcher, R., *The Writing of Royalism 1628–1660* (Cambridge, 2001).

Winship, M. P., 'Freeborn (Puritan) Englishmen and Slavish Subjection: Popish Tyranny and Puritan Constitutionalism, c. 1570–1606', *EHR*, 124 (2009), pp. 1050–74.

— 'Algernon Sidney's Calvinist Republicanism', *JBS*, 49 (2010), pp. 753–73.

Wiseman, S., '"Adam, the Father of All Flesh": Porno-Political Theory in and After the English Civil War', in J. Holstun (ed.), *Pamphlet Wars. Prose in the English Revolution* (1992), pp. 134–57.

Wootton, D., *Divine Right and Democracy* (1986).

Zagorin, P., *A History of Political Thought in the English Revolution* (1954).

— *The Court and the Country. The Beginning of the English Revolution* (1969).

Zaller, R., 'The Figure of the Tyrant in English Revolutionary Thought', *Journal of the History of Ideas*, 54 (1993), pp. 585–610.

Zuckert, M. P., *Natural Rights and the New Republicanism* (Princeton, 1994).

DOCTORAL THESES

Boster, T., *"Better To Be Alone Than In Ill Company' Jeremy Collier The Younger: Life And Works, 1650–1726'*, PhD Thesis, University of Pittsburgh, 2006.

Petrie, S., 'Sir Roger Twysden 1597–1672: A Re-appraisal of His Life and Writings', PhD Thesis, University of Kent, 2006.

Index

absolute monarchy 53, 59–62, 67–71,
    73–6, 108–10, 117, 129, 145–6, 174,
    229n115, 247
absolutism 4, 7, 13, 50n184, 90n231,
    130n5, 147, 157n52, 190, 205n53,
    240, 247–8
Adam and Eve 30–1, 46n111, 66, 127,
    215–17, 225n12
Adamite paradigm 3, 5, 70–4, 94–9,
    109–12, 149–51, 190–3, 213–14,
    222–4, 248–9
Ady, Thomas 48n145
Ainsworth, Henry 36
Alford, Edward 85n141, 134n99
Alford, Stephen 126, 140n216–17
allegiance 213, 221, 234, 238–9, 246,
    248, 249
Alsted, Johann Heinrich 136n138
Althusius, Johannes 61, 136n138
Ammirato, Scipione 71
ancient Rome 52, 53, 56, 58, 75–6, 99,
    112, 118, 199, 216–17, 221
Anderson, Henry 200
Andrea of Isernia 137n172
Andrewes, Lancelot 41n31, 100n5, 123,
    139n195, 139n201
anti-Catholicism 53, 56, 57, 60, 61, 63,
    104
Aquinas, Thomas 24
arbitrary power 5, 74, 99, 110–11, 152,
    158n56, 170, 172, 188–9, 201, 218,
    223–4, 227n75, 240
Aristotle 3, 23, 40n26, 68, 72, 110,
    132n63, 163, 218
Arminianism 54, 60, 61, 63, 80n51,
    83n92, 154, 247
Arundel, Thomas Howard, Earl of 57,
    82n63
Ashcraft, Richard 173

Ashwell, George 174
Astell, Mary 46n116, 204
atheism 168, 176, 232, 233
Atkyns, Sir Robert 235
Atwood, William 177n24, 236–8,
    242–3n28–30, 243n42
Aubrey, John 29
Aucher, John 199

Bacon, Francis 175
Bancroft, Bishop Richard 192
Barclay, John 5, 87n160
Barclay, William 14n18
Bargrave, Isaac 40n21, 63, 145, 154
Barrow, Isaac 198
Barston, John 152
Becanus, Martin 91
Bellarmine, Robert 2, 67, 77, 91, 92–5,
    99, 100n2, 128, 166, 247
Belloy, Pierre de 93
Bèze, Théodore de 64, 100n2, 192, 249
Bible 2, 25, 45n105, 62, 64, 72, 96, 166
billeting troops 54, 107, 113, 114, 131n37
Bilson, Thomas 192
bishops 53, 161–2, 179n42
Blackwood, Adam 5, 87n160
Blount, Charles 188–9, 194
Blount, Thomas 27
Bodin, Jean 2, 3, 28, 48n144, 128,
    132n62, 170, 198
Bohun, Edmund 187, 193, 212–23,
    224n2–3, 225n9–10, 225n21–2,
    226n29, 226n33, 227n63
Bolton, Edmund 88n183
Bond of Association (1584) 126,
    140n219
Bostridge, Ian 47n141
Brady, Robert 192, 195, 197, 206n71,
    236, 240

Bramhall, John 135n124
Brathwaite, Richard 53
Brutus 52, 118, 199
Buchanan, George 64, 67, 87n160, 107, 108, 191, 204n38
Buckeridge, John 72, 100n5, 138n188
Buckingham, George Villiers, Duke of 52, 53, 57, 60, 61, 63, 64, 65, 78n10, 85n135–6, 106–7, 125, 134n113, 152
Burgess, Glenn 4, 7, 86n144, 150, 151, 159n76
Burghley, Lord 126
Burton, Henry 53
Burton, Thomas 37, 173
Butler, Samuel 175–6, 183n140

Cajetan, Cardinal 24, 97
Calvin, John 24, 67, 166–7
Calvinism 35, 65, 81n53, 144, 191
Camden, William 28, 29, 159n78
Carleton, Sir Dudley 52
Catholicism 25, 27, 36, 54, 126, 145, 188, 191
Cecil, Robert 108
Charles I, king 22, 27, 61, 62, 83n104, 106, 108, 125, 156n25
    Buckingham and 85n136, 152
    discontent with 54, 55
    imprisonment and execution of 171, 192
    military campaigns 145, 152
    Parliament and 113–16, 134n113, 145
    Patriarcha and 2, 10, 23, 65–6, 146–8
    'Personal Rule' period 107, 125, 188
    taxation and 88n181, 115, 156n36, 178n29
    van Dyck portrait of 129, 142n248, 151
    weakness of 141n242
Charles II, King 27, 160n89, 188, 196, 200, 202n4, 208n99, 219, 231, 232, 241, 244n57
China 215, 226n37
Church of England 28, 29, 81n53, 167, 168, 232, 243n42

Cicero 52, 53, 54, 58, 62, 118, 139n193
Civil War 38, 77, 90n229, 164–6, 170–1, 181n101, 241
Clarendon, Earl of 87n155, 169, 177n29
Clark, Peter 56, 79n35, 80n43, 82n63
Clark, William 27
Clegg, Cyndia S. 109
Clément, Jacques 91
Cogswell, Thomas 90n229, 152
Coiro, Ann Baynes 108
Coke, Sir Edward 113, 169, 174
Coke, Sir John 114
Collier, Jeremy 207n71, 218, 239, 244n52
Collins, Samuel 123, 139n195
Collinson, Patrick 115, 140n217
common law 35, 71, 75, 109, 111–12, 115, 150, 169, 170, 238
Constable, Robert 191
constitutionalism 60, 74, 99, 117, 169
Contarini, Alvise 53 130–1n24
contracts 35–6, 37, 127, 170, 236
contractualists 5, 7, 14n16, 72, 89n193, 172, 192, 223
corruption 53, 57–8, 62, 151
Coryton, William 114, 115, 116, 133n86, 133n94
Cotgrave, Randle 52, 77n7
Cotton, Sir Robert 22, 28
Cowell, John 109, 131n46
Craig, Thomas 121
Cromwell, Oliver 38, 162, 182n112, 223
Crossman, Samuel 197
Culpeper, Sir Cheyney 28
Culpeper, Sir John 164, 177n29–30
Culpeper, Sir Thomas 26, 43n66
Curll, Walter 54–5
Cust, Richard 76, 78n12, 84n128, 106, 115, 131n31, 145, 147, 148

Daly, James 6–7, 16n37, 88n178, 154n1, 157n56, 194, 202n13, 206n71, 226n29, 229n115, 239
Dave, John 100n2
Davis, Colin 81n54
Del Rio, Martin 35, 36, 49n155

democracy 54, 70, 71, 75–6, 92 *see also*
    popular government; mixed
    government
Dering, Sir Edward 26, 28, 44n85,
    79n33, 164, 168
D'Ewes, Simonds 131n37, 164
Digges, Sir Dudley 60, 135n124
Diggs, Thomas 180n83
divine right of kings 3, 5, 14n17, 93,
    96, 108, 145, 155n111, 189, 230n117,
    236–8, 243n42
Dixon, Reverend Robert 168
Donne, John 29
Dorislaus, Isaac 106
Downam, George 25
Dryden, John 193, 240
Dugdale, Sir William 208n99
Duke, Sir Edward 26
Duppa, Brian 175

Edmondes, Sir Thomas 27
Effiat, Marquis d' 106, 140n211
Eliot, Sir John 85n141, 113
Elizabeth, Princess (Stuart) 105, 124,
    125, 147, 152
Elizabeth I, Queen 21, 54, 90n232, 106,
    117, 125, 126, 152
Erle, Sir Walter 113
Eve 30, 46n111, 66, 127, 147, 215, 225n12
Everitt, Alan 10, 77n2
Exclusion Crisis (1679-81) 2, 7, 120,
    187, 190, 196, 201n1, 219, 223,
    229n113, 240, 246, 248
excommunication 90n232, 93
Ezell, M. 45n105

Fairfax, Sir Thomas 171
Falkner, William 223, 240
Felton, John 53
Fenton, Roger 24–5, 42n31, 42n34–5
Filmer, Sir Robert 6–8, 26, 39n4,
    79n36, 86n144, 87n164, 120, 121,
    141n237, 164
    books owned by 22, 40n15, 40n27,
        204n44, 251–3
    in Cambridge and London 28–30

death of 38, 164
friendship with Peter Heylyn 161–4,
    167
imprisonment 165–6, 168–9,
    178n34, 178n38
influence of 173–6, 205n58,
    206–7n71, 209–10n113, 209n101,
    238–41
Kentish literati and 6, 26–9
life and family 21–3, 26, 38, 55–6
meticulous scholarship of 23,
    40n26, 89n192
political views of 203n28
religious sympathies of 29
on theology 166–9
works by
    *An Advertisement to the Jurymen
        of England* 33–8, 47n141
    *The Anarchy of a Limited or
        Mixed Monarchy* 28, 67, 76,
        170, 174, 175, 192
    *Directions for Obedience to Gover-
        nours* 172–3
    The Free-Holders Grand Inquest
        74, 99, 117, 169, 180n70, 235
    In Praise of the Vertuous Wife
        30–3, 37, 166
    *The Necessity of the Absolute Power
        of all Kings* 28, 47n140, 170,
        174–5, 197, 203n31, 229n101
    *Observations Concerning the
        Originall of Government* 171–2
    *Observations Upon Aristotles
        Politiques Touching Forms of
        Government* 110, 172, 176
    *Of the Blasphemie against the
        Holy-Ghost* 166, 167, 178n41
    Of the Sabeth 168
    Patriarcha, see under Patriarcha
    Quaestio Quodlibetica 23–6, 32,
        37, 41–2n30–1, 176
    Theologie: or Divinity 168–9
    Touching marriage and adultery
        45n105
    Treatises on Rebellion (disputed)
        157–8n56

Filmer family 21–3, 26, 27, 29, 38,
    80n41, 164, 165–6, 178n36
Finch, Francis 26
Finch, John 57
Fisher, Ambrose 28–9
Fitzherbert, Thomas 123
Flatman, Thomas 194
Fludd, Robert 28
Forced Loan policy (1626-7) 54, 107, 113,
    134n113, 144–5
Forsett, Edward 123, 153
Fortescue, Sir John 132n68
France 83–4n104, 215, 249
Frankland, Thomas 208n99
Frederick V, Elector Palatine 105, 124,
    125, 147, 152
'freeborn Englishmen,' rights of 9, 53,
    62, 63, 77, 152, 153, 236
freedom of speech 85n141, 107, 113,
    115–18, 135n119, 136n137, 141n243
Fuller, Thomas 54, 79n32

Garnet, Father Henry 91
Gee, Edward 175, 183n134
Gilbert, Samuel 198
Gipps, Thomas 198
Glanville, Sir John 113
Glorious Revolution (1688) 187, 225n9,
    235–9
Goddard, Guybon 175
Goddard, Thomas 206n71, 209n113,
    223, 229n115
Goldie, Mark 156n30, 204n46,
    207n79, 225n10, 244n55
governance 5, 11, 31–2, 71, 73, 92,
    109–10, 172, 215
Grant, John 29
Greenleaf, William H. 4, 14n13, 111
Gretser, Jacob 91
Grotius, Hugo 171, 172, 225n9
Gunpowder Plot (1605) 91, 191,
    209n101, 249
Gustavus Adolphus of Sweden 87n149,
    125, 146–7

Haillan, Bernard de Girard du 249

Hales, John 178n41, 181n98
Hales, Matthew 235
Hall, John 175
Harrington, James 163
Harris, Tim 228n94, 229n113
Harrison, William 159n78
Hart, Vaughan 74
Hartlib, Samuel 28
Hayward, Sir John 5, 87n160, 121,
    209n105
Henrietta Maria, Queen 27, 125, 129
Henry, Prince of Wales 105, 108,
    124–5
Henry III, King of France 83n104, 91,
    195, 249
Henry IV, King of France 87n149,
    90n232, 91, 100n4, 195, 249
Herbert, George 29
hereditary succession 58–9, 76, 94,
    96, 112, 121–2, 189, 192, 193,
    207n74, 219, 221, 225n10, 240
Heylyn, Peter 57, 120–1, 137n171,
    160n85, 161–4, 167, 177n15,
    177n22, 188, 240, 242n25
Heywood, Thomas 151
Hickes, George 193, 204n39, 223, 240,
    243n29
Hirst, Derek 14n20, 50n184, 83n98,
    130n14, 131n37, 138n189
Hobbes, Thomas 2, 5, 49n156, 126,
    128, 136n140, 136n142, 147, 148,
    156n30, 195, 240, 244n59
    Leviathan 74, 159n80, 171, 172,
    182n104, 201
Hooker, Richard 3, 28, 235
Hoskyns, John 135n131
Hotman, François 57, 64
House of Commons 27, 60, 105, 109,
    113–14, 117, 134n113, 169–70,
    227n63
House of Lords 105, 161–2, 169
Houston, Alan Craig 239–40
Hunt, Thomas 192, 194–5, 200,
    207n72, 207n74
Hunton, Philip 170

imprisonment without cause 54, 113, 114, 115
Isham, Sir Justinian 175

James, Duke of York (James II) 140 n219, 153, 189–90, 199, 208n99, 219, 225n9, 231, 236, 238
James I, King 2, 23, 29, 88n187, 108, 212, 240
   absolute/arbitrary power 110–11
   attack on Jesuits 91, 95
   on danger of 'popularity' 54, 104–6
   'fatherly care' 122
   foreign policy 105, 120, 125, 147, 152
   knighthood policy 57–8
   mystery of kingship 128, 141n238
   Oath of Allegiance conflict 86n146, 91
   parliamentary opposition to 130n14
   works by 35, 36, 104–6, 108, 122, 152
Jenkins, David 202n14, 203n22
Jesuits 35, 36, 66, 67, 77, 90n232, 94–9, 121, 124, 130n17, 170, 191–2, 195, 204n41–3, 205n51, 217, 240, 248
Johnson, Cornelius 27–8
Johnson, Samuel 192, 238, 242–3n29
Johnston, Nathaniel 210n113, 223
Jones, William 188
Jonson, Ben 23, 28, 29, 52, 152
Julius Caesar 61, 118, 199

Kellison, Matthew 100n3
Kennett, White 197–8
kingship 71, 74, 108, 124, 126, 128, 141n238, 149, 240
Kishlansky, Mark 115, 134n113
knighthood 57–8, 117
Knights, Mark 190, 202n16, 204n37
Knolles, Richard 28
König, Reinhard 61
Kynaston, Sir Francis 116–21, 126, 135n128, 135n132–3, 137n154, 147, 148, 153

LaCapra, Dominick 12

Lake, Peter 82n61, 104, 129n1
Lambarde, William 22, 251, 252
Langbaine, Gerard 244n50
Laslett, Peter 6, 16n42, 21, 40n19, 86n146, 146, 157n56, 173, 178n37, 244n55, 253n3
Laud, William, Archbishop of Canterbury 145, 148, 155n19, 159–60n84, 168
Leighton, Alexander 52–3
L'Estrange, Sir Roger 189, 193, 194–6, 198, 206n63, 207n75, 207n79, 234, 237, 240, 244n57
Leyland, John 159n78
Liebenthal, Christian 61
Littleton, Edward 113
Livy 54, 118
Lloyd, Humphrey 139n193
Locke, John 1, 2, 6, 7, 10, 13, 154, 159n83, 173, 187, 190, 193, 213, 222, 230n116–17, 248, 250
The London Gazette 191, 231, 232, 233, 234, 241n2
Louis XIII, King 27, 106
Lovelace, Richard 26, 27
Lucan 52
Luther, Martin 16n53, 81n53
Lynche, Richard 22
Lythe, Henry 39n12

Mackenzie, Sir George 206n71, 209–10n113, 223, 229n115
Magna Carta (1215) 75, 113, 114
Mahlberg, Gaby 13n7, 160n89, 222, 245n61
Maidstone, battle of (1648) 171
Major, John 191
Malet, Sir Thomas 164, 168
Manwood, Sir Peter 28
Mariana, Juan de 92, 100n10, 192
Marsham, Sir John 26, 27
martyrdom 30, 118, 153, 219–20
Mary I, Queen 55, 57, 90n229, 140n218
Mary Queen of Scots 30
Maxwell, John 124, 139n205, 240

May, Thomas 52
Mayney, Sir John 27
Maynwaring, Roger 10, 145, 154,
160n84, 163
Melanchthon, Philipp 59
Middleton, Thomas 90n232
Milton, Anthony 137n171, 147, 160n85,
177n9
Milton, John 171, 172
Mitchell, James 204n39
mixed government 28, 56, 67, 107,
110, 111, 131n38, 172, 174–5, 188,
207n79
Mocket, Richard 122–3, 138–9n190
monarchomachs 61, 94, 107, 117, 191,
248
monarchy 94–6, 219, 220
'father of the fatherland' 112, 149,
193, 197, 214, 247–8
land and 159n78
laws and 69, 72, 99, 102n70, 111
opposition to 54–5, 87n155, 104–6,
125, 190, 215, 232
papal authority and 93, 94, 95,
100n3, 191
trust 115–16, 151, 188
see also Adamite paradigm; divine
right; kingship
Monson, Sir John 191, 203n33
Montaigne, Bishop George 58, 145
Morison, Richard 153
Mosaic law 25, 49n163, 168
Mossom, Robert, Bishop of Derry
123–4
MPs (members of parliament) 53, 55,
56, 57, 60, 62, 70, 85n141, 105,
113–18, 151, 188, 189, 200, 219,
248
Murray, Anthony 22

Nalson, John 193, 199–200, 205n51,
206n71, 208n88
Naseby, battle of (1645) 169
national identity 5, 14n20, 63, 77, 112,
126, 150, 159n78, 240
nationalism 152

natural rights 71, 89n193, 162, 170, 192,
197, 223
Nedham, Marchamont 203n32
Nero, Emperor 70, 88n183
Netherlands 52, 172, 176, 197, 200
Neville, Sir Henry 52, 160n89, 198,
200, 222–3
Newman, Gerald 151
Nimrod 73, 97, 110, 139n205
Noah 22, 97, 149, 216, 239
Norman Conquest (1066) 56, 57, 169
North, Sir Roger 113, 114, 115, 116
Northleigh, John 193, 200–1, 220, 223

Oakley, Francis 111
Oath of Allegiance (1606) 2, 86n146,
91, 93, 122, 239
Ogle, Sir John 52
Owen, David 191–2

Palatinate 54, 105, 120, 125, 147, 152
Palmer, Herbert 60
pamphlets 120, 128, 144–5, 202n10, 221
papism 84n107
Pareus, David 144
Parker, Henry 162, 170, 188
Parliament 2, 5–6, 26, 27, 31–2, 53, 60,
63, 70, 126, 150, 223, 238
Charles I and 64, 107, 116, 146, 188
Charles II and 188, 190
disputes 130n6, 130n14
elections 53, 55, 60, 164
factions in 81n59
impeachment of Buckingham
85n136
James I and 138n189
patriotism in 68, 113–19, 152–3
parricide 91–2, 100n4, 120, 121, 124,
148, 191, 195, 199, 201, 220, 231,
234, 248
Parsons, Robert 67, 87n160, 121, 123,
138n174n175, 191, 192, 245n64
passive obedience 225n10, 236, 243n42
Pateman, Carole 150
paternalism 14n22
pater patriae 6, 9, 11, 17n59, 74, 108, 116,

119, 121–4, 135n124, 137–8n172, 151,
153, 157n56, 158n58, 175, 197–200,
208n98–9, 213–14, 216, 239
Patriarcha (Filmer) 1–2, 37–9, 66–77,
110, 121, 127, 154, 156n41
attempt to publish (1632) 2, 10, 23,
65–6, 146, 154, 163, 177n22, 247
political context of 144–8, 190
publication of (1680) 153–4, 189–90,
193, 214, 219, 222, 246
secularity of 154, 160n84, 240
see also Heylyn; Locke; Sidney;
Tyrrell
patriarchalism 1, 3–7, 55, 59, 68–72,
121, 189, 246–50
Atwood on 236–8
Bohun's rehabilitation of 212–24
Exclusion crisis period 190–3
Glorious Revolution and 235–9
Jesuitism and 94–9, 100n5
Kynaston 116, 117, 118–20, 121
patriotism and 51–77, 116–24,
219–24
Tory propaganda and 194–6, 200–1
patriotism 1, 38, 51, 67–8, 125, 149–50,
193–4, 246, 248
Bond of Association 126
conspiracies 231–3
country 52–65, 70, 76–7
Kynaston on 119–20
monarchical nature of 143, 151–3
Parliament and 113–16
patriarchalism and 51–77, 116–24,
219–24
see also Jesuits
patriots 38–9, 51–3, 61, 67–8, 77, 107,
116, 118–19, 124, 126, 153, 193–4,
217–18, 219, 231–4, 236, 247–8
Pelling, Edward 194, 198
Pembroke, Philip Herbert, fourth Earl
of 29, 78n10
Pembroke, William Herbert, third Earl
of 52
Perkins, William 35–7, 48n153, 49n163
Petition of Right (1628) 61, 107, 113, 118,
133n86, 197

petitions 187, 188, 189, 202n4, 202n17,
221
Petyt, William 197, 236
Phelips, Sir Robert 113
Philip II of Spain 57, 90n229, 140n218
Phillips, Fabian 211n132
Philopatris 193–4, 206n63
Piers, William 178n31
Plato 3, 23, 32, 54, 72, 74, 132n63
Plessis-Mornay, Philippe du 64
Pocock, John 17n63, 130n5
Ponet, John 125, 140n216
Pope, temporal authority of 2, 77,
87n161, 90–9, 102n46, 121, 123,
191, 198, 247
popery 61, 81n53, 84n107, 104, 145, 188,
192, 200, 201, 203n28, 204n46,
246
Popish Plot (1678-81) 197, 219, 232–3
popular government 7, 51, 75–6, 99,
144, 150, 158n56, 170, 172, 193,
203n28, 237
popularity 38, 54–5, 75, 91, 104–6, 119,
144, 192, 196, 246
Presbyterians 174, 175, 204n39, 214,
223
primogeniture 58–9, 76, 96, 226n33
private property rights 110, 144
Protestantism 53, 60, 81n53, 104, 105,
125, 126, 146–7
Prynne, William 99, 169–70, 208n98
Puritanism 55, 57, 60, 63–4, 67, 80n51,
81n53, 81n61, 84n128, 104–7, 121,
191–2, 204n41–3, 205n51, 240

Raleigh, Sir Walter 157n52, 251
Randolph, Edmund 26
Randolph, Thomas 23
Ravaillac, François 91, 204n39
Reading, John 168
republicanism 52, 59, 65, 106, 118, 121,
160n89, 200–1, 216–18, 220
resistance theory 108, 117, 136n138,
144–5, 173, 195, 204n49, 223
Reynolds, John 105–6, 130n17
Ribadeneyra, Petro de 91

Rich, Sir Nathaniel 113, 114
Richard II (Shakespeare) 151
Rider, Matthew 191
Roman law 96–7
   see also ancient Rome
Rous, Francis 83n92
royal prerogative 9, 53, 55, 62, 70,
   81n54, 99, 104–5, 109, 113–19,
   128, 144, 153, 188, 189, 221
Royston, Richard 33, 169, 170, 172,
   209n100, 244n55
Russell, Conrad 77n4, 83n95, 103n73
Russell, John 52
Rutt, John Tovill 183n132
Rye House Plot (1683) 198–9, 231–2

Sâ, Emmanuel de 91
St Augustine 24
St Leger, Anthony 171, 181n94
Salmasius (Claude de Saumaise) 41n31,
   171, 172
Salvetti, Amerigo 107, 131n31
Sancroft, Archbishop 224n3
Sanderson, Robert 123
Sandys, George 29
Sandys, Sir Edwin 27, 28, 44n82, 57,
   60, 170
Saravia, Hadrian 16n47, 72, 252
Sarpi, Paolo 43n69
Schochet, Gordon 3–4, 6, 16n37, 150,
   154n1, 157n56, 203n33, 224n3
Scott, Charles 55
Scott, Edward 57
Scott, Jonathan 187, 203n29
Scott, Sir Reginald 34, 48n144, 48n145,
   55–6
Scott, Thomas 17n58, 39, 55–7, 66–8,
   76, 77, 79n36, 80n43, 116, 128–9,
   247
   on Arminian threat 83n92
   on billeting 107, 131n37
   diary kept by 51, 56, 79n40
   radicalism 81n54
   religious identity 80–1n53
   on 'succession crisis' 201n1
   treatise by 9, 51, 57–65, 82n63

Scottish Parliament 105
sedition 54–5, 67, 75, 105, 118, 231–2
Selden, John 28, 43n68, 86n146,
   224n3, 235
Seneca 58, 118, 213
Settle, Elkanah 200, 208–9n99,
   210n116–17
Sforce, Lodovic 64, 85n137
Shaftesbury, Earl of 210n116, 221,
   227n75, 228n95
Sharpe, James 204n39
Sharpe, Kevin 108, 126, 129, 149, 150,
   248
Sherlock, William 223, 238–40
Sibthorpe, Robert 10, 145, 154, 160n84,
   163
Sidney, Algernon 1, 6, 65, 154, 159n82,
   160n89, 163, 187, 193, 196, 199,
   200, 201, 212, 222, 231, 238
Sixtus V, Pope 90n232, 91
Skinner, Quentin 12–13
Skynner, Augustine 178n38
Slatyer, William 22
Somers, John 223
Sommerville, Johann P. 7, 40n19,
   41n31, 86n146, 155n11, 157n56,
   250n1
Somner, William 22
sovereignty 2, 4, 5, 54–5, 69–72,
   88n178, 112, 118, 128, 199, 213,
   223, 238
Spain 52, 60, 105–6, 125, 152
standing army 172, 218–19, 227n72,
   227n75
Starkey, Ralph 119, 137n154
Streater, John 175
Suarez, Francisco 2, 77, 91, 95–9, 128,
   141n231, 192, 204n38, 247
Sugge, Tristram 174

taxation 54, 88n181, 115, 156n36, 164,
   178n29
Temple, William 197
Terre Rouge, Jean de 121
Test Bill 227n75
Thanet, Earl of 28

Thirty Years War (1618-48) 125, 152
Thompson, Anthony B. 146, 148
Timpler, Clemens 136n138
Tom Tell Troath 120, 137n161
Tories 193–6, 200–1, 203n28, 219,
    228n94, 240
Towers, John, Bishop of Peterborough
    162
Tuck, Richard 86n146, 100n5, 181n101
Tufton, Sir John 27
Tuvil, Daniel 46n113
Twysden, Sir Roger 22–4, 26, 27, 28,
    43n68–71, 164–5, 174
Twysden, Sir William 22
tyrannicide 9, 92, 136n140, 191,
    204n46
tyranny 2, 52, 53, 54, 61–3, 110, 217–18
    opposition to 63–4, 67, 84n128,
        102n47, 106, 107, 124, 144, 248
Tyrrell, James 1, 6, 156n30, 187, 193,
    198, 214–15, 221–3, 226n33

Ultramontanists 99, 124, 170, 192,
    249
Underdown, David 55
usury 21, 23–6, 32, 37, 41–2n30–1, 174

van Dyck, Anthony 129, 142n248, 151
Vasquez, Gabriel 91
Venice 172, 176, 200
Vitoria, Francisco de 97

Walker, Clement 174–5
Walker, John 199
Walsingham, Sir Francis 126
Walton, Izaac 29
Ward, Lee 16n53, 141n233
Weckherlin, Georg Rudolph 65–6,
    87n149, 146, 147, 148
Weil, Rachel 141n228, 245n61
Weldon, Anthony 165–6, 178n35
Wentworth, Thomas 147, 148
Whigs 6, 187, 192, 202n13, 203n28,
    207n72, 219, 221, 223, 228,
    230n117, 241
William and Mary 225n9, 236, 239
Williams, John, Bishop of Lincoln 162,
    177n8
Wilson, Dr Thomas 162
Wilson, John 199
Winship, Michael P. 90n227, 134n115
witchcraft 21, 33–8, 47n141, 48n144–5,
    49, 167
Wither, George 129
Womock, Laurence 206n71
Wood, Anthony à 168, 180n70
Wotton, Sir Henry 135n131
Wren, Matthew 155n10, 155n19
Wyatt, G. 40n20
Wyatt, Sir Thomas 55, 57, 90n229

Zachary, Pope 93
Zuckert, Michael 88n180

Milton Keynes UK
Ingram Content Group UK Ltd.
UKHW042140120224
437711UK00012B/60